THE BABY BOOMERS GROW UP

Contemporary Perspectives
on Midlife

Edited by

Susan Krauss Whitbourne
University of Massachusetts Amherst

Sherry L. Willis
Pennsylvania State University

LAWRENCE ERLBAUM ASSOCIATES, PUBLISHERS
2006   Mahwah, New Jersey   London

Lawrence Erlbaum Associates, Inc., Publishers
10 Industrial Avenue
Mahwah, New Jersey 07430
www.erlbaum.com

Cover design by Tomai Maridou

Library of Congress Cataloging-in-Publication Data

p. cm.

Includes bibliographical references and index.
ISBN 0-8058-4875-4 (cloth : alk. paper)
ISBN 0-8058-4876-2 (pbk. : alk. paper)

2006
—dc22

2006000000
CIP

Printed in the United States of America
10   9   8   7   6   5   4   3   2   1

THE BABY BOOMERS GROW UP

Contemporary Perspectives
on Midlife

Contents

Preface   vii
Susan Krauss Whitbourne and Sherry L. Willis

**PART ONE   BABY BOOMERS: DEMOGRAPHIC AND
             THEORETICAL PERSPECTIVES**

1   Demography of the Baby Boomers   3
        David J. Eggebeen and Samuel Sturgeon

2   Social, Historical, and Developmental Influences
        on the Psychology of the Baby Boom at Midlife   23
        Abigail J. Stewart and Cynthia M. Torges

3   Studying Baby Boom Cohorts Within a Demographic
        and Developmental Context: Conceptual
        and Methodological Issues   45
        Duane F. Alwin, Ryan J. McCammon, and Scott M. Hofer

PART TWO   PHYSICAL AND MENTAL HEALTH ISSUES

4   Menopause: Recent Research Findings   75
        Nancy E. Avis and Sybil Crawford

5   Mental Health Among the Baby Boomers   111
     Jennifer R. Piazza and Susan Turk Charles

PART THREE   PSYCHOSOCIAL ISSUES

6   Identity Processes and the Transition to Midlife
     Among Baby Boomers   149
     Kelly M. Jones, Susan Krauss Whitbourne,
     and Karyn M. Skultety

7   Daily Life Stressors of Early and Late Baby Boomers   165
     David M. Almeida, Joyce Serido, and Daniel McDonald

8   The View From the Driver's Seat: Sense of Control
     in the Baby Boomers at Midlife   185
     Marilyn McKean Skaff

9   Cognitive Functioning in the Baby Boomers: Longitudinal
     and Cohort Effects   205
     Sherry L. Willis and K. Warner Schaie

PART FOUR   FUNCTIONING IN CONTEXT

10   The Baby Boomers and Their Parents: Cohort
     Influences and Intergenerational Ties   237
     Karen Fingerman and Megan Dolbin-MacNab

11   Perspectives on Close Relationships Among
     the Baby Boomers   261
     Rosemary Blieszner and Karen Roberto

12   Employment and the Baby Boomers: What Can We Expect
     in the Future?   283
     Sara J. Czaja

13   Summary and Future Directions   299
     Susan Krauss Whitbourne and Sherry L. Willis

Author Index   311

Subject Index   333

Preface

Susan Krauss Whitbourne
Sherry L. Willis

The aim of this volume is to examine development in middle age from the perspective of the Baby Boomers, a unique cohort now in midlife. The babyboom cohorts in the U.S. are defined as the cohorts born in the years 1946 to 1962. They are the largest cohorts ever to enter middle age in Western society. They currently represent approximately one third of the total U.S. population.

The Baby Boomers, an imposing force in society from the time of their entry into youth, continue to exert a powerful impact on the media, fiction, movies, and even popular music. As they enter the years normally considered to represent midlife, they are redefining how we as a society regard adults in their middle and later years. Just as they challenged the existing norms and values when they were teenagers and young adults, the Baby Boomers are questioning the standards and expectations for behavior of people in their 50s and 60s. They are healthier than previous generations of middle-aged adults, better educated, and in possession of more disposable income. A formidable target of marketers, the Baby Boomers are willing and able to avail themselves of products that will help them preserve their youthful appearance and approach to life. From Botox to designer jeans, the Baby Boomers seem ready, willing, and able to take advantage of products that will allow them to hold onto their identities for as long as possible. As the song says, the Baby Boomers seem to be adhering to the creed "I won't grow up!"

Why do the Baby Boomers refuse to grow old gracefully? Are they simply vain and superficial? Are they obsessed with control, seeking to determine the fate of their bodies and the changes that accompany the aging process? Or are they simply the first generation to take advantage of advancements in health, fitness, and cosmetic surgery that would have appealed to their elders had these advances been made in earlier decades? We know that many in this cohort were the fortunate beneficiaries of a growing economy in the post World War II years that made it possible for their families to enjoy new levels of affluence. However, their generation produced the inventors of technological innovations that transformed society. Having made these bold advances, do they now fear becoming irrelevant as their children's generation takes over the reins of business and industry? At the heart of these questions is the basic premise that the Baby Boomers are in fact different; due to a confluence of unique historical and social conditions, this generation will not endure the downward trajectories usually associated with growing older. They will continue to "question authority," even now, when they have become the "authority!"

As fascinating as these questions are from the standpoint of this particular generation, it is only in the last century that middle age, the period from approximately ages 40 to 65, has come into its own as a normative developmental period in the human life span. In 1900, the average life expectancy for both men and women was less than fifty years of age. Hence, the average individual did not fully experience the middle years as they are currently defined. Given the recency of the midlife period in the human life course and the unprecedented size of the baby-boom cohorts, it is likely that the Baby Boomers will significantly impact the manner in which middle age is conceptualized and studied far into the future, when their own middle-aged children will be puzzling over the challenges of providing for this large cohort's health and financial needs.

This volume has three unique features that distinguish it from other research on middle age. First, the authors of each chapter focus on what is known regarding the baby-boom cohorts in areas such as stress, menopause, family relationships, and cognitive functioning. The authors specify the particular issues and concerns relevant to the Baby Boomers rather than summarizing all of the existing literature on a topic. For example, data are presented on menopause that take into account the secular trends in health care that differentially impact the experience of menopause for different cohorts of midlife women. The recent debate on hormone replacement therapy is an example of a health issue having a unique impact on the cohorts now in middle age. Second, the authors, where possible, address developmental change across the approximately two and one half decades spanning what is typically defined as middle age; they examine the quantitative and qualitative changes occurring from the forties to the fifties and sixties rather than looking at all midlife adults as one group. It is important to differentiate between the leading-edge Boomers (e.g., birth cohorts in 1940s) and the trailing-edge Boomers (e.g., birth cohorts in the 1960s). Third, the authors consider variations within the baby-boom cohort, recognizing that they are not a uniform group in terms of social class, race, and education. What follows are, we hope, the most comprehensive and up-to-date reviews of the major issues facing this cohort as it develops through midlife and beyond.

PART ONE

Baby Boomers: Demographic
and Theoretical Perspectives

CHAPTER ONE

Demography of the Baby Boomers

David J. Eggebeen
Samuel Sturgeon
Pennsylvania State University

INTRODUCTION

It is appropriate that this book on the Baby Boomers at midlife includes a chapter on demographic characteristics, given that, at root, the Baby Boom was, and remains, a singular demographic event. Simply put, the Baby Boom was a fifteen-year splurge of births that emerged in the aftermath of World War II. It was a splurge because it represented a big reversal from long-term trends in fertility. A change, we might add, that was completely unexpected by those whose job it was to know these things (demographers). Ironically, despite this mistaken call, the Baby Boom phenomenon has probably done more than anything else to popularize demographic perspectives and approaches to understanding social change.

This chapter will begin with a brief review of this singular demographic event, its causes, and its early characteristics and consequences. The second part of this chapter will be a description of these Baby Boomers at midlife using demographic data drawn from various Current Population Surveys (CPS). Two key themes will drive the discussion: diversity and change. Baby Boomers are not a homogeneous bunch.[1] We will explore variations among

---

[1] For the purposes of this chapter we will follow convention and define the Baby Boom era as births beginning in 1946 and ending in 1964, recognizing, of course, that these dates are somewhat arbitrary (see Bouvier, 1980 for a good demographic analysis of when to demarcate the Baby Boom).

Baby Boomers by gender, race, and socioeconomic status (SES). We also will differentiate between the leading-edge Baby Boomers and those that followed. Specifically, we will compare the experiences of men and women, Blacks, Whites, and Hispanics, college educated and non–college educated, Baby Boomers born in 1947–1949 (leading-edge), Baby Boomers born in 1953–1955 (intermediate), and those born on the trailing edge of the Baby Boom era (1960–1962). Our focus will be on work, marriage, living arrangements, and individual resources as these Baby Boomers enter and move through middle age. Finally, we will end this chapter with some speculations about the near future.

WHO ARE THE BABY BOOMERS?

In 1943 two prominent demographers, Warren Thompson and Pascal Whelpton, following accepted sociological theory, predicted that the U.S. population would not only stop growing, but would start to decline (Bouvier & De Vita, 1991). Less than five years later this prediction was in tatters. Starting in 1946, births began to surge. Just under a million more births took place in 1947 than had taken place in 1945. The number of births climbed each year, and, starting in 1954, annual births exceeded four million for the next eleven years (National Center for Health Statistics, 2003). Thompson and Whelpton predicted that the U.S. population would be 147 million in 1970. The actual count was 204 million. The difference between these numbers—47 million—is why those born between 1946 and 1964 are so fascinating. These excess births have been blamed for many of our nation's problems—and many of its successes (Bouvier & De Vita, 1991). The profound cultural and economic dislocations of the past few decades are often traced back to the Baby Boomers (Easterlin, 1987; Macunovich, 2002).

What caused this Baby Boom? Demographers and others who study social change still are not in agreement on this. Until 1946, birth rates had been steadily declining since the turn of the century. It was clear to scholars why this was happening. Increased urbanization and modernization worked to transform American society away from its traditional and rural roots. American society and culture was increasingly characterized by individualism, rationalism, and a flexible, adaptable family structure that was in-tune with a modern, industrial-based economy. Smaller families were expected to become widespread. So why did America experience this sudden and unprecedented departure?

Two popular explanations for the Baby Boom are that the end of World War II brought home troops who made up for lost time, and that the Baby Boom represented a return to large families. Demographic facts do not support either pattern. Births did spike soon after the end of the war, along with marriages and divorces, clearly a response to demobilization, but this explains only the rise in births in the later years of the 1940s. Birth rates continued to rise through the 1950s, remaining high for nearly twenty years after 1945, suggesting other causes than merely the end of World War II were in play.

Neither was the Baby Boom a result of a return to traditional, large families. Work by Charles Westoff (1978) and others showed clearly that large families (four or more children) contributed little to the Baby Boom. What happened was that more individuals married, married sooner, had children sooner, had children tightly spaced, and more likely had two or three children (Bean, 1983; Bouvier & De Vita, 1991).

Why this change in marriage and childbearing? Scholars generally point to three sets of factors: demographic, economic, and social. Many view the booming post-war economy as a major factor. This historically unprecedented growth in housing, education, transportation and manufacturing created jobs—lots of jobs. Incomes grew at a rapid rate; prosperity was widespread (Levy, 1987). However, this extra income, as some have noted, was not expended on consumer goods or luxury items, but on extra children (Bouvier & De Vita, 1991). In a word, families "bought" a third child because they could afford them.

Sociocultural changes also contributed to the Baby Boom (Jones, 1980). The terrible dislocations of World War II—the massive mobilization of men into the armed forces, but also the restrictions on domestic life and widespread female labor force participation on the home front—created the conditions for a sharp increase in domesticity in the post-war years (Mintz & Kellogg, 1988). Not surprisingly, marriages increased, and they happened at earlier ages. Half of all women marrying for the first time in the early part of the baby-boom years were teenagers (Bouvier & De Vita, 1991). Given the early ages at marriage, the pace of childbearing increased. Having the two expected children at a younger age than previous cohorts, combined with the relative affluence of many couples, set up the conditions for what Charles Westoff (1978) called "a relaxation of contraceptive vigilance." Thus, unwanted fertility, in the form of couples having a child beyond their stated preferences, was a major contributor to the Baby Boom.

Richard Easterlin (1987) has proposed the most comprehensive explanation of the baby-boom phenomenon. This theory is built on two key aspects: relative cohort size and relative income. Easterlin argues that the size of one's birth cohort is a major influence on one's life chances, because cohort size has a lot to say about the social and economic climate of society. The comparatively small birth cohorts of the 1930s benefited from less competition in schools and in the job market. Better pay and quicker promotions marked the work trajectories of the 1930s birth cohorts as they moved through adulthood. Because they were born during the Great Depression, their early lives tended to be marked by deprivation or economically modest lifestyles, leading, Easterlin argued, to relatively modest or simple tastes for consumer goods in adulthood. High income, combined with modest expectations for the good life meant many members of these 1930s cohorts developed an optimistic outlook on life—freeing them to not only marry, but to marry younger. Freeing them not only to have children, but to have more of them (Easterlin, 1987). Easterlin's theory has proven useful to understand the marital and fertility behavior of the Depression-era birth cohorts and the subsequent marital and fertility behavior of the relatively large baby-boom cohorts (Easterlin, 1987; Macunovich, 2002). This theory, however, has not been without its critics, and its ability to account for the behavior of the "baby bust" birth cohorts (1970s) remains to be seen (Bean, 1983; Butz & Ward, 1979; Russell, 1982).

What have been the consequences of this massive surge in births? To begin to appreciate the context of the social changes typically traced to the baby-boom cohorts, it is helpful to see what has happened to the age structure of the American population since 1950. Figure 1.1 displays a series of age pyramids for each decade from 1950 through 1980, 1989, 1995, and 2002, then projections forward to 2030. We have included 1989, 1995, and 2002 because these years mark when the leading, intermediate, and trailing cohorts of the Baby Boom entered middle age by turning 40.

These graphs clearly show the distinctive size of the baby-boom cohort relative to the preceding and following cohorts. Comparing one panel to the next clearly shows the movement of the Baby Boomers through the age structure. In 1950, there were approximately 11 million 10- to 14- year-olds. The 1970 pyramid shows nearly double that number. From flooded maternity wards, to overcrowded classrooms, to the centrality of teenage culture, and the tight labor markets, the Baby Boomers have dominated social, economic, and cultural life in America, as many authors, scholars, and pundits have noted (cf. Jones, 1980; Macunovich, 2002; Russell, 2001).

The last three panels of Fig. 1.1 project what the age structure will look like over the next 30 years. Of course the size of the baby-boom cohorts at these three time points cannot be predicted with complete accuracy, given the necessity of making assumptions about immigration patterns and mortality trends. Nevertheless, these pyramids display, in broad strokes, what lies ahead. Over time, we see that the age pyramids will become more like rectangles, as the size of the elderly population will grow spectacularly relative to the other age groups. The implications of the aging of the baby-boom cohorts have received a significant amount of attention, little of it optimistic. Scholars and others warn of increased competition between young and old dependents for scarce public resources, looming financial crises surrounding the Social Security system, and concern over who, and at what cost, will meet the projected

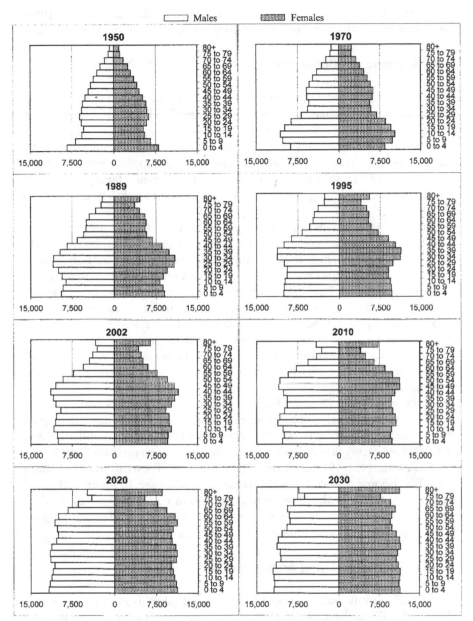

Source: All reported populations and population projections are taken from the International Database.

FIG. 1.1. The movement of baby-boom cohorts through population age–sex pyramids.

caregiving needs (cf. Alt, 1998; Hardy & Kruse, 1998; Pillemar & Suitor, 1998). Our focus in this chapter, however, is on these Baby Boomers at middle age.

Baby Boomers at Middle Age

Our portrait of the Baby Boomers is built on data drawn from the 1989, 1995, and 2002 Current Population Surveys (CPS). The CPS is a nationally representative survey of the residential noninstitutionalized population that has been conducted monthly for more than 50 years. It is the primary source of the official government statistics on employment and unemployment. The data come from the March round, also known as the Annual Demographic File, which contains the demographic information relevant for describing the Baby Boomers.

These data present several advantages. First, the CPS files are representative. The sampling universe is the civilian noninstitutional population of the United States living in housing units and members of the Armed Forces living in civilian housing units on a military base or in a household not on a military base. These files are large. For each year, anywhere from 50,000 to 60,000 households were interviewed. Our analytical samples range from 6,511 to 11,301, allowing us to directly compare various subgroups within each cohort. An additional advantage is the uniform way that questions are structured, making the data comparable over time. Finally, because the CPS has been administered yearly since 1968 to the present, it is possible to observe both inter- and intracohort changes.

We draw on three CPS files for this investigation. The 1989 file is used because this year reasonably approximates the entry into middle age (turning 40) for the leading edge Baby Boomers—those born 1947–1949. In similar fashion, the 1995 CPS survey is used because this is when the intermediate Baby Boomers, those born 1953–1955, turned 40, and the 2002 CPS best captures the trailing edge Baby Boomers (born 1960–1962) entering middle age. In addition, the 1995 and the 2002 CPS files also allow us to document intracohort changes, in effect, covering an approximately 15-year span of middle age for the leading edge cohort, and about a ten-year span for the intermediate cohort.

Marital Status and Living Arrangements

Parents of Baby Boomers—those who reached adulthood in or soon after World War II—embraced marriage as no other generation before or after. However, their children, especially the leading edge of the Baby Boom, experienced young adulthood in the context of the social ferment of the 1960s (Bouvier & De Vita, 1991). Among the many aspects of society and culture that came under scrutiny were the family and marriage-centered lifestyles of their parents. The marital behavior of the Baby Boomers represented a turning point in marriage trends in incidence, timing, and dissolution. From the mid-1960s onward, marriage rates began to decline, the timing of first marriage began to climb, and divorce rates rapidly increased. We can see evidence of some of these trends in Table 1.1.

There are two notable trends in these data. First, across all three racial/ethnic groups we see that the proportion married declines within cohorts as well as across cohorts. Quite reasonably, the proportion of the leading-edge cohort that is currently married declines. For Blacks and Whites, this decline appears to be mainly because of divorce. For Hispanics, however, widowhood seems to be the culprit. We also see evidence that a smaller proportion of Baby Boomers entered middle age married. For example, nearly 77% of Whites in the leading-edge cohort were married at the beginning of middle age compared to 71% of the trailing-edge cohort.

TABLE 1.1
Marital Status of Baby Boomers by Cohort and Race

| | Age of Respondent | | | | | | | | |
| | 40–42 | | | 47–49 | | | 53–55 | | |
Birth Cohort	White	Black	Hisp.	White	Black	Hisp.	White	Black	Hisp.
Leading									
(1947–1949)									
Married	76.6	58.2	72.8	74.8	55.4	68.1	72.5	46.1	69.3
Widowed	1.2	3.4	1.0	1.6	4.1	3.5	3.0	7.2	4.3
Sep./Div.	16.0	23.1	20.0	16.8	22.7	19.7	18.8	29.2	18.6
Nev. Mar.	6.2	15.3	6.2	6.9	17.8	8.8	5.8	17.6	7.8
Middle									
(1953–1955)									
Married	73.7	46.4	69.3	72.5	46.7	69.0			
Widowed	0.8	2.1	1.3	1.3	4.4	2.5			
Sep./Div.	15.7	29.2	17.8	17.2	27.2	16.7			
Nev. Mar.	10.0	22.3	11.6	9.1	21.6	11.8			
Trailing									
(1960–1962)									
Married	71.4	47.2	66.0						
Widowed	1.0	1.4	1.5						
Sep./Div.	12.4	20.4	14.7						
Nev. Mar.	12.4	31.0	17.8						

Source: 1989, 1995, 2002 Current Population Surveys. Data are weighted. Numbers in table are percentages.
Terms: Sep./Div.: Separated or divorced.
Nev. Mar.: Never married.
Hisp.: Hispanic.

Second, there are stark racial/ethnic differences in marriage among Baby Boomers. Despite the declines noted above, marriage remains the dominant experience of Whites and Hispanics, at least to this point in middle age. In contrast, less than half of African Americans are married at the start of middle age in both the middle and trailing-edge cohorts. Having never married by age 40 has become particularly common among African Americans, more than doubling from 15% to 31% across cohorts.

To what extent might this decline in marriage be offset by the growth of cohabitation? Table 1.2 contains estimates of the proportion of Baby Boomers currently cohabiting. Since the CPS did not begin asking about cohabitation until 1995, we cannot estimate its prevalence for the leading-edge cohort at age 40. Overall, the proportion of Baby Boomers cohabiting at any given time appears relatively small, never exceeding 4%. These data suggest that Baby Boomers may have instigated the popularity of cohabitation starting in the 1970s, but they did not sustain these relationships over the long term. There are modest cohort differences, with the trailing-edge Baby Boomers the most likely to be cohabitors.

Table 1.3 displays a number of characteristics of the living arrangements of Baby Boomers. As one might expect, there are significant changes across mid-

TABLE 1.2
Cohabiting Status of Baby Boomers by Cohort and Age

Birth Cohort	40–42	47–49	53–55
Leading			
(1947–1949)			
Married	—	72.6	69.7
Cohabiting	—	2.0	2.9
Single	—	25.3	27.4
N	—	6,234	7,190
Middle			
(1953–1955)			
Married	71.4	71.1	
Cohabiting	2.8	3.0	
Single	25.8	25.9	
N	6,967	9,370	
Trailing			
(1960–1962)			
Married	70.9		
Cohabiting	3.9		
Single	25.2		
N	11,307		

Source: 1989, 1995, and 2002 Current Population Survey. Data are weighted. Numbers in table are percentages.

TABLE 1.3

Living Arrangements of Baby Boomers, by Cohort and Age

Birth Cohort	Age of Respondent					
	40–42		47–49		53–55	
	Males	*Females*	*Males*	*Females*	*Males*	*Females*
Leading						
(1947–1949)						
% living alone	10.8	5.7	11.5	9.7	11.4	16.2
Avg. HH size	3.47	3.52	3.17	3.02	2.72	2.44
% with children	64.9	69.0	47.9	39.3	24.0	40.8
Avg. No. of children	1.3	1.3	0.8	0.6	0.4	0.3
% with elderly dep.	5.5	4.8	7.2	6.9	6.8	9.1
Middle						
(1953–1955)						
% living alone	10.4	5.9	12.6	10.5		
Avg. HH size	3.48	3.17	3.13	2.98		
% with children	62.4	71.3	46.9	41.7		
Avg. No. of children	1.3	1.4	0.8	0.6		
% with elderly dep.	7.9	5.3	7.2	7.4		
Trailing						
(1960–1962)						
% living alone	12.5	7.2				
Avg. HH size	3.44	3.55				
% with children	60.9	70.6				
Avg. No. of children	1.3	1.4				
% with elderly dep.	6.9	5.5				

Source: 1989, 1995, and 2002 Current Population Surveys. Data are weighted.

Terms: % living alone: Proportion of Baby Boomers living in household alone.

Avg. HH size: Average number of persons living in household of respondent.

% with children: Proportion of Baby Boomers who are living in household that contains a household member less than 18 years of age.

Avg. No. of children: Average number of household members who are less than 18 years of age.

% with elderly dep: Proportion of Baby Boomers living in a household that contains at least one person aged 65 or older.

dle age, and these changes are different for men and women. Living alone is rare among Baby Boomers. However, there are pronounced gender differences in the trends over time. The proportion of men living alone remained fairly constant, at about 11%, both across middle age and across the three cohorts. Women, in contrast, are less likely to be living alone (about 6%) at the beginning of middle age, but increasingly likely to be living alone over time.

For instance, the proportion of leading-edge women living alone nearly triples from 5.7% at ages 40 to 42 to 16.2% at ages 53 to 55. Gender differences in divorce and remarriage are likely behind this, given that men are more likely to be married at each time point (analyses not shown). Also, the proportion of women with children in the home declines slower over time than for men and the proportion with an elderly relative in the home grows faster, suggesting that these shifts are not the primary reason for the increasing proportion of women living alone.

Average household size at the beginning of middle age remains constant across cohorts, but, not surprisingly, shows evidence of decline within the leading-edge and middle cohorts. A major reason for this is nest-leaving. Children are a part of the home experience of the majority of Baby Boomers at the beginning of middle age. However, there is some evidence of the declining experience of coresident children for men across cohorts noted by others (Eggebeen, 2002), from 65% among the leading-edge cohort to 61% among the trailing-edge. Among the leading-edge men, living with children moves from common to rare as individuals age from their 40s to their mid 50s. The proportion of leading-edge women living with children also declines, but a sizable proportion (41%) remain coresident parents while in their mid 50s.

Finally, there is some evidence that Baby Boomers, especially those now in their mid-50s, are increasingly likely to have coresident relatives. The overall proportion of multigenerational baby-boomer households remains small, and the increase over time is not significant enough to offset the loss of children from the home.

Social and Economic Resources

Beyond the family, schools probably were the most profoundly affected by the onset of the Baby Boom (Bouvier & De Vita, 1991). Starting with elementary schools, then junior high and high schools, educational institutions struggled to accommodate the legions of children. Between 1955 and 1975, enrollments in elementary and secondary schools shot up 41% (U.S. Bureau of the Census, 1991). The onslaught continued beyond high school. College enrollments had already begun to rise soon after World War II, as the fathers of the Baby Boomers took advantage of the GI Bill to extend their schooling, and the Baby Boomers flocked to colleges and universities in even larger droves. Between 1965 and 1980, college enrollments more than doubled, from 5.9 million to 12 million students. As a result, the Baby Boomers far exceeded previous cohorts in their level of education.

Table 1.4 displays the distribution of Baby Boomers by level of education achieved by middle age. Two patterns stand out. The starkest trend is the remarkable differences by race/ethnicity in levels of completed education.

TABLE 1.4

Level of Education of Baby Boomers by Cohort and Race

	Age of Respondent								
	40–42			47–49			53–55		
Birth Cohort	White	Black	Hisp.	White	Black	Hisp.	White	Black	Hisp.
Leading									
(1947–1949)									
<HS	9.2	21.6	43.0	7.7	22.6	44.7	7.4	18.6	46.3
HS	37.7	39.6	30.0	30.8	34.6	27.7	31.4	33.7	25.1
SC	22.1	23.9	16.2	28.3	28.2	17.8	27.9	28.9	16.9
C+	31.1	15.0	10.8	33.2	14.7	9.9	33.2	18.9	11.6
Middle									
(1953–1955)									
<HS	7.8	18.2	39.4	5.7	15.8	40.6			
HS	33.0	35.3	29.5	32.1	32.5	27.6			
SC	29.1	31.7	20.6	29.5	32.3	18.0			
C+	30.1	14.9	10.5	32.7	19.5	13.8			
Trailing									
(1960–1962)									
<HS	7.1	12.8	36.4						
HS	33.5	35.4	30.2						
SC	28.3	34.4	19.7						
C+	31.1	17.5	13.8						

Source: 1989, 1995, 2002 Current Population Surveys. Data are weighted. Numbers in table are the percentages.

Terms: <HS:　Respondent has less than 12 years of completed education.

　　　 HS:　Respondent has 12 years of completed education.

　　　 SC:　Respondent has 13–15 years of completed education.

　　　 C+:　Respondent as 16 or more years of completed education.

Among leading-edge Baby Boomers, Whites are twice as likely as African Americans to hold college degrees and three times as likely as Hispanic Americans. The differences in the proportion that are poorly educated are even more disturbing. Fewer than 10% of leading-edge Whites are high school dropouts compared to about one fifth of African Americans and 43% of Hispanic Americans. There is some evidence, however, that the racial gap among Baby Boomers has narrowed. There are clear declines across cohorts in the proportion of both African Americans and Hispanic Americans that are high school dropouts. The proportion with college degrees, however, has increased only modestly. The implications of these disparate trends in education are reflected in the patterns of labor force participation (Table 1.5) and, most significantly, in family incomes (Table 1.7).

Finishing school, the leading-edge Baby Boomers entered the labor market in the late 1960s. Between 1965 and 1970, nearly 8.4 million workers were added to the labor force, an eleven percent increase (U.S. Bureau of the Census, 1991). An additional 10 million workers were added between 1970 and 1975, and another 13 million by 1980. All told, the U.S. labor force grew a phenomenal 42% between 1965 and 1980.

Table 1.5 displays the labor force status of the three middle age baby-boom cohorts. At age 40, African Americans and Hispanic Americans are about twice as likely as Whites to not be in the labor force in the leading and middle cohorts. This gap is significantly smaller for the trailing-edge cohort, however. About two out of three white Americans work full-time (worked at least 35 hours per week for at least 50 weeks in the previous year), with little discernible trend within or across cohorts. In contrast, Blacks in the leading-edge cohort show a decline in the proportion working full-time across middle age from 63% to 55%.

Male and female Baby Boomers show very different patterns of labor force attachment as depicted in Table 1.6. At middle age, men are strongly anchored

TABLE 1.5

Labor Force Participation of Baby Boomers by Cohort and Race

| | Age of Respondent | | | | | | | | |
| | 40–42 | | | 47–49 | | | 53–55 | | |
Birth Cohort	White	Black	Hisp.	White	Black	Hisp.	White	Black	Hisp.
Leading									
(1947–1949)									
Not in LF	11.4	17.3	20.3	12.2	18.7	25.1	17.7	28.0	26.9
P/T	23.6	19.6	25.5	22.2	20.5	23.1	18.8	16.7	18.1
F/T	65.0	63.1	54.2	65.7	60.8	51.8	63.6	55.3	55.0
Middle									
(1953–1955)									
Not in LF	11.9	23.2	23.1	13.4	21.6	19.7			
P/T	25.1	21.0	26.2	19.0	18.0	21.5			
F/T	63.0	55.8	50.7	67.5	60.5	58.8			
Trailing									
(1960–1962)									
Not in LF	13.0	19.5	19.6						
P/T	20.7	18.3	19.8						
F/T	66.3	62.2	60.7						

Source: 1989, 1995, 2002 Current Population Surveys. Data are weighted. Numbers in table are percentages.

Terms: Not in LF: Respondent was not in the labor force the previous year.
          P/T: Respondent worked in previous year, but less than 35 hours per week or less than 50 weeks.
          F/T: Respondent worked at least 35 hours per week for at least 50 weeks in previous year.

TABLE 1.6
Labor Force Participation of Baby Boomers by Cohort and Gender

	Age of Respondent					
	40–42		47–49		53–55	
Birth Cohort	Male	Female	Male	Female	Male	Female
Leading						
(1947–1949)						
Not in LF	6.6	19.2	8.5	19.3	14.3	24.9
P/T	15.6	31.1	14.0	29.7	14.3	22.7
F/T	77.8	49.7	77.5	51.0	71.4	52.5
Middle						
(1953–1955)						
Not in LF	8.3	20.4	9.3	20.2		
P/T	16.9	32.0	14.0	24.2		
F/T	74.8	47.6	76.8	55.6		
Trailing						
(1960–1962)						
Not in LF	8.2	20.8				
P/T	14.3	25.8				
F/T	77.6	53.4				

Source: 1989, 1995, 2002 Current Population Surveys. Data are weighted. Numbers in table
are percentages.

Terms: Not in LF: Respondent was not in the labor force the previous year.
   P/T: Respondent worked in previous year, but less than 35 hours per
     week or less than 50 weeks.
   F/T: Respondent worked at least 35 hours per week for at least 50 weeks
     in previous year.

in full-time work, with some declines in the leading-edge cohort after age 50.
In contrast, only about half of the female Baby Boomers in the leading-edge
cohort began middle age as full-time workers. In contrast to their male counterparts, however, there is a slight increase in those working full-time across
middle age. Women's attachment to the labor force as full-time workers, not
surprisingly, is somewhat higher in the trailing-edge cohort, although there remain significant gender differences.

These patterns of education and labor force behavior are the major deter-
minant of the income distributions we observe in Table 1.7. Despite the common stereotype of Baby Boomers as an affluent generation (Bouvier & De
Vita, 1991), we see considerable economic diversity at middle age. Perhaps the
starkest difference is by race/ethnicity. White Baby Boomers show clear advantages in income relative to African Americans and Hispanic Americans.
Whites are twice as likely at any age or cohort as either Blacks or Hispanics to

EGGEBEEN AND STURGEON

TABLE 1.7

Family Income of Baby Boomers by Cohort and Race

| | Age of Respondent | | | | | | | | |
| | 40–42 | | | 47–49 | | | 53–55 | | |
Birth Cohort	White	Black	Hisp.	White	Black	Hisp.	White	Black	Hisp.
Leading (1947–1949)									
<15,000	6.1	19.3	16.0	6.3	17.2	21.0	8.0	19.5	14.9
15–30,000	11.6	20.9	23.2	11.1	23.5	24.1	10.9	20.0	22.0
30–45,000	15.2	19.9	21.1	14.7	16.5	19.5	12.8	16.5	20.0
45–60,000	16.7	13.4	14.9	14.5	14.9	10.7	14.5	13.1	10.5
60–75,000	15.7	9.5	10.0	13.5	9.4	10.0	12.0	9.9	11.0
75–100,000	17.4	10.0	7.8	17.3	8.1	7.6	14.8	10.4	10.7
100,000+	17.3	6.9	7.0	22.4	10.4	7.1	27.1	10.5	10.9
Middle (1953–1955)									
<15,000	7.5	21.9	21.8	6.5	17.8	15.8			
15–30,000	13.0	21.9	23.8	10.9	19.4	18.4			
30–45,000	16.0	16.9	18.1	12.3	18.1	17.9			
45–60,000	16.2	15.2	14.0	13.9	12.9	14.1			
60–75,000	14.9	9.7	8.5	11.8	11.1	10.6			
75–100,000	16.3	9.7	7.9	18.0	10.5	12.0			
100,000+	16.1	4.7	5.9	26.6	10.3	11.2			
Trailing (1960–1962)									
<15,000	6.6	17.6	17.2						
15–30,000	11.2	19.7	21.9						
30–45,000	14.3	20.0	19.3						
45–60,000	14.3	12.5	12.8						
60–75,000	13.3	10.6	9.9						
75–100,000	17.4	11.0	9.7						
100,000+	22.9	8.6	9.2						

Source: 1989, 1995, 2002 Current Population Survey. Data are weighted. Numbers in table are percentages. Incomes are adjusted by CPI-U to make them comparable across years.

have earned at least $75,000. Similarly, Whites are only half as likely as Blacks or Hispanics to have earned less than $30,000 in the previous year. The magnitude of this race/ethnic gap does not appear to lessen across cohorts. There is some evidence that all three groups experience growth in incomes over time, however. Slightly more than one-third of Whites earned $75,000 or more at the beginning of middle age. By their mid-fifties, 42% of white Baby Boomers were earning this much income. Black and Hispanic Baby Boomers in the leading-edge cohort also showed gains over time in the group earning the highest incomes, although the gap between race/ethnic groups does not lessen.

Family income is also likely to be very different depending on how couples decide who will work. Although there are many possible permutations, we will focus on three common strategies: (a) couples where both are full-time in the labor force, (b) couples where one spouse works full-time and the other part-time or less, and (c) couples where there is no full-time worker, and either one or both spouses work part-time or are retired. For all three cohorts, the most common strategy is for married couples to rely on one full-time worker. Slightly more than half of married couples begin middle age utilizing this strategy (data not shown), and this proportion declines over time. The next most common arrangement, dual-worker couples, represents 36% of 40- to 42- year-olds among the leading and middle cohorts, and 40% among the trailing-edger's. Finally, the proportion of couples not significantly attached to the labor force is comparatively small in middle age (12% or less) across all the cohorts, and tends to vary over time.

The choices couples make about who works clearly matter (Table 1.8). Across all three cohorts, dual-worker couples have dramatically higher incomes. Alrcady at age 40, approximately half of these couples report incomes in excess of $75,000, compared to less than a third of couples with only one full-time worker and only 11% to 19% of couples with no full-time worker. Furthermore, the proportion of dual-worker couples in the top income brackets climbs over time, increasing, for the leading-edge cohort, from 51% to nearly 63%.

Furthermore, between forty-one and fifty-three percent, depending on the cohort, of Baby Boomers aged 40 to 42 who are not significantly attached to the labor force have incomes below $30,000. The proportion with very low income does significantly change across middle age for the leading-edge cohort.

CONCLUSIONS

What have we learned from these data about the Baby Boomers at middle age? First and foremost, these data underscore the substantial diversity among Baby Boomers. One of the most fundamental axes of differentiation is race. Differences between the races, most notably black/white differences, in marriage, education, labor force participation, and income are so stark as to make broad generalizations about Baby Boomers as a whole erroneous. Furthermore, viewing these race differences separately obscures their interaction. For example, the distinctly higher levels of white Baby

TABLE 1.8

Family Income of Baby Boomer Married Couples by Labor Force Participation

	Age of Respondent								
	40–42			47–49			53–55		
Cohort	<=P/T	One F/T	Both F/T	<=P/T	One F/T	Both F/T	<=P/T	One F/T	Both F/T
Leading (1947–1949)									
<15,000	20.0	2.5	1.0	23.8	2.0	<1.0	18.4	2.1	<1.0
15–30,000	24.9	10.1	3.4	24.5	9.2	2.3	25.2	9.4	1.8
30–45,000	20.6	18.1	8.9	19.6	17.8	7.1	15.4	14.2	7.4
45–60,000	14.5	21.1	15.8	10.6	16.9	12.9	13.4	16.3	11.6
60–75,000	7.5	16.7	20.3	6.3	15.8	16.9	7.9	13.7	15.9
75–100,000	6.7	15.4	26.6	7.2	16.3	25.4	8.8	16.8	19.8
100,000+	5.6	16.0	24.0	8.1	22.3	34.9	11.0	27.4	43.0
Middle (1953–1955)									
<15,000	24.2	2.2	1.1	17.6	2.3	<1.0			
15–30,000	28.8	11.4	3.5	24.9	8.3	1.3			
30–45,000	17.6	17.3	9.7	15.4	13.1	5.8			
45–60,000	11.9	21.0	16.7	10.5	15.9	11.6			
60–75,000	6.1	17.3	20.7	9.5	14.5	16.1			
75–100,000	4.7	14.7	26.0	10.1	19.1	26.0			
100,000+	6.8	16.2	22.5	12.2	26.9	38.7			
Trailing (1960–1962)									
<15,000	20.7	1.9	<1.0						
15–30,000	20.3	9.4	1.8						
30–45,000	18.4	16.1	8.7						
45–60,000	14.2	16.4	16.0						
60–75,000	7.3	15.5	18.1						
75–100,000	9.0	18.5	24.8						
100,000+	10.2	22.3	30.3						

Source: 1989, 1995, 2002 Current Population Survey. Data are weighted. Numbers in table are percentages. Incomes are adjusted by CPI-U to make them comparable across years.

Terms: <=P/T: Both spouses worked less than 35 hours per week or less than 50 weeks in previous year.

One F/T: Only one spouse worked at least 35 hours per week for at least 50 weeks in previous year.

Both F/T: Both spouses worked at least 35 hours per week for at least 50 weeks in previous year.

Boomers with high education and living as married couples is a major reason they dominate the proportion of Baby Boomers in two-earner couples—and why they are overrepresented in the top income groups.

The second important axis of differentiation evident in these data is socioeconomic. The stereotype of Baby Boomers as being more likely than previous generations to be highly educated is true. However, the demographic reality is that only a minority of Baby Boomers has college degrees; most are relatively poorly educated at a time when education has become increasingly more important as the vehicle to well paying jobs. These differences in education form the basis for substantial disparities in family income. It is true that, as a group, Baby Boomers are better off than their parents. Averages, however, obscure the fact that even at middle age, substantial fractions of Baby Boomers have low or modest incomes. In a word, there is strong demographic evidence to argue that there are essentially two groups of Baby Boomers—the haves and have-nots.

A second finding is that there appear to be only modest differences between the leading-edge and trailing-edge Baby Boomers, at least for the demographic characteristics examined in these data. This is somewhat surprising, given the attention this difference is given by others. Of course, it is reasonable to suppose that the more substantial cohort differences lie in factors like attitudes, values, and relationship qualities and dynamics, rather than what was examined with these data (marital status, education, living arrangements, work, and income). Intercohort differences may also widen as the middle- and trailing-edge cohorts move deeper into middle age.

What lies ahead for America's Baby Boomers? Most analysts have focused on the implications or challenges of the large number of Baby Boomers entering old age. The aging of the workforce, the potential increases in social expenditures, the rising need for caregiving, and, of course, the threat of the Baby Boomers to the viability and solvency of the Social Security system are some of the challenges typically discussed, usually without much optimism. This demographic determinism is, however, somewhat simplistic. Some of the most important factors that will shape their lives as elderly people—economic upturn or downturns, social instability, and cultural change—have essentially unpredictable or unknowable consequences.

Nevertheless, there are some clues in the current patterns that can give us some hints about what may lie ahead. We can assume, for example, that for the next 10 or 25 years, the Baby Boomers will continue to build on the foundation laid in middle age for their retirement years. The Baby Boomers who are most advantaged at middle age—those who are highly educated, with good jobs that provide excellent health insurance and pension plans, and high incomes, and who are married with children—will undoubtedly be well positioned to weather economic, cultural, and social turmoil as they enter old age. We estimate these represent about 40% of Whites, but only about 20% of Blacks and 15 to 20% of Hispanics, respectively.

On the other hand, those Baby Boomers that lack two or more of these advantages—perhaps 20% of these cohorts—are likely to face a less predictable, more uncertain future. It is the future of these Baby Boomers that will be most affected by the emerging debates about how to allocate scarce resources between the dependent young and the dependent elderly.

REFERENCES

Alt, P. M. (1998). Future directions for public senior services: Meeting divergent needs. *Generations, 22,* 29–33.

Bean, F. D. (1983). The Baby Boom and its explanations. *Sociological Quarterly, 24,* 353–365.

Bouvier, L. F. (1980). America's Baby Boom generation: The fateful bulge. *Population Bulletin, 35*(1), 1–36.

Bouvier, L. F., & De Vita, C. J. (1991). The Baby Boom—Entering middle age. *Population Bulletin, 46*(3), 1–34.

Butz, W. P., & Ward, M. P. (1979). Will US fertility remain low? A new economic interpretation. *Population and Development Review, 5*(4), 663–688.

Easterlin, R. (1987). *Birth and fortune: The impact of numbers on personal welfare.* Chicago: University of Chicago Press.

Eggebeen, D. (2002). The changing course of fatherhood: Men's experiences with children in demographic perspective. *Journal of Family Issues, 23,* 486–505.

Hardy, M. A., & Kruse, K. S. (1998). Realigning retirement income: The politics of growth. *Generations, 22,* 22–28.

Jones, L. Y. (1980). *Great expectations: America and the Baby Boom generation.* New York: Coward, McCann & Geoghegan.

Levy, F. (1987). *Dollars and dreams: The changing American income distribution.* New York: Russell Sage Foundation.

Macunovich, D. J. (2002). *Birth quake: The Baby Boom and its aftershocks.* Chicago: University of Chicago Press.

Mintz, S., & Kellogg, S. (1988). *Domestic revolutions: A social history of American family life.* New York: Free Press.

National Center for Health Statistics. (2003). *Live births by age of mother and race: 1930–1998.* http://www.cdc.gov/nchs/data/natality/mage33tr.pdf

Pillemar, K., & Suitor, J. J. (1998). Baby Boom families: Relations with aging parents. *Generations, 22,* 65–69.

Russell, C. (2001). *The Baby Boom: Americans aged 35 to 54.* Ithaca, NY: New Strategist Publications.

Russell, L. B. (1982). *The Baby Boom generation and the economy.* Washington, DC: Brookings.

U.S. Bureau of the Census. (1991). *Statistical abstract of the United States: 1991* (111th ed.). Washington, DC.

Westoff, C. F. (1978). Some speculations on the future of marriage and fertility. *Family Planning Perspectives, 10*(2), 79–83.

CHAPTER TWO

Social, Historical, and Developmental Influences on the Psychology of the Baby Boom at Midlife

Abigail J. Stewart
Cynthia M. Torges
University of Michigan

Many generations are given names and identities, perhaps increasingly, as journalists and marketers see generations as potential niches in the market of readers and consumers. Most generations are well known for something they accomplished or experienced as young adults. The Generation of 1914 fought World War I (Wohl, 1979); the Greatest Generation fought World War II and then created the civic culture of the 1950s (Brokaw, 1998); the Generation of 1968 were student activists worldwide (Passerini, 1996). But the defining fact about the baby-boom generation (some of whom also became members of the Generation of 1968) was that it was born. This was viewed as socially consequential at the time and ever after—because of the impact on education, health care, labor force activity, and so on. In this chapter we examine a different issue. We consider the psychological meaning of generation in the lives of those people who actually composed the Baby Boom. To do that, we consider briefly what the Baby Boom felt like to those who created it and, much more extensively, what it has felt like to those who populated it. We also consider what we know about the significance of generation in individual psychology. Our treatment will begin from the assumption that a birth cohort (group of people born at the same time) like the Baby Boom becomes a generation (a birth cohort defined by its shared social history) when it is viewed as one by others, and by its own members (see Alwin, McCammon, & Hofer, chap. 3, this volume). The Baby Boom qualifies on both counts. Finally, we examine how the meaning of generation changes over the course of adulthood, at least into middle age.

WHAT IS THE BABY BOOM?

The baby-boom generation is made up of about 76 million people who happened to be born between 1946 and 1964. The overall number of U.S. births per year had dropped below 2.5 million in the late 1930s and stayed low until after the War, when it climbed steeply; it peaked above 4.0 million per year between 1956 and 1961 (when it declined fairly steeply through the 1960s). Early Boomers (those born between 1946 and 1954) were born during the years when the birthrate was climbing, and the late Boomers (those born between 1955 and 1964) were born when the Baby Boom had been recognized and was beginning to level off (these data are drawn from CBO, 1993).

The fact of a large increase in the birthrate had inevitable consequences for everyday life. For example, one woman born in the 1940s said about that time:

> I did not have any romantic image [of family life]. I grew up in a double triple-decker [a three-story apartment building], with triple-deckers stacked along, and everyone was having babies. This was the 50s! And they cried all the time. And people yelled all the time. That was my view of kids—they cry all the time, they trap you, they foreclose options, and they're a heck of a lot of trouble, and they drive you nuts. (quoted in Stewart, 1994)

Many people have commented that members of large cohorts may suffer from crowding throughout their lives—their parents may have trouble getting them into nursery schools, they may attend overcrowded elementary schools, they may face stiff competition for college and in the labor force, and so forth (see for example, Easterlin, 1987; CBO, 1993). Some have speculated that large cohorts should face economic scarcity, due to the competition for limited resources (Welch, 1979; Easterlin, 1987). Some features of the Baby Boomer's life experiences, then, derive fairly directly from the mere size of their cohort.

Other features of the Baby Boomer's life experiences may derive from other aspects of U.S. social history during the period in which they were raised. For example, Light (1988) points out that the Baby Boom was accompanied by a housing boom, in which certain construction codes dictated that the kinds of physical spaces in which children were raised if their families moved into new houses or apartments, were very similar. Goulden (1976) noted that "the American Gas Association, a trade group, persuaded the entire appliance industry to agree upon standard sizes for both kitchen cabinets and appliances, maintaining that a streamlined kitchen would not belong exclusively to the housewife who could afford custom workmanship" (p. 137). Thus, as Light points out, "if the Baby Boomers do not remember exactly the same political events, they will always remember the same kitchen" (p. 111). He goes on to specify that:

five shared experiences may unite them. They were part of a silent revolution in social values. . . . They were raised with great expectations about their future. . . . They witnessed history through the unifying image of television. They experienced social crowding which fueled their desire for individual distinction. And they shared the fears brought on by a new generation of cold-war weapons. (pp. 111–112)

Different writers identify different key experiences and focus on different aspects of them (for example, is the key unifying experience the fear of devastation or the Cold War opposition between the U.S. and Russia?). Moreover, some experiences seem to have obvious affective or psychological implications (e.g., great expectations about the future), but even these are ambiguous in their consequences. Does having "great expectations about the future" lead to narcissism? Optimism? Both?

THE PSYCHOLOGICAL IMPLICATIONS OF BEING A PART OF THE BABY BOOM

We suspect that the psychologically important features of Baby Boomers' early life experience may be found in the historical processes that created the population surge itself. First, and most crucial: World War II ended. A large cohort of young men and women who had deferred personal lives set up house and populated those houses with babies (Stewart & Malley, 2004); this cohort literally produced the Baby Boom. World War II cast a longer or shorter shadow over the next period in these families' lives depending on the parents' experiences during the war (of combat, of the military, of the labor force, of dislocation and loss).

The economic circumstances of the postwar period in the U.S.—that is, enormous and rapid economic growth and prosperity—were no doubt also responsible for the sustained population surge over twenty years. These economic conditions were coupled with policies and programs (e.g., the G.I. bill, the expansion of consumer credit and home mortgages) that ensured their widespread impact particularly on White, middle-class and upwardly-mobile Americans (Cohen, 2003; Coontz, 1992). Economic growth and prosperity, in combination with long-term processes of urbanization, led to the expansion of residential suburbs around large cities, and a new suburban lifestyle (O'Neill, 1986). Finally, all of these things together created intensified gender differentiation in baby-boom families. As Friedan (1963) understood, the new suburban lifestyle required women to be at home to greet their children at lunchtime, and to monitor their play after school. Suburban housing was located too far from urban centers of labor force opportunities to make even part-time work easily compatible with these demands for childrearing. Moreover, many families formed during and after World War II welcomed the chance to build a domestic life that had been deferred by war responsibilities on the front and at home (Chafe, 1972; Hartmann, 1982; May, 1988). This combination of factors (demobilization, economic prosperity, suburbanization and intensified gender pressures) shaped the public life of the U.S. and the home lives of Baby Boomers during their formative years.

In addition, there were more specific or particular social experiences that were widely shared. It is difficult to know how important any given experience is, or how consequential for later life stages. For example, the Baby Boom was famously exposed to air raid drills in which children were taught to "duck and cover" their heads in anticipation of a nuclear attack. It is simply a social historical fact that this training went on in American public schools during the period in which many Baby Boomers went to school (see Garrison, 1994; May, 1988). It is reasonable to argue, based on facts like this, that the childhoods of Baby Boomers were filled with specific anxiety-provoking images that might have shaped some of their ideas about the future. But for how long would these images continue to affect Baby Boomers' life experiences in distinctive ways? Should we expect that this early experience had enduring consequences beyond the impact of later experiences, including experiences of the end of the Cold War? What about after the September 11 attack on the World Trade Center in New York City? Did Baby Boomers react to that later threat with memories of the childhood Cold War practices more than did other generations? To our knowledge, this has not been studied, but a focus on the psychological meaning of generation would suggest that one important meaning of generation or cohort—perhaps for all cohorts—is that certain experiences are formative and remain lifelong reference points when subsequent events occur.

One well-studied example of this kind of reference point is the Kennedy assassination. All generations alive at the time tended to experience this event as a "vivid" or "flashbulb" memory (Brown & Kulik, 1977; Neisser, 1982; Pillemer, 1984; Rubin & Kozin, 1984). People felt the importance of the event at the time, and subsequently remembered where they were and what they were doing when they heard about it. Early Baby Boomers were young adolescents at the time, and late Baby Boomers were children. It is likely that for both groups this experience was formative in a different way than it was for middle-aged adults (many of whom in fact compared their responses to their feelings at the time of President Roosevelt's death in 1945—thus demonstrating that they already had a reference experience).

INSIDE THE BABY BOOM

As we have seen, it is possible to think about features of the baby-boom experience that may be very general, and to think of the Baby Boom as having an identity as a generation. Nevertheless, there are some critical distinctions in the experience of Baby Boomers—experiences that divide the cohort into different groups. Mannheim (1952) defines these groups within a generation as *generation units*.

> The generation unit represents a much more concrete bond than the actual generation as such. Youth experiencing the same concrete historical problems may be said to be part of the same actual generation; while those groups within the same actual generation which work up the material for their common experiences in different specific ways, constitute separate generation units (p. 304). . . . These [generation units] are characterized by the fact that they do not merely involve a loose participation by a number of individuals in a pattern of events shared by all alike though interpreted by the different individuals differently, but an identity of responses, a certain affinity in the way in which all move with and are formed by their common experiences. (p. 306)

Generation units may be defined by features of social structure (like gender and social class) that recur in many generations. They are created, though, not out of those structures per se, but out of the specific sharing of experiences of social history that some groups have and others do not.

For example, different groups within the Baby Boom experienced events such as the Vietnam War differently. Some Baby Boomers experienced the war as soldiers (either by voluntary enlistment or draft), whereas others experienced it as protesters. Such differences in experience may in turn create differences in worldviews (or strengthen preexisting differences); Vietnam veterans likely have quite different perceptions and expectations of the world than do people who protested the war.

Likewise, Baby Boomers experienced events of the sixties and seventies differently depending on their race. For instance, both black and white Americans point to the assassination of John Kennedy as a "flashbulb memory," but African Americans name the assassinations of Martin Luther King Jr. and Malcolm X much more often than do Whites (Brown & Kulik, 1977). We also speculate that the degree to which race serves as a generation unit, that is, a focus of conscious identification, depends on the race in question. Many Blacks had similar experiences as targets of discrimination, prejudice and fewer opportunities based on their race; those common experiences supported the development of a sense of common fate among Blacks. Although Whites accrued material and social advantages from their race, they were largely unaware of that fact, and therefore had little basis for the development of a conscious identification as a generation unit (see Frankenberg, 1993).

As we outlined previously, early and late Boomers experienced events differently based on their developmental stage when events occurred; hence, birth placement also creates generation units. Stewart and Healy (1989) propose that social events experienced in childhood shape an individual's fundamental expectations and values, whereas social events experienced later, during young adulthood, shape a person's identity (see Duncan & Agronick, 1995; Schuman & Scott, 1989 for evidence supporting this notion). Hence, the dramatic social events of the 60s and 70s (the Civil Rights movement, women's and gay liberation movements, and Vietnam War) were the context for the development of expectations about the future for late Boomers. However, for the early boomers, these events contributed to their identity and consequently helped to form their political commitments.

This difference in experience between the early and late Boomers also explains some of the variation in generational identity across the Baby Boom. Early Boomers, because they experienced extremely politicizing events when they were struggling to form their own identities, may attach both political and personal meaning to their sense of generation (Erikson, 1968). Stewart and Healy (1986) draw on the life of Vera Brittain to illustrate how influential social events (World War I in her case) experienced during this stage can catalyze and form a person's political identity and commitment. Attaching one's identity to politicizing events that also have a powerful personal impact enhances one's identification with one's generation; thus, early Boomers should identify with their generation more than late Boomers.

We theorize that this tendency to identify with one's generation is also influenced by personality. Broadly speaking, some people tend to understand themselves in the context of a larger picture; they see their own lives interconnected or woven within the lives and events around them. Others experience themselves as unique and distinct from the happenings surrounding them. Vera Brittain exemplifies the former orientation when she notes that her father feels "nothing but contempt" for her but also observes that this dynamic is not unique to her; she laments that this is the social condition all women must endure (Stewart & Healy, 1986). This tendency to interpret one's own life circumstances and experiences in the light of larger social and political meanings is an individual difference that creates differences within all generations.

It follows, then, that Baby Boomers are heterogeneous in how much they identify with their generation. Nevertheless, as a whole, Baby Boomers, and early Boomers in particular, should have more horizontal identification with their own generation than vertical identification with their parents'. Consequently Baby Boomers are less apt than members of other cohorts to identify with their parents' values and beliefs or to transmit them to their own children (Stewart & Healy, 1989; Stewart, 2003). In addition, people with horizontal identification tend to encourage social change rather than invest in the status quo. Baby Boomers demonstrate this phenomenon in the multitude of ways in which they disagreed with their parents' generation on topics varying from school integration to business–labor evaluations (Jennings, Stoker, & Bowers, 1999).

MIDLIFE ISSUES

Our focus in this chapter is on the generation of Baby Boomers at midlife. In thinking about this generation's particular experience at midlife, it is helpful to consider those features that have been identified as generally important at midlife regardless of cohort (Hunter & Sundel, 1989; Kalish, 1989; Lachman, 2001; Lachman & James, 1997; Whitbourne, 1986; Whitbourne, Zuschlag, Elliot, & Waterman, 1992; Willis & Reid, 1999).

The Psychology of Middle Aging

First, one of the psychological hallmarks of midlife is supposed to be generativity, or a preoccupation with creating or preserving something that may contribute to the larger society and that may endure beyond one's own life span as a legacy (Erikson, 1963, 1969; McAdams & de St. Aubin, 1998; Rossi, 2001). Of course this intensifies a focus on cross-generational care—preserving valuable traditions, skills and values from the past generation, and strengthening the capacities of the next generation. It is also in middle age that new demands for caregiving may emerge on two sides: not only from offspring, but also from aging parents (Climo & Stewart, 2003; Ryff & Seltzer, 1996). This new need for caregiving from the older generation both creates new demands for support from midlife adults and also makes them the responsible caregivers of those both older and younger than they are.

Identity, or a sense of persistent personal selfhood within a larger web of social connections, was first recognized by personality theorists as a critical feature of adolescence (not middle age; see Erikson, 1968). However, recent research has shown that identity is often an important issue in midlife, perhaps because it may be challenged, revised, and/or affirmed or strengthened and consolidated in this period (Stewart, Ostrove, & Helson, 2001; Zucker, Ostrove, & Stewart, 2002).

A third important psychological issue in midlife is one's relationship to authority, or status. Midlife is conventionally a period of maximum expertise and accomplishment, and associated with that expertise and accomplishment is an internal sense of authority and competence, or confident power (see Stewart & Vandewater, 1998). Neugarten and Berkowitz (1964) assumed that this quality was commonly acquired in professional-level occupations, but many studies have found that both social class and work experience are unrelated to the development of this quality (see Miner-Rubino, Winter, & Stewart, 2004; Stewart, Ostrove, & Helson, 2001). At the same time, many writers have suggested that midlife carries with it the first serious intimations of mortality in the form of anxiety about physical decline and death (Jaques, 1965; Gullette, 1997).

Middle Age as a Long Life Stage

The psychological characteristics of midlife have been studied without much attention to the possibility that middle age is long and not uniform (Staudinger & Bluck, 2001; Stewart & Vandewater, 1998). Usually defined as beginning around age 40 and ending in the early 60s, this is at least a two-decade life stage, likely to be different at the beginning than at the end. For example, Stewart and Vandewater (1999) argue that regrets about "paths not taken" that are acknowledged in the late 30s can be addressed via life changes (career changes, divorces, marriages, becoming a parent), but that regrets acknowledged in the late 50s more often cannot. There is little research that makes a clear distinction between early and late middle age, but we suspect the need to do so will be increasingly recognized (see also Stewart & Ostrove, 1998; Stewart & Vandewater, 1998). Wherever we can, we will attempt to differentiate the psychology of early middle age of Baby Boomers from that of later middle age.

THE INTERSECTION OF DEVELOPMENT AND SOCIAL HISTORY: IMPLICATIONS FOR THE PSYCHOLOGY OF THE BABY BOOM GENERATION

As we have seen, Stewart and Healy (1989) argued that the socio-historical circumstances encountered during childhood shape background assumptions about life and the social world. Thus, as Elder (1974) showed, "children of the Great Depression" grew up under conditions of economic scarcity and carried an assumption of scarcity forward even into affluent times. Few psychologists have systematically examined "the psychology of generations," so we have little empirical evidence about this hypothesis for other cohorts. However, Twenge (2000) has demonstrated that—across cohorts sampled in the 1950s through the 1990s—indicators of social conditions during childhood correlate substantially with children's scores on anxiety, and less with adults'. By thinking through the nature of the historical experience coinciding with each life stage, we can derive some reasonable hypotheses about the psychology of this particular generation.

Childhood

The Baby Boom's childhood (1946–1970) took place, in contrast to that of the Greatest Generation, under conditions of economic expansion (including dramatic increases in white collar employment) that were metaphorically paralleled by expansion into outer space. This current of optimistic expansion was complicated by other powerful social currents of isolationism and anxiety about the Cold War and enemies (particularly communist ones) within and without, and military and political security. At least one social historian of the period has argued that "containment" of powerful and threatening forces characterized the adult psychology of the 1950s as well as the foreign policy (May, 1988). It is difficult to know quite how children were influenced by these complex social and political phenomena, and surely they were not influenced in any uniform manner. Although the beginning of this period (immediate postwar) and the end (particularly the late sixties) were not identical, most members of the Baby Boom generation—whether born early or late—were influenced to some degree by this long period of peace, prosperity and Cold War.

The Significance of Peace and Prosperity. The impact of a prolonged period of peace (including peaceful relations between labor and management) combined with economic expansion would appear to have the clearest and most homogeneous psychological impact, perhaps in part because of its sharp contrast with the long period of the Great Depression followed by World War II. Many American children—regardless of their family background—grew up during the Baby Boom with an expectation of nearly limitless economic growth and opportunity. This kind of expectation might breed a certain level of optimism, confidence and sense of entitlement (Coontz, 1997). Sociologist Wini Breines (1992) wrote, for example:

> It is not surprising, then, that the optimism for which Americans have been notorious was in full flower in the 1950s. . . . Many 1950s memories exude this certainty and confidence. Backyard barbecues, family television watching, and soda fountains tell of easy times. . . . Americans, it appears, felt secure and content. . . . The students who grew up in the fifties . . . shared this self-assurance. (pp. 4–5)

The Impact of Competition. At the same time, the context of the Cold War and the dramatic population growth in a single generation combined to create growing conditions for the development of a level of competitiveness and individualism that was remarkable even for American society. In addition, the powerful postwar commitment to the ideology of the U.S. as a melting pot was challenged by increased racial and ethnic contact resulting from northern migration of African Americans and the flight of white ethnics from homogeneous urban neighborhoods to more ethnically diverse, if racially segregated, suburbs (Gleason, 1992). Faced with crowded schools and the looming expectation of a crowded college and labor market, baby-boom children struggled for individual recognition and distinction. Anxiety about threats from dangerous others could only enhance the usual national preference for self-reliance and individualism (see Breines, 1992). Indeed, Twenge (2000) found that samples of baby-boom children scored higher on indices of anxiety than children (tested at comparable ages) born before the boom. Baby-boom children's life experiences contrasted sharply with their parents' childhood and adult experience of profound national missions (in response to the Depression and World War II), unifying experiences, and pressure for conformity both in terms of the development of large-scale national organizations and the domestic sphere (reflected in the development of "organization men" as well as an ideology of the perfect housewife; see, e.g., Riesman, 1950; Whyte, 1956; O'Neill, 1986). Baby-boom children experienced each other at best as everpresent competitors in a battle for resources; at worst as potential threats in a dangerous world. When they reached adulthood, the Baby Boom was roundly criticized by many cultural critics for being "narcissistic" and a "me" generation incapable of building community (Bellah, 1985; Lasch, 1978).

Adolescence

Many writers have commented on the fact that the Baby Boomers' adolescence coincided with the turbulent 1960s and early 1970s (Farber, 1994; Gitlin, 1987). The leading edge of the cohort came of age in the late sixties and early seventies, while the trailing edge were adolescents in the late seventies and early eighties (and therefore children during the earlier tumultuous periods). These were surely different times.

Adolescence for the Leading Edge. In the earlier period national disunity was overt, racial divisions were open, and the country was at war in Vietnam. The early 1960s remained expansionist and optimistic during the New Frontier, but the assassination of President Kennedy in 1963 and the growing racial tension and war in Vietnam all marked a much more polarized and conflict laden time (see Conway, 1997). Student movements arose on college campuses as access to higher education increased for women, minorities and less affluent students. These students—along with many people not in college—increasingly mobilized around the civil rights movement, the anti-war movement, and eventually the women's movement. Through the early 1970s those movements acted as crucibles for a generation of student activists, and as a focus for ideological debate about the direction of national policy.

Adolescence for the Trailing Edge. By the late 1970s the war had ended, and both the Civil Rights and women's movements slowly receded from national political debate, while continuing to leave lasting changes in social and cultural life. Stewart, Settles and Winter (1998) showed that these movements were felt to be formative not only for college students who were activists at the time, but also for those who were "engaged observers"—students who were interested, concerned and attentive, but not active. These two groups included a large majority of the former college students they studied.

Implications of Student/Youth Activism.   A substantial literature has focused on the later life course consequences of having been an activist during this entire period. Virtually all of that literature suggests differences between those who were activists and those who were not activists even before their political engagement; however, it is also evident that participating in social protest has life course consequences that endure (Cole & Stewart, 1996; Cole, Zucker, & Ostrove, 1998; Dickstein, 1992; Franz & McClelland, 1994; McAdam, 1989; Jennings, 1987; Ostrove, 1999; Sherkat & Blocker, 1997; Stewart & McDermott, 2004). For example, Sherkat (1998) found that student activists were less involved with traditional religion before college (and after), but he also showed that student activists resisted the *traditionalization* of religious schemas that characterized other groups in the population during the 1970s and early 80s.

Implications of War.   The period of polarized national debate about major issues that characterized the Baby Boomers' adolescence provided a stark contrast to the much more unified, conformist and suppressed national politics of the 1950s (Gitlin, 1987; Farber, 1994). Moreover, like many other generations asked to go to war, this generation felt defined by that experience (Pennebaker & Banasik, 1997)—a different experience from some previous war generations in part because of the lack of national consensus about the war itself (see Wohl, 1979 on the generation of 1914 and Brokaw, 1998 on the World War II generation).

Key Role of Discontinuity Between Childhood and Adolescence.   We have argued that the Baby Boom was somewhat defined and shaped by its demography and its early life experience during its childhood. It was, though, its adolescence that provided the kind of sharp discontinuity between childhood and adolescent social conditions that Stewart and Healy suggest creates *generational identity*. The collective experiences of war and social movements helped create a number of separate and often complementary generational units within the Baby Boom—people who shared a particular experience of those best and worst of times.

As adolescents who were members of this generation formed their own individual identities during this period, many of them identified with others (of the same gender, race, or class) with whom they shared these formative and shaping experiences (see Neisser, 1982; Conway, 1997, for related arguments). These factors created the conditions for a generation of individuals whose powerful childhood sense of initiative, optimism and entitlement was both tested by exposure to frightening social chaos at home and at war, and affirmed and strengthened by the success of social movements and many aspects of the national missions at home and abroad. These factors also created the conditions for the development of narcissists who became individuals with well developed collective identities, or identifications with groups who shared a certain set of experiences or statuses within the culture (see Gaskell & Wright, 1997, for a parallel analysis of the role of "Thatcherism" in England). One of the collective identities they developed was Baby Boomers itself, and it took on much richer social meaning and content than its merely demographic origins implied. This identity included engagement with politics and collective identities, even protest, as well as a variety of associations with movements in music, art and culture (see especially Farber, 1994).

Young Adulthood

The Political Environment.   For most of the Baby Boomers' adolescence a Democrat was President; in contrast, Republican Presidents were running a country whose postwar economic boom was over for most of their young adult lives—regardless of whether they were early or late Boomers. Richard Nixon was elected in 1968 and until January 1993, Republicans occupied the White House, except for four short years of the Carter Presidency. The earliest Boomers turned 21 at the beginning of this period of Republican Presidents, and the latest did at the end. For most boomers, then, the increasingly conservative 70s and 80s corresponded with the period in which they were building "life structures" (Levinson, Darrow, Klein, Levinson, & McKee, 1978) including jobs, families and community lives. During these decades the national focus turned to avoiding a repetition of our failed imperialist adventure in Vietnam and maintaining (and expanding) our affluence. As one observer commented:

> . . . as economic issues became more pressing in the early seventies, a conservative reaction set in, including a middle-class tax rebellion, and Ronald Reagan sprang forth as its spokesman and beneficiary. More traditional values—religion, family, patriotism—came to the fore, and many Americans recoiled from the carnivalesque instability of those times. (Dickstein, 1992, p. 14)

The Personal Focus.   The developmentally appropriate focus of the baby-boom generation on domestic or private life was compatible with this national agenda. At the same time, given the activist and collectivist values that emerged in conjunction with the social movements of the late sixties, this inward turn was discontinuous with the generation's own past and with some core values that had animated it in youth. In a study of the leading edge of the Australian baby-boom cohort, Riggs and Turner (2000) argue that this disjunction produced "short term pessimism about community issues and optimism for their personal futures" (p. 87). Stewart and Healy (1989) predict that early adulthood is generally a period in which social changes—such as the changes toward inclusion of women and minorities in full citizenship—may affect individual life choices and opportunities, but core values and personal identities remain relatively stable.

This prediction was tested most clearly by a spate of commentators and formal studies showing that the baby-boom generation remained distinctive throughout adulthood in its embrace of social responsibility and communal values (Cole & Stewart, 1996; Cole, Zucker, & Ostrove, 1998; Dickstein, 1992; Franz & McClelland, 1994; McAdam, 1989; Jennings, 1987; Ostrove, 1999; Sherkat & Blocker, 1997). Dickstein (1992) noted that in young adulthood the Baby Boom "disappeared into families, guilds, and professions in every area of society" (p. 18). And yet, at the end of that period, former activists were different from earlier generations of former activists.

> There were no signs of the dramatic deconversions that had marked the middle-aging of the Old Left. Few of these radicals were still politically active but many had become socially concerned writers, editors, teachers, filmmakers, or labor organizers, bringing old commitments into new professional lives. Others had gone in for local activism, serving on school boards or community boards, organizing campaigns to stop a highway from being built or open land from being developed. Few, it seemed, had just gone for the money, despite the Gilded Age ethics of the Reagan years. It was clear that some sense of communal responsibility would continue to shape the remainder of their active lives. (p. 19)

Middle Age

Maintaining Generational Distinctiveness.   It is consequential for theories about middle age that Baby Boomers continue to look distinctive as a generation in middle age. This observation suggests both that generations may truly carry their earlier histories with them into the future, and that notions of universal personality developmental pressures must be understood in the context of evidence for cohort differences. Let us consider the four personality dimensions identified earlier as key features of personality in midlife: generativity and caregiving, confident power (or authoritativeness), identity, and psychological orientation to aging and death (see Stewart, Ostrove, & Helson, 2001; Zucker, Ostrove, & Stewart, 2002; Miner-Rubino, Winter, & Stewart, 2004). If these four issues dominate middle aging for all generations, how might they be distinctive in the experience of Baby Boomers?

General Personality Developmental Patterns in the Particular Development of the Baby Boom.   If it is true, as Dickstein (1992) and many others (e.g., Cole & Stewart, 1996) have suggested, that Baby Boomers had an unusually pronounced sense of social responsibility, then it would seem that generativity, though developmentally normative in middle age for all cohorts, should be particularly pronounced for them. As Dickstein put it, "As members of this generation have moved into positions of authority, their ideals have transformed institutions as well as individual lives" (p. 19). In their relationship to caregiving for their elders (a particularly prominent issue for them as their parents' generation enjoys much longer life spans than previous generations), Baby Boomers have been found to share in the cultural norms about filial responsibility, with adult daughters in this generation quite likely to provide direct care for nearby elders (Caputo, 2002).

Identity could be seen as a constant issue for members of the Baby Boom, as they sought to develop distinctiveness in their large cohort. In fact, their negative identities (narcissistic, the "me" generation) were often caricatures of a relentless search for personal meaning and self-expression. Most important, perhaps women born during the Baby Boom were the first generation of women encouraged—often after their adolescence—to develop their own individual identities (see Hulbert & Schuster, 1993, on the *transitional generation*). Moreover, the high levels of labor market participation and divorce they encountered in adulthood required them to do so even when they were disinclined. We expect, then, that women of the baby-boom generation—especially women in the leading edge—may be particularly focused on issues of identity in middle age (Helson, Stewart, & Ostrove, 1995).

Equally, if the women's movement had the kind of sustained impact on the life course of the women of this generation that many have suggested (see Echols, 1994; DuPlessis & Snitow, 1998), then women should be particularly likely to develop increased authoritativeness or confident power over the course of early adulthood. This makes sense in light of Twenge's (1997; 2001) finding that later cohorts of women were higher in masculine qualities of assertiveness and confidence than were baby-boomer women during their college years. Women of the baby-boom generation may have developed confidence over their life course to a level that younger women reach much earlier (see Stewart & Ostrove, 1998). In contrast, baby-boom men—raised to normative gender demands for early adult masculinity—may experience middle age as providing some release from demands for the performance of male authority or some decline in status and authority (Gullette, 1997; Thompson, 1994). Indeed, Twenge found fewer differences between baby-boom men and later cohorts' masculinity scores, and none in their femininity or assertiveness.

Perhaps this generation's relationship to mortality—to aging and death—is actually less gendered than the other psychological dimensions. In this domain the issues raised by social class—by differential demands for physical labor and strength over the life course, and differential access to health resources too—will be more important (see Miner-Rubino, Winter, & Stewart, 2004). In short, the generation units that matter in the psychology of midlife may be different for different personality developmental themes.

Impact of Distinctive Features of the Baby Boom Generation in Middle Age

A Long Generation. There are, of course, other issues about the Baby Boom at midlife about which we can speculate and examine data. The Baby Boom is a long generation (born over 15 years) that cannot possibly be homogeneous. We have noted some differences in the way that the leading and trailing edges of the generation intersect with social history. Surely these are consequential. The leading edge was grown up at the beginning of the long Republican 70s and 80s, but the trailing edge were just arriving at adulthood. It is not unreasonable to ask whether the key disjunction in at least some of the trailing-edge Boomers' experience was between the turbulent social-change-oriented late sixties and early seventies (coinciding with late childhood and early adolescence) and the materialist neoconservative seventies and eighties (coinciding with late adolescence and early adulthood). For these later born members of the generation, the identity-formative experiences may have come with the turn inward, not with the powerful collectivist movements of the late sixties. We need more research that would help establish the meaningful psychological distinctions based on a social historical approach that divides different cohorts within this long generation.

A Long Life Stage. It is equally true that middle age is long. If it extends at least from 40 to somewhere in the 60s, it seems likely that this 25-year agescape is marked by some changes. Stewart and Vandewater (1998) suggest, for example, that generativity may peak in middle age, but it may actually decline for much of it, as individuals come to terms with their own declining personal role in the social or collective future. Equally, Stewart and Vandewater (1999) examined the implications of regret in early middle age (that is, at age 37) as a motivator of "midcourse corrections" or major life changes. In contrast, in recent research Torges, Stewart, and Miner-Rubino (2005) have examined the implications of regret in late middle age (at age 60) for a process of life review or "coming to terms" with past choices and experiences that cannot be undone or reversed. The tasks of early and later middle aging are different, and the strengths that are required may also be different. The first study showed that the capacities to mobilize energy, assess alternatives and make instrumental choices are critical in early middle age; the second showed that capacities to reflect on alternatives, transform experiences into wisdom, and identify the lessons learned from life may be much more important later.

Social Structure and Social Identities. It seems very clear that social structure matters in middle aging for all generations, but the baby-boom generation's shaping experiences underscored the importance of these kinds of social groups as sources of identification: women, racial and ethnic groups, lesbians and gay men, social classes (see Baruch & Brooks-Gunn, 1984; Farrell & Rosenberg, 1981). All of these social categories or identities were understood by at least some Boomers as not merely abstract positions in a social hierarchy or collections of disparate individuals, but rather potential collectivities endowed with agency on their own behalf. In middle age these collective identities remain, even as the accretion of individualized life experiences sharpens individuals' sense of their own distinctiveness. Thus, for example, the very subject matter of regret is profoundly shaped by gender, and to a lesser extent by social class, with women and people of working class backgrounds both reporting more regrets about lack of education, and women reporting more regret about lack of pursuit of career opportunities (Torges, Stewart, & Miner-Rubino, 2005).

Material circumstances—opportunities, stresses, challenges—are clearly associated with these social structures, and they too affect middle aging particularly through their effects on physical health and longevity. Here social class (like race) exacts its very personal toll in the poor health and shortened life span of the less affluent (Adler, Boyce, Chesney, Cohen, Folkman, Kahn, & Syme, 1994; Ostrove & Adler, 1998; Ostrove, Feldman, & Adler, 1999). These issues loom larger and larger for the baby-boom generation, as the country remains paralyzed by a national failure of will to address the need for a national system of health care and health insurance that could provide a minimum standard of health for all Americans as they age.

CONCLUSIONS

It seems unavoidable to conclude by paraphrasing Kluckhohn & Murray (1953, p. 53) on individual personality: in some ways the Baby Boomers' middle age is like all generations' middle age; in some ways it's like some other generations' middle age; and in some ways it's like no other generation's middle age. By considering the intersection of this generation's life course with social history, we have put some specificity into that very general claim. We have some theoretical leads, and some evidence from personal memories and historians' accounts. What we don't have is very much empirical evidence that compares this generation's experience to another's in equivalent terms. Of course it is very difficult to collect data that permit us to do this (though Twenge has found imaginative ways to use meta-analysis of data that already exist).

We should be designing studies that would allow us to compare the current generation of middle-aged Baby Boomers—using the same measures given to past samples—to earlier generations of middle aged members of the Greatest Generation and the Silent Generation (that came of age in the fifties; see Stewart, 2003; Twenge, 1997, 2000, 2001 for examples). And of course we should be planning studies that will be carried forward by the next generation, to compare the middle aging of the baby-boom generation to that of its younger siblings and its children (see Gerson, 2002; Jennings, 2002; Twenge, 1997, 2000, 2001 for examples). It is only by investing now in comparative studies of the psychology of generations that we can develop an understanding that would allow us confidently to assess the particular meaning of one life stage in any generation's life course—even the Baby Boom's.

ACKNOWLEDGMENTS

The authors are grateful to Christa McDermott, Perry Silverschanz, Allison G. Smith, Timothy Stewart-Winter, Susan Whitbourne, Sherry Willis and David G. Winter for their helpful comments on earlier versions of this manuscript.

REFERENCES

Adler, N. E., Boyce, T., Chesney, M. A., Cohen, S., Folkman, S., Kahn, R. L., & Syme, S. L. (1994). Socioeconomic status and health: The challenge of the gradient. *American Psychologist, 49*, 15–24.

Baruch, G., & Brooks-Gunn, J. (Eds.). (1984). *Women in midlife*. New York: Plenum.

Bellah, R. N. (1985). Habits of the heart: Individualism and commitment in American life. Berkeley: University of California Press.

Breines, W. (1992). *Young, white and miserable: Growing up female in the fifties*. Boston: Beacon.

Brokaw, T. (1998). *The greatest generation*. New York: Random House.

Brown, R., & Kulik, J. (1977). Flashbulb memories. *Cognition, 5*, 73–99.

Caputo, R. K. (2002). Adult daughters as parental caregivers: Rational actors versus rational agents. *Journal of Family and Economic Issues, 23*, 27–50.

CBO (Congressional Budget Office). (1993, September). *Baby Boomers in retirement: An early perspective*. Washington, DC: U.S. Government Printing Office.

Chafe, W. H. (1972). *The American woman: Her changing social, economic, and social roles, 1920–1970*. New York: Oxford University Press.

Climo, A. H., & Stewart, A. J. (2003). Eldercare and personality development in middle age. In J. Demick & C. Andreolotti (Eds.), *Handbook of adult development* (pp. 443–457). New York: Kluwer/Academic/Plenum.

Cohen, L. (2003). *A consumer's republic: The politics of mass consumption in postwar America*. New York: Knopf.

Cole, E. R., & Stewart, A. J. (1996). Meanings of political participation among Black and White women: Political identity and social responsibility. *Journal of Personality and Social Psychology, 71*, 130–140.

Cole, E. R., Zucker, A. N., & Ostrove, J. (1998). Political participation and feminist consciousness among women activists of the 1960s. *Political Psychology, 19*, 349–371.

Conway, M. (1997). The inventory of experience: Memory and identity. In J. W. Pennebaker, D. Paez, & B. Rime (Eds.), *Collective memory of political events: Social psychological perspectives* (pp. 21–46). Mahwah, NJ: Lawrence Erlbaum Associates.

Coontz, S. (1992). *The way we never were: American families and the nostalgia trap.* New York: Basic.

Coontz, S. (1997). *The way we really are: Coming to terms with America's changing families.* New York: Basic.

Dickstein, M. (1992). After utopia: The 1960s today. In B. L. Tischler (Ed.), *Sights on the sixties* (pp. 13–24). New Brunswick, NJ: Rutgers University Press.

Duncan, L., & Agronick, G. (1995). The intersection of life stage and social events: Personality and life outcomes. *Journal of Personality and Social Psychology, 69,* 558–568.

DuPlessis, R. B., & Snitow, A. (Eds.). (1998). *The feminist memoir project: Voices from women's liberation.* New York: Three Rivers Press.

Easterlin, R. A. (1987). *Birth and fortune: The impact of numbers on personal welfare.* Chicago: University of Chicago Press.

Echols, A. (1994). Nothing distant about it: Women's liberation and sixties radicalism. In D. Farber (Ed.), *The sixties: From memory to history* (pp. 149–174). Chapel Hill: University of North Carolina Press.

Elder, G. H. (1974). *Children of the Great Depression.* Chicago: University of Chicago Press.

Erikson, E. (1963). *Childhood and society.* New York: W. W. Norton.

Erikson, E. (1968). *Identity: Youth and crisis.* New York: W. W. Norton.

Erikson, E. (1969). *Gandhi's truth.* New York: W. W. Norton.

Farber, D. (Ed.). (1994). *The sixties: From memory to history.* Chapel Hill: University of North Carolina Press.

Farrell, M., & Rosenberg, S. (1981). *Men at midlife.* Dover, MA: Auburn House.

Frankenberg, R. (1993). *White women race matters: The social construction of whiteness.* Minneapolis: University of Minnesota Press.

Franz, C., & McClelland, D. C. (1994). The life course of women and men active in social protests of the 1960s: A longitudinal study. *Journal of Personality and Social Psychology, 66,* 196–205.

Friedan, B. (1963). *The feminine mystique.* New York: W. W. Norton.

Garrison, D. (1994). "Our skirts gave them courage": The Civil Defense Peace Movement in New York City, 1955–1961. In J. Meyerowitz (Ed.), *Not June Cleaver: Women and gender in postwar America, 1945–1960* (pp. 201–226). Philadelphia: Temple University Press.

Gaskell, G. D., & Wright, D. B. (1997). Group differences in memory for a political event. In J. W. Pennebaker, D. Paez, & B. Rime (Eds.), *Collective memory of political events: Social psychological perspectives* (pp. 175–190). Mahwah, NJ: Lawrence Erlbaum Associates.

Gerson, K. (2002). Moral dilemmas, moral strategies, and the transformation of gender: Lessons from two generations of work and family change. *Gender & Society, 16,* 8–28.

Gitlin, T. (1987). *The sixties: Years of hope, days of rage.* New York: Bantam.

Gleason, P. (1992). *Speaking of diversity: Language and ethnicity in twentieth-century America.* Baltimore: Johns Hopkins University Press.

Goulden, J. (1976). *The best years: 1945–1950.* New York: Atheneum.

Gullette, M. M. (1997). *Declining to decline: Cultural combat and the politics of the midlife.* Charlottesville: University Press of Virginia.

Hartmann, S. (1982). *The home front and beyond: American women in the 1940s.* Boston: Twayne Publishers.

Helson, R., Stewart, A. J., & Ostrove, J. (1995). Identity in three cohorts of women. *Journal of Personality and Social Psychology, 69,* 544–557.

Hulbert, K. D., & Schuster, D. T. (Eds.). (1993). *Women's lives through time: Educated American women of the twentieth century.* San Francisco: Jossey-Bass.

Hunter, K., & Sundel, M. (Eds.). (1989). *Midlife myths: Issues, findings and practical implications.* Newbury Park, CA: Sage.

Jaques, E. (1965). Death and the mid-life crisis. *International Journal of Psychoanalysis, 46,* 502–514.

Jennings, K. (1987). Residues of a movement: The aging of the American protest generation. *American Political Science Review, 81,* 365–382.

Jennings, M. K. (2002). Generation units and the student protest movement in the United States: An intra- and intergenerational analysis. *Political Psychology, 23,* 303–324.

Jennings, M. K., Stoker, L., & Bowers, J. (1999, September). *Politics across generations: Family transmission reexamined.* Paper presented at the 1999 American Political Science Association Convention, Atlanta, Georgia.

Kalish, R. (Ed.). (1989). *Midlife loss: Coping strategies.* Newbury Park, CA: Sage.

Kluckhohn, C., & Murray, H. A. (1953). Personality formation: The determinants. In C. Kluckhohn, H. A. Murray, & D. M. Schneider (Eds.), *Personality in nature, society and culture* (pp. 53–67). New York: Knopf.

Lachman, M. E. (Ed.). (2001). *Handbook of midlife development.* New York: Wiley.

Lachman, M. E., & James, J. B. (Eds.). (1997). *Multiple paths of midlife development.* Chicago: University of Chicago Press.

Lasch, C. (1978). *The culture of narcissism.* New York: W. W. Norton.

Levinson, D. J., Darrow, C. M., Klein, E. B., Levinson, M. H., & McKee, B. (1978). *The seasons of a man's life.* New York: Ballantine Books.

Light, P. C. (1988). *Baby Boomers.* New York: W. W. Norton.

Mannheim, K. (1952). *Essays on the sociology of knowledge.* New York: Oxford University Press.

May, E. T. (1988). *Homeward bound: American families in the Cold War era.* New York: Basic.

McAdam, D. (1989). The biographical consequences of activism. *American Sociological Review, 54,* 744–760.

McAdams, D. P., & de St. Aubin, E. (1998). *Generativity and adult development.* Washington, DC: American Psychological Association.

Miner-Rubino, K., Winter, D. G., & Stewart, A. J. (2004). Gender, social class, and the subjective experience of aging: Self-perceived personality change from early adulthood to late midlife. *Personality and Social Psychology Bulletin, 30,* 1599–1610.

Neisser, U. (1982). Snapshots or benchmarks? In U. Neisser (Ed.), *Memory observed: Remembering in natural contexts* (pp. 43–48). San Francisco: Freeman.

Neugarten, B. L., & Berkowitz, H. (1964). *Personality in middle and late life: Empirical studies.* New York: Atherton Press.

O'Neill, W. (1986). *American high: The years of confidence: 1945–1960.* New York: Free Press.

Ostrove, J. M. (1999). A continuing commitment to social change: Portraits of activism throughout adulthood. In M. Romero & A. J. Stewart (Eds.), *Women's untold stories: Breaking silence, talking back, voicing complexity* (pp. 212–226). New York: Routledge.

Ostrove, J., & Adler, N. E. (1998). The relationship of socio-economic status, labor force participation, and health among men and women. *Journal of Health Psychology, 3,* 451–463.

Ostrove, J. M., Feldman, P., & Adler, N. E. (1999). Relations among socioeconomic status indicators and health for African-Americans and Whites. *Journal of Health Psychology, 4,* 451–463.

Passerini, L. (1996). *Autobiography of a generation: Italy, 1968.* Middletown, CT: Wesleyan University Press.

Pennebaker, J. W., & Banasik, B. L. (1997). On the creation and maintenance of collective memories: History as social psychology. In J. W. Pennebaker, D. Paez, & B. Rime (Eds.), *Collective memory of political events* (pp. 3–19). Mahwah, NJ: Lawrence Erlbaum Associates.

Pillemer, D. B. (1984). Flashbulb memories of the assassination attempt on President Reagan. *Cognition, 16,* 63–80.

Riesman, D. (1950). *The lonely crowd.* New Haven, CT: Yale University Press.

Riggs, A., & Turner, B. S. (2000). Pie-eyed optimists: Baby-boomers the optimistic generation? *Social Indicators Research, 52,* 73–93.

Rossi, A. S. (Ed.). (2001). *Caring and doing for others: Social responsibility in the domains of family, work, and community.* Chicago: University of Chicago Press.

Rubin, D., & Kozin, M. (1984). Vivid memories. *Cognition, 16,* 81–95.

Ryff, C. D., & Seltzer, M. M. (Eds.). (1996). *The parental experience in midlife.* Chicago: University of Chicago Press.

Schuman, H., & Scott, J. (1989). Generations and collective memories. *American Sociological Review, 54,* 359–381.

Sherkat, D. E. (1998). Counterculture or continuity? Competing influences on Baby Boomers' religious orientation and participation. *Social Forces, 76,* 1087–1114.

Sherkat, D. E., & Blocker, T. J. (1997). Explaining the political and personal consequences of protest. *Social Forces, 75,* 1049–1076.

Staudinger, U., & Bluck, S. (2001). A view on midlife development from life-span theory. In M. E. Lachman (Ed.), *Handbook of midlife development* (pp. 3–39). New York: Wiley.

Stewart, A. J. (1994). The women's movement and women's lives: Linking individual development and social events. In A. Lieblich & R. Josselson (Eds.), *The narrative study of lives: Exploring identity and gender* (Vol. 2, pp. 230–250). Thousand Oaks, CA: Sage.

Stewart, A. J. (2003). Gender, race and generation in a midwest high school: Using ethnographically informed methods in psychology. *Psychology of Women Quarterly, 27,* 1–11.

Stewart, A. J., & Healy, J. M. (1986). The role of personality development and experience in shaping political commitment: An illustrative case. *Journal of Social Issues, 42*(2), 11–31.

Stewart, A. J., & Healy, J. M. (1989). Linking individual development and social changes. *American Psychologist, 44*(1), 30–42.

Stewart, A. J., & Malley, J. E. (2004). Women of the greatest generation. In C. Daiute & C. Lightfoot (Eds.), *Narrative analysis: Studying the development of individuals in society* (pp. 223–244). Thousand Oaks, CA: Sage.

Stewart, A. J., & McDermott, C. (2004). Civic engagement, political identity and generation in developmental context. *Research in Human Development, 1*(3), 189–203.

Stewart, A. J., & Ostrove, J. M. (1998). Women's personality in middle age: Gender, history and mid-course correction. *American Psychologist, 53,* 1185–1194.

Stewart, A. J., Ostrove, J., & Helson, R. (2001). Middle aging in women: Patterns of personality change from the 30s to the 50s. *Journal of Adult Development, 8,* 23–37.

Stewart, A. J., Settles, I. H., & Winter, N. J. G. (1998). Women and the social movements of the 1960s: Activists, engaged observers, and nonparticipants. *Political Psychology, 19,* 63–94.

Stewart, A. J., & Vandewater, E. A. (1998). The course of generativity. In D. P. McAdams & E. de St. Aubin (Eds.), *Generativity and adult development: Psychosocial perspectives on caring for and contributing to the next generation* (pp. 75–100). Washington, DC: American Psychological Association Press.

Stewart, A. J., & Vandewater, E. A. (1999). "If I had it to do over again . . .": Midlife review, midcourse corrections, and women's well-being in midlife. *Journal of Personality and Social Psychology, 76,* 270–283.

Thompson, E. H., Jr. (1994). *Older men's lives.* Thousand Oaks, CA: Sage.

Torges, C., Stewart, A. J., & Miner-Rubino, K. (2005). Personality after the prime of life: Men and women coming to terms with regrets. *Journal of Research in Personality, 39*(1), 148–165.

Twenge, J. (1997). Changes in masculine and feminine traits over time: A meta-analysis. *Sex Roles, 36,* 305–325.

Twenge, J. (2000). The age of anxiety? The birth cohort change in anxiety and neuroticism, 1952–2993. *Journal of Personality and Social Psychology, 79,* 1007–1021.

Twenge, J. (2001). Changes in women's assertiveness in response to status and roles: A cross-temporal meta-analysis, 1931–1993. *Journal of Personality and Social Psychology, 81,* 133–145.

Welch, F. (1979). Effects of cohort size on earnings: The Baby Boom babies' financial bust. *Journal of Political Economy, 87,* S65–S97.

Whitbourne, S. K. (1986). *Adult development.* New York: Praeger.

Whitbourne, S. K., Zuschlag, M. K., Elliot, L. B., & Waterman, A. S. (1992). Psychosocial development in adulthood: A 22-year sequential study. *Journal of Personality and Social Psychology, 63*(2), 260–271.

Whyte, W. H. (1956). *The organization man.* New York: Simon and Schuster.

Willis, S. L., & Reid, J. (Eds.). (1999). *Life in the middle: Psychological and social development in middle age.* New York: Academic.

Wohl, R. (1979). *The generation of 1914.* Cambridge, MA: Harvard University Press.

Zucker, A. N., Ostrove, J. M., & Stewart, A. J. (2002). College-educated women's personality development in adulthood: Perceptions and age differences. *Psychology and Aging, 17,* 236–244.

CHAPTER THREE

Studying Baby Boom Cohorts Within a Demographic and Developmental Context: Conceptual and Methodological Issues[1]

Duane F. Alwin
Pennsylvania State University

Ryan J. McCammon
University of Michigan

Scott M. Hofer
Pennsylvania State University

> **co·hort** (kō′ hôrt), *n.* **1.** a group or company: *She has a cohort of admirers.* **2.** a companion or associate. **3.** one of the ten divisions in an ancient Roman legion, numbering from 300 to 600 soldiers. **4.** any group of soldiers or warriors. **5.** an accomplice; abettor: *he got off with probation, but his cohorts got ten years apiece.* **6.** a group of persons sharing a particular statistical or demographic characteristic: *the cohort of all children born in 1980.* **7.** *Biol.* An individual in a population of the same species. [1475-85; < MF *cohorte* < L *cohort-* (s. of *cohors*) farmyard, armed force (orig. from a particular place or camp), cohort, retinue, equiv. to *co-* co- + *hort* (akin to *hortus* garden); r. late ME *cohors* < L nom. sing.]
>
> —*Webster's New Universal Unabridged Dictionary.*
> Barnes and Noble Books (1996)

INTRODUCTION

The term *cohort* is used in many ways. In the field of epidemiology a cohort is simply a group of people that is studied over time, regardless of the temporal attributes of their birth. In psychology and sociology, by contrast, cohort is often used synonymously with the term *generation* to refer to a group of people

---

[1] An expanded version of this chapter can be found at http://www.personal.psu.edu/faculty/d/f/dfa2.

born about the same time. And in demography, a cohort is, as implied by the definition from *Webster's*, a group of people born in the same calendar year.

A somewhat more general approach would define a cohort as a group of people who have shared some critical experience during the same interval of time. For example, people who enter college in a given year are referred to as an entering cohort and those who graduate in the same year would be called a graduating cohort. Or, those persons marrying in a given year are called a marriage cohort. In each case, there is an event or experience in common that defines the cohort. When the cohort-defining event is birth then the term cohort is often used as shorthand for birth cohort, which refers to all persons born in the same year. This is the way we use the term in this chapter (see also Alwin & McCammon, 2003).[2]

Members of a birth cohort share the experience of the life cycle, that is, they experience birth, infancy and childhood, reach adolescence, grow into early adulthood, and mature into midlife and old age during the same historical time. In this sense, members of a birth cohort share a social history, that is, they experience the same historical events and the opportunities and constraints posed by society at a given time in history. Defined in this way, knowing a person's cohort membership may be thought to index the unique historical period in which a group's common experiences are embedded, but as we have elsewhere argued and discuss next, this does not necessarily make a "cohort" (or a set of cohorts) a "generation" (see Alwin & McCammon, 2003).

This chapter reviews issues involving the conceptualization of cohort (and related concepts) and discusses the methodological issues involved in the translation of an interest in studying the life experiences of the baby-boom cohorts into research design and analysis. First, we begin with a discussion of the concept of cohort as a theoretical tool in the analysis of social change, distinguishing it from other concepts, such as generation. Second, we review the demographic context for a consideration of the phenomenon of the Baby Boom and its potential for influencing the makeup of society. Third, we review the *age–period–cohort model* for studying social and individual change and clarify the nature of effects of "aging, cohort and historical period" as used in the demographic literature. In this context we discuss the difficulties of clearly identifying the effects of these factors using the kinds of research designs routinely available in social and behavioral science. Finally, we review two major forms of data analysis employed to study data from multiple-cohort designs: (1) the decomposition of social trends into components representing cohort replacement and net social change, and (2) the use of growth-modeling techniques to study within-individual change.

---

[2]Using annual time periods is completely arbitrary. We could define cohorts in terms of months, or two-year intervals, etc., but the common definition employs the annual metric.

WHAT ARE COHORT EFFECTS?

Because members of a birth cohort share the experience of the life cycle, it is possible that the unique intersection of biography and history produce what demographers refer to as *cohort effects*, effects that contribute to social change through processes of *cohort replacement*. We return to a more complete discussion of these topics later in the chapter, but suffice it to say at this stage in our discussion that a cohort effect refers to a distinctive formative experience that members of a birth cohort (or set of birth cohorts) share that lasts—and indelibly marks them—throughout their lives. For example, people who grew up during the Great Depression of the 1930s may have different ideas about money than those who grew up in more prosperous times (Inglehart, 1977). Or, the women who were the first to have exercised their political enfranchisement in the U.S. after the 19th Amendment was passed in the early part of the 20th century may have taken voting more seriously throughout their lives and reported higher rates of voter turnout (Firebaugh & Chen, 1995). Or, children growing up during the "second demographic transition" may have very different perspectives on the nature of marriage, family and gender-based social roles than did their parents (Lesthaeghe, 1983, 1995; Amato & Booth, 1997). There are many other examples of potential cohort effects, although as we shall point out later, it is very difficult to draw firm conclusions from empirical data about such phenomena, given the confounding of cohort effects with age effects. Their potential confounding with other effects, however, does not mean they do not exist, only that it is difficult to adduce evidence on their behalf.

In keeping with this line of thought, we would argue that the unique historical and social events happening during the period of youth undoubtedly play a strong role in shaping human lives. Certainly, some eras and social movements provide particularly distinctive experiences for youth during particular times. The Civil Rights and feminist movements of the 1960s and 1970s, the political ideologies formed during Roosevelt's New Deal in the 1930s and 1940s, the 1973 Pro-Choice Supreme Court decision in *Roe vs. Wade*, or the environmentalist movement of the 1970s and 1980s, are all examples of particular historical stimuli to the development of such worldviews during specific historical periods (see, e.g., Alwin, Cohen, & Newcomb, 1991; Firebaugh & Davis, 1988; Schuman, Steeh, Bobo, & Krysan, 1997; Scott, 1998; Scott, Alwin, & Braun, 1996; Mason & Lu, 1988; Roof, 1999). It is not, however, simply the influence of these historical and social events on society that interests us here—it is their distinctive impact on the youth of the period. As Norman Ryder (1965) put it, ". . . the potential for change is concentrated in the cohorts of young adults who are old enough to participate directly in the movements impelled by change, but not old enough to have become committed to an occupation, a residence, a family of procreation, or a way of life" (p. 848).

Cohort effects, thus, refer to the impact of historical events and processes on individual lives, particularly during the formative years. As Modell (1989) notes, however, we need not limit our conception of cohort effects to this sort of one-way relationship between history and the individual. He argues for "a socio-historical approach to the life course" that focuses as well on "the way those altered individual experiences *aggregated* to constitute a new *context* for others living through these changes" (p. 22). The reactions of some cohorts to their historical experiences often become normative patterns that, once rationalized by society, influence the lives of later cohorts. In this sense cohort effects can be thought of as both direct and indirect. He uses the example of dating patterns among youth in American society to illustrate this point, and his analysis shows that adolescent dating, an invention of the 1920s (invented mainly by adolescent women), became a normative pattern among adolescents of the 1950s and 1960s, one which he argues actually constrained the choices that young women could make (Modell, 1989).

In addition to experiencing a unique piece of history during their formative years, members of a birth cohort share the experience of the cohort itself; the distinctive aspects of the cohort, e.g. its size or its level of education, are something unique to the cohort. Some of these distinctive attributes of cohorts may have a powerful impact upon their social experiences. One example of this is the phenomenon of cohort size. For example, in a path-breaking series of studies, Easterlin (1987) argues the numerically large set of birth cohorts making up the Baby Boom are at a significant socioeconomic disadvantage relative to that of their predecessors, simply because of their size. The number of persons born in a particular year, thus, has far-reaching consequences, given its effects on competition for jobs and the strain it produces on the opportunity structure. Easterlin (1987) argues that relative cohort size affects not only the economic well-being of cohort members, but many features of the family and individual functioning, including fertility rates. Individuals in large cohorts will be less likely to marry and more likely to put off having children. Mothers will be more likely to work outside the home, and as young adults they will be more likely to experience psychological stress and feelings of alienation.[3]

GENERATIONS AND COHORTS

The formative years for each new cohort are often thought to exert a powerful force in their lives, and behavioral scientists often theorize that how people think about the social world around them may depend as much on what is happening in the world at the time they were growing up as it does on what is

---

[3]For a review of the current status of research on the *Easterlin effect*, see Pampel (1993).

happening in the present. In a highly cited treatise titled "The Problem of Generations" written in the 1920s, the German sociologist Karl Mannheim (1952) argued that having shared the same formative experiences contributes to a unique worldview or frame of reference that can be a powerful influence throughout one's life. In Mannheim's (1952) words, "Even if the rest of one's life consisted of one long process of negation and destruction of the natural world view acquired in youth, the determining influence of those early impressions would still be predominant" (p. 298). Similarly, the Spanish sociologist José Ortega y Gasset (1933, p. 15) wrote that "generation is the most important conception in history," arguing that each generation has a special mission even if it goes unachieved (see Kertzer, 1983, p. 128). Each generation resolves issues of identity in its own way, however, and it may be difficult to generalize about generational phenomena. Psychoanalyst Erik Erikson (1988), put it this way:

> No longer is it merely for the old to teach the young the meaning of life . . . it is the young who, by their responses and actions, tell the old whether life as represented by the old and presented to the young has meaning; and it is the young who carry in them the power to confirm those who confirm them and, joining the issues, to renew and to regenerate or to reform and to rebel. (p. 21)

We agree that the "unique slice of history" in which one reaches maturity can have lasting effects on large segments of birth cohorts, but we would also suggest that the effects of cohort membership do not automatically imply the existence of "generations" in the sense of Mannheim (1927/1952). According to White (1992) cohorts only become "actors" when they cohere enough around historical events, in both their own and others' eyes, to be called "generations." In this sense, we would distinguish between cohorts and generations, in that the former refers to effects attributable to having been placed by one's birth in a particular historical period, whereas a generation is "a joint interpretive construction which insists upon and builds among tangible cohorts in defining a style recognized from the outside and from within" (White, 1992, p. 31). Through such mechanisms cohort effects are given life through these interpretive and behavioral aspects. There is, thus, an "identity" component associated with the concept of generation, as made explicit in the work of Mannheim (1927/1952) and Ortega y Gasset (1933) that may be difficult to isolate when studying cohort differences and their tendencies to persevere.

Generations are groups of people sharing a distinctive culture or identity by virtue of having experienced the same historical events at approximately the same time in their lives. As such, generations are distinct historical phenomena, which do not map neatly to birth cohort, or even to a fixed number of birth cohorts. Unlike cohort, generations do not enjoy a fixed metric that easily lends itself to statistical analysis. Rather, the distinction between generations is a matter of quality, not degree, and the temporal location of their boundaries cannot be easily identified, particularly without the context of a set of particular analytic questions. Roscow (1978) suggests that incisive historical events may distinguish generations, but that when such events "are soft and indistinct, (generations) . . . may be clearest at their centers, but blurred and fuzzy at the edges. They may remain so as long as transitional events are still gathering force, but a new (generation) . . . has not yet blossomed" (p. 69). Similarly, Mannheim (1927/1952) suggests that distinctive generations may fail to materialize for long periods of time should economic and social conditions remain stable, such that "largely static . . . communities like the peasantry display no such phenomenon as new generation units sharply set off from their predecessors . . . the tempo of change is so gradual that new generations evolve . . . without any visible break" (Mannheim, 1927/1952, p. 309).[4]

One must be also careful in the interpretation of members of cohorts as if they were monolithic, homogenous groupings of individuals, representing a generation in the sense meant by generational theorists. Instead, in many ways we see these cohorts as divided into what Mannheim (1927/1952) called *generational units*, the division of a set of cohorts by social position and level of involvement in the events of the day. How these subgroupings are identified and understood is clearly contingent on the substantive questions at hand, as generations do not exist in a vacuum, operating in the same way at all times for all members. Rather, like all sociological factors, cohort experiences differ by social position and the corresponding differential experience of events based on those contexts. The Civil Rights movement in the United States was largely carried out by the youth of the era, and there are clear generational identities associated with the movement, but the content of this identity obviously varies along geographic and racial dimensions (see McAdam, 1988). Similarly, the Vietnam War was a defining experience for the so-called baby-boom generation, but the imprint of the war on the identity of a conscientious objector who fled the country was vastly different from his shared cohort counterpart who experienced the war as a soldier in Hanoi (Hagan, 2001). Both may have generational identities linked to the war, but those identities are far from uniform. In contrast to cohorts, which have extremely broad coverage and precise boundaries, but lack specific explanations for the phenomena to which they are related, generations lack specific boundaries and are meaningful in their distinctiveness largely as subpopulations, but offer the potential of being used as powerful explanations in and of themselves for distinctive patterns of attitudes, beliefs, and behaviors (see Alwin & McCammon, 2003).

Finally, we note that the concept of generation has more than one meaning and its multiplicity of meanings can produce confusion. It is also used as a *kinship* term, designating the relationships between individuals who have a com-

---

[4]See Alwin & McCammon (2003) for a more detailed discussion of these issues.

mon ancestor. As a term denoting kinship relations, a generation consists of a single stage or degree in the natural line of descent. Thus, within a given family, generations are very clearly defined, and while generational replacement is more or less a biological inevitability within families (assuming continuous life cycle processes), the replacement of generations in this sense does not correspond in any neat manner to the historical process at a macro-social level because of individual differences in fertility (i.e., individuals do not all replace themselves at the same rate, or at all) and the fact that the temporal gap between generations is variable across families. The common reference to cohort effects as a *generational phenomenon* is probably derived from the presumption that historically based experiences shape individuals in a way that sets them apart from the parental generation. Because of this potential confusion of meanings, we prefer the term *birth cohort* for what many others refer to as generations in the historical sense of the term. This is especially true in the present case, as it can hardly be argued that there is a baby-boom generation, although there may be generational phenomena within these cohorts.

THE BABY BOOM COHORTS IN DEMOGRAPHIC CONTEXT

The focus of this book is on one particular set of cohorts, known as the baby-boom cohorts or Boomers. As a demographic phenomenon, the Baby Boom was a clear disruption of an otherwise monotonic decline in fertility over the previous two centuries in American society. From the point of view of examining the demographic makeup of modern society and its change, one cannot ignore the potential impact of the Baby Boom and its aftermath. What was remarkable about the Baby Boom, however, was not simply the fact that vast numbers of children were born within a relatively short span of history, but also the fact that they were born to a relatively small group of women. The production of a bulge in the age composition of society by a group of women themselves born roughly between 1915 and 1940 would have potentially dramatic impacts on society (Alwin, 1998, 2002).

It was not just that the baby-boom cohorts were larger than those that preceded them—they were also larger than those that followed. Birth rates have reached an all-time low throughout the industrialized world, with many European countries now experiencing unprecedented levels of fertility that are below replacement (Morgan, 2003). As noted earlier, fertility declines have, of course, occurred throughout most of the 20th century and before, so the post–Baby Boom readjustments to lower birth rates were not so much revolutionary as they were a continuation of a rather long-term trend toward lower birth rates (Teitelbaum & Winter, 1985). What was remarkable was not so much the fertility level achieved during the baby-boom era but rather its timing and the intensity of the increase. In fact, fertility levels at the height of the

Baby Boom reached parity with similar levels experienced in American society during the latter part of the nineteenth century.

Any definition of the Baby Boom is somewhat arbitrary. Most everyone agrees it began after World War II and lasted some fifteen-plus years, through the early 1960s. A more precise definition, based on crude birth rates and total fertility rates might define the Baby Boom as those born between approximately 1946 and 1963 (see Morgan, 1996). The crude birth rate peaked in 1947 and had all but subsided by 1962. The total fertility rate was about 3.1 in 1947 and 3.6 in 1962, whereas it was about 2.5 in 1946 and 1966.

Although we often refer to the Baby Boom as a set of cohorts born during a particular historical period, the actual Baby Boom was an experience that occurred to their mothers and fathers as much as it did to them. We can refer to differences between the Baby Boomers and their parents as a generational effect—but such differences confound both cohort differences and age differences. Several studies have drawn comparisons between generations—in sense of kinship groups (e.g., Biblarz, Bengtson, & Bucur, 1996; Rossi & Rossi, 1990)—employing multi-generational data, but such research designs are not very useful for identifying cohort effects (see Alwin & McCammon, 2003, pp. 28–29).

As a social phenomenon, those born during the baby-boom years share a unique social history, reaching adulthood in the mid-1960s through the late 1970s, but it would be a mistake to assume that the experiences of the baby-boom cohorts were in any sense homogeneous, either within or between cohorts. The first cohorts of the Baby Boom, thus, reached age 21 in 1968 at the height of the Vietnam War protests, the assassination of Dr. Martin Luther King, Jr., and presidential candidate Senator Robert Kennedy. During their formative years, they experienced a unique slice of American history, specifically the Civil Rights movement, the Vietnam War and the turbulent period of student protests against the war, the sexual revolution, the influx of drugs into American culture, the Nixon years and the Watergate scandal, the post Watergate malaise, and the feminist movement. The later born baby-boom cohorts may have been influenced by these events, but their lives were less immediately affected by the historical events of the 1960s and 1970s. The last cohorts of the Baby Boom reached age 21 in 1983, during the ascendancy of the Republican Party and the early years of the Reagan era. For some purposes it therefore makes sense to break the baby-boom cohorts into two parts, those born 1947 to 1954, and those born 1955 to 1962 (see Alwin, 1998).

THE BABY BOOM COHORTS IN COMPARATIVE PERSPECTIVE

Several things about the lives of individuals have a bearing on how society changes. Indeed, demographic theories of social change rest on the assumption that society changes as a function of two sets of mechanisms: (1) through the succession of cohorts, and (2) through changes undergone by individuals (Ryder, 1965; Firebaugh, 1992). Thus, society changes (paradoxically) both because individuals change and because they remain stable. The stable component of individuals reflects the indelible influences of historically based formative experiences, as discussed previously (if such exist), whereas the component representing changes to individuals is usually associated with the effects of aging and period influences.

These several types of influences can be visualized with respect to Fig. 3.1, which depicts the intersection of biographical and historical time in the lives of four birth cohorts (see Riley, 1973). These groups are distinguished by their origins with respect to historical time. The members of Cohort A originated at the turn of the twentieth century, those born into Cohort B originated in 1920, and so forth. Cohort D contains individuals who were part of the baby-boom cohorts. Society, at any given time, is a reflection of its cohorts—so, for example, in 1940 Cohorts A, B, and C (among others who went before) were present in any depiction of the nature of society, but not Cohort D. Similarly, in 2000 Cohort A is no longer represented, but B, C and D are (along with subsequent cohorts), each at a different stage in the life cycle.

We noted in the above discussion that cohort effects result from the intersection of biographical and historical time. Thus, when historical events and processes have a unique impact on a particular cohort because it is experiencing the impressionable period of youth at a particular time, we speak of the result as a cohort effect. The assumption of most theories of cohort replacement is that it is the phase of youth when individuals are the most vulnerable to the impact of such historical influences, but this is an empirical question.[5] If, for a particular outcome, there are no differences in the effects of such influences across persons at different life phases, then it may be difficult to argue that there are cohort effects that will result in social change via cohort succession. On the other hand, if cohort effects of the sort defined above exist (that is, differences in experiences that result in persistent intercohort differences), then society will change as the cohort composition of society shifts.

The previous discussion is intended to illustrate the meaning of the concept *cohort replacement* or *cohort succession*. That is, over historical time later-born cohorts replace earlier-born ones, and to the extent that there are differences due to cohort effects, this will be reflected in the way society changes. Where one set of cohorts is especially large—like the Baby Boomers—its lifestyle dominates the social spectrum as it passes through the life cycle. Baby Boomers' taste in music and clothes (or debt), for example, disproportionately shapes the nature of the culture.

---

[5]There is no logical necessity for cohort effects to be limited to the impact of historical factors on cohorts during their youth, but this is the manner in which they are most often conceptualized because of the assumption that youth is the most impressionable period of the human life cycle.

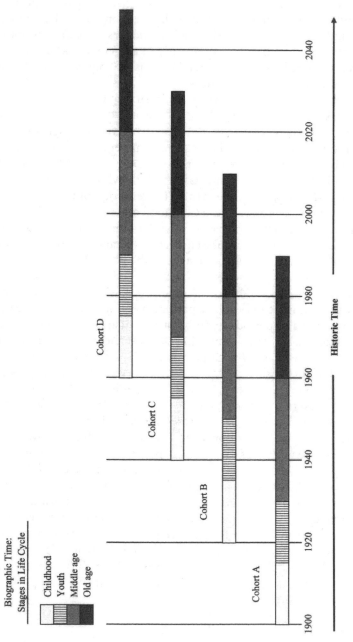

FIG. 3.1.   Intersection of biographic and historic time.

Figure 3.1 also portrays the passage of biographical time within each of the hypothetical cohorts. It illustrates that biographical time is literally embedded in historical time. For each cohort we have arbitrarily depicted four life phases or stages: childhood, youth, middle age and old age. This is clearly an oversimplification, but the intent is to present the course of development or maturation as a type of change to individuals that occurs in biographical time. Any such change can be attributed to aging or life cycle changes resulting from some combination of biological, psychological and social mechanisms that produce within-individual change. Influences of development, maturation, and aging are usually identified with differences within individuals (and between age groups) linked to their getting older, becoming more mature due to having lived more of life, or because of physical or cognitive change. For simplicity, in the present discussion, we refer to all of these as effects of aging.

Another source of individual change that is confounded with aging, as we shall see later, is identified as *period effects*, changes that come about through individuals' responses to historical events and processes happening in historical time. So, for example, when an entire society is affected by historical events—and not just young persons—then we speak of effects of history or period. If all members of society are caught up in and are affected by a set of historical events, such as a war, an economic depression, or a social movement, the widespread changes that occur are referred to as period effects. The Civil Rights movement, for example, may have changed ideas about race for all Americans, not just those birth cohorts growing up in the 1960s. If it affected primarily the young it would be called a cohort effect, but if it affected all cohorts it would be seen as a period effect. Of course, both could be happening. Not only were the youngest cohorts of women and men affected by the Feminist movement of the 1970s and 1980s, the movement might also have influenced the views of almost everyone living in the society during that time. There is clearly a fine line between what should be considered a cohort versus a period effect, but it usually comes down to who is affected by the events in question. In some cases it is impossible for most members of society to remain unaffected by historical events or social changes. Take the changes in the economy, or the influence of computers on society, for example. Or, consider the impacts of an event in more recent history—the September 11, 2001 terrorist attacks on the World Trade Center in New York and the Pentagon in Washington, DC. These events had a profound effect on virtually all members of American society, regardless of their year of birth.

RESEARCH DESIGN ISSUES

In the previous discussion we clarified the distinction between effects of aging, cohort, and period factors in the lives of individuals. These distinctions are consistent with a vast literature that has dealt with these issues, across disciplines over several decades (e.g., Baltes, 1968; Glenn, 2003, 2004; Mason & Fienberg, 1985; Riley, 1973; Ryder, 1965; Schaie, 1965, 1984). These are of critical importance in the present case because researchers investigating phenomena linked to the lives of the baby-boom cohorts may wish to draw inferences about the effects of these factors in the lives of these cohorts. In the remainder of the chapter we focus on two related sets of issues: (1) research design issues, and (2) the analysis of data gathered from such designs. In this discussion we consider the following designs: (a) the general repeated cross-sectional design and repeated measures longitudinal design, (b) the *synthetic cohort* cross-sectional design, (c) the single cohort repeated measures design, (d) the multiple-cohort repeated measures design, and (e) the longitudinal cohort sequential design. In the course of this discussion, we focus on two primary sets of analytic tools for analyzing multiple-cohort data: (1) a discussion of techniques for decomposing secular trends into net change (i.e., within-cohort change) and cohort replacement components, and (2) the use of growth models to study within-person change.

The Identification of Age, Period and Cohort Effects

In order to illustrate the nature of the effects of aging, period, and cohort, we configure such effects within the framework of the typical longitudinal research design in which observations are made on multiple occasions. In Table 3.1 we array the data by time and age, following the convention of the standard cohort table in which intervals of age correspond to intervals of observation (see Glenn, 2003, pp. 466–467). This may be thought of either in terms of: (a) a repeated cross-sectional longitudinal design, which observes the same co-

TABLE 3.1
Age, Period and Cohort Effects in the Standard Cohort Table

| Age | Year of Study (Period) | | | |
	1970	1980	1990	2000
20–29	$A_1 + P_1 + C_4$	$A_1 + P_2 + C_3$	$A_1 + P_3 + C_2$	$A_1 + P_4 + C_1$
30–39	$A_2 + P_1 + C_5$	$A_2 + P_2 + C_4$	$A_2 + P_3 + C_3$	$A_2 + P_4 + C_2$
40–49	$A_3 + P_1 + C_6$	$A_3 + P_2 + C_5$	$A_3 + P_3 + C_4$	$A_3 + P_4 + C_3$
50–59	$A_4 + P_1 + C_7$	$A_4 + P_2 + C_6$	$A_4 + P_3 + C_5$	$A_4 + P_4 + C_4$
60–69	$A_5 + P_1 + C_8$	$A_5 + P_2 + C_7$	$A_5 + P_3 + C_6$	$A_5 + P_4 + C_5$
70–79	$A_6 + P_1 + C_9$	$A_6 + P_2 + C_8$	$A_6 + P_3 + C_7$	$A_6 + P_4 + C_6$
80–89	$A_7 + P_1 + C_{10}$	$A_7 + P_2 + C_9$	$A_7 + P_3 + C_8$	$A_7 + P_4 + C_7$

C_1 = born 1971 to 1980 C_6 = born 1921 to 1930
C_2 = born 1961 to 1970 C_7 = born 1911 to 1920
C_3 = born 1951 to 1960 C_8 = born 1901 to 1910
C_4 = born 1941 to 1950 C_9 = born 1891 to 1900
C_5 = born 1931 to 1940 C_{10} = born 1881 to 1890

horts over time (but not the same individuals), or (b) a repeated measures (or panel) longitudinal design, which observes the same individuals over time (Duncan & Kalton, 1987). The present discussion applies equally to both. We consider them separately when we consider modes of analysis subsequently in the chapter.

Table 3.1 cross-classifies categories of age by occasion of measurement, and these categories are arrayed such that cohort groups can be followed along the diagonals of the table. Within the cells of the table we have placed the notation that depicts the effects of age (A), period (P) and cohort (C) that are reflected in the observations for each cell. The effect A_1 represents, for example, the effect of being in the youngest age group, the effect P_2 represents the effect associated with being measured at the second occasion of measurement (in this case 1980), and C_4 represents the effect of membership in the cohorts born in 1941–1950, and so forth.

Table 3.1 illustrates several things: (a) any data point in the cross-classification of age with time contains a combination of effects of age, period and cohort; (b) cross-sectional differences among age groups confound cohort and age effects, that is, comparisons of any two age groups at a particular occasion of measurement yields a difference that is due to a combination of effects of age differences and cohort differences; (c) cross-time comparisons for any cohort group confounds age and period effects, that is, for a given cohort category cross-time comparisons yield differences that are a joint function of age differences and period effects; and (d) cross-time comparisons for any age group confounds cohort and period effects, that is, comparison of a given age group, say ages 20 to 29, in successive surveys yields a difference that is due to a combination of effects of cohort differences and time of survey differences. These observations embody the classic age–period–cohort identification problem for which there is no statistical solution (see Mason & Fienberg, 1985). We illustrate some of these problems in our discussion of several research designs often used to examine the effects of cohort, the effects of aging, or the effects of period.

To capture the nature of the identification problem, we assume from the above discussion that variables representing the three main sets of factors can be thought of as affecting the mean levels of variables observed in the cells of the above tables: aging (A), historical time or period (P), and birth cohort (C). These are conceptual categories of variables representing rich and complex sets of influences that operate primarily through (a) processes of aging and life cycle changes, (b) processes influencing specific cohorts, and (c) those effects due to the distinctiveness of the time of measurement or historical period. The problem is, however, that within a given occasion of measurement, A (age) and C (cohort) are perfectly correlated. And in a series of repeated cross-sections, within cohorts, A (age) and P (time period) are perfectly correlated (Mason & Fienberg, 1985). Because

$$Age = Period - Cohort \; (A = P - C)$$

it is rarely possible to separate the influences of aging, cohorts, and time periods using longitudinal data in any purely exploratory fashion. One needs to be able to impose a strong set of assumptions about the nature of one or more of these three sources of variation—aging, cohorts and periods—in order to identify these separate influences unequivocally. By turning to supplementary types of data, what Converse (1976) called *side information*, assumptions about the nature of certain historical, aging, or cohort processes, it may be possible to simplify the problem. If one can make strong theoretical assumptions about the nature of certain influences, for example, setting either cohort, aging, or period effects to zero, it is possible to creatively interpret longitudinal data with the goal of identifying cohort phenomena when they exist. Short of such strong assumptions, it is usually not possible to cleanly disentangle these processes empirically from such data alone.[6]

Cross-Sectional Synthetic Cohort Designs

The framework developed above allows us to illustrate a number of implications of the identification problem for common research designs used to draw inferences about age, period or cohort effects (see Mason & Fienberg, 1985, pp. 59–66). For example, one of the most simple (and probably most flawed) designs for studying aging involves the construction of a *synthetic cohort* from cross-sectional comparisons of age groups. Note that examples of this design are embedded in the longitudinal design depicted in Table 3.1—any column of Table 3.1 represents such a design. In the minds of those who apply such a design, differences among age groups are often thought to be a result of processes that vary as a function of where the person is along a continuum of development or aging, linked to the passage of biographic time. Or in other cases the differences may be thought to reflect cohort differences alone.

It is very common for investigators to look at a cross-section of adults in American society, drawing comparisons between age groups and interpreting them either in terms of aging differences or cohort differences. It is not uncommon these days for comparisons to be drawn between baby-boom cohorts and those cohorts who went before or who came after on the basis of such data. Based on what we have presented here, it should be clear that such

---

[6]There are a number of excellent discussions of the identification problem referred to here (e.g., Mason & Fienberg, 1985; Glenn, 1976, 2004). Some literature focuses on possible statistical solutions (see Mason, Mason, Winsborough, & Poole, 1973). Although there is some value to considering these alternatives, the most productive initiatives with respect to the identification problem are those that find direct measures of theoretically relevant period or cohort influences (e.g., Farkas, 1977; O'Brien, 2000).

comparisons easily confuse cohort differences with the possibility that they might instead reflect differences due to experience or maturity (i.e., aging), or vice versa. Earlier-born cohorts not only grew up in a different era, they are now also older and more experienced. By contrast, cohorts born more recently are younger and have less experience. So, if one is looking at a phenomenon that is influenced both by the amount of experience one has as well as the particular slice of history in which one participated when growing up, the results of empirical analyses can be quite puzzling.

As one can see from the cells in any column of Table 3.1, any comparison of two age groups, e.g. the youngest and the oldest, involves the confounding of both age and cohort effects. Consider the comparisons involved for the year 2000 (the entries in the far right column in Table 3.1). The difference between these two groups in the variable observed in the cells of the table amounts to the following:

$$[(A_7 + P_4 + C_7) - (A_1 + P_4 + C_1)]$$
$$= [(A_7 + C_7) - (A_1 + C_1)] = [(A_7 - A_1) + (C_7 - C_1)]$$

The algebra here illustrates that this design controls for period effects, in the sense that only one occasion of measurement is represented in this table, which drop out in the comparisons among rows of the table. Any inference, however, that the difference reflects age effects alone, or for that matter cohort effects alone, might be grossly mistaken (see Riley, 1973). Such designs are quite common, regardless of their problems. For example, in research on cognitive aging it is very common for researchers to observe cognitive test performance in older adults and compare the results with the performance of college students (e.g., Park, Smith, Lautenschlager, Earles, Frieske, Zwahr, & Gaines, 1996). Such work has two serious flaws. The first flaw is the one noted here involving the confounding of aging and cohort effects in making inferences about aging, and the second involves the failure to obtain a representative sample of the population to which the generalizations are intended to apply.

Single Cohort Designs

Another common design that can be viewed within the framework of the larger longitudinal design shown above (in Table 3.1) is the single cohort design, of which there are a number of examples.[7] Several famous British longitudinal studies of single birth cohorts fit this design. The 1970 British Cohort Study, for example, followed all children born April 5 to 11, 1970 in England,

---

[7]In some cases such studies involve multiple adjacent birth cohorts, but are considered to be single-cohort studies because the cohorts are treated as if they were from a single cohort.

Scotland and Wales, assessed at ages 5, 10, 16, 26 and 30 (Bynner, Ferri, & Shepherd, 1997). Another such study, begun in 1946, studied all births occurring in Britain during one week and observing them nineteen times since birth—ten times in childhood and adolescence, and nine times in adult life (Wadsworth, 1991). The Detroit Longitudinal Study sampled all first, second, and fourth parity births in the Detroit metropolitan area in the month of July, 1961 and used this as a basis for studying fertility decision making among the mothers using multiple surveys across time (Freedman, Thornton, Camburn, Alwin, & Young-DeMarco, 1988). The children were, however, not studied until they were 18 years of age, missing most of their developmental milestones.

By studying individuals over their lives such studies can be highly informative with respect to whether youth is a particularly impressionable period relative to other times, an assumption common to cohort replacement theory. One of the classic studies in sociology that illustrates this point was carried out in the 1930s and 1940s by Theodore Newcomb at Bennington College, then a newly formed women's college in southwestern Vermont. The young women who attended Bennington at that time—from cohorts born between 1912 and 1923—came primarily from conservative backgrounds. By contrast, the faculty members were notably progressive in their economic and political views. Newcomb observed that the longer the young women stayed at Bennington, the more their political and economic views changed in the direction of the more liberal faculty. He concluded that young adulthood is constituted in terms of an openness to identity formation and change and that the individual's immediate environment plays a powerful role in shaping their views (Newcomb, 1943). His theoretical insights into the processes by which responses to social change are shaped by the individual's immediate environment have since become incorporated into social psychological perspectives on human development. It is now commonplace to assume that an individual's reference groups mediate and interpret the influences of social and political events (see Newcomb, Koenig, Flacks, & Warwick, 1967; Alwin, Cohen, & Newcomb, 1991).

Such designs have the serious limitation that they cannot distinguish the effects of aging from the effects of history. As can be seen from the comparison of cells in any row of Table 3.1, if one is studying the changes in a single cohort (or set of cohorts) over time, effects that might otherwise be attributable to aging are confounded with period effects, and disentangling the two sets of influences can be exceedingly difficult. Taking the cohorts born 1941–1950 as a concrete illustration, and comparing two occasions of measurement, say the observations obtained in 1970 and 2000, we have the following:

$$[(A_4 + P_4 + C_4) - (A_1 + P_1 + C_4)] = [(A_4 + P_4) - (A_1 + P_1)]$$
$$= [(A_4 - A_1) + (P_4 - P_1)]$$

This algebra illustrates that this design controls for cohort effects, inasmuch as only one set of cohorts is represented here, but any inference that the above difference reflects age effects alone, or for that matter period effects alone, must be drawn carefully (see Riley, 1973). Despite their clear problems, as our discussion shows, such designs are quite common and can be very useful for studying within-individual change, despite the inability to disentangle the effects of aging and period.

Multiple Cohort Designs

Some of the limitations of longitudinal studies of a single cohort (or set of cohorts) can be remedied by studying more than one cohort or group of cohorts, but there are still major problems of confounding of age, period and cohort effects. This is an increasingly prevalent design in use by researchers wishing to study age differences within a longitudinal framework (e.g., Hofer & Sliwinski, 2001; Hofer, Sliwinski, & Flaherty, 2002; Martin, Grünendahl, & Martin, 2001). To illustrate some of the potential limitations of this design, we can compare two cohort groups from Table 3.1—those born 1941 to 1950 (ages 20 to 29 in 1970) and those born 1911 to 1920 (ages 50 to 59 in 1970). These particular cohorts were chosen because the later-born cohorts will be ages 50 to 59 by the last occasion of measurement (in 2000), which is the same age as the other set of cohorts at the first occasion of measurement. This design illustrates the same two issues of confounding observed above in the synthetic cohort design and the single cohort design (see above): (1) cross-sectional differences among age groups confound cohort and age effects, and (2) cross-time comparisons for any cohort group confounds age and period effects.

Cohort Sequential Designs

A design that has a long history of research in education is the *cohort sequential* design, which observes a sequence of cohorts (or groups of cohorts) over a fixed number of occasions of measurement, attempting to reach some conclusions about the effects of age, period and cohort on variables of interest. This design is a multiple cohort design, staggered in time, in which the first observation of each cohort group occurs when they are of similar age (or stage). One such use of this design is O'Malley, Bachman, and Johnston's (1988) analysis of trends in substance use among young Americans enrolled in school during the senior year, followed up over several occasions of measurement. Each year they obtain data on a representative sample of high school seniors, following each group at annual intervals in successive years.

Based on the lessons learned in our discussion of Table 3.1, one can construct the parameters describing age, period and cohort effects in such a design involving four cohort groups each observed at four occasions of measurement over their life cycles (say at ages 20 to 29, 30 to 39, 40 to 49 and 50 to 59). In such a design, the particular occasions of measurement and age ranges were chosen arbitrarily because the substantive focus of the study and practical design considerations will govern these choices. In many applications of this design, the subsequent observations continue indefinitely. Although this design is an improvement over some of the other designs given above, it still confounds aging effects with period influences and aging and cohort effects within time. The creative display and interpretation of such data can, however, often provide strong hints regarding what factors are likely to be generating the data, but there is no statistical solution, as above, to the confounding of age, period and cohort effects.

ANALYSIS OF MULTIPLE COHORT DATA

In the discussion of Table 3.1 we commented that the general framework within which we have considered issues of research design applies equally to: (a) repeated cross-sectional longitudinal designs, which gather observations on the same cohorts over time (but not the same individuals); or to (b) repeated measures (or panel) longitudinal designs, which observe the same individuals over time (see Duncan & Kalton, 1987). All of the previous research designs discussed in the foregoing are special cases of one or the other of these two general designs, and therefore one or the other of the following sections will be of relevance to any one of those more specialized designs.

The Decomposition of Change in Repeated Measures Designs

Earlier in the chapter we argued that it is not possible to identify the unique effects of aging, cohort and period in the types of data we normally collect, unless we are willing to make some rather strong assumptions about the nature of some of those effects. Short of identifying these unique effects, we can, as we will demonstrate in this section, identify two components of change: change due to *cohort replacement* and change that occurs within cohorts, or *intracohort change*. We can illustrate this using the comparisons shown in Table 3.2, involving the systematic comparison of the 1990 and 2000 columns of Table 3.1, which presents a standard decomposition of columns in the standard cohort table into age-specific and cohort-specific net change. We use the notation Δ_1 to represent age-specific *net change*, that is, the difference in the two samples, net of age. As can be seen in the table, this is formed by subtracting the 1990 from the 2000 observations within rows of the table. The weighted average of these differences will equal the overall difference between the 1990

TABLE 3.2

Decomposition of Columns in the Standard Cohort Table
Into Age-Specific and Cohort-Specific Net Change

| Age | Year of Study (Period) | | Δ_1 | Δ_2 |
	1990	2000		
20–29	$A_1 + P_3 + C_2$	$A_1 + P_4 + C_1$	$(P_4 - P_3) + (C_1 - C_2)$	—
30–39	$A_2 + P_3 + C_3$	$A_2 + P_4 + C_2$	$(P_4 - P_3) + (C_2 - C_3)$	$(A_2 - A_1) + (P_4 - P_3)$
40–49	$A_3 + P_3 + C_4$	$A_3 + P_4 + C_3$	$(P_4 - P_3) + (C_3 - C_4)$	$(A_3 - A_2) + (P_4 - P_3)$
50–59	$A_4 + P_3 + C_5$	$A_4 + P_4 + C_4$	$(P_4 - P_3) + (C_4 - C_5)$	$(A_4 - A_3) + (P_4 - P_3)$
60–69	$A_5 + P_3 + C_6$	$A_5 + P_4 + C_5$	$(P_4 - P_3) + (C_5 - C_6)$	$(A_5 - A_4) + (P_4 - P_3)$
70–79	$A_6 + P_3 + C_7$	$A_6 + P_4 + C_6$	$(P_4 - P_3) + (C_6 - C_7)$	$(A_6 - A_5) + (P_4 - P_3)$
80–89	$A_7 + P_3 + C_8$	$A_7 + P_4 + C_7$	$(P_4 - P_3) + (C_7 - C_8)$	$(A_7 - A_6) + (P_4 - P_3)$

C_1 = born 1971 to 1980 C_6 = born 1921 to 1930
C_2 = born 1961 to 1970 C_7 = born 1911 to 1920
C_3 = born 1951 to 1960 C_8 = born 1901 to 1910
C_4 = born 1941 to 1950 C_9 = born 1891 to 1900
C_5 = born 1931 to 1940 C_{10} = born 1881 to 1890

and 2000 occasions of measurement. The notation Δ_2 is used to represent co-hort-specific or intracohort change, formed by subtracting elements in the di-agonals of the table that pertain to the same cohort. The weighted average of these differences reflects the average amount of within-cohort change over the time period studied (see Alwin & Scott, 1996).

As can be seen from the analytic scheme presented in Table 3.2, the compo-nent representing age-specific net change, or Δ_1, is composed of two parts, dif-ferences in period effects and differences in cohort effects. Similarly the com-ponent representing cohort-specific change, or Δ_2, is also composed of two parts, differences in age effects and differences in period effects. In other words, Δ_1 confounds period and cohort effects and Δ_2 confounds age and pe-riod. Only if one can make some strong assumptions about the nature of some of these effects can one arrive at an identification of the other effects. For example, if one were in a position to assume that there were no period effects occurring between 1990 and 2000 in the variable of interest, which may be plausible in some circumstances, then one could interpret Δ_1 purely in terms of cohort differences and Δ_2 in terms of aging. Or, if one were in a position to assume there were no age effects, then Δ_2 would be interpretable purely in terms of period effects, and the identification of the P coefficients would per-mit the resolution of the cohort effects from the age-specific differences. Finally, if one were in a position to assume there were no cohort effects operat-ing in this table, then Δ_1 would be entirely made up of period effects, the identi-fication of which could be used to identify the age effects from Δ_2. We should stress, however, that whatever assumptions one makes must be made consistently across the entire table, and it is not possible to make one set of assumptions for the purpose of identifying coefficients in one column and then make another set of assumptions in order to identify coefficients in another. Such an approach, which was articulated early in the literature on age–period–cohort effects (see Schaie, 1965), is inherently flawed, as can be seen through an examination of the analytic scheme presented in Table 3.2.

There is a multivariate analogue to the tabular presentation that we have applied to the standard cohort table here (see Alwin & Scott, 1996). Such an approach may oversimplify reality, in the sense that it presents certain assumptions about linearity and additivity, but it is a very useful research strategy that can have substantial benefits. The approach we illustrate here, due to Firebaugh (1989), is basically similar in its overall intent to the approach used above, in that the goal is to decompose net social change into two components, cohort replacement and intracohort change. The basic idea is to first regress the variable of interest on survey year and cohort (birth year), as follows:

$$y = b_0 + b_1 \text{ Year} + b_2 \text{ Cohort} + e$$

The slopes from the estimation of this equation are then used to estimate the cohort replacement and intracohort change components, defined as:

$$\text{Intracohort change (IC)} = b_1 (t_T - t_1), \text{ and}$$

$$\text{Cohort replacement (CR)} = b_2 (\overline{C}_T - \overline{C}_1)$$

where $t_T - t_1$ represents the amount of historical time elapsed between time 1 and time T, $\overline{C}_T$ is the mean birth year at time T, and $\overline{C}_1$ is the mean birth year at time 1. As Firebaugh (1989) notes, due to the fact that the model is often misspecified in positing linearity and additivity of year and cohort, the two components rarely sum to $\overline{Y}_T - \overline{Y}_1$. But, "the discrepancy should not be large; a large discrepancy suggests that the effects of year (intracohort, the period–age effect) and cohort (intercohort, the cohort–age effect) are not linear–additive" (p. 253). After comparing this method with other techniques that decompose differences of means across time, Firebaugh (1989) concluded that the linear decomposition method expressed above provides reasonably good estimates of cohort turnover and intracohort influences on means.[8]

Studying Within-Person Change Using Growth Models

In the foregoing we argued that it is not possible to identify the unique effects of aging, cohort and period in longitudinal data, unless one is willing to make

---

[8]See Rodgers (1990) for a critique of this approach.

some rather strong assumptions about the nature of some of those effects. The argument applies equally to designs involving repeated cross-sections, where data are collected on the same cohorts over time, as well as to designs involving repeated measures on the same persons. In the previous section we demonstrated that two components of change can be identified: change due to cohort replacement and change that occurs within cohorts, or intracohort change. These methods can also be applied to the case where repeated measures of variables of interest are observed on the same individuals within a longitudinal design—typically referred to as *repeated measures designs*. However, such analyses are rarely applied in such cases because the interest in these designs is in the changes of persons, i.e. *within-person change,* rather than changes within cohorts. In this section we develop a set of models that are appropriate when the interest is in studying within-person change, namely, growth curve models.

State-of-the-art methods of growth curve analysis are rooted in the historical concerns of educational and psychological researchers with the measurement and analysis of change (Harris, 1963). Early fixed-effects ANOVA models were formulated for repeated measures designs involving two or more groups of different subjects in which each subject had measurements on two or more occasions (Lindquist, 1953). These early statistical models focused explicitly on within-person change, although notions of growth or development were fairly primitive in these early statistical treatments. Early methodological contributions concentrated primarily on the problems and limitations of difference scores for assessing change (Lord, 1963; Cronbach & Furby, 1970).

More recently, modern statistical models for the analysis of growth (and decline) were stimulated in part by early applications of growth curve analysis to the measurement of change (Rogosa, Brandt, & Zimowski, 1982). Somewhat parallel developments occurred with respect to the analysis of change using causal models of change in panel data (Heise, 1969, 1970; Wiley & Wiley, 1970; Kessler & Greenberg, 1981; Jöreskog, 1974, 1979). This separate regression-based tradition for the analysis of change grew out of causal modeling and structural equation developments in sociology and econometrics (see Alwin, 1988); however, a major shortcoming with this approach is that it focused primarily on interindividual differences rather than intraindividual change and had no readily available way to incorporate trends in means and individual-level trajectories of change.

In recent years, pioneering work has taken place to bring these two traditions together into models of individual growth that can be conceptualized within the general framework offered by structural equation models (SEM) or covariance structure analysis (e.g., Meredith & Tisek, 1990; McArdle, 1986, 1988, 1991; McArdle & Anderson, 1990; McArdle & Bell, 2000; McArdle & Epstein, 1987; McArdle & Hamagami, 1992, 2001; Willett & Sayer, 1994). Given that the formulation of LGC models can be embedded in the general SEM approach, they also have a natural kinship to confirmatory factor models and models for factorial invariance (Alwin & Jackson, 1979, 1981; Alwin, 1988; Jöreskog, 1971a, 1971b; McArdle & Bell, 2000). Moreover, LGC models can also be viewed as a special application of multilevel models in which occasions of measurement are nested within persons (Bryk & Raudenbush, 1992; Goldstein, 1995; Hox, 2000).

There are several alternate ways to construct individual latent growth models (e.g., Willett & Sayer, 1994; McArdle & Bell, 2000). One approach is to specify a within-person (i.e., intra-individual) model for individual change over time. These are often referred to as *time-based* or *occasion-based* models. These models represent a stepping-off point for all growth models, regardless of their complexity. In addition, using longitudinal data from multiple birth cohorts (the so-called accelerated longitudinal design), it is possible to combine a series of simple cohort-specific time-based models (in which time and age are perfectly collinear) into what would be thought of in the SEM literature as a multiple-group model (see Miyazaki & Raudenbush, 2000 for an HLM-based specification of this approach). This is an extremely adaptable design that allows for the specification of age trajectories and the testing of cohort differences therein (see Alwin, Hofer, & McCammon, 2005).

Growth analyses aspire to estimate patterns of aging, while at the same time taking cohort differences in levels and slopes into account, whereas the interpretation of the results in these terms comes at the expense of the assumption of the absence of period effects in these data. Although the assumption of "no period effects" may make a great deal of sense in the examination of scores over such a short period of time (see Alwin & McCammon, 1999, 2001), this may not always be the case (see Freedman, Aykan, & Martin, 2001; Rodgers, Ofstedal, & Herzog, 2003). And certainly in other substantive domains, such an assumption may provide questionable conclusions (Glenn, 2003).

CONCLUSIONS

In this chapter we review several conceptual and methodological issues for the study of baby-boom birth cohorts within a framework that integrates demographic and developmental considerations. Our discussion is relevant to cohort studies in general and focuses on several issues involving the conceptualization of cohort and related concepts. We argue that such a consideration of the conceptual background for the study of cohorts and their change is essential for any treatment of the key methodological issues involved in the translation of an interest in studying the life experiences of birth cohorts into research design and analysis.

Our chapter begins with a discussion of the concept of cohort as a theoretical tool in the analysis of social change and stresses the critical differences between the concept as used in this chapter and somewhat more popular ideas such as generation, taking care to observe the essential differences in the meaning of the two concepts. This theoretical framework provides a context for a consideration of the baby-boom cohorts as a demographic phenomenon and their potential for influencing the makeup of society. We argue, however, that drawing inferences about the differences in the ways the baby-boom cohorts have aged or matured into midlife, or the ways in which their mean levels or patterns of change have differed from the cohorts that preceded them or those that followed is complicated by some basic limitations in what is possible in the framework of standard research designs.

We argue that a systematic and rigorous approach to the study of cohort differences and cohort change must confront the basic age–period–cohort identification problem, and our review focuses on the difficulties inherent in the study of social and individual change. We attempt to clarify the nature of effects of aging, cohort and historical period as used in the developmental and demographic literatures, and within this framework we review the limitations to identifying the effects of these factors using the kinds of research designs routinely available in social and behavioral science. Despite these limitations, we have taken the view that it is possible nonetheless to find meaning in data drawn from multiple cohort designs, and we review two major research strategies: (1) the decomposition of social trends into components representing cohort replacement and within-cohort change, and (2) the use of growth modeling techniques to study within-individual change. These strategies can be creatively employed to organize longitudinal data and clarify the range of possible inferences.

ACKNOWLEDGMENTS

Support for this research was received from a research grant (AG-20099-03) for the project Latent Growth Models of Cognitive Aging from the National Institute on Aging (D. F. Alwin and W. L. Rodgers, Principal Investigators). The research assistance of Pauline Mitchell is gratefully acknowledged.

REFERENCES

Alwin, D. F. (1988). Structural equation models in research on human development and aging. In K. W. Schaie, R. T. Campbell, W. Meredith, & S. C. Rawlings (Eds.), *Methodological issues in aging research* (pp. 71–170). New York: Springer.

Alwin, D. F. (1998). The political impact of the Baby Boom: Are there persistent generational differences in political beliefs and behavior? *Generations, 22*, 46–54.

Alwin, D. F. (2002). Generations X, Y and Z: Are they changing America? *Contexts, 1*, 42–51.

Alwin, D. F., Cohen, R. L., & Newcomb, T. M. (1991). *Political attitudes over the life span: The Bennington women after fifty years.* Madison: University of Wisconsin Press.

Alwin, D. F., Hofer, S. M., & McCammon, R. J. (2005). Modeling the effects of time: Integrating demographic and developmental perspectives. In R. H. Binstock & L. K. George (Eds.), *Handbook of aging and the social sciences* (6th ed., pp. 20–38). New York: Academic Press.

Alwin, D. F., & Jackson, D. J. (1979). Measurement models for response errors in surveys: Issues and applications. In K. F. Schuessler (Ed.), *Sociological methodology 1980* (pp. 68–119). San Francisco: Jossey-Bass.

Alwin, D. F., & Jackson, D. J. (1981). Applications of simultaneous factor analysis to issues of factorial invariance. In D. J. Jackson & E. F. Borgatta (Eds.), *Factor analysis and measurement in sociological research* (pp. 249–279). Beverly Hills, CA: Sage.

Alwin, D. F., & McCammon, R. J. (1999). Aging versus cohort interpretations of intercohort differences in GSS vocabulary scores. *American Sociological Review, 64,* 272–286.

Alwin, D. F., & McCammon, R. J. (2001). Aging, cohorts and verbal ability. *Journal of Gerontology: Social Sciences, 56B,* S151–S161.

Alwin, D. F., & McCammon, R. J. (2003). Generations, cohorts, and social change. In J. T. Mortimer & M. Shanahan (Eds.), *Handbook of the life course* (pp. 2–49). New York: Plenum.

Alwin, D. F., & Scott, J. (1996). Attitude change—Its measurement and interpretation using longitudinal surveys. In B. Taylor & K. Thomson (Eds.), *Understanding change in social attitudes* (pp. 75–106). Aldershot, UK: Dartmouth.

Amato, P., & Booth, A. (1997). *Generation at risk: Growing up in an era of family upheaval.* Cambridge, MA: Harvard University Press.

Baltes, P. B. (1968). Longitudinal and cross-sectional sequences in the study of age and generation effects. *Human Development, 11,* 145–171.

Biblarz, T. J., Bengtson, V. L., & Bucur, A. (1996). Social mobility across three generations. *Journal of Marriage and Family, 58,* 188–200.

Bryk, A. S., & Raudenbush, S. W. (1992). *Hierarchical linear models: Applications and data analysis methods.* Newbury Park, CA: Sage.

Bynner, J., Ferri, E., & Shepherd, P. (1997). *Twenty-something in the 1990s: Getting on, getting by, getting nowhere.* Aldershot: Ashgate.

Converse, P. E. (1976). *The dynamics of party support: Cohort analyzing party identification.* Beverly Hills, CA: Sage.

Cronbach, L. J., & Furby, L. (1970). How should we measure "change"—Or should we? *Psychological Bulletin, 74,* 68–80.

Duncan, G. J., & Kalton, G. (1987). Issues of design and analysis of surveys across time. *International Statistical Review, 55,* 7–117.

Easterlin, R. A. (1987). *Birth and fortune: The impact of numbers on personal welfare.* Chicago: University of Chicago Press.

Erikson, E. H. (1988). Youth: Fidelity and diversity. *Daedalus, 117,* 1–24.

Farkas, G. (1977). Cohort, age, and period effects upon the employment of white females: Evidence for 1957–1968. *Demography, 14,* 33–42.

Firebaugh, G. (1989). Methods for estimating cohort replacement effects. In C. C. Clogg (Ed.), *Sociological methodology 1989* (pp. 243–262). Oxford: Blackwell.

Firebaugh, G. (1992). Where does social change come from? Estimating the relative contributions of individual change and population turnover. *Population Research and Policy Review, 11,* 1–20.

Firebaugh, G., & Chen, K. (1995). Vote turnout of Nineteenth Amendment women: The enduring effect of disenfranchisement. *American Journal of Sociology, 100,* 972–996.

Firebaugh, G., & Davis, K. E. (1988). Trends in anti-black prejudice, 1972–1984: Region and cohort effects. *American Journal of Sociology, 94,* 251–272.

Freedman, D., Thornton, A., Camburn, D., Alwin, D. F., & Young-DeMarco, L. (1988). The life history calendar: A technique for collecting retrospective data. In C. C. Clogg (Ed.), *Sociolog-*

3. CONCEPTUAL AND METHODOLOGICAL ISSUES

ical methodology 1988 (Vol. 18, pp. 37–68). Washington, DC: American Sociological Association.

Freedman, V. A., Aykan, H., & Martin, L. G. (2001). Aggregate changes in severe cognitive impairment among older Americans: 1993 and 1998. *Journal of Gerontology: Social Sciences, 56B*, S100–S111.

Glenn, N. D. (1976). Cohort analysts' futile quest: Statistical attempts to separate age, period, and cohort effects. *American Sociological Review, 41*, 900–905.

Glenn, N. D. (2003). Distinguishing age, period, and cohort effects. In J. T. Mortimer & M. J. Shanahan (Eds.), *Handbook of the life course* (pp. 465–476). New York: Kluwer Academic/Plenum Publishers.

Glenn, N. D. (2004). *Cohort analysis* (2nd ed.). Thousand Oaks, CA: Sage.

Goldstein, H. (1995). *Multilevel statistical models* (2nd ed.). New York: Halsted.

Hagan, J. (2001). *Northern passage: American Vietnam War resisters in Canada.* Cambridge, MA: Harvard University Press.

Harris, C. W. (1963). *Problems in measuring change.* Madison: University of Wisconsin Press.

Heise, D. R. (1969). Separating reliability and stability in test–retest correlations. *American Sociological Review, 34*, 93–101.

Heise, D. R. (1970). Causal inference from panel data. In E. F. Borgatta & G. W. Bohrnstedt (Eds.), *Sociological methodology 1970* (pp. 3–27). San Francisco: Jossey-Bass.

Hofer, S. M., & Sliwinski, M. J. (2001). Understanding ageing: An evaluation of research designs for assessing the interdependence of ageing-related changes. *Gerontology, 47*, 341–352.

Hofer, S. M., Sliwinski, M. J., & Flaherty, B. P. (2002). Understanding ageing: Further commentary on the limitations of cross-sectional designs for ageing research. *Gerontology, 48*, 22–29.

Hox, J. (2000). Multilevel analyses of grouped and longitudinal data. In T. D. Little, K. U. Schnabel, & J. Baumert (Eds.), *Modeling longitudinal and multilevel data: Practical issues, applied approaches and specific examples* (pp. 15–32). Mahwah, NJ: Lawrence Erlbaum Associates.

Inglehart, R. (1977). *The silent revolution: Changing values and political styles among western publics.* Princeton, NJ: Princeton University Press.

Jöreskog, K. G. (1971a). Statistical analysis of sets of congeneric tests. *Psychometrika, 36*, 109–133.

Jöreskog, K. G. (1971b). Simultaneous factor analysis in several populations. *Psychometrika, 36*, 409–426.

Jöreskog, K. G. (1974). Analyzing psychological data by structural analysis of covariance matrices. In R. C. Atkinson, D. H. Krantz, R. D. Luce, & P. Suppes (Eds.), *Contemporary developments in mathematical psychology* (Vol. 2, pp. 1–56). San Francisco: Freeman.

Jöreskog, K. G. (1979). Statistical estimation of structural models in longitudinal developmental investigations. In J. R. Nesselroade & P. B. Baltes (Eds.), *Longitudinal research in the study of behavior and development* (pp. 303–374). New York: Academic Press.

Kertzer, D. I. (1983). Generation as a sociological problem. In R. H. Turner & J. F. Short, Jr. (Eds.), *Annual review of sociology* (pp. 125–149). Palo Alto, CA: Annual Reviews Inc.

Kessler, R. C., & Greenberg, D. F. (1981). *Linear panel analysis.* New York: Academic Press.

Lesthaeghe, R. (1983). A century of demographic and cultural change in Western Europe: An exploration of underlying dimensions. *Population and Development Review, 9*, 411–435.

Lesthaeghe, R. (1995). The second demographic transition in western countries: An interpretation. In K. O. Mason & A.-M. Jensen (Eds.), *Gender and family change in industrialized countries* (pp. 17–62). Oxford: Clarendon Press.

Lindquist, E. F. (1953). *Design and analysis of experiments in psychology and education.* Boston: Houghton Mifflin.

Lord, F. M. (1963). Elementary models for measuring change. In C. W. Harris (Ed.), *Problems in measuring change* (pp. 21–38). Madison: University of Wisconsin Press.

Mannheim, K. (1952). The problem of generations. In P. Kecskemeti (Ed.), *Essays in the sociology of knowledge* (pp. 276–322). Boston: Routledge & Kegan Paul. (Original work published 1927)

Martin, M., Grünendahl, M., & Martin, P. (2001). Age differences in stress, social resources, and well-being in middle and older age. *Journal of Gerontology: Psychological Sciences, 56,* P214–P222.

Mason, K. O., & Lu, Y. (1988). Attitudes toward women's familial roles: Changes in the United States, 1977–1985. *Gender and Society, 2,* 39–57.

Mason, K. O., Mason, W. M., Winsborough, H. H., & Poole, W. K. (1973). Some methodological issues in the analysis of archival data. *American Sociological Review, 38,* 242–258.

Mason, W. M., & Fienberg, S. E. (1985). *Cohort analysis in social research: Beyond the identification problem.* New York: Springer-Verlag.

McAdam, D. (1988). *Freedom summer.* New York: Oxford University Press.

McArdle, J. J. (1986). Latent variable growth within behavior genetic models. *Behavior Genetics, 16,* 163–200.

McArdle, J. J. (1988). Dynamic but structural equation modeling of repeated measures data. In J. R. Nesselroade & R. B. Cattell (Eds.), *The handbook of multivariate experimental psychology* (Vol. 2, pp. 561–614). New York: Plenum Press.

McArdle, J. J. (1991). Structural models of developmental theory in psychology. *Annals of Theoretical Psychology, 7,* 139–160.

McArdle, J. J., & Anderson, E. (1990). Latent variable growth models for research on aging. In J. E. Birren & K. W. Schaie (Eds.), *Handbook of the psychology of aging* (3rd ed., pp. 21–44). New York: Academic Press.

McArdle, J. J., & Bell, R. Q. (2000). An introduction to latent growth models for developmental data analysis. In T. D. Little, K. U. Schnabel, & J. Baumert (Eds.), *Modeling longitudinal and multilevel data: Practical issues, applied approaches and specific examples* (pp. 69–107). Mahwah, NJ: Lawrence Erlbaum Associates.

McArdle, J. J., & Epstein, D. (1987). Latent growth curves within developmental structural equation models. *Child Development, 58,* 110–133.

McArdle, J. J., & Hamagami, F. (1992). Modeling incomplete longitudinal and cross-sectional data using latent growth structural models. *Experimental Aging Research, 18,* 145–166.

McArdle, J. J., & Hamagami, F. (2001). Latent difference score structural models for linear dynamic analyses with incomplete longitudinal data. In L. M. Collins & A. G. Sayer (Eds.), *New methods for the analysis of change* (pp. 139–175). Washington, DC: American Psychological Association.

Miyazaki, Y., & Raudenbush, S. W. (2000). Tests for linkage in multiple cohorts in an accelerated longitudinal design. *Psychological Methods, 5,* 44–63.

Modell, J. (1989). *Into one's own.* Berkeley: University of California Press.

Morgan, S. P. (1996). Characteristic features of modern American fertility. In J. B. Caterline, R. D. Lee, & K. A. Foote (Eds.), *Fertility in the United States: New patterns, new theories* (pp. 19–63). New York: The Population Council.

Morgan, S. P. (2003). *Is very low fertility inevitable in America? Insights and Porecasets from an integrative model of fertility.* Unpublished presidential address to the Population Association of America.

Newcomb, T. M. (1943). *Personality and social change: Attitude formation in a student community.* New York: Dryden Press.

Newcomb, T. M., Koenig, K. E., Flacks, R., & Warwick, D. P. (1967). *Persistence and change: Bennington College and its students after 25 years.* New York: Wiley.

O'Brien, R. M. (2000). Age-period-cohort-characteristic models. *Social Science Research, 29,* 123–139.

O'Malley, P. M., Bachman, J. G., & Johnston, L. D. (1988). Period, age, and cohort effects on substance use among young Americans: A decade of change, 1976–1986. *American Journal of Public Health, 78*, 1315–1321.

Ortega y Gasset, J. (1933). *The modern theme*. New York: Norton.

Pampel, F. C. (1993). Relative cohort size and fertility: The socio-political context of the Easterlin Effect. *American Sociological Review, 58*, 496–514.

Park, D. C., Smith, A. D., Lautenschlager, G., Earles, J., Frieske, D., Zwahr, M., & Gaines, C. (1996). Mediators of long-term memory performance across the life-span. *Psychology and Aging, 11*, 621–637.

Riley, M. W. (1973). Aging and cohort succession: Interpretations and misinterpretations. *Public Opinion Quarterly, 37*, 774–787.

Rodgers, W. L. (1990). Interpreting the components of time trends. In C. C. Clogg (Ed.), *Sociological methodology* (Vol. 20, pp. 421–446). Oxford, England: Blackwell.

Rodgers, W. L., Ofstedal, M. B., & Herzog, A. R. (2003). Trends in scores on tests of cognitive ability in the elderly U.S. population, 1993–2000. *Journal of Gerontology: Social Sciences, 58B*, S338–S346.

Rogosa, D., Brandt, D., & Zimowski, M. (1982). A growth curve approach to the measurement of change. *Psychological Bulletin, 92*, 726–748.

Roof, W. C. (1999). *Spiritual marketplace: Baby Boomers and the remaking of American religion*. Princeton, NJ: Princeton University Press.

Roscow, I. (1978). What is a cohort and why? *Human Development, 21*, 65–75.

Rossi, A. S., & Rossi, P. H. (1990). *Of human bonding: Parent–child relations across the life course*. New York: Aldine de Gruyter.

Ryder, N. B. (1965). The cohort as a concept in the study of social change. *American Sociological Review, 30*, 843–861.

Schaie, K. W. (1965). A general model for the study of developmental problems. *Psychological Bulletin, 64*, 92–107.

Schaie, K. W. (1984). Historical time and cohort effects. In K. A. McCluskey & H. W. Reese (Eds.), *Life-span developmental psychology: Historical and generational effects* (pp. 1–15). New York: Academic Press.

Schuman, H., Steeh, C., Bobo, L., & Krysan, M. (1997). *Racial attitudes in America: Trends and interpretations*. Cambridge, MA: Harvard University Press.

Scott, J. (1998). Generational changes in attitudes to abortion: A cross-national comparison. *European Sociological Review, 14*, 177–190.

Scott, J., Alwin, D. F., & Braun, M. (1996). Generational changes in gender role attitudes: Britain in cross national perspective. *Sociology, 30*, 471–492.

Teitelbaum, M. S., & Winter, J. M. (1985). *The fear of population decline*. Orlando, FL: Academic Press.

Wadsworth, M. E. J. (1991). *The imprint of time: Childhood, history, and adult life*. Oxford, UK: Clarendon.

White, H. (1992). Succession and generations: Looking back on chains of opportunity. In H. A. Becker (Ed.), *Dynamics of cohort and generations research* (pp. 31–51). Amsterdam: Thesis Publishers.

Wiley, D. E., & Wiley, J. A. (1970). The estimation of measurement error in panel data. *American Sociological Review, 35*, 112–117.

Willett, J. B., & Sayer, A. G. (1994). Using covariance structure analysis to detect correlates and predictors of individual change over time. *Psychological Bulletin, 116*, 363–381.

PART TWO

Physical and Mental Health Issues

CHAPTER FOUR

Menopause: Recent Research Findings

Nancy E. Avis
Wake Forest University School of Medicine

Sybil Crawford
University of Massachusetts Medical Center

INTRODUCTION

Why Menopause Is Important

Menopause is experienced by half of the population that reaches midlife. It is a prominent biological marker in the aging process and potentially has an important physiological, psychological, and sociological impact on women. As such, it is an important event in women's lives to include in any overview of midlife. Further, menopause is big business. Pharmaceutical companies aggressively market medications for menopausal symptoms and postmenopausal health and menopause clinics continue to sprout up around the country.

During the last decade, interest in menopause has skyrocketed. Much of this newfound interest can be attributed to the current baby-boom generation of women who began approaching menopause. This large cohort of women grew up asserting more control over their reproductive lives and encouraged frank and open discussion of previously taboo topics. Furthermore, with the increased attention to and promotion of hormone therapy (HT), menopausal women are faced with making decisions that could ultimately affect the rest of their lives. In the past, women had little control over menopause and it required little active involvement. Now, with menopause increasingly implicated as a risk factor for subsequent disease, and numerous options available for preventing these diseases, menopause has become a time requiring active decision making by women. Furthermore, with new data on the risks of hormone therapy, Baby Boomers are thrown into a quandary of what to do about menopausal symptoms and prevention of long-term chronic diseases. Menopause is thus a very salient topic for baby-boom women.

Overview of Chapter

Many articles, chapters, and books have been written describing the epidemiology, symptoms, and cultural attitudes associated with menopause. These publications, however, present research conducted largely on women who were pre-Baby Boomers. The purpose of this chapter is to present findings from more recent studies conducted on women considered part of the baby-boom generation (born between the years 1946 and 1964) and where possible, to compare this newer research to that conducted on previous cohorts. In addition, most of the earlier research was conducted almost entirely on Caucasian women. More recent research has begun to include women of diverse ethnicities. Throughout this chapter, we present new research and compare findings across racial/ethnic groups. First, we describe the changing view of menopause among women and health care practitioners. We then review aspects of the menopausal transition, and finally discuss treatments for menopausal symptoms and postmenopausal health.

CHANGING VIEWS OF MENOPAUSE AMONG WOMEN AND HEALTH CARE PRACTITIONERS

Historical Perspective

Menopause has been viewed through the ages as a sign of sin and decay, psychological loss, and more recently as a deficiency disease (Kaufert & McKinlay, 1985; McCrea, 1983). It was often assumed that menopause was inevitably accompanied by hot flashes, sweats, prolonged menstrual irregularities, vaginal dryness and a host of other symptoms, including depression, irritability, weight gain, insomnia, dizziness, and loss of interest in sex. Much of this perception is derived from early research based on clinical samples of women who sought treatment for menopause-related problems. In the 1980s several large community-based studies provided much-needed scientific data on menopause among more representative samples, and these studies dispelled some misperceptions. A more detailed historical view is provided by Avis (1999, 2000).

The view of menopause as a deficiency disease is no longer in vogue. Women have objected to the use of this term for a naturally occurring process and menopause is no longer viewed as a disease. Part of this change in nomenclature can be attributed to the feminism of Baby Boomers who found this terminology both ageist and sexist (Bell, 1990; Rostosky & Travis, 2000).

New Research Now Focusing on the Baby-Boom Generation

There are a number of reasons why women who are part of the baby-boom generation are likely to have a different response to menopause than did their predecessors. In general, this has been a generation of women who have grown up discussing topics that were previously thought to be taboo or too personal to talk about in public. Baby Boomers talk more freely about pregnancy, sex, breast cancer, and reproductive topics than did their parents or grandparents. Menstrual products are commonly advertised in magazines and on television. This generation has also grown up with a certain skepticism about pharmaceutical treatments and has seen the negative consequences of such so-called miracle drugs as thalidomide and diethylstilbestrol (DES). Finally, this is also a generation of women for whom health information is readily available and as a result, they expect to be actively involved in health care decisions. Along with the rise of the Internet, health information is disseminated quickly and widely. The rise of feminism has also changed the way women approach the medical profession and vice versa.

Racial/Ethnic Differences

Although the baby-boomer cohort is often referred to as a homogenous group of women, this is clearly not the case. As mentioned, previous research on menopause has focused largely on Caucasian women. We know little about the menopausal experience of non-Caucasian women. Most cross-cultural research has been anthropological in nature and/or only conducted within a single culture. Rarely have multiple racial/ethnic groups been included in a single study in numbers large enough to make comparisons. Some observational longitudinal studies such as the Healthy Women's Study (Matthews, Kelsey, Meilahn, Kuller, & Wing, 1989), Massachusetts Women's Health Study (Avis & McKinlay, 1995), the Melbourne Women's Midlife Health Project (Dennerstein, Smith, Morse, Burger, Green, Hopper, & Ryan, 1993), and the Seattle Midlife Women's Health Study (Mitchell & Woods, 1996) have included African Americans, Asians, and/or Hispanics. However, these groups have not been included in numbers large enough to analyze as a group.

Two recent studies have focused on comparisons of two racial/ethnic groups. One is a study of late reproductive-aged Caucasian and African-American women from Philadelphia County, Pennsylvania (Grisso, Freeman, Maurin, Garcia-Espana, & Berlin, 1999). The other is the Australian Longitudinal Study on Women's Health, which compared participants aged 45 to 50 born in Australia with women born elsewhere, mostly in Asia (Brown, Bryson, Byles, Dobson, Lee, Mishra, & Schofield, 1998). Other studies that have large numbers of non-Caucasian women such as the Women's Health

Initiative (WHI), the Postmenopausal Health Disparities Study in Oklahoma (Gavaler, Bonham-Leyba, Castro, & Harman, 1999) and the Women's Health Trial: Feasibility Study in Minority Populations (Lewis, George, Fouad, Porter, Bowen, & Urban, 1998), focus on postmenopausal women.

The ongoing Study of Women's Health Across the Nation (SWAN) is providing for the first time some of the best data on racial/ethnic differences of women transitioning through menopause. The SWAN study also provides some of the best data on the baby-boomer cohort. Because we refer to the SWAN study often in this chapter, we describe it in detail below.

Description of SWAN

Funded primarily by the National Institute on Aging, with additional funding from the National Institute of Nursing Research, the Office of Research on Women's Health, the Center for Complementary and Alternative Medicine and the U.S. Department of Defense, SWAN is a prospective, multidisciplinary study of the natural history of menopause and the menopausal transition being conducted at seven different sites. The primary goals of SWAN are to describe the chronology of, and the normal variation in, the biologic and psychosocial characteristics of the menopause transition, to distinguish age-related changes from menopause-related changes, and to describe the health and risk factors after menopause among community and/or population-based samples of women of various racial/ethnic backgrounds.

As part of the SWAN design, each site recruited Caucasian women for approximately half of its sample, and a specific non-Caucasian group for the other half. SWAN includes non-Hispanic Caucasian (seven sites), African-American (four sites), Chinese (one site), Hispanic (one site) and Japanese (one site) women at the seven study sites. SWAN consists of three phases: focus groups (phase I), a cross-sectional survey (phase II), and the longitudinal cohort (phase III). Investigators have already begun the ninth follow-up (annual) interviews of the longitudinal (phase III) portion of the study.

Phase I (Focus Groups). In September 1994 phase I of SWAN was initiated with 27 focus groups consisting of approximately 195 pre-, peri- and postmenopausal women from the study's target ethnic groups. The focus groups, which were carried out during the first year, were conducted to direct the study design and protocols, and to ensure the relevance and the appropriateness of the protocols to the multi-ethnic cohort.

Phase II (Cross-Sectional Study). The cross-sectional survey had two main purposes: (1) to identify and recruit eligible women into the longitudinal cohort, and (2) to provide a snapshot of women at midlife that included their health, lifestyles, symptoms, age at natural menopause and prevalence of surgical menopause. Fifteen-minute interviews (primarily by telephone) were conducted with more than 16,000 women, ages 40 to 55 (born 1939–1954), from all five of the target ethnic groups: Caucasians (7,772, 48.5%), African Americans (4,383, 27.4%), Hispanics (including Mexican) (1,955, 12.2%), Japanese (854, 5.3%) and Chinese (651, 4.1%). Interviews also were conducted with women who identified themselves as belonging partly, but not primarily, to one of the target ethnic groups. These interviews provided investigators with cross-sectional data not only on women who would be entering the cohort (pre- or very early perimenopausal), but also on surgically menopausal women, on those already well into the transition, and on postmenopausal women.

Phase III (Longitudinal Cohort Study). The longitudinal cohort study is the major focus of SWAN and addresses the primary research questions. A total of 3,302 women (approximately 450 at each of the seven sites) from the cross-sectional sample were enrolled in the longitudinal cohort study. The women ranged in age from 42 to 52 years at baseline (born 1943–1953), reported having menses within the past 3 months, had an intact uterus and at least one ovary and were not taking exogenous reproductive hormones. An extensive battery of examinations was undertaken with each woman at baseline. Participants have returned for 2-hour visits at each of nine annual follow-ups. Annual study visits include a wide range of measures, including hormones, bone density (five sites), cardiovascular risk factors, symptoms, menstrual bleeding, health care utilization, quality of life, attitudes towards menopause, sexual functioning, and a range of psychosocial measures. The inclusion of all five racial/ethnic groups in a single study facilitates multiple between-group comparisons regarding menopause and health. We will be returning to SWAN in our discussion of specific aspects of menopause.

MENOPAUSAL TRANSITION

This next section focuses on aspects of the menopausal transition including age of menopause, attitudes towards menopause, and symptoms experienced. The focus is primarily on more recent research and how Baby Boomers might compare to earlier cohorts. We begin with a definition of the various stages of the menopausal transition.

Definition of Menopause

The various defining points and indicators of menopausal status have evolved over the years as we learn more about the complex physiological changes that occur during this transition. Indicators used include age, menstrual bleeding patterns, and levels of reproductive hormones. Although early studies employed chronologic age as an indicator of natural menopause (Bungay, Vessey, & McPherson, 1980; Rostosky & Travis, 1996; Sowers & LaPietra, 1995), the variability in the age at final menstrual period (FMP) has shown that chronologic age is a very unsatisfactory proxy variable for postmenopausal status (McKinlay, Brambilla, & Posner, 1992; Soules, Sherman, Parrott, Rebar, Santoro, Utian, & Woods, 2001).

Epidemiological studies have based definitions of menopause status on reported menstrual bleeding patterns and gynecological surgery. The standard epidemiological definition of natural menopause is twelve consecutive months of amenorrhea in the absence of surgery or other cause (e.g., pregnancy, radiation therapy) that would terminate menstruation (Magursky, Mesko, & Sokolik, 1975; Treloar, 1974; World Health Organization, 1981). It is important to note that the point at which a woman experiences her FMP can only be determined retrospectively after twelve consecutive months of amenorrhea. Prospectively collected information on the date of the FMP is preferable to retrospective recall, as the latter is subject to recall error, increasingly so with greater time elapsed since the FMP (Cramer & Xu, 1996; McKinlay, Jefferys, Thompson, 1972).

Traditionally, perimenopause refers to that period of time immediately prior to the menopause, when the endocrinological and clinical features of approaching menopause commence, through the first year after the final menstrual period. It is characterized by increased variability in menstrual cycles, skipped menstrual cycles, and changes in hormone levels (World Health Organization, 1996). Operationally, perimenopause has been a difficult period to define, with definitions often being inconsistent (Crawford, 2000; Mitchell, Woods, Mariella, 2000). Until recently it was considered the entire time period from increased menstrual cycle irregularity to FMP. However, this is a wide time period and the median duration of perimenopause is roughly 4 years (McKinlay et al., 1992; Treloar, 1981). The recently held Stages of Reproductive Aging Workshop (STRAW) advocated distinguishing the early and late menopausal transitions (Soules et al., 2001). STRAW has recommended the adoption of early perimenopause to be defined as increased menstrual irregularity, but bleeding in the past 3 months and late perimenopause to be defined as 3 to 11 months of amenorrhea. This distinction was already being made by SWAN. Generally, women progress from early to late perimenopause, but some women seesaw between states (Mitchell et al., 2000; Soules et al., 2001).

Reproductive hormones, particularly follicle-stimulating hormone (FSH), also have been used to classify women with respect to menopause status. A cutoff of 35–40 IU/I for FSH is often employed in both clinical practice and in research studies as indicative of postmenopausal status (Goldenberg, Grodin, Rodbard, & Ross, 1973; Wilson & Foster, 1992). A cutoff of 10–20 IU/l has also been taken as indicating perimenopause (Cooper & Baird, 1995). Hormone concentrations, however, vary widely both within and across women during perimenopause and also change as a function of chronologic age (Burger, 1994a, 1994b, 1996; Reame, Kelche, Beitins, Yu, Zawacki, & Padmanabhan, 1996). Consequently, although average values of hormone levels exhibit general trends during the perimenopause, no single cutoff value—particularly for use with a single serum sample—is likely to yield an accurate classification of menopause status for an individual woman (Stellato, Crawford, McKinlay, & Longcope, 1998).

One of SWAN's goals is to refine the current definitions of menopausal stages by combining data from a number of sources, including annual serum hormones and menstrual bleeding and symptoms from monthly diaries, as well as daily urinary hormones for one menstrual cycle annually in a subset of participants who were pre- or early perimenopausal at the first annual follow-up visit, the start of recruitment for this substudy.

It is crucial to distinguish natural from surgical or induced menopause. The latter has been defined by the WHO (1981, 1996) as the cessation of menses due to removal of the uterus and at most one ovary, or removal of both ovaries with or without removal of the uterus. Surgically menopausal women differ in a number of respects from other women, including lower age, greater access to health care, and lower general levels of health (Johannes & Avis, 1996; McKinlay, 1994; McKinlay, Brambilla, Avis, & McKinlay, 1991; Sowers & LaPietra, 1995). Their menopausal experiences may differ from those of other women for these reasons, and also because of differences in rapidity and timing of changes in reproductive hormone concentrations (Bush, 1990; Sowers & LaPietra, 1995). Consequently, surgically menopausal women are often treated as a separate stratum in study design and analyses (McKinlay, 1994). In describing the menopause experience, this chapter refers to the experience of natural menopause, unless otherwise specified.

Factors Related to Age of Menopause and Secular Trends

The median age at the final menstrual period is between 50 and 52 years (Brambilla & McKinlay, 1989; McKinlay, Bifano, & McKinlay, 1985; McKinlay, 1996), and 80% of women experience their last menstrual period between 45 and 55. It is hypothesized that menopause occurs after a certain level of oocyte depletion (Cramer, Xu, & Harlow, 1995). Consequently, factors affecting the size of the initial pool of follicles or the rate of depletion may influence the timing of the menopause. In particular, smoking appears to have an adverse impact on oocytes (Baron, La Vecchia, & Levi, 1990); current smokers reach menopause 1 to 2 years earlier than nonsmokers or past smokers (McKinlay et al., 1985; Cramer, Harlow, Xu, Fraer, & Barbieri, 1995; Bromberger et al., 1997; Gold et al., 2001).

Higher parity and use of oral contraceptives, but not age at menarche, have been found to be related to a later age at menopause (Whelan, Sandler, McConnaughey, & Weinberg, 1990; Gold et al., 2001). A later age at menopause also has been linked to higher weight and better nutrition (associated with socioeconomic status) during gestation or early childhood (Bromberger et al., 1997; Hardy & Kuh, 2002; Lawlor, Ebrahim, & Smith, 2003), and to higher consumption of phytoestrogens (Avis, Kaufert, Lock, McKinlay, & Vass, 1993). However, these factors are not as consistently found across studies as is smoking.

A secular trend in the age at menopause would have important health-related consequences, including changes in the period for childbearing and contraception, and in lifetime exposure to endogenous estrogen and its consequences for diseases such as breast cancer and osteoporosis. Research findings, however, are mixed. Studies outside the United States have reported small but statistically significant increases over time in the age at menopause, thought to be linked to improvements in general health and changes in nutrition, e.g., increased fat consumption (Kono, Sunagawa, Higa, & Sunagawa, 1990; Nagata, Kawakami, & Shimizu, 1997; Rodstrom & Bengtsson, 2003; van Noord & Kaaks, 1991; van Noord, Dubas, Dorland, Boersma, & te Velde, 1997; Boldsen & Jeune, 1990; Varea, Bernis, Montero, Arias, Barroso, & Gonzalez, 2000). Other investigators have contended that there is little or no secular trend (Bengtsson et al., 1979; WHO, 1981; McKinlay et al., 1985), in contrast to other reproductive-related variables such as age at menarche or age at first birth (Morabia & Costanza, 1998), which appear to be more strongly influenced by living conditions (Thomas, Renaud, Benefice, de Meeus, & Guegan, 2001).

Compared with earlier cohorts in the United States, Baby Boomers have lower overall pregnancy rates and delayed first and second births (Ventura & Mosher, 2000), factors that could accelerate the transition to menopause. On the other hand, Baby Boomers are more likely to have used oral contraceptives than earlier cohorts (Dawson, 1990). Baby Boomers have also experienced general secular trends including reduced smoking, higher body mass index, and higher total calories and fat consumption (Bauman, Suchindran, & Murray, 1999; CDC, 2004a, 2004b; Flegal, Carroll, Ogden, & Johnson, 2002), all of which might increase the age at menopause. Thus, it is difficult to forecast changes in the distribution of the age at menopause for Baby Boomers compared with earlier cohorts. However, based on the consistency of the age at menopause in past studies and the relatively small changes observed in recent studies, any such changes are likely to be slight. Given the age range at which menopause occurs, it is premature to have definitive empirical findings on the age at menopause in Baby Boomers, but future data from projects such as SWAN will be very informative in this regard.

Racial/ethnic differences in age at menopause vary across studies, but are generally relatively small (Harlow & Signorello, 2000). Several studies found an earlier menopause—by 6 to 12 months—for black women compared with non-Hispanic Caucasians in Africa and the United States (MacMahon & Worcester, 1966; Frere, 1971; Kwawukume, Ghosh, & Wilson, 1993; Bromberger et al., 1997), but there was no difference in three other studies (Gold et al., 2001; Brett & Cooper, 2003; Cooper, Baird, & Darden, 2001). Some studies found an earlier menopause in Latinas than in non-Hispanic Caucasians (Garrida-Latorre, Lascano-Ponce, Lopez-Carillo, & Hernandez-Avila, 1996), although two other studies found no significant differences after adjustment for confounding factors (Gold et al., 2001; Brett & Cooper, 2003). Results comparing Chinese and Japanese with non-Hispanic Caucasians also are mixed (Gold et al., 2001; Boulet, Oddens, Lehert, Vemer, & Visser, 1994; Tamada & Iwasaki, 1995).

Racial/ethnic differences in factors such as diet and socioeconomic status in childhood—which are often not accounted for—may explain any racial/ethnic variability in age at menopause. Assessment of such differences is complicated by the relative lack of research including multiple racial and ethnic groups in the same study. Differences across studies in racial and ethnic comparisons may reflect different methodologic approaches rather than racial or ethnic differences per se (Sievert & Hautaniemi, 2003).

Surgical Menopause

Hysterectomy is the most frequently performed nonobstetric surgery for women in the United States (Lepine, Hillis, Marchbanks, Koonin, Morrow, Kieke, & Wilcox, 1997). Roughly one third of women will undergo this procedure by age 60, with the highest rate in women aged 40 to 44 (Wilcox, Koonin, Pokras, Strauss, Xia, & Peterson, 1994), well below the median age of natural menopause. Approximately half of hysterectomies are accompanied by a bilateral oophorectomy, occurring most often in women aged 45 to 54 (Wilcox et al., 1994). Overall, rates of hysterectomy have remained relatively stable over the past several decades (Brett, Marsh, & Madans, 1997; Keshavarz, Hillis, & Kieke, 2002; Lepine et al., 1997), suggesting that rates for Baby Boomers will be similar to those for earlier cohorts. Compared with non-Hispanic Caucasians, African Americans have somewhat higher hysterectomy rates (Wilcox et al., 1994; Lepine et al., 1997; Kjerulff, Guzinski, Langenberg, Stolley, Moye, & Kazadjian, 1993; Gold et al., 2001); are more likely to have a hysterectomy for fibroids (Weaver, Hynes, Goldberg, Khuri, Daley, & Henderson, 2001; Lepine et al., 1997); and tend to be younger at surgery (Keshavarz et al., 2002). Hispanics appear to have fewer hysterectomies than non-Hispanic Caucasians (Brett & Higgins, 2003).

Attitudes Towards Menopause

Attitudes, perceptions, and expectations are part of the psychosocial phenomena surrounding menopause (Avis, 1996). Both women in midlife and health professionals believe that attitudes play a role in the experience of menopause (Cowan, Warren, & Young, 1985) with results from longitudinal studies supporting this belief (Avis & McKinlay, 1991; Avis, Crawford, & McKinlay, 1997; Hunter, 1990; Matthews, 1992). The stereotypical notion is that women view menopause quite negatively, but research on women's attitudes towards menopause, conducted across a wide range of populations and cultures, has not found such negativity among mid-aged women. In 1963 Neugarten published a classic paper (Neugarten, Wood, Kraines, & Loomis, 1963) showing that women's attitudes towards menopause were much more positive than the medical community believed. Since then, researchers have studied women's attitudes towards menopause among women in many countries.

Menopausal status also has an impact on attitudes, with postmenopausal and older women consistently expressing more positive feelings about menopause than younger women (Avis & McKinlay, 1991; Abraham, Llewellyn-Jones, & Perz, 1994; Frey, 1981; Neugarten et al., 1963; Sommer et al., 1999; Wilbur, Miller, & Montgomery, 1995). However, studies in other countries have not found that menopausal status is associated with attitudes (Olofsson & Collins, 2000)

In the cross-sectional component of SWAN, women were asked a series of 10 statements concerning menopause and aging. For each statement, women were asked if they agreed, felt neutral, or disagreed. Because SWAN included women who are considered pre–Baby Boomers, as well as women considered part of the baby-boom generation, we were able to compare responses to the attitudes questions for the pre-Boomers (born 1939–1945) and Boomers (born 1946–1954). Table 4.1 shows the percentage of women by Boomer status who agreed with each of the attitudes questions, both unadjusted and adjusted for menopausal status (since pre-Boomers are older and more likely to be postmenopausal). In general, Baby Boomers were less positive towards menopause. They were less likely to feel that women who no longer have menstrual periods feel free and independent (67% vs. 71%); that menopause does not require medical attention (25% vs. 28%); that women with little free time hardly notice the menopause (30% vs. 37%); and that going through menopause is a positive experience (43% vs. 46%). They were more likely to agree that during menopause they did (or expected to) become irritable or depressed (37% vs. 31%); that they felt, or would feel, regret when their periods stopped (16% vs. 14%); and they do not, or did not, know what to expect with menopause (48% vs. 45%). On the other hand, Baby Boomers had slightly more positive attitudes toward aging. They were more likely to agree that the older a women is, the more valued she is (61% vs. 59%), and less likely to agree that a women is

TABLE 4.1
Unadjusted and Adjusted[a] Percent of Women in SWAN Who Agreed
With Different Attitudinal Statements by Baby Boomer Status

	Unadjusted		Adjusted	
Attitude	Pre-Boomer	Boomer	Pre-Boomer	Boomer
The older a woman is, the more valued she is.	60.4	59.9	58.8	60.5
A women is less attractive after menopause.	13.8****	11.5	13.9**	11.4
Women who no longer have menstrual periods feel free and independent.	74.8****	64.9	70.8***	67.3
Menopause is a midlife change that generally does not need medical attention.	29.6****	24.5	28.1**	24.7
Women with little free time hardly notice menopause.	38.5****	30.1	37.3****	30.4
Overall, going through the menopause or change of life will be, or was, a positive experience for me.	47.3****	41.9	45.7*	42.5
As I age, I feel worse about myself.	14.9	15.8	15.0	15.7
During the menopause or the change of life, I became, or expect to become, irritable or depressed.	32.5****	36.5	31.4****	37.0
I will feel, or felt, regret when my periods stopped for the last time.	13.1****	16.0	13.8***	15.8
I don't, or didn't, know what to expect with the menopause.	45.1****	47.4	45.3**	47.5

[a]Adjusted for menopausal status.
*p < .05. **p < .01. ***p < .001. ****p < .0001.

less attractive after menopause (11% vs. 14%). It is important to note that in most cases, the differences in these percentages are actually quite small and may only be significant because of the large sample. In general, only small percentages of women (<20%) thought women are less attractive after menopause, that women feel worse about themselves as they age, and would feel regret when their menstrual periods stopped.

It is also worth comparing these results to previous studies based on pre-Boomer women. The Massachusetts Women's Health Study (MWHS) asked some of the same questions in 1982–1985 to women who were born between 1927 and 1937 (Avis & McKinlay, 1991). The women in the MWHS were much more likely to agree that women become depressed or irritable during menopause (71%), but also more likely to agree that women with many interests do not notice the menopause (76%). There was little difference between cohorts in women feeling regret when their periods stopped (16.7% in MWHS). This suggests that over time women have come to learn that depression is not an inevitable component of menopause. It is not surprising that in the 1990s, with increasing media attention to menopause, fewer women feel that busy women are less likely to notice the menopause.

Cross-cultural studies typically find that U.S. women have more negative attitudes towards menopause (Avis, 1996). Within the United States, the few studies that have included African-American women have found that they have a more positive attitude than that expressed by Caucasian women (Holmes-Rovner, Padonu, Kroll, Rovner, Talarczyk, & Rothert, 1996; Padonu et al., 1996; Standing & Glazer, 1992; Sommer et al., 1999). SWAN also found that African-American women were significantly more positive in their attitudes. The Chinese and Japanese women had the least positive attitudes, with the less acculturated Chinese and Japanese women (those who were educated in their native country and completed the interview in their native language) having the most negative attitudes.

Symptoms

A number of symptoms such as headaches, joint pain, dizzy spells, vaginal dryness, sleep disturbance, anxiety, and irritability have been attributed to the menopause, but only vasomotor symptoms (hot flashes and night sweats) have been related directly to menopausal status (Avis et al., 2001; WHO, 1981; Greene & Cooke, 1980; McKinlay & Jefferys, 1974; Neugarten & Kraines, 1965).

Vasomotor Symptoms. Estimates of the incidence of hot flashes from population studies in the United States and worldwide have ranged from 24 to 93 percent (Kronenberg, 1990). Some discrepancies in the prevalence of hot flash reporting reflect inconsistencies in research methodology, as well as study populations. Age ranges and menopause status of the women studied differ; some studies are based on patient samples whereas others are general population samples; and the specific symptom questions and the timeframe also differ. However, even within study or controlling for methodology, a high degree of variability of symptom reporting is found among women, thus suggesting considerable individual variation in symptom experience.

There are sparse longitudinal data on the age and menopause status at which hot flashes begin and how long they last. McKinlay et al. (1992) reported data from the Massachusetts Women's Health Study (MWHS) on the relationship of hot flashes to the menopause transition showing that hot flash reporting peaked just prior to menopause (i.e., 12 months of amenorrhea). These findings contradicted the widely held clinical impression that hot flashes began to increase after the last menstrual period, but are consistent with data from the SWAN cross-sectional survey which found the highest rate of vasomotor symptom reporting among late perimenopausal women (Gold,

Sternfeld, & Kelsey, 2000). Longitudinal analyses of vasomotor symptom reporting over the menopausal transition are currently being conducted among the SWAN cohort and will soon be forthcoming.

Some women report never experiencing hot flashes, whereas others report experiencing hot flashes throughout the day. There are limited data on factors that may predispose women to hot flashes. Thin women may have more hot flashes because they have higher levels of sex hormone binding globulin and their circulating estrogen is less biologically active, although SWAN found that greater body mass index was positively related to hot flashes. Interestingly, SWAN found that the association between estriadiol (E2) and body mass index (BMI) varies according to menopausal status (Randolph et al., 2004) which may explain some of the inconsistent findings. Other factors thought to be related to hot flashes include stress (Bromberger et al., 1997; Dennerstein et al., 1993; Swartzman, Edelberg, & Kemmann, 1990); smoking (Avis et al., 1997; Gold et al., 2000; Dennerstein, Dudley, Hopper, Guthrie, & Berger, 2000); lower socioeconomic status (Avis et al., 1997; Gold et al., 2000; Schwingl, Hulka, & Harlow, 1994); negative attitudes prior to menopause (Avis & McKinlay, 1991; Avis et al., 1997; Hunter, 1990); greater symptom reporting in general (Avis et al., 1997); and less physical activity (Gold et al., 2000). Women who smoke are thought to have a higher prevalence of vasomotor symptoms because of the anti-estrogenic effects of smoking.

Studies have consistently found racial/ethnic differences in reports of vasomotor symptoms. African-American women have been found to have greater frequency of hot flash reporting (Gold et al., 2000; Avis et al., 2001), and Asian women consistently have less (Avis et al., 1993, 2001; Gold et al., 2000). Whether the low incidence of vasomotor symptoms reflects cultural, psychological, or physiological differences, or some combination of all three, requires further examination. Japanese women may not perceive these heat changes as remarkable and/or they may experience them at a much lower rate, possibly due to the much lower fat content in their diets. Another hypothesis is that the low rate of hot flash reporting among Japanese women may be due to a higher proportion of phytoestrogens in their diet (Adlercreutz, Hamalainen, Gorbach, & Grodin, 1992).

Without knowing more about factors related to vasomotor symptoms, it is difficult to surmise how Baby Boomers might compare to previous cohorts. Table 4.2 compares reports of hot flashes/night sweats for women in the SWAN cohort with those of the earlier MWHS sample. Note that the MWHS did not distinguish between early and late perimenopause; these women are all classified as perimenopausal. Since the MWHS consisted largely of non-Hispanic Caucasian women, for comparison purposes, we have also broken out this group of women from SWAN. Based on these comparisons, the SWAN women report hot flashes/night sweats at slightly higher rates, which is mostly seen in the pre and late perimenopausal women. The higher rate

TABLE 4.2

Comparison of Hot Flash/Night Sweat Reporting
in the Past 2 Weeks for Women in the MWHS and SWAN

| | MWHS[a] | | SWAN, All Ethnicities | | SWAN, Caucasians Only | |
Menopausal Status	N	% Reporting HF	N	% Reporting HF	N	% Reporting HF
Surgical	2234	44.4	2617	46.0	1089	37.9
Postmenopause	2444	42.6	2190	44.2	1092	39.2
Late Perimenopause	—	—	553	58.1	281	57.7
Early Perimenopause	—	—	2164	39.5	1070	34.6
Perimenopause	2127	37.3	—	—	—	—
Premenopause	977	13.8	2123	22.4	925	21.0
N	7802	34.8	9647	39.6	4458	35.2

[a]Reported in Avis et al. (1993).

among the premenopausal women may reflect an increased sensitivity to or expectation of hot flashes among baby-boomer women. The higher rate among the late perimenopausal women highlights the important of distinguishing between these stages. The rate of hot flash/night sweat reporting between the two samples is remarkably similar for the surgical and postmenopausal women, although the Caucasian SWAN women report lower rates than the overall SWAN sample.

Although frequency of hot flash reporting among Baby Boomers is likely to be similar to that of previous cohorts, it is possible that the Baby Boomers may differ in terms of how bothersome they find hot flashes. At this point there are no published papers that address this question, but these data will be available from SWAN.

Depression and Mood.   Numerous studies have examined the association between menopausal status and mood, yet findings from these studies are inconsistent. Although most community-based studies have not found an association between menopausal status and depressive mood, several studies have found a higher rate of depressed mood in the perimenopause (Avis, 2000; Bromberger, Harlow, Avis, Kravitz, & Cordal, 2004).

Data from the SWAN cross-sectional study showed that the presence of psychological distress (irritability, depression, and tension) in the previous 2 weeks was greater among early perimenopausal women than among pre or postmenopausal women (Bromberger et al., 2001). Baseline data from the SWAN cohort (that included only pre and early perimenopausal women) looked at four symptoms: irritability, nervousness, frequent mood changes, and feeling blue or depressed (Bromberger et al., 2003). These analyses found that rates of all of these symptoms were higher in the perimenopausal women than among premenopausal women. However, when analyses adjusted for major covariates and confounders then early perimenopausal women no longer had significantly higher odds of feeling blue.

In an attempt to examine possible cohort differences, we compared data from SWAN with those of the MWHS similar to the comparison for hot flashes. Table 4.3 shows that 35.9% of women in the MWHS (aged 45 to 55) reported feeling blue or depressed in the past two weeks while 39.8% of SWAN women in this age range reported feeling blue or depressed. In both samples, symptom reporting varied by menopausal status with the highest rates among women who had a surgical menopause (39.1% in the MWHS and 42.5% in SWAN) and in the perimenopause (38.1% in MWHS and 40.6% in late perimenopause for SWAN). In general, symptom reporting of feeling blue or depressed was higher in the SWAN cohort than the MWHS. This is particularly apparent among the premenopausal women, which may reflect increased demands and stress on women. The differences between the two samples does not seem to be due to ethnic differences.

The Center for Epidemiologic Studies–Depression (CES–D) Scale has been used as a measure of depressive symptoms. The SWAN study found an overall prevalence of 24% of the sample reporting scores ≥ 16, the usual cut-point for depressive symptoms (Bromberger et al., 2004). Women with irregular menstrual cycles had a higher rate of depressive symptoms in unadjusted analyses. In multivariate analyses, depressive symptoms were significantly related to education, poorer self-assessed health, more physical symptoms, stress, and low social support, but not irregular cycles. More women in SWAN were classified as having depressive symptoms than in the MWHS. Overall rates of depression among women in the MWHS averaged around 12% (see McKinlay, McKinlay, & Brambilla, 1987). These differences are not explained by the different racial/ethnic compositions of the samples, as the Caucasian women in SWAN had a rate of 22.3%.

TABLE 4.3

Comparison of Reporting Feeling Blue or Depressed
in the Past 2 Weeks for Women in the MWHS and SWAN

	MWHS[a]		SWAN, All Ethnicities		SWAN, Caucasians Only	
Menopausal Status	N	% Reporting Blue or Depressed	N	% Reporting Blue or Depressed	N	% Reporting Blue or Depressed
Surgical	2234	39.1	2621	42.5	1089	40.9
Postmenopause	2444	33.8	2196	37.8	1095	36.5
Late Perimenopause	—	—	554	40.6	281	38.8
Early Perimenopause	—	—	2173	36.0	1077	41.3
Perimenopause	2127	38.1	—	—	—	—
Premenopause	977	29.1	2139	36.0	933	38.2
N	7802	35.9	9683	39.8	4475	39.2

[a]Reported in Avis et al. (1993).

From these comparisons, it is not possible to explain why these rates are different, but they clearly suggest that middle aged women are currently reporting more symptoms and are more likely to be depressed than did middle aged women in previous years.

Sleep. Sleep difficulties among women increase with age beginning around midlife. However, it is unknown whether this increased difficulty in sleep is due to aging, physical problems, psychosocial problems, hormonal changes, or night sweats. The SWAN cross-sectional survey found that 38% of women reported difficulty sleeping in the past two weeks (Kravitz et al., 2003). Age-adjusted rates were highest in the women who were late perimenopausal (45.4%) and surgically postmenopausal (47.6%). Menopausal status was still significantly associated with difficulty sleeping even after controlling for vasomotor and psychological symptoms and self-assessed health.

Memory. Like sleep disturbances, memory complaints have also been thought to be associated with menopause (Woods, Mitchell, & Adams, 2000). However, the extent to which estrogen loss affects memory and cognitive functioning during and after the menopausal transition is unknown. Two longitudinal studies, SWAN and the Melbourne Women's Midlife Health Project (MWMHP) have examined change in cognitive function as women transition through menopause. The Chicago site of SWAN assessed working memory and perceptual speed and found small but significant *increases* over time during the premenopausal and perimenopausal phases (Meyer et al., 2003). Cognitive functioning is also being assessed in the entire SWAN cohort and those data should be available soon. The MWMHP also found no effect of menopause on episodic verbal memory (Henderson, Guthrie, Dudley, Burger, & Dennerstein, 2003). The Seattle Midlife Women's Health Study looked at memory functioning among perimenopausal women divided into early, middle, and late perimenopause and found little difference in perceived memory functioning among the different stages (Woods et al., 2000). Thus, although women often report memory problems during the perimenopause, objective measures of cognitive functioning have shown no negative effect of menopause.

Impact of Menopause on Chronic Conditions

The role of natural menopause in chronic conditions largely has been inferred indirectly from studies of exogenous rather than endogenous hormones (Sowers & LaPietra, 1995; Bradsher & McKinlay, 2000; Derby, 2000). Direct evidence regarding natural menopause is relatively sparse and somewhat inconclusive, but is strongest and most consistent for bone density. Bone loss accelerates after the final menstrual period (Reeve et al., 1999), but it is unclear when bone loss starts in relation to the menopausal transition (Sowers & LaPietra, 1995; Bradsher & McKinlay, 2000). Few studies have been conducted regarding endogenous hormones and cardiovascular disease risk, and results vary across studies (Derby, 2000). The few studies of natural menopause and urinary incontinence also have yielded mixed results (Gold et al., 2000; Sherburn, Guthrie, Dudley, O'Connell, & Dennerstein, 2001; Sampselle, Harris, Harlow, & Sowers, 2002). Studies of osteoarthritis find little association with menopause status after adjustment for factors such as age and body mass index (Sowers, 2000). Moreover, little data exist regarding ethnic variation in menopause-related changes in chronic conditions (Derby, 2000).

Inconsistencies across studies are likely due to a number of methodological issues (Sowers & LaPietra, 1995; Bradsher & McKinlay, 2000; Derby, 2000; Sowers et al., 2000). These include problems regarding sampling, such as small sample sizes, drawing participants from menopause clinics, and cross-sectional rather than longitudinal comparisons—the former may be subject to cohort effects, particularly with use of historical controls, and cannot indicate temporal associations. Other methodological issues involve measurement and statistical analysis, including: inadequate duration of follow-up for conditions that may take years to develop; insufficient frequency of measurements for assessing within-woman change; inadequate adjustment for confounding factors; lack of premenopausal baseline data; and imprecision in measurement of menopause status or of the chronic conditions. SWAN was designed to address these issues, by following a large multi-ethnic community-based sample of pre- and early perimenopausal women through the menopausal transition, making annual prospective measurements of menopause status and endogenous hormones as well as numerous confounding factors and chronic conditions (Sowers et al., 2000; Avis & Crawford, 2001).

TREATMENTS FOR MENOPAUSAL SYMPTOMS AND POSTMENOPAUSAL HEALTH

Since the late 1960s with the publication of *Feminine Forever*, clinicians increasingly recommended that all menopausal women begin taking estrogen and continue taking it throughout their lives. Over the years, the list of purported benefits from exogenous hormone therapy (HT) continued to grow so that estrogen truly appeared to be a miracle drug that could prevent cardiovascular disease, osteoporosis, Alzheimer's disease, and colorectal cancer, and in general improve women's quality of life, although possibly increase a woman's risk of breast cancer. However, for Baby Boomers in the midst of the menopausal transition, the message is drastically changing. Within less than two years, data from several large clinical trials have totally changed the prevailing view of the benefits of estrogen (Rossouw et al., & Writing Group for the Women's Health Initiative Investigators, 2002; Herrington & Klein, 2003) and left Baby Boomers in a quandary. Results from recent randomized clinical trials are discrepant from conclusions of earlier observational studies, particularly regarding cardiovascular disease (CVD). Use of HT is declining while interest in alternatives is increasing, although many women perceive a lack of sufficient information on this issue, particularly from their health care providers. It is also interesting to note a change in terminology. Although previously referred to as hormone *replacement* therapy, the preferred term is now just hormone therapy. This reflects a consciousness change reflecting the current view that it is natural for hormone levels to be lower postmenopause.

Risks and Benefits of Hormone Therapy

Cardiovascular Disease.   The effect of HT varies for different cardiovascular risk factors; thus, its overall influence may be either helpful or harmful (Ho & Mosca, 2002). In contrast to observational studies that showed a lower risk of cardiovascular disease (CVD) among ever-users of HT (Grodstein & Stampfer, 1995; Stampfer, Colditz, Willett, Manson, Rosner, Speizer, & Hennekens, 1991; O'Keefe, Kim, Hall, Cochran, Lawhorn, & McCallister, 1997), recent randomized clinical trials in postmenopausal women suggest a lack of benefit and possible harm, particularly during the first year of treatment (Herrington & Klein, 2003). Results are generally consistent across a number of both primary and secondary prevention trials with a variety of CVD-related outcomes and hormone preparations (Herrington & Klein, 2003). These include the estrogen plus progestin (E + P) component of the Women's Health Initiative (WHI) (Manson et al., & Women's Health Initiative Investigators, 2003), the Heart and Estrogen/progestin Replacement Study (HERS) (Hulley et al., 1998), the Estrogen Replacement and Atherosclerosis (ERA) study (Herrington et al., 2000), and a number of other studies (e.g., Clarke, Kelleher, Lloyd-Jones, Slack, & Schofiel, 2002; Cherry et al., 2002; Angerer, Stork, Kothny, Schmitt, & von Schacky, 2001; Waters et al., 2002; Hodis et al., & Women's Estrogen–Progestin Lipid-Lowering Hormone Atherosclerosis Regression Trial Research Group, 2003; Simon et al., 2001; Viscoli et al., 2001).

Several possibilities might explain the startling different findings between earlier observational studies and recent randomized trials. These include the selection to HT bias, biologic factors, and the timing of initiation. HT users, particularly long-term users, differ in a number of ways from other women such that benefits of HT might be overestimated in observational studies (Sotelo & Johnson, 1997). For example, users tend to be healthier prior to initiation of HT, are more compliant with medication, and tend to have more contact with the health care system so that any disease is more likely to be treated (Grimes & Lobo, 2002; Grodstein, Clarkson, & Manson, 2003)

Alternatively, differences between observational studies and clinical trials may be due to biologic factors. HT's cardioprotective effects appear to be greater in women with less atherosclerosis or cardiovascular risk (Clarkson, Anthony, Morgan, 2001; Grodstein et al., 2003; Hodis et al., 2001; Karim et al., 2005), and beginning HT years after the onset of menopause may reduce its cardioprotective effects (Clarkson et al., 2001). Thus, it is unclear whether randomized clinical trial results in older women regarding lack of HT benefit apply to younger women with less atherosclerosis who initiate HT closer to menopause (Grimes & Lobo, 2002). Nevertheless, the recent highly publicized findings from the WHI and other studies have not provided consistent evidence that HT can prevent cardiovascular disease, which has discouraged women from taking HT for primary prevention.

Breast Cancer. One of the primary potential risks associated with long-term HT use is breast cancer, which is clearly a hormonally mediated disease, related to markers of hormonal status such as age of menarche, pregnancy, and age of natural and surgical menopause affecting risk (Howe & Rohan, 1993). In the WHI, E + P increased the overall risk of breast cancer and the risk of invasive cancer by 24% relative to placebo (Chlebowski et al., & WHI Investigators, 2003), and almost doubled the rate of abnormal mammograms after one year, i.e., even after short-term use. Among invasive cases, the E + P participants had larger cancers, tumors were more likely to be node-positive, and were diagnosed at a more advanced stage, suggesting a generally less favorable prognosis. A recent study of HT in breast cancer survivors was terminated earlier than planned, due to an increased risk of new breast cancer in the treated group (Holmberg, Anderson, & HABITS Steering and Data Monitoring Committees, 2004).

Bone. One area in which HT has consistently been found to be beneficial is in preventing bone loss. A recent meta-analysis of 57 randomized clinical trials of HT in postmenopausal women indicated a consistent protective effect on bone mineral density, with differences in 2-year percent change in bone density of 4.1% for the forearm, 4.5% for the femoral neck (hip), and 6.8% for the lumbar spine (Wells et al., & The Osteoporosis Research Advisory Group, 2002). At three years of follow-up in the WHI (E + P trial), the mean difference in bone density between the E + P and placebo arms was 3.6% for the hip and 4.5% for the lumbar spine (Cauley et al., & Women's Health Initiative Investigators, 2003). HT also has been linked to reductions in fractures, with a relative risk of 0.66 for vertebral fractures and a relative risk of 0.87 for nonvertebral fractures (Wells et al., 2002). In the WHI, E + P reduced hip fracture relative to placebo by one-third, and the total fracture risk by 24% (Cauley et al., 2003). When considering other chronic diseases, however, there was no net benefit of E + P compared with placebo, even for participants with a high fracture risk. Although HT can prevent bone loss, other alternatives, such as the bisphosphonates, appear to have fewer risks associated with them.

Cognitive Functioning. Despite evidence that HT may benefit cognition and dementia through mechanisms such as neuronal effects and enhancement of neurotransmitters (Wise, Dubal, Wilson, Rau, & Bottner, 2001), population-based randomized controlled trials have not shown a benefit of HT on cognitive functioning.

The WHI Memory Study found no evidence that E + P is protective of cognitive function in healthy postmenopausal women aged 65+. The average increase in the modified Mini Mental Status Examination was statistically significantly lower in E + P participants but the overall difference was not clinically meaningful (Rapp et al., & WHIMS Investigators, 2003). Results from the HERS study are consistent with this finding (Grady et al., 2002). Compared with placebo, women in the E + P arm of WHI also were more than twice as likely to be diagnosed with probable dementia (Shumaker et al., & WHIMS Investigators, 2003).

However, epidemiologic results have been contradictory due to methodological issues such as inaccurate recall of HT exposure, a healthy user bias, small sample sizes, and limited tests of cognitive function (Yaffe, Sawaya, Lieburburg, & Grady, 1998). Further, most studies have not separated the effect of HT on cognitive function from its effect on symptom relief (particularly sleep). A recent review indicated a positive impact on cognitive performance in perimenopausal women, perhaps due to relief of menopausal symptoms, but no benefit in asymptomatic women (Yaffe et al., 1998).

Colorectal Cancer. The overall risk of colorectal cancer in the WHI was approximately 40% lower in the E + P arm than in the placebo arm, with a much lower risk of local disease (Chlebowski et al., 2004). The reduction in risk is consistent with findings from observational studies (Grodstein, Newcomb, & Stampfer, 1999) and with results from HERS (Hulley et al., & HERS Research Group, 2002), although the mechanism for such a reduction is not clear. The WHI also found, however, that cancers in the E + P participants were more likely to have lymph-node involvement, had a higher average number of positive nodes, and were diagnosed at a more advanced stage. Despite the reduction in colorectal cancer, the risks of E + P outweighed its benefits even in subgroups at high risk for colorectal cancer (Chlebowski et al., 2004).

Symptoms and Quality of Life. HT remains the most effective treatment identified to date for vasomotor symptoms, and short-term low-dose use continues to be recommended by the North American Menopause Society (2004). However, this benefit in terms of symptom relief has not been translated into improving general quality of life. The WHI found at one year of follow-up there were no statistically significant differences between E + P and placebo in general health, vitality, mental health, depressive symptoms, or sexual satisfaction (Hays et al., & Women's Health Initiative Investigators, 2003). Although women in the E + P group had statistically significantly less sleep disturbance, bodily pain, and better physical functioning, these effects were not large enough to be clinically important. In women aged 50 to 54 with moderate/severe vasomotor symptoms at baseline—a group who might be expected to have a treatment-related difference in quality of life due to symptoms—vasomotor symptoms and sleep were better in the E + P arm, but there were no other significant differences in quality of life despite relief of vasomotor symptoms. However, the investigators have noted that the majority of women who agreed to enroll in the WHI did not have severe symptoms. These results are consistent with those of the ERA trial (Sherman & Shumaker, 2003). In addition, both the ERA and HERS trials found that exogenous estrogen was linked to greater urinary incontinence (Sherman & Shumaker, 2003; Grady et al., & HERS Research Group, 2001), consistent with recent observational results (Grodstein, Lifford, Resnick, & Curhan, 2004).

Risks and Benefits. The results of these recent trials have clearly changed the risk/benefit equation for hormone therapy. HT is the best treatment option for menopausal symptoms, but its potential long-term negative consequences are causing more women to question its benefits. One of the biggest issues now for Baby Boomers is the search for alternatives to HT, as discussed below.

ATTITUDES, TRENDS IN USE, AND DECISION MAKING REGARDING MENOPAUSAL THERAPIES

Even prior to the publication of results from HERS and WHI, women were aware of the risks and side effects of HT. Up to 30% of prescriptions went unfilled, and almost half of users discontinued within one year (Ettinger, Li, & Klein, 1996). Common concerns include breast cancer and side effects such as headaches, nausea, weight gain, and menstrual bleeding (Newton, LaCroix, Leveille, Rutter, Keenan, & Anderson, 1997; Reece, Theroux, & Taylor, 2002; Theroux & Taylor, 2003). Many women see menopause as a natural process that may not require treatment, particularly with an unnatural therapy such as HT (Newton et al., 1997; Kang, Ansbacher, & Hammoud, 2002; Bonetta, Cheung, & Stewart, 2001). Several studies have found that, compared with non-Hispanic Caucasians, African Americans or women from more traditional cultures are more likely to see menopause as natural and not requiring medical intervention (Sampselle, Harlow, Skurnick, Brubaker, & Bondarenko, 2002; Bonetta et al., 2001; Pham, Grisso, & Freeman, 1997).

As a result of recent clinical trial findings, women's concerns about negative effects of HT are likely to increase, with a corresponding decline in HT use. A recent survey found that over half of women aged 40 to 79 were personally worried about the impact of the WHI findings (Breslau et al., 2003). Mirroring heightened concerns, HT use decreased slightly after the publication of results from HERS and the ERA trial, with a much larger decrease following the WHI announcement in July 2002 (Hersh et al., 2004; Haas, Kaplan, Gerstenberg, & Kerlikowski, 2004; Ettinger, Grady, Tosteson, Pressman, & Macer, 2003; Grady, Ettinger, Tosteson, Pressman, & Macer, 2003). Prescriptions for lower-dose Premarin (0.3 mg/day) increased slightly in the second half of 2002, suggesting possible attempts at tapering, i.e., lowering of the dose (Hersh et al., 2004).

In contrast to HT, interest in and use of alternative therapies has been increasing (Warren, Shortle, & Dominguez, 2002), with this trend likely to accelerate. Such therapies are viewed favorably—and sometimes preferred to HT—by many women, due in part to a belief that they are safe and have fewer side effects than HT because they are natural (Warren et al., 2002; Newton, Buist, Keenan, Anderson, & LaCroix, 2002; Seidl & Stewart, 1998; Fogel & Woods, 1995). This may be particularly true for the current generation of menopausal women (Fogel & Woods, 1995). Users of these therapies see them as effective for menopausal symptoms and health (Newton et al., 2002; Seidl & Stewart, 1998; Kam, Dennehy, & Tsourounis, 2002), although this may be related to selection bias (Newton et al., 2002), and few randomized clinical trials have been conducted. Use of alternative therapies also has been linked to a desire for personal control over one's own health (Seidl & Stewart, 1998; Richter, Corwin, Rheaume, & McKeown, 2001), a concern more common among Baby Boomers than in previous generations.

These alternatives include other pharmaceutical agents, herbal or dietary remedies, and behavioral therapies. Pharmaceutical agents have included clonidine, antidepressants, veralipride, Bellargal, and progestational agents. Unfortunately, many of these agents are ineffective or have a high incidence of side effects (Loprinzi, Kubler, & Sloan, 2000).

With many of the prescription medications having limited efficacy and multiple side effects, women have turned to over-the-counter natural products to treat menopausal symptoms (Kronenberg, O'Leary Cobb, & McMahon, 1994; Beal, 1998). Many women are attracted to phytomedicines as a more natural remedy (Wade, Kronenberg, Kelly, & Murphy, 1999). Currently there is a national trend towards using these alternative agents for alleviation of hot flashes. These products include St. John's wort, vitamin E, black cohosh, dong quai, ginseng, evening primrose oil, motherwort, licorice, wild yam, red clover, and soy derivatives (Kronenberg & Fugh-Berman, 2002). Black cohosh has been found to have a modest effect on hot flashes in trials lasting six months or less. Although few adverse events have been reported, the long-term safety (mainly estrogenic stimulation of the breast or endometrium) of black cohosh is unknown and not enough data exist to support a recommendation for its use in this country (NCCAM website, 2002). Soy is a popular alternative for relieving hot flashes, but the evidence for its effectiveness is mixed (Albertazzi et al., 1998; Burke et al., 2003; Quella, Loprinzi, & Barton, 2000). A 12-week double-blind cross-over design clinical trial of 177 women found no evidence that soy was more effective than placebo (Quella et al., 2000). Burke and colleagues (2003) also did not find beneficial effects of soy. Although soy markedly diminished moderate to severe hot flashes in a double-blind, placebo-controlled trial of 104 postmenopausal women, side effects such as gastrointestinal problems, food intolerance, and constipation were experienced by a significant number of participants (Albertazzi et al., 1998). Further, soy-based diets are questionable for use in women with breast cancer because of their estrogenic activity (Lucerno & McCloskey, 1997). In a review of 29 randomized controlled clinical trials of complementary and alternative medicine therapies for hot flashes, Kronenberg and Fugh-Berman (2002) did not find evidence that other herbs and nutritional supplements evidence were beneficial, a conclusion also supported by another recent review (Huntley & Ernst, 2003). Many of these alternative therapies have not been shown to be effective and are not regulated by the Food and Drug Administration. A further problem is that the identity of the compounds and the mechanism of action are unknown (Kronenberg & Fugh-Berman, 2002).

Behavioral therapies such as paced respiration (slow, deep breathing), relaxation techniques, and regular exercise have also been studied. There is suggestive but inconclusive evidence that paced respiration (Freedman & Woodward, 1992; Freedman, Woodward, & Brown, 1995), regular physical exercise (Hammar, Berg, & Lindgren, 1990; Ivarsson, Spetz, & Hammar, 1998), and applied relaxation (Wijma, Melin, Nedstrand, & Hammar, 1997) decrease the frequency of hot flashes. However, the research on these therapies is limited; most studies have been small and of short duration.

A number of studies indicate that many women are dissatisfied with the information on menopausal therapies—both amount and quality—received from health care providers, including HT risks and benefits and alternatives to HT (Ettinger et al., 2003; National Committee for Quality Assurance, 2001; Theroux & Taylor, 2003; Newton et al., 1998). For example, in a recent survey, only one-third of women reported receiving good or excellent counseling regarding menopause and HT (National Committee for Quality Assurance, 2001). In another survey, just over one-third of women received any menopausal information from their physicians (Utian & Schiff, 1994). A study of racial differences found that 60% of African Americans received no menopausal information from their physicians, compared with 40% of Caucasians (Pham et al., 1997). In the same study, Caucasians were twice as likely to have discussed their menopausal symptoms with their physician, or to be asked about their symptoms by the physician; 23% of Caucasians received recommendations for HT, compared with no African Americans.

A majority of women in many studies report that their primary source of menopausal information is a source other than their health care provider, including the Internet, magazines and books, television and radio, friends and family, and health food store employees (Conboy, Domar, & O'Connell, 2001; Utian & Boggs, 1999; Pham et al., 1997; Theroux & Taylor, 2003; Utian & Schiff, 1994). Consequently, many women are making decisions regarding therapies independently of their health care providers, despite a perceived or actual lack of information (Ettinger et al., 2003; Newton et al., 1997, 1998; Connelly, Ferrari, Hagen, & Inui, 1999). For Baby Boomers currently approaching or experiencing the menopause transition, high-quality studies are needed to provide accurate information on alternatives to HT, including effectiveness and side effects for short- and long-term use.

SUMMARY

The ways that Baby Boomers approach menopause will undoubtedly be different from women of previous generations. They will talk about it, read about it, and spend money on various products to reduce symptoms and long-term consequences. It is too early to tell whether all of this attention will actually alter women's experience of menopause in terms of symptoms and other consequences.

The Study of Women's Health Across the Nation (SWAN) is the first study to simultaneously evaluate multiple aspects of menopause-related changes in a multiracial/ethnic community-based sample of women. The study promises to provide unique data on the menopause experience, and to give clinicians a broader, more balanced understanding of the changes that occur as women transition from pre- to postmenopause. We are already learning from SWAN that the menopausal transition varies physiologically and psychologically for different racial/ethnic groups of women.

Treatment for menopausal symptoms and long-term consequences are undergoing rapid changes. Hormone therapy, long considered an elixir to prolong youth and well-being is no longer the wonder drug it was once thought to be. As women seek alternatives to HT, scientific studies on new approaches to symptom management will proliferate. These are indeed uncertain times for Baby Boomers who will once again be on the forefront of change.

ACKNOWLEDGMENTS

The Study of Women's Health Across the Nation (SWAN) was funded by the National Institute on Aging (U01 AG012495, U01 AG012505, U01 AG012531, U01 AG012535, U01 A012539, U01 AG012546, U01 AG012553, U01 AG012554), the National Institute of Nursing Research (U01 NR04061), and the NIH Office of Research on Women's Health.

REFERENCES

Abraham, S., Llewellyn-Jones, D., & Perz, J. (1994). Changes in Australian women's perception of the menopause and menopausal symptoms before and after the climacteric. *Maturitas*, *20*, 121–128.

Adlercreutz, H., Hamalainen, O., Gorbach, S., & Grodin, B. (1992). Dietary phytoestrogens and the menopause in Japan. *Lancet*, *339*, 123–133.

Albertazzi, P., Pansini, F., Bonaccorsi, G., Zanotti, L., Forini, E., & de Aloysio, D. (1998). The effect of dietary soy supplementation on hot flashes. *Obstetrics and Gynecology*, *91*(1), 6–11.

Angerer, P., Stork, S., Kothny, W., Schmitt, P., & von Schacky, C. (2001). Effect of oral postmenopausal hormone replacement on progression of atherosclerosis. *Arteriosclerosis, Thrombosis, and Vascular Biology*, *21*(2), 262–268.

Avis, N. E. (1996). Women's perceptions of the menopause. *European Menopause Journal*, *3*, 80–84.

Avis, N. E. (1999). Women's health at midlife. In S. L. Willis & J. D. Reid (Eds.), *Middle aging: Development in the third quarter of life*. San Diego: Academic Press.

Avis, N. E. (2000). Is menopause associated with mood disturbances? In R. A. Lobo, J. Kelsey, & R. Marcus (Eds.), *Menopause: Biology and pathology*. New York: Academic Press.

Avis, N., & Crawford, S. (2001). SWAN: What it is and what we hope to learn. *Menopause Management*, *10*, 8–15.

Avis, N. E., Crawford, S., & McKinlay, S. M. (1997). Psychosocial, behavioral and health factors related to menopause symptomalogy. *Women's health: Research on gender, behavior and policy. Maturitas*, *26*, 175–184.

Avis, N. E., Kaufert, P. A., Lock, M., McKinlay, S. M., & Vass, K. (1993). The evolution of menopausal symptoms. *Balliere's Clinical Endocrinology and Metabolism*, *7*(1), 17–32.

Avis, N. E., & McKinlay, S. M. (1991). A longitudinal analysis of women's attitudes towards the menopause: Results from the Massachusetts Women's Health Study. *Maturitas*, *13*, 65–79.

Avis, N. E., & McKinlay, S. M. (1995). The Massachusetts Women's Health Study: An epidemiological investigation of the menopause. *Journal of American Medical Women's Association*, *50*(2), 45–50.

Avis, N. E., Stellato, R., Crawford, S., Bromberger, J., Ganz, P., Cain, V., & Jagawa-Singer, M. (2001). Is there a menopausal syndrome? Menopause status and symptoms across ethnic groups. *Social Science and Medicine*, *52*, 345–356.

Baron, J., La Vecchia, C., & Levi, F. (1990). The antiestrogen effect of cigarette smoking in women. *American Journal of Obstetrical Gynecology*, *162*, 502–514.

Bauman, K. E., Suchindran, C. M., & Murray, D. M. (1999). The paucity of effects in community trials: Is secular trend the culprit? *Preventative Medicine*, *28*(4), 426–429.

Beal, M. W. (1998). Women's use of complementary and alternative therapies in reproductive health care. *Journal of Nurse Midwifery*, *43*(3), 224–234.

Bell, S. (1990). Sociological perspective on the medicalization of menopause. *Annals of the New York Academy of Sciences*, *592*, 173–178.

Bengtsson, C., Lindquist, O., & Redvall, L. (1979). Is the menopausal age rapidly changing? *Maturitas*, *1*(3), 159–164.

Boldsen, J., & Jeune, B. (1990). Distribution of age at menopause in two Danish samples. *Human Biology*, *62*(2), 291–300.

Bonetta, C., Cheung, A. M., & Stewart, D. E. (2001). Italian-Canadian women's views of menopause: How culture may affect hormone use. *Medscape Women's Health ejournal*, *6*(5), 4.

Boulet, M. J., Oddens, B. J., Lehert, P., Vemer, H. M., & Visser, A. (1994). Climacteric and menopause in seven south-east Asian countries. *Maturitas*, *19*, 157–176.

Bradsher, J., & McKinlay, S. (2000). Distinguishing the effects of age from those of menopause. In R. Lobo, J. Kelsey, & R. Marcus (Eds.), *Menopause: Biology and pathobiology* (pp. 203–211). San Diego: Academic Press.

Brambilla, D. J., & McKinlay, S. M. (1989). A prospective study of factors affecting age at menopause. *Journal of Clinical Epidemiology, 42*, 1031–1039.

Breslau, E. S., Davis, W. W., Doner, L., Eisner, E. J., Goodman, N. R., Meissner, H. I., Rimer, B. K., & Rossouw, J. E. (2003). The hormone therapy dilemma: Women respond. *Journal of American Medical Women's Association, 58*(1), 33–43.

Brett, K., & Cooper, G. (2003). Associations with menopause and menopausal transition in a nationally representative US sample. *Maturitas, 45*, 89–97.

Brett, K., & Higgins, J. (2003). Hysterectomy prevalence by Hispanic ethnicity: Evidence from a national survey. *American Journal of Public Health, 93*, 307–312.

Brett, K. M., Marsh, J. V. R., & Madans, J. H. (1997). Epidemiology of hysterectomy in the U.S.: Demographic and reproductive factors in a nationally representative sample. *Journal of Women's Health, 6*, 309–316.

Bromberger, J. T., Assmann, S. F., Avis, N. E., Schocken, M., Kravitz, H. M., & Cordal, A. (2003). Persistent mood symptoms in a multiethnic community cohort of pre- and perimenopausal women. *American Journal of Epidemiology, 158*(4), 347–356.

Bromberger, J., Harlow, S., Avis, N. E., Kravitz, H. M., & Cordal, A. (2004). The role of multiple factors in ethnic differences in the prevalence of elevated depressive symptoms of midlife women: The Study of Women's Health Across the Nation (SWAN). *American Journal of Public Health.*

Bromberger, J. T., Matthews, K. A., Kuller, L. H., Wing, R. R., Meilahn, E. N., & Plantinga, P. (1997). A prospective study of the determinants of age at menopause. *American Journal of Epidemiology, 145*, 124–133.

Bromberger, J. T., Meyer, P. M., Kravitz, H. M., Sommer, B., Cordal, A., Powell, L., Ganz, P. A., & Sutton-Tyrrell, K. (2001). Psychologic distress and natural menopause: A multiethnic community study. *American Journal of Public Health, 91*(9), 1435–1442.

Brown, W. J., Bryson, L., Byles, J. E., Dobson, A. J., Lee, C., Mishra, G., & Schofield, M. (1998). Women's Health Australia: Recruitment for a national longitudinal cohort study. *Women Health, 28*(1), 23–40.

Bungay, G. T., Vessey, M. P., & McPherson, C. K. (1980). Study of symptoms in middle life with special reference to the menopause. *British Medical Journal, 281*, 181–183.

Burger, H. G. (1994a). The menopause: When is it all over or is it? *Australian and New Zealand Journal of Obstetrics and Gynecology, 34*, 293–295.

Burger, H. G. (1994b). Diagnostic role of follicle-stimulating hormone (FSH) measurements during the menopausal transition: An analysis of FSH, oestradiol and inhibin. *European Journal of Endocrinology, 130*, 38–42.

Burger, H. G. (1996). The endocrinology of the menopause. *Maturitas, 23*, 129–136.

Burke, G. L., Legault, C., Anthony, M., Bland, D., Morgan, T. N., Naughton, M. J., Leggett, K., Washburn, S. A., & Vitolins, M. Z. (2003). Soy protein and isoflavone effects on vasomotor symptoms in peri and postmenopausal women: The Soy Estrogen Alternative Study. *Menopause, 10*(2), 147–153.

Bush, T. L. (1990). The epidemiology of cardiovascular disease in postmenopausal women. *Annals of the New York Academy of Sciences, 592*, 263–271.

Cauley, J. A., Robbins, J., Chen, Z., Cummings, S. R., Jackson, R. D., LaCroix, A. Z., LeBoff, M., Lewis, C. E., McGowan, J., Neuner, J., Pettinger, M., Stefanick, M. L., Wactawski-Wende, J., Watts, N. B., & Women's Health Initiative Investigators. (2003). Effects of estrogen plus progestin on risk of fracture and bone mineral density: The Women's Health Initiative randomized trial. *The Journal of the American Medical Association, 290*(13), 1729–1738.

CDC. (2004a). Prevalence of cigarette use among 14 racial/ethnic populations—United States, 1999–2001. *Morbidity and Mortality Weekly Report CDC Surveillance Summary, 53*(3), 1–4.

CDC. (2004b). Trends in intake of energy and macronutrients—United States, 1971–2000. *Morbidity and Mortality Weekly Report CDC Surveillance Summary, 53*(4), 80–82.

Cherry, N., Gilmour, K., Hannaford, P., Heagerty, A., Khan, M. A., Kitchener, H., McNamee, R., Elstein, M., Kay, C., Seif, M., Buckley, H., & ESPRIT Team. (2002). Oestrogen therapy for prevention of reinfarction in postmenopausal women: A randomised placebo controlled trial. *Lancet, 360*(9350), 2001–2008.

Chlebowski, R. T., Hendrix, S. L., Langer, R. D., Stefanick, M. L., Gass, M., Lane, D., Rodabough, R. J., Gilligan, M. A., Cyr, M. G., Thomson, C. A., Khandekar, J., Petrovitch, H., McTiernan, A., & WHI Investigators. (2003). Influence of estrogen plus progestin on breast cancer and mammography in healthy postmenopausal women: The Women's Health Initiative randomized trial. *The Journal of the American Medical Association, 289*(24), 3243–3253.

Chlebowski, R. T., Wactawski-Wende, J., Ritenbaugh, C., Hubbell, F. A., Ascensao, J., Rodabough, R. J., Rosenberg, C. A., Taylor, V. M., Harris, R., Chen, C., Adams-Campbell, L. L., White, E., & Women's Health Initiative Investigators. (2004). Estrogen plus progestin and colorectal cancer in postmenopausal women. *New England Journal of Medicine, 350*(10), 991–1004.

Clarke, S., Kelleher, J., Lloyd-Jones, H., Slack, M., & Schofiel, P. M. (2002). A study of hormone replacement therapy in postmenopausal women with ischaemic heart disease: The Papworth HRT atherosclerosis study. *British Journal of Obstetrics and Gynecology, 109*(9), 1056–1062.

Clarkson, T. B., Anthony, M. S., & Morgan, T. M. (2001). Inhibition of postmenopausal atherosclerosis progression: A comparison of the effects of conjugated equine estrogens and soy phytoestrogens. *The Journal of Clinical Endocrinology and Metabolism, 86*, 41–47.

Conboy, L., Domar, A., & O'Connell, E. (2001). Women at mid-life: Symptoms, attitudes, and choices, an internet based survey. *Maturitas, 38*, 129–136.

Connelly, M. T., Ferrari, N., Hagen, N., & Inui, T. S. (1999). Patient-identified needs for hormone replacement therapy counseling: A qualitative study. *Annals of Internal Medicine, 131*, 265–268.

Cooper, G. S., & Baird, D. D. (1995). The use of questionnaire data to classify peri- and premenopausal status. *Epidemiology, 6*, 625–628.

Cooper, G., Baird, D., & Darden, F. R. (2001). Measures of menopausal status in relation to demographic, reproductive, and behavioral characteristics in a population-based study of women aged 35–49 years. *American Journal of Epidemiology, 153*, 1159–1165.

Cowan, G., Warren, L. G., & Young, J. L. (1985). Medical perceptions of menopausal symptoms. *Psychology of Women Quarterly, 9*, 3–14.

Cramer, D. W., Harlow, B. L., Xu, H., Fraer, C., & Barbieri, R. (1995). Cross-sectional and case-controlled analyses of the association between smoking and early menopause. *Maturitas, 22*, 79–87.

Cramer, D., & Xu, H. (1996). Predicting age at menopause. *Maturitas, 23*, 319–326.

Cramer, D., Xu, H., & Harlow, B. L. (1995). Does incessant ovulation increase risk for early menopause? *American Journal of Obstetrics and Gynecology, 172*, 568–573.

Crawford, S. L. (2000). Epidemiology: Methodologic challenges in the study of menopause. In R. Lobo, J. Kelsey, & R. Marcus (Eds.), *Menopause: Biology and pathobiology* (pp. 159–174). San Diego, CA: Academic Press.

Dawson, D. (1990). Trends in use of oral contraceptives—Data from the 1987 National Health Interview Survey. *Family Planning Perspective, 22*(4), 169–172.

Dennerstein, L., Dudley, E. C., Hopper, J. L., Guthrie, J. R., & Burger, H. G. (2000). A prospective population-based study of menopausal symptoms. *Obstetrics and Gynecology, 96*(3), 351–358.

Dennerstein, L., Smith, A. M. A., Morse, C., Burger, H., Green, A., Hopper, J., & Ryan, M. (1993). Menopausal symptoms in Australian women. *The Medical Journal of Australia, 159,* 232–236.

Derby, C. (2000). Cardiovascular pathophysiology. In R. Lobo, J. Kelsey, & R. Marcus (Eds.), *Menopause: Biology and pathobiology* (pp. 229–243). San Diego, CA: Academic Press.

Ettinger, B., Grady, D., Tosteson, A. N., Pressman, A., & Macer, J. L. (2003). Effect of the Women's Health Initiative on decisions to discontinue postmenopausal hormone therapy. *Obstetrics and Gynecology, 102,* 1225–1232.

Ettinger, B., Li, D., & Klein, R. (1996). Continuation of postmenopausal hormone replacement therapy: Comparison of cyclic versus continuous combined schedules. *Menopause, 3,* 185–189.

Flegal, K. M., Carroll, M. D., Ogden, C. L., & Johnson, C. L. (2002). Prevalence and trends in obesity among US adults, 1999–2000. *The Journal of the American Medical Association, 288,* 1723–1727.

Fogel, C., & Woods, N. (1995). *Women's health care.* Thousand Oaks, CA: Sage.

Freedman, R. R., & Woodward, S. (1992). Behavioral treatment of menopausal hot flashes: Evaluation by ambulatory monitoring. *American Journal of Obstetrics and Gynecology, 167,* 436–439.

Freedman, R. R., Woodward, S., & Brown, B. (1995). Biochemical and thermoregulatory effects of behavioral treatment for menopausal hot flashes. *Menopause, 2,* 211–218.

Frere, G. (1971). Mean age at menopause and menarche in South Africa. *South African Journal of Medical Science, 36,* 21–24.

Frey, K. (1981). Middle-aged women's experience and perceptions of menopause. *Women's Health, 6,* 24–36.

Garrida-Latorre, F., Lascano-Ponce, E., Lopez-Carillo, L., & Hernandez-Avila, M. (1996). Age of natural menopause among women in Mexico City. *International Journal of Gynecology and Obstetrics, 53,* 159–166.

Gavaler, J. S., Bonham-Leyba, M., Castro, C. A., & Harman, S. E. (1999). The Oklahoma postmenopausal women's health study: Recruitment and characteristics of American Indian, Asian, Black, Hispanic and Caucasian women. *Alcohol, Clinical and Experimental Research, 23,* 220–223.

Gold, E., Bromberger, J., Crawford, S., Samuels, S., Greendale, G. A., Harlow, S. C., & Skurnick, J. (2001). Factors associated with age at natural menopause in a multiethnic sample of midlife women. *American Journal of Epidemiology, 153,* 865–874.

Gold, E. B., Sternfeld, B., & Kelsey, J. L. (2000). Relation of demographic and lifestyle factors to symptoms in a multi-racial/ethnic population of women 40–55 years of age. *American Journal of Epidemiology, 152,* 436–473.

Goldenberg, R. L., Grodin, J. M., Rodbard, D., & Ross, G. T. (1973). Gonadotropins in women with amenorrhea. *American Journal of Obstetrics and Gynecology, 116,* 1003–1012.

Grady, D., Brown, J. S., Vittinghoff, E., Applegate, W., Varner, E., Snyder, T., & Heart and Estrogen/Progestin Replacement Study Research Group. (2001). Postmenopausal hormones and incontinence: The Heart and Estrogen/Progestin Replacement Study. *Obstetrics and Gynecology, 97*(1), 116–120.

Grady, D., Ettinger, B., Tosteson, A. N., Pressman, A., & Macer, J. L. (2003). Predictors of difficulty when discontinuing postmenopausal hormone therapy. *Obstetrics and Gynecology, 102,* 1233–1239.

Grady, D., Yaffe, K., Kristof, M., Lin, F., Richards, C., & Barrett-Connor, E. (2002). Effect of postmenopausal hormone therapy on cognitive function: The Heart and Estrogen/Progestin Replacement Study. *American Journal of Medicine, 113,* 543–548.

Greene, J. G., & Cooke, D. J. (1980). Life stress and symptoms at the climacterium. *British Journal of Psychiatry, 136,* 486–491.

Grimes, D. A., & Lobo, R. A. (2002). Perspectives on the Women's Health Initiative trial of hormone replacement therapy. *Obstetrics and Gynecology, 100*(6), 1344–1353.

Grisso, J., Freeman, E., Maurin, E., Garcia-Espana, B., & Berlin, J. A. (1999). Racial differences in menopause information and the experience of hot flashes in the late reproductive years. *Journal of General Internal Medicine, 14*, 98–103.

Grodstein, F., Clarkson, T. B., & Manson, J. E. (2003). Understanding the divergent data on postmenopausal hormone therapy. *New England Journal of Medicine, 348*(7), 645–650.

Grodstein, F., Lifford, K., Resnick, N. M., & Curhan, G. C. (2004). Postmenopausal hormone therapy and risk of developing urinary incontinence. *Obstetrics and Gynecology, 103*(2), 254–260.

Grodstein, F., Newcomb, P., & Stampfer, M. (1999). Postmenopausal hormone therapy and the risk of colorectal cancer: A review and meta-analysis. *American Journal of Medicine, 1096*, 574–582.

Grodstein, F., & Stampfer, M. (1995). The epidemiology of coronary heart disease and estrogen replacement in postmenopausal women. *Progress in Cardiovascular Diseases, 38*, 199–210.

Haas, S., Kaplan, C. P., Gerstenberg, E. P., & Kerlikowski, K. (2004). Changes in the use of postmenopausal hormone therapy after the publication of clinical trial results. *Annals of Internal Medicine, 140*, 184–188.

Hammar, M., Berg, G., & Lindgren, R. (1990). Does physical exercise influence the frequency of postmenopausal hot flushes? *Acta Obstetricia et Gynecologica Scandinavica, 69*, 409–412.

Hardy, R., & Kuh, D. (2002). Does early growth influence timing of the menopause? Evidence from a British birth cohort. *Human Reproduction, 17*(9), 2474–2479.

Harlow, B., & Signorello, L. (2000). Factors associated with early menopause. *Maturitas, 35*, 3–9.

Hays, J., Ockene, J. K., Brunner, R. L., Kotchen, J. M., Manson, J. E., Patterson, R. E., Aragaki, A. K., Shumaker, S. A., Brzyski, R. G., LaCroix, A. Z., Granek, I. A., Valanis, B. G., & Women's Health Initiative Investigators. (2003). Effects of estrogen plus progestin on health-related quality of life. *New England Journal of Medicine, 348*(19), 1839–1854.

Henderson, V. W., Guthrie, J. R., Dudley, E. C., Burger, H. G., & Dennerstein, L. (2003). Estrogen exposures and memory at midlife: A population-based study of women. *Neurology, 60*, 1369–1371.

Herrington, D., & Klein, K. (2003). Randomized clinical trials of hormone replacement therapy for treatment or prevention of cardiovascular disease: A review of the findings. *Atherosclerosis, 166*, 203–212.

Herrington, D. M., Reboussin, D. M., Brosnihan, K. B., Sharp, P. C., Shumaker, S. A., Snyder, T. E., Furberg, C. D., Kowalchuk, G. J., Stuckey, T. D., Rogers, W. J., Givens, D. H., & Waters, D. (2000). Effects of estrogen replacement on the progression of coronary-artery atherosclerosis. *New England Journal of Medicine, 343*, 522–529.

Hersh, A. L., Stefanick, M. L., & Stafford, R. S. (2004). National use of postmenopausal hormone therapy: Annual trends and response to recent evidence. *Journal of the American Medical Association, 291*, 47–53.

Ho, J. E., & Mosca, L. (2002). Postmenopausal hormone replacement therapy and atherosclerosis. *Current Atherosclerosis Reports, 4*(5), 387–395.

Hodis, H. N., Mack, W. J., Azen, S. P., Lobo, R. A., Shoupe, D., Mahrer, P. R., Faxon, D. P., Cashin-Hemphill, L., Sanmarco, M. E., French, W. J., Shook, T. L., Gaarder, T. D., Mehra, A. O., Rabbani, R., Sevanian, A., Shil, A. B., Torres, M., Vogelbach, K. H., Selzer, R. H., & Women's Estrogen–Progestin Lipid-Lowering Hormone Atherosclerosis Regression Trial Research Group. (2003). Hormone therapy and the progression of coronary-artery atherosclerosis in postmenopausal women. *New England Journal of Medicine, 349*(6), 535–545.

Hodis, H. N., Mack, W. J., Lobo, R. A., Shoupe, D., Sevanian, A., Mahrer, P. R., Selzer, R. H., Liu, C. H., & Azen, S. P. (2001). Estrogen in the Prevention of Atherosclerosis: A randomized, double-blind, placebo-controlled trial. *Annals of International Medicine, 135*, 939–953.

Holmberg, L., Anderson, H., & HABITS Steering and Data Monitoring Committees. (2004). HABITS (hormonal replacement therapy after breast cancer—is it safe?), a randomised comparison: Trial stopped. *Lancet, 363,* 453–455.

Holmes-Rovner, M., Padonu, G., Kroll, J., Rovner, D. R., Talarczyk, G., & Rothert, M. (1996). African-American women's attitudes and expectations of menopause. *American Journal of Preventive Medicine, 12,* 420–423.

Howe, G. R., & Rohan, T. E. (1993). The epidemiology of breast cancer in women. In J. Lorrain (Ed.), *Comprehensive management of menopause* (pp. 39–51). New York: Springer-Verlag.

Hulley, S., Furberg, C., Barrett-Connor, E., Cauley, J., Grady, D., Haskell, W., Knopp, R., Lowery, M., Satterfield, S., Schrott, H., Vittinghoff, E., Hunninghake, D., & Heart and Estrogen/Progestin Replacement Study Research Group. (2002). Noncardiovascular disease outcomes during 6.8 years of hormone therapy Heart and Estrogen/progestin Replacement Study follow-up (HERS II). *The Journal of the American Medical Association, 288,* 58–66.

Hulley, S., Grady, D., Bush, T., Furberg, C., Herrington, D., Riggs, B., & Vittinghoff, E. (1998). Randomized trial of estrogen plus progestin for secondary prevention of coronary heart disease in postmenopausal women. *The Journal of the American Medical Association, 280,* 605–613.

Hunter, M. S. (1990). Somatic experience of the menopause: A prospective study. *Psychosomatic Medicine, 52,* 357–367.

Huntley, A. L., & Ernst, E. (2003). Soy for the treatment of perimenopausal symptoms: A systematic review. *Maturitas, 47*(1), 1–9.

Ivarsson, T., Spetz, A. C., & Hammar, M. (1998). Physical exercise and vasomotor symptoms in post menopausal women. *Maturitas, 29,* 139–146.

Johannes, C. B., & Avis, N. E. (1996). The short-term health consequences of hysterectomy. *Journal of Women's Health, 5,* 278.

Kam, I., Dennehy, C., & Tsourounis, C. (2002). Dietary supplement use among menopausal women attending a San Francisco health conference. *Menopause, 9*(1), 72–78.

Kang, H., Ansbacher, R., & Hammoud, M. (2002). Use of alternative and complementary medicine in menopause. *International Journal of Gynecology and Obstetrics, 79,* 195–207.

Karim, R., Mack, W. J., Lobo, R. A., Hwang, J., Liu, C.-R., Liu, C.-H., Sevanian, A., & Hodis, H. N. (2005). Determinants of the effect of estrogen on the progression of subclinical atherosclerosis: Estrogen in the Prevention of Atherosclerosis Trial. *Menopause, 12*(4), 366–373.

Kaufert, P. A., & McKinlay, S. M. (1985). Estrogen Replacement Therapy: The production of medical knowledge and the emergence of policy. In E. Lewin & V. Olesen (Eds.), *Women, health and healing: Toward a new perspective* (pp. 113–138). New York: Tavistock.

Keshavarz, H., Hillis, S., & Kieke, B. (2002, July 12). Hysterectomy surveillance—United States, 1994–1999. In *Surveillance Summaries, Morbidity and Mortality Weekly Report (MMWR), 51*(SS-5), 1–8.

Kono, S., Sunagawa, Y., Higa, H., & Sunagawa, H. (1990). Age of menopause in Japanese women: Trends and recent changes. *Maturitas, 12*(1), 43–49.

Kravitz, H. M., Ganz, P. A., Bromberger, J. T., Powell, L., Sutton-Tyrrell, K., & Meyer, P. M. (2003). Sleep difficulty in women in midlife: A community survey of sleep and the menopausal transition. *Menopause, 10*(1), 19–28.

Kronenberg, F. (1990). Hot flashes: Epidemiology and physiology. *Annals of the New York Academy of Sciences, 592,* 52–86.

Kronenberg, F., & Fugh-Berman, A. (2002). Complementary and alternative medicine for menopausal symptoms: A review of randomized, controlled trials. *Annals of Internal Medicine, 137,* 805–813.

Kronenberg, F., O'Leary Cobb, J., & McMahon, D. (1994). Alternative medicine for menopausal problems: Results of a survey [Abstract]. *Menopause, 1,* 171–172.

Kwawukume, E., Ghosh, T., & Wilson, J. (1993). Menopausal age of Ghanaian women. *International Journal of Gynecology and Obstetrics, 40*, 151–155.

Lawlor, D., Ebrahim, S., & Smith, G. (2003). The association of socio-economic position across the life course and age at menopause: The British Women's Heart and Health Study. *British Journal of Obstetrics and Gynecology, 110*(12), 1078–1087.

Lepine, L., Hillis, S., Marchbanks, P., Koonin, L., Morrow, B., Kieke, B., & Wilcox, L. (1997, August 8). Hysterectomy surveillance—United States. 1980–1993. In *CDC Surveillance Summaries, Morbidity and Mortality Weekly Report (MMWR), 46*(SS-4), 1–15.

Lewis, C., George, V., Fouad, M., Porter, V., Bowen, D., & Urban, N. (1998). Recruitment strategies in the women's health trial: Feasibility study in minority populations. *Controlled Clinical Trials, 19*(5), 461–476.

Loprinzi, C. L., Kubler, J. W., & Sloan, J. A. (2000). Venlafaxine in management of hot flashes in survivors of breast cancer: A randomized controlled trial. *Lancet, 356*, 2059–2063.

Lucerno, M. A., & McCloskey, W. W. (1997). Alternatives to estrogen for the treatment of hot flashes. *The Annals of Pharmacotherapy, 31*, 915–917.

MacMahon, B., & Worcester, J. (1966). Age at menopause: United States 1960–1962. *US Vital and Health Statistics, 2*(19), 1–19.

Magursky, V., Mesko, M., & Sokolik, L. (1975). Age at menopause and onset of the climacteric in women of Martin District. *International Journal of Fertility, 20*, 17–23.

Manson, J., Hsia, J., Johnson, K., Rossouw, J., Assaf, A., Lassern, N., Trevisan, M., Black, H., Heckbert, S., Detrano, R., Strickland, O., Wong, N., Crouse, J., Stein, E., Cushman, M., & Women's Health Initiative Investigators. (2003). Estrogen plus Progestin and the risk of coronary heart disease. *New England Journal of Medicine, 349*(6), 523–534.

Matthews, K. A. (1992). Myths and realities of the menopause. *Psychosomatic Medicine, 54*, 1–9.

Matthews, K., Kelsey, S., Meilahn, E., Kuller, L., & Wing, R. (1989). Educational attainment and behavioral and biologic risk factors for coronary heart disease in middle-aged women. *American Journal of Epidemiology, 129*, 1132–1144.

McCrea, F. (1983). The politics of menopause: The discovery of a deficiency disease. *Social Problems, 31*, 111.

McKinlay, J. B., McKinlay, S. M., & Brambilla, D. (1987). The relative contributions of endocrine changes and social circumstances to depression in mid-aged women. *Journal of Health and Social Behavior, 28*, 345–363.

McKinlay, S. M. (1994). Issues in design, measurement, and analysis for menopause research. *Experimental Gerontology, 29*, 479–493.

McKinlay, S. M. (1996). The normal menopause transition: An overview. *Maturitas, 23*, 137–145.

McKinlay, S. M., Bifano, N. L., & McKinley, J. B. (1985). Smoking and age at menopause in women. *Annals of Internal Medicine, 103*, 350–356.

McKinlay, S. M., Brambilla, D. J., Avis, N. E., & McKinley, J. B. (1991). Women's experience of the menopause. *Current Obstetrics and Gynecology, 1*, 3–7.

McKinlay, S. M., Brambilla, D. J., & Posner, J. G. (1992). The normal menopause transition. *American Journal of Human Biology, 4*, 37–46.

McKinlay, S. M., & Jefferys, M. (1974). The menopausal syndrome. *British Journal of Preventive Social Medicine, 28*, 108–115.

McKinlay, S., Jefferys, M., & Thompson, B. (1972). An investigation of the age at menopause. *Journal of Biosocial Sciences, 4*, 161–173.

Meyer, P. M., Powell, L. H., Wilson, R. S., Everson-Rose, S. A., Kravitz, H. M., Luborsky, J. L., Madden, T., Pandey, D., & Evans, D. A. (2003). A population-based longitudinal study of cognitive functioning in the menopausal transition. *Neurology, 61*, 801–806.

Mitchell, E. S., & Woods, N. F. (1996). Symptom experiences of midlife women: Observations from the Seattle Midlife Women's Health Study. *Maturitas, 25*, 1–10.

Mitchell, E. S., Woods, N. F., & Mariella, A. (2000). Three stages of the menopausal transition from the Seattle Midlife Women's Health Study: Toward a more precise definition. *Menopause, 7*(5), 334–349.

Morabia, A., & Costanza, M. (1998). International variability in ages at menarche, first livebirth, and menopause. World Health Organization Collaborative Study of Neoplasia and Steroid Contraceptives. *American Journal of Epidemiology, 148*(12), 1195–1205.

Nagata, C., Kawakami, N., & Shimizu, H. (1997). Trends in the incidence rate and risk factors for breast cancer in Japan. *Breast Cancer Research and Treatment, 44*, 75–82.

National Center for Complementary and Alternative Medicine (NCCAM). (2002). *Questions and answers about black cohosh and the symptoms of menopause.* Retrieved from http://ods.od.nih.gov/factsheets/blackcohosh.html

National Committee for Quality Assurance. (2001). Retrieved March 16, 2004, from http://www.ncqa.org/somc2001/MENOPAUSE/SOMC_2001_MOM.html

Neugarten, B. L., & Kraines, R. J. (1965). Menopausal symptoms in women of various ages. *Psychosomatic Medicine, 27*, 266–273.

Neugarten, B. L., Wood, V., Kraines, R. J., & Loomis, B. (1963). Women's attitudes toward the menopause. *Vitae Human, 6*, 140–151.

Newton, K., LaCroix, A., Leveille, S., Rutter, C., Keenan, N., & Anderson, L. (1997). Women's beliefs and decisions about hormone replacement therapy. *Journal of Women's Health, 6*, 459–465.

Newton, K., LaCroix, A., Leveille, S., Rutter, C., Keenan, N., & Anderson, L. (1998). The physician's role in women's decision making about hormone replacement therapy. *Obstetrics & Gynecology, 92*, 580–584.

Newton, K. M., Buist, D. S., Keenan, N. L., Anderson, L. A., & LaCroix, A. Z. (2002). Use of alternative therapies for menopause symptoms: Results of a population-based survey. *Obstetrics & Gynecology, 101*(1), 205.

North American Menopause Society. (2004). Treatment of menopause-associated vasomotor symptoms: Position statement of The North American Menopause Society. *Menopause, 11*(1), 11–33.

O'Keefe, J. J., Kim, S., Hall, R., Cochran, V., Lawhorn, S., & McCallister, B. (1997). Estrogen replacement therapy after coronary angioplasty in women. *Journal of the American College of Cardiology, 29*, 1–5.

Olofsson, A. S., & Collins, A. (2000). Psychosocial factors, attitude to menopause and symptoms in Swedish perimenopausal women. *Climacteric, 3*(1), 33–42.

Padonu, G., Holmes-Rovner, M., Rothert, M., Schmitt, N., Knoll, J., Rovner, D. R., Talarczyk, G., Breer, L., Ranson, S., & Gladney, E. (1996). African-American women's perception of menopause. *American Journal of Health Behavior, 20*, 242–251.

Pham, K. T. C., Grisso, J. A., & Freeman, E. W. (1997). Ovarian aging and hormone replacement therapy: Hormonal levels, symptoms, and attitudes of African-American and White women. *Journal of General Internal Medicine, 12*, 230–236.

Quella, S. K., Loprinzi, C. L., & Barton, D. L. (2000). Evaluation of soy phytoestrogens for the treatment of hot flashes in breast cancer survivors: A North Central Cancer Treatment Group trial. *Journal of Clinical Oncology, 18*, 1068–1074.

Randolph, J. F., Jr., Sowers, M., Bondarenko, I. V., Harlow, S. D., Luborsky, J. L., & Little, R. J. (2004). Change in estradiol and follicle-stimulating hormone across the early menopausal transition: Effects of ethnicity and age. *Journal of Clinical Endocrinology and Metabolism, 89*(4), 1555–1561.

Rapp, S., Espeland, M., Shumaker, S., Henderson, V., Brunner, R., Manson, J., Gass, M., Stefanick, M., Lane, D., Hays, J., Johnson, K., Coker, L., Dailey, M., Bowen, D., & Women's Health Initiative Memory Study Investigators. (2003). Effect of estrogen plus progestin on global cognitive function in postmenopausal women. The Women's Health Initiative Memory Study: A randomized controlled trial. *Journal of the American Medical Association, 289*(20), 2663–2672.

Reame, N. E., Kelche, R. P., Beitins, I. Z., Yu, M. Y., Zawacki, C. M., & Padmanabhan, V. (1996). Age effects of follicle-stimulating hormone and pulsatile luteinizing hormone secretion across the menstrual cycle of women. *Journal of Clinical Endocrinology and Metabolism, 81*, 1512–1518.

Reece, S., Theroux, R., & Taylor, K. (2002). Weighing the cons and pros: Women's reasons for discontinuing hormone replacement therapy. *Health Care Women International, 23*, 19–32.

Reeve, J., Walton, L., Russell, L., Lunt, M., Wolman, R., Abraham, R., Justice, J., Nicholls, A., Wardley-Smith, B., Green, J., & Mitchell, A. (1999). Determinants of the first decade of bone loss after menopause at spine, hip and radius. *Quarterly Journal of Medicine, 92*, 261–273.

Richter, D., Corwin, S., Rheaume, C., & McKeown, R. (2001). Perceptions of alternative therapies available for women facing hysterectomy or menopause. *Journal of Women & Aging, 13*(4), 21–37.

Rodstrom, K., & Bengtsson, C. (2003). Evidence for a secular trend in menopausal age: A population study of women in Gothenburg. *Menopause, 10*(6), 538–543.

Rossouw, J. E., Anderson, G. L., Prentice, R. L., LaCroix, A. Z., Kooperberg, C., Stefanick, M. L., Jackson, R. D., Beresford, S. A., Howard, B. V., Johnson, K. C., Kotchen, J. M., Ockene, J., & Writing Group for the Women's Health Initiative Investigators. (2002). Risks and benefits of Estrogen plus Progestin in healthy postmenopausal women: Principal results from the Women's Health Initiative randomized controlled trial. *Journal of the American Medical Association, 288*(3), 321–333.

Rostosky, S. S., & Travis, C. B. (1996). Menopause research and the dominance of the biomedical model 1984–1994. *Psychology Women Quarterly, 66*, 295–312.

Rostosky, S. S., & Travis, C. B. (2000). Menopause and sexuality: Ageism and sexism unite. In C. B. Travis & J. W. White (Eds.), *Sexuality, society, and feminism. Psychology of women* (pp. 181–209). Washington, DC: American Psychological Association.

Sampselle, C., Harlow, S., Skurnick, J., Brubaker, L., & Bondarenko, I. (2002). Urinary incontinence predictors and life impact in ethnically diverse perimenopausal women. *Obstetrics and Gynecology, 100*, 1230–1238.

Sampselle, C., Harris, V., Harlow, S., & Sowers, M. (2002). Midlife development and menopause in African American and Caucasian women. *Health Care for Women International, 23*, 351–363.

Schwingl, P. J., Hulka, B. S., & Harlow, S. (1994). Risk factors for menopausal hot flashes. *Obstetrics and Gynecology, 84*, 29–34.

Seidl, M., & Stewart, D. (1998). Alternative treatments for menopausal symptoms. *Canadian Family Physician, 44*, 1271–1276.

Sherburn, M., Guthrie, J., Dudley, E., O'Connell, H., & Dennerstein, L. (2001). Is continence associated with menopause? *Obstetrics and Gynecology, 98*, 628–633.

Sherman, A., Shumaker, S., Sharp, P., Reboussin, D. M., Kancler, C., Walkup, M., & Herrington, D. M. (2003). No effect of HRT on health-related quality of life in postmenopausal women with heart disease. *Minerva Ginecologica, 55*(6), 511–517.

Shumaker, S., Legault, C., Rapp, S., Thal, L., Wallace, R., Ockene, J., Hendrix, S., Jones, B., III, Assaf, A., Jackson, R., Kotchen, J., Wassertheil-Smoller, S., Wactawski-Wende, J., & Women's Health Initiative Memory Study Investigators. (2003). Estrogen plus Progestin and the incidence of dementia and mild cognitive impairment in postmenopausal women. The Women's Health Initiative Memory Study: A randomized controlled trial. *Journal of the American Medical Association, 289*(20), 2651–2662.

Sievert, L., & Hautaniemi, S. (2003). Age at menopause in Puebla, Mexico. *Human Biology, 75*(2), 205–226.

Simon, J., Hsia, J., Cauley, J., Richards, C., Harris, F., Fong, J., Barrett-Connor, E., & Hulley, S. (2001). Postmenopausal hormone therapy and risk of stroke: The Heart and Estrogen-Progestin Replacement Study (HERS). *Circulation, 103*(5), 620–622.

Sommer, B., Avis, N., Meyer, P., Ory, M., Madden, T., Kagawa-Singer, M., Mouton, C., Rasor, N. O., & Adler, S. (1999). Attitudes toward menopause and aging across ethnic/racial groups. *Psychosomatic Medicine, 61,* 868–875.

Sotelo, M., & Johnson, S. (1997). The effects of hormone replacement therapy on coronary heart disease. *Endocrinology and Metabolism Clinics of North America, 26,* 313–328.

Soules, M. R., Sherman, S., Parrott, E., Rebar, R., Santoro, N., Utian, W., & Woods, N. (2001). Executive summary: Stages of Reproductive Aging Workshop (STRAW). *Fertility and Sterility, 76*(5), 874–878.

Sowers, M. (2000). Osteoarthritis and menopause. In R. A. Lobo, J. Kelsey, & R. Marcus (Eds.), *Menopause: Biology and pathobiology* (pp. 535–542). San Diego: Academic Press.

Sowers, M., Crawford, S., Sternfeld, B., Morganstein, D., Gold, E., Greendale, G. A., Evans, D., Neer, R., Matthews, K., Sherman, S., Lo, A., Weiss, G., & Kelsey, J. (2000). Design, survey sampling and recruitment methods of SWAN: A multi-center, multi-ethnic, community-based cohort study of women and the menopausal transition. In R. A. Lobo, J. Kelsey, & R. Marcus (Eds.), *Menopause: Biology and pathobiology* (pp. 175–188). San Diego, CA: Academic Press.

Sowers, M. R., & LaPietra, M. T. (1995). Menopause: Its epidemiology and potential association with chronic diseases. *Epidemiologic Reviews, 17,* 287–302.

Stampfer, M., Colditz, G., Willett, W., Manson, J., Rosner, B., Speizer, F., & Hennekens, C. (1991). Postmenopausal estrogen therapy and cardiovascular disease. Ten-year follow-up from the Nurses' Health Study. *New England Journal of Medicine, 325,* 756–762.

Standing, T. S., & Glazer, G. (1992). Attitudes of low-income clinic patients toward menopause. *Health Care Women International, 13,* 271–280.

Stellato, R., Crawford, S., McKinlay, S., & Longcope, C. (1998). Can follicular stimulating hormone be used to define menopause? *Endocrine Practice, 4,* 137–141.

Swartzman, L. C., Edelberg, R., & Kemmann, E. (1990). Impact of stress on objectively recorded menopausal hot flashes and on flash report bias. *Health Psychology, 9,* 529–545.

Tamada, T., & Iwasaki, H. (1995). Age at natural menopause in Japanese women. *Nippon Sanka Fujinka Gakkai Zasshi, 47,* 947–952.

Theroux, R., & Taylor, K. (2003). Women's decision making about the use of hormonal and nonhormonal remedies for the menopausal transition. *Journal of Obstetrics, Gynecology, and Neonatal Nursing, 32,* 712–723.

Thomas, F., Renaud, F., Benefice, E., de Meeus, T., & Guegan, J. (2001). International variability of ages at menarche and menopause: Patterns and main determinants. *Human Biology, 73*(2), 271–290.

Treloar, A. E. (1974). Menarche, menopause and intervening fecundability. *Human Biology, 46,* 89–107.

Treloar, A. E. (1981). Menstrual cyclicity and the pre-menopause. *Maturitas, 3,* 249–264.

Utian, W., & Boggs, P. (1999). The North American Menopause Society 1998 Menopause Survey. Part I: Postmenopausal women's perceptions about menopause and midlife. *Menopause, 6*(2), 122–128.

Utian, W., & Schiff, I. (1994). NAMS–Gallup survey on women's knowledge, information sources, and attitudes to menopause and hormone replacement therapy. *Menopause, 1,* 39–48.

van Noord, P., Dubas, J., Dorland, M., Boersma, H., & te Velde, E. (1997). Age at natural menopause in a population-based screening cohort: The role of menarche, fecundity, and lifestyle factors. *Fertility & Sterility, 68,* 95–102.

van Noord, P., & Kaaks, R. (1991). The effect of wartime conditions and the 1944–45 Dutch famine on recalled menarcheal age in participants of the DOM breast cancer screening project. *Annals of Human Biology, 18,* 57–70.

Varea, C., Bernis, C., Montero, P., Arias, S., Barroso, A., & Gonzalez, B. (2000). Secular trend and intrapopulational variation in age at menopause in Spanish women. *Journal of Biosocial Science, 32*(3), 383–393.

Ventura, S., Mosher, W., Curtin, S. C., Abma, J. C., & Henshaw, S. (2000). Trends in pregnancy and pregnancy rates by outcome: Estimates for the United States, 1976–96. National Center for Health Statistics. *Vital Health Statistics, 21*(56), 2000.

Viscoli, C., Brass, L., Kernan, W., Sarrel, P., Suissa, S., & Horwitz, R. (2001). A clinical trial of Estrogen-replacement therapy after ischemic stroke. *New England Journal of Medicine, 345*, 1243–1249.

Wade, C., Kronenberg, F., Kelly, A., & Murphy, P. A. (1999). Hormone-modulating herbs: Implications for women's health. *Journal of American Medical Women's Association, 54*(4), 181–183.

Warren, N., Shortle, B., & Dominguez, J. (2002). Use of alternative therapies in menopause. Best practices. *Obstetrics and Gynecology, 16*(3), 411–448.

Waters, D., Alderman, E., Hsia, J., Howard, B., Cobb, F., Rogers, W., Ouyang, P., Thompson, P., Tardif, J., Higginson, L., Bittner, V., Steffes, M., Gordon, D., Proschan, M., Younes, N., & Verter, J. (2002). Effects of hormone replacement therapy and antioxidant vitamin supplements on coronary atherosclerosis in postmenopausal women: A randomized controlled trial. *Journal of the American Medical Association, 288*(19), 2432–2440.

Weaver, F., Hynes, E., Goldberg, J., Khuri, S., Daley, J., & Henderson, W. (2001). Hysterectomy in Veterans Affairs Medical Centers. *Obstetrics and Gynecology, 97*(6), 880–884.

Wells, G., Tugwell, P., Shea, B., Guyatt, G., Peterson, J., Zytaruk, N., Robinson, V., Henry, D., O'Connell, D., Cranney, A., Osteoporosis Methodology Group, & The Osteoporosis Research Advisory Group. (2002). Meta-analysis of the efficacy of hormone replacement therapy in treating and preventing osteoporosis in postmenopausal women. *Endocrine Review, 23*(4), 529–539.

Whelan, E. A., Sandler, D. P., McConnaughey, R., & Weinberg, C. R. (1990). Menstrual and reproductive characteristics and age at natural menopause. *American Journal of Epidemiology, 131*(4), 625–632.

Wijma, K., Melin, A., Nedstrand, E., & Hammar, M. (1997). Treatment of menopausal symptoms with applied relaxation: A pilot study. *Journal of Behavior Therapy and Experimental Psychiatry, 28*(4), 251–261.

Wilbur, J., Miller, A., & Montgomery, A. (1995). The influence of demographic characteristics, menopausal status, and symptoms on women's attitudes toward menopause. *Women and Health, 23*, 19–39.

Wilcox, L., Koonin, L., Pokras, R., Strauss, L., Xia, Z., & Peterson, H. (1994). Hysterectomy in the United States, 1988–1990. *Obstetrics and Gynecology, 83*(4), 549–555.

Wilson, J. D., & Foster, D. W. (1992). *Williams textbook of endocrinology* (Vol. 8). Philadelphia: Saunders.

Wise, P., Dubal, D., Wilson, M., Rau, S., & Bottner, M. (2001). Minireview. Neuroprotective effects of estrogen—New insights into mechanisms of action. *Endocrinology, 142*, 969–973.

Woods, N. F., Mitchell, E. S., & Adams, C. (2000). Memory functioning among midlife women: Observations from the Seattle Midlife Women's Health Study. *Menopause, 7*(4), 257–265.

World Health Organization. (1981). *Research on the menopause* (WHO Technical Services Report Series 670). Geneva.

World Health Organization. (1996). *Research on the menopause in the 1990s* (WHO Technical Services Report Series No. 866). Geneva.

Yaffe, K., Sawaya, G., Lieberburg, I., & Grady, D. (1998). Estrogen therapy in postmenopausal women: Effects on cognitive function and dementia. *Journal of the American Medical Association, 279*(9), 688–695.

CHAPTER FIVE

Mental Health Among the Baby Boomers

Jennifer R. Piazza
Susan Turk Charles
University of California, Irvine

The first half of the twentieth century presented a paradox for human survival. As two world wars and an economic depression brought chaos and devastation, scientific and medical advances were increasing overall life expectancy by stemming the tide of deaths from acute diseases such as influenza, pneumonia, and tuberculosis. After this tumultuous beginning, the second half of the century ushered in renewed hope and new life. Between 1946 and 1964, the United States experienced an unprecedented increase in birth rate (see chap. 1, this volume). The new generation, termed Baby Boomers, was born into a world of relative peace and prosperity. Economic and social stability translated into higher levels of education, improved standards of living, better physical health, and increased life expectancy.

Despite increases in the standard of living, advances in the second half of the twentieth century have not translated into improved psychological well-being for the Baby Boomers in comparison to their predecessors. Higher educational attainment, greater income, and medical advances are all related to improved mental health, yet Baby Boomers report lower levels of well-being than earlier-born cohorts. In addition, Baby Boomers have higher rates of several psychological disorders when compared to previous generations. This phenomenon has been demonstrated across studies of Europeans and European Americans; for cohorts born since the end of World War II, prevalence rates of mental illnesses such as depression and substance abuse appear to be increasing and age of onset seems to be decreasing (Klerman et al., 1985; Weissman, Bruce, Leaf, Florio, & Holzer, 1991; Wittchen, Knauper, & Kessler, 1994).

This chapter discusses the mental health of the Baby Boomers, a heterogeneous group whose births spanned 18 years and who were raised during a time of scientific growth and cultural change. As a result of the time period in which they were raised, any discussion of research findings concerning the mental health of the Baby Boomers needs to be placed within its proper historical and developmental context. In the first section, we present the prevalence and incidence rates for several psychological disorders including mood disorders, anxiety disorders, substance use disorders, schizophrenia, and dementia. Although prevalence rates for some of these disorders appear to be increasing in more recently born cohorts, other disorders do not display such consistent or ominous trends. After this descriptive first section, we temper these findings with a review of methodological issues to be considered when interpreting this research.

Following this section, we focus on sociological and psychological factors that may have influenced the observed cohort-related trends in mental health. We first present the diathesis/stress model to describe how sociological and psychological factors fit into a larger framework of mental health determinants. We then discuss three psychosocial factors, consisting of intragroup competition, increased consumerism, and increased feelings of alienation and personal threat, posited to influence trajectories of mental health over time. We conclude this chapter by discussing the potential impact of age-related changes on the trajectory of mental health. In this section, we suggest that understanding mental health from a life-span perspective is imperative when predicting and preparing for the future mental health of this influential generation.

THE PICTURE OF MENTAL HEALTH ACROSS COHORTS

The Historical Context of Mental Health Research

The end of World War II brought not only the beginning of the Baby Boom, but also a burgeoning of the empirical study of mental health. Researchers had studied mental disorders for centuries, but the recognition of psychology as a science and the organization of an empirical study of mental health grew rapidly in the years following World War II. During this time, the U.S. Army was forming a classification system to organize types of disorders observed among veterans of the recent war. The World Health Organization took this nomenclature into account when, for the first time, they included mental disorders in their international classification system of medical diseases (ICD–6) in 1949. In the same year, the American Psychological Association sponsored the historic Boulder, Colorado conference where they formalized the need for empirical research to inform clinical psychology training in the scientist-practitioner model. The American Psychiatric Association, which had begun efforts in 1917 to classify severe psychiatric and neurological conditions, published the first Diagnostic and Statistical Manual of Mental Disorders in 1952. Specific diagnostic criteria, however, would have to wait until the third edition of this manual, published in 1980 (American Psychiatric Association, 1994).

The rather nascent state of an organized system to study mental health limits our literature review. Hospital admissions for psychiatric disorders were recorded years before the Baby Boomers were born, but studies outlining specific diagnostic criteria are rare. Moreover, criteria for diagnoses and hospital admission change over time, as do treatment standards, which are shaped by economics and advances in therapeutic treatments. As a result, the study of cohort differences for psychological disorders is generally limited to cross-sectional analyses. The study of subclinical indicators of mental health, such as well-being, has an even shorter history (Diener, Suh, Lucas, & Smith, 1999), and is also largely based on cross-sectional research.

Well-Being

In cross-sectional studies of well-being, the Baby Boomers, now middle-aged adults, score more negatively than do older adults. They report lower levels of happiness (Mroczek & Kolarz, 1998) and longer periods of distress in their daily lives when compared to their older counterparts (Carstensen, Pasupathi, Mayr, & Nesselroade, 2000). In addition, sense of control, a factor related to overall well-being, is higher among older adults relative to the middle-aged Baby Boomers (Lachman & Weaver, 1998). On these indices, the Baby Boomers fare poorly when compared to people from earlier-born cohorts.

When Baby Boomers are compared to younger adults, however, they are relatively advantaged, as they score more positively on mental health indicators than do their younger counterparts (Keyes & Ryff, 1999). In terms of specific aspects of well-being, middle-aged Baby Boomers report greater autonomy and environmental mastery than do younger adults (Ryff, 1989, 1991), albeit similar levels of control (Lachman & Weaver, 1998). Although researchers posit that developmental changes are related to increases in emotion regulation and well-being (Carstensen & Charles, 1998; Mroczek & Spiro, 2003), these age-related changes do not rule out the possibility of a cohort effect.

Psychological Disorders

Several studies of psychological disorders mirror the trends found in studies of well-being and life satisfaction. For many disorders, such as depression and substance abuse, the Baby Boomers tend to have higher rates than their predecessors but lower rates than the cohorts following them (Kessler et al., 1994; Lavori et al., 1987). More generally, among all cohorts born after World War II, there appears to be an increase in rates of several mental disorders and a decrease in age of onset (Klerman et al., 1985; Klerman & Weissman, 1989; Regier, Rae, Narrow, Kaelber, & Schatzberg, 1988; Twenge, 2000).

These trends are apparent in Caucasian samples from Western countries (e.g., Angst, 1985; Hagnell, Lanke, Rorsman, & Oejesjoe, 1982; Kessler et al., 1994; Regier et al., 1988), but are not universal. Studies of Mexican Americans in the Los Angeles area (Karno et al., 1987), Puerto Ricans living in their homeland (Canino et al., 1987), and Koreans living in both Seoul and the surrounding rural communities (Lee, Kovak, & Rhee, 1987) reveal different patterns across cohorts (see review by Klerman & Weissman, 1989). Among Puerto Ricans and Koreans, rates of mental disorders appear to be higher in cohorts born prior to 1960, and for Mexican Americans rates appear to be stable across cohorts. The nonuniversality of these trends is informative given that the apparent rise in mental illness cannot be fully attributed to artifactual explanations, such as memory bias on the part of older adults (Klerman & Weissman, 1989). Moreover, the failure to find linear, increasing rates with time among these samples may point to differences in psychosocial factors related to increases in mental disorders.

The following section highlights several psychological disorders. Mood disorders, anxiety disorders, and substance use disorders are the most common forms of psychopathology among community-dwelling adults in the United States (Kessler et al., 1994) and are also some of the most widely studied. Schizophrenia is also included, as this disorder is arguably one of the most debilitating and often requires hospitalization. Finally, we briefly mention dementia. We do not discuss cohort effects for this disorder, but include this disease because of its relevance to an aging population.

Mood Disorders: Major Depressive Disorder. Current one-year prevalence rates for major depressive episodes are 6.5% for adults between the ages of 18 and 54, and 3.7% for adults over the age of 55 (U.S. Department of Health and Human Services, 1999). Although this figure varies considerably across studies (e.g., Kessler et al., 1994; Kessler et al., 2003; Regier et al., 1988), younger cohorts generally report higher rates of depression when compared to older cohorts, a trend that both preceded and now follows the Baby Boomers (e.g., Lewinsohn, Rohde, Seeley, & Fischer, 1993). In one study, for example, the probability of reporting depression increased 5% for males and 7% for females with each successive year of birth between 1930 and 1959 (Lavori et al., 1987). Similar patterns have been confirmed in a population-based study in Sweden, where rates of depression, particularly among people in their late 20s and 30s, were higher in 1957–1972 than in 1947–1952 (Hagnell et al., 1982).

In the United States, researchers have noted a demarcation between cohorts born before and after World War II, with those born after World War II being at an elevated risk for depression (e.g., Klerman et al., 1985; Klerman & Weissman, 1989). In fact, Lewinsohn and colleagues (1993) found that the probability of experiencing a major depressive episode by the age of 34 was 10 times greater in the cohort born between 1945 and 1954 than for the cohort born between 1905 and 1914. Similarly, in a replication of the National Comorbidity Study conducted between 2001 and 2003, Kessler and colleagues (2005) found that rates of major depressive disorder were higher in cohorts born after 1940 compared with those born before 1940.

Across studies, a linear trend emerges for adults over the age of 25, with each successive cohort at a higher risk for major depressive disorder than their predecessors. When adults between the ages of 18 and 24 are included in these analyses, quadratic trends often appear. Because younger adults between the ages of 18 and 24 have not yet reached the age when major depression is most often diagnosed, their lower rates may be misleading. Rates would most likely increase if people were queried after their mid and late twenties, when this disorder commonly occurs. Thus a censoring effect (examining people prior to the onset of symptom/disorder) may drive these findings. Indeed, a number of studies reveal a linear trend when the younger age groups are excluded. Table 5.1 presents a review of these studies.

In addition to increasing prevalence rates, the age of incidence (i.e., the first episode) appears to be decreasing in cohorts born after World War II (e.g., Burke, Burke, Rae, & Regier, 1991; Cross-National Collaborative Group, 1992; Kessler et al., 1994; Kessler et al., 2003; Klerman, 1976; but see Murphy, Sobol, Neff, Olivier, & Leighton, 1984). For example, Klerman and colleagues (1985) found that age of onset for depression decreased with each successive cohort born throughout the 1900s, with the youngest age of onset found in those born after 1950.

Mood Disorders: Bipolar Disorder I and II. Bipolar disorder and mania are relatively rare, but current studies suggest cohort effects for these disorders as well. For people between the ages of 18 and 54, the estimated one-year prevalence rates of bipolar I (mania only or mixed mania and depression) and bipolar II (depression and hypomania) are 1.1% and .6%, respectively. For people over the age of 55, rates drop to .2% for bipolar I and .1% for bipolar II (U.S. Department of Health and Human Services, 1999). Similar to depression, cohorts born after 1940 have higher prevalence rates (presented in Table 5.2) and accelerated onset ages (Burke et al., 1991; Rice et al., 1987). In one study, for example, the highest lifetime prevalence rates of both bipolar I and II were found in people born between 1938 and 1952, who were approximately 30 to 44 years of age at the time of data collection. Individuals aged 18 to 29, born approximately between the years 1953 and 1964, had the second highest lifetime prevalence rates, although their rates may have been underestimated as age of onset is commonly in the late twenties and early thirties. For both disorders, rates were much lower in the two cohorts born before 1938 (Weissman et al., 1991). Other studies show similar results: rates of bipolar disorder are higher in cohorts born after 1935 compared to those born before 1935 (Lasch, Weiss-

TABLE 5.1

Summary of Studies Examining Depressive Disorders

Study	N	Ages Examined (approx.)	Birth Cohorts or Years Examined^ (approx.)	Peak Age(s) (approx.)	Peak Cohort(s) (approx.)	Trend	Assess.	Sex	Country
MAJOR DEPRESSIVE DISORDER									
Lifetime Prevalence/Risk									
Bland et al. (1988)	3,258	18–65+	pre 1919–1966	—	—	No trend	I	M/F	Canada
Blazer et al. (1994)	8,098**	15–54	1937–1976	—	—	Stable	I	M/F	U.S.
Canino et al. (1987)	1,513	18–64	1920–1966	—	—	Stable	I	M/F	P.R.
Coryell et al. (1992)	965	<20–60+	pre 1920–post 1960	<40	post 1940	Increase	I	M/F	U.S.
Cross Nat. Coll. Group	43,268*	18–65+	pre 1905–post 1955	varies‡	varies†	Increase†	I	M/F	Various°
Gershon et al. (1987)	823	18–65+	pre 1910–1959	18–36	1940–1959	Increase	I	M/F	U.S.
Karno et al. (1987)	1,243*	18–65+	pre 1894–1966	—	—	Stable	I	M/F	U.S.
Kessler et al. (2005)	9,282	18–60+	pre 1940–1985	30–59	1940–1969	Quadratic	I	M/F	U.S.^M
Klerman et al. (1985)	2,289	<25–72+	pre 1910–post 1950	—	—	Increase	I	M/F	U.S.
Lavori et al. (1987)	1,144	19–52	1930–1959	19–30	1950–1959	Increase	I	M/F	U.S.
Lewinsohn et al. (1993)	2,032	<18–65+	1900–1959	—	—	Increase	I	M/F	U.S.
Regier et al. (1988)	18,571*	18–65+	pre 1905–1964	25–44	1937–1956	Quadratic	I	M/F	U.S.
Robins et al. (1984)	9,543*	18–65+	pre 1905–1964	25–44	1937–1956	Quadratic	I	M/F	U.S.
Simon et al. (1995)	5,603	18–65	1927–1974	18–25	1967–1974	Increase	I	M/F	Various■
Weissman & Myers (1978)	511	18–65+	pre 1910–1950	26–45	1931–1950	Increase	I	M/F	U.S.
Weissman et al. (1984)	2,003	18–45+	pre 1935–1960	30–44	1935–1949	Quadratic	I	M/F	U.S.
Wickramaratne et al. (1989)	10,640*	18–65+	1905–1965	25–44	1935–1955	Quadratic	I	M/F	U.S.

MAJOR DEPRESSIVE DISORDER (cont.)

One-Year Prevalence

Study	N	Age	Period			Trend		Sex	Country
Weissman et al. (1988)	18,571*	18–65+	pre 1905–1964	18–44	1937–1964	Quadratic	I	M/F	U.S.

Six-Month Prevalence

Study	N	Age	Period			Trend		Sex	Country
Bland et al. (1988)	3,258	18–65+	pre 1919–1966	—	—	No trend	I	M/F	Canada
Canino et al. (1987)	1,513	18–64	1920–1966	—	—	Stable	I	M/F	P.R.

One-Month Prevalence

Study	N	Age	Period			Trend		Sex	Country
Blazer et al. (1994)	8,098**	15–54	1937–1976	15–44	1946–1976	Increase	I	M/F	U.S.
Regier et al. (1988)	18,571*	18–65+	pre 1905–1964	25–44	1937–1956	Quadratic	I	M/F	U.S.

Current Prevalence

Study	N	Age	Period			Trend		Sex	Country
Murphy et al. (1984)	2,125	18–65+	1952–1970^	—	—	Stable	I	M/F	Canada
Murphy et al. (2000)	3,600	18–65+	1952–1992^	—	—	Stable	I	M/F	Canada
Sturt et al. (1984)	165	15–65	1971, 1976, 1981^	—	—	Decrease	HR	M/F	U.K.
Weissman & Myers (1978)	511	18–65+	pre 1910–1950	46–65	1911–1930	Quadratic	I	M/F	U.S.

SEVERE DEPRESSION

Lifetime Prevalence/Risk

Study	N	Age	Period			Trend		Sex	Country
Hagnell et al. (1982)	2,550	<9–80+	1947–1972^	—	—	Decrease	I	M/F	Sweden

(Continued)

TABLE 5.1
Summary of Studies Examining Depressive Disorders (*Continued*)

Study	N	Ages Examined (approx.)	Birth Cohorts or Years Examined^ (approx.)	Peak Age(s) (approx.)	Peak Cohort(s) (approx.)	Trend	Assess.	Sex	Country
MILD/MODERATE DEPRESSION									
Lifetime Prevalence/Risk									
Hagnell et al. (1982)	2,550	<9–80+	1947–1972^	—	—	Increase	I	M/F	Sweden
One-Month Prevalence									
Blazer et al. (1994)	8,098**	15–54	1937–1976	15–44	1946–1976	Quadratic	I	M/F	U.S.
Current Prevalence									
Angst (1985)	64,816	—	1920–1982^	—	—	Increase	HA	M/F	Switz.

^ Years Examined
* Data derived from the Epidemiologic Catchment Area (ECA) Program
** Data derived from the National Comorbidity Survey (NCS)
‡ Varies according to country
† Excluding Hispanic samples
° The United States, Canada, Germany, Lebanon, Italy, France, New Zealand, Taiwan
M Mexican Americans
■ Turkey, Greece, India, Germany, The Netherlands, Nigeria, Germany, the United Kingdom, Japan, France, Brazil, Chile, the United States, China, Italy
I: Interview
HR: Hospital Records
HA: Hospital Admissions
P.R.: Puerto Rico

TABLE 5.2

Summary of Studies Examining Bipolar Disorders and Mania

Study	N	Ages Examined (approx.)	Birth Cohorts or Years Examined^ (approx.)	Peak Age(s) (approx.)	Peak Cohort(s) (approx.)	Trend	Assess.	Sex	Country
MANIA									
Lifetime Prevalence/Risk									
Regier (1988)	18,571*	18–65+	pre 1905–1964	18–44	1937–1964	Increase	I	M/F	U.S.
Robins et al. (1984)	9,543*	18–65+	pre 1905–1964	18–44	1937–1964	Increase	I	M/F	U.S.
One-Month Prevalence									
Lasch et al. (1990)	17,827*	18–65+	pre 1905–1964	18–46	1935–1964	Increase	I	M/F	U.S.
Current Prevalence									
Angst (1985)	64,816	—	1920–1982^	—	—	Increase	HR	M/F	Switz.
Eagles & Whalley (1985)	—	—	1969–1978^	—	—	Stable	HD	M/F	Scotland
Joyce (1987)	—	<20–55+	1974–1984^	—	—	Increase	HA	M/F	N.Z.
BIPOLAR DISORDER									
Lifetime Prevalence									
Kessler et al. (2005)	9,282	18–60+	pre 1940–1985	18–29	1970–1985	Increase	I	M/F	U.S.
One-Year Prevalence									
Weissman et al. (1988)	18,571*	18–65+	pre 1905–1964	18–44	1937–1964	Increase	I	M/F	U.S.

^ Years Examined

* Data derived from the Epidemiologic Catchment Area (ECA) Program

I: Interview

HR: Hospital Records

HD: Hospital Discharge Data

HA: Hospital Admissions

N.Z.: New Zealand

man, Wickramaratne, & Bruce, 1990), and in cohorts born after 1940 compared to those born before 1940 (Gershon, Hamovit, Guroff, & Nurnberger, 1987). Recent evidence from the National Comorbidity Survey replication provides continued support for this trend, with rates of bipolar disorder higher in more recently born cohorts (Kessler et al., 2005).

Age of onset also appears to be decreasing in more recently born cohorts. Rice and colleagues (1987) found that the youngest age of onset for cohorts born before the mid-1930s was 20, whereas cohorts born after 1955 had much younger onset ages. Similarly, Burke et al. (1991) reported a younger age of onset for people born between 1937 and 1952 compared to those born between 1917 and 1936, suggesting that the Baby Boomers were continuing a trend that preceded them.

Anxiety Disorders.

Anxiety Disorders.   Similar to the aforementioned disorders, rates of anxiety, both in terms of subclinical symptoms and diagnosed disorders, are higher in younger and middle-aged adults than they are in older adults. In a meta-analysis examining reports of anxiety among college students from 1952 to 1992, Twenge (2000) found that anxiety levels increased nearly one standard deviation between the two time points, with this increase beginning in the 1950s among college students.

Diagnosed anxiety disorders are common in the population, but as in the case of depression, prevalence rates exhibit an age-related pattern (see review by Gatz, Kasl-Godley, & Karel, 1996). One-year prevalence rates are 16.4% for adults between the ages of 18 and 54, and 11.4% for adults over the age of 55 (U.S. Department of Health and Human Services, 1999). In several studies, prevalence rates of generalized anxiety disorders, as well as other less prevalent anxiety disorders such as obsessive-compulsive disorder and panic disorder, are higher in the Baby Boomers than in earlier-born cohorts (Kessler et al., 2005; Regier et al., 1988; Robins et al., 1984; see Table 5.3). In cohorts born after the Baby Boomers, however, evidence is mixed, with some studies demonstrating continued increases in rates of anxiety disorders (Kessler et al., 1994) and others reporting stability in successive cohorts (Regier et al., 1988). This apparent contradiction in the literature may stem from small differences in diagnostic criteria. For example, one study showed that social phobia characterized by nonspeaking fears increased in more recently born cohorts, whereas social phobia with only speaking fears remained stable across cohorts (Heimberg, Stein, Hiripi, & Kessler, 2000).

Temporal trends in age of onset for anxiety disorders are also inconsistent across diagnoses. Although the modal age of onset for obsessive-compulsive disorder is younger for cohorts born after 1950, the constellation of phobias shows the opposite pattern, with age of onset actually higher for cohorts born after 1950. In contrast, age of onset for panic disorder has remained relatively stable across birth cohorts (Burke et al., 1991).

TABLE 5.3
Summary of Studies Examining Anxiety Disorders

Study	N	Ages Examined (approx.)	Birth Cohorts or Years Examined^ (approx.)	Peak Age(s) (approx.)	Peak Cohort(s) (approx.)	Trend	Assess.	Sex	Country
ANXIETY									
Lifetime Prevalence/Risk									
Canino et al. (1987)	1,513	18–64	1920–1966	45–64	1920–1939	Decrease	I	M/F	P.R.
Kessler et al. (1994)	8,098**	15–54	1936–1976	—	—	Stable	I	M/F	U.S.
Kessler et al. (2005)	5,692	18–60+	pre 1940–1985	30–44	1955–1969	Quadratic	I	M/F	U.S.
One-Year Prevalence									
Kessler et al. (1994)	8,098**	15–54	1936–1976	15–24	1967–1976	Increase	I	M/F	U.S.
Offord et al. (1996)	8,116	15–64	1926–1975	15–24	1966–1975	Increase	I	M/F	Canada
Six-Month Prevalence									
Canino et al. (1987)	1,513	18–64	1920–1966	45–64	1920–1939	Stable	I	M/F	P.R.
One-Month Prevalence									
Regier et al. (1988)	18,571*	18–65+	pre 1905–1964	18–44	1937–1964	Stable§ / Increase	I / I	M / F	U.S. / U.S.
Current Prevalence									
Murphy et al. (1984)	2,125	18–65+	1952–1970^	—	—	Stable	I	M/F	Canada
Meta-Analysis									
Twenge (2000) Sample 1	40,192	18–22	1952–1993^	—	—	Increase	SR	M/F	U.S.
Twenge (2000) Sample 2	12,056	9–17	1952–1993^	—	—	Increase	SR	M/F	U.S.

^ Years Examined
* Data derived from the Epidemiologic Catchment Area (ECA) Program
** Data derived from the National Comorbidity Survey (NCS)
§ Stable until the age of 65, then a significant decline
I: Interview
SR: Self-Report
P.R.: Puerto Rico

Substance Use Disorders.   For a cohort who frequently heard Timothy Leary's advice to "turn on, tune in, drop out," higher rates of substance use may seem unsurprising. For rates of illicit drug and alcohol abuse, the Baby Boomers far exceed older cohorts, with several studies demonstrating younger onset ages (Helzer, Burnam, & McEvoy, 1991; Burke et al., 1991) and higher prevalence rates for cohorts born after 1950 (see Table 5.4). In a comparison of cohorts born throughout the twentieth century, rates of substance abuse and substance dependence were highest in the cohort born between 1953 and 1964. People born between 1938 and 1952 had the second highest prevalence rates, whereas the lowest prevalence rates were found among the two oldest cohorts: those born prior to 1917, and between 1917 and 1936 (Burke et al., 1991).

Alcohol-related problems follow a similar pattern, with rates of alcohol abuse considerably higher among people born after 1940 compared to those born before 1940 (Rice et al., 2003). Results from a study based on a national survey of over 40,000 people also show higher rates of alcohol abuse and dependence among people born after 1947 (Grant & Hartford, 1994). When comparing cohorts prior to the Baby Boomers, the trend for more recently born cohorts to have higher prevalence rates remains; those born between 1937 and 1945 reported drinking more than those born at the beginning of the twentieth century, after controlling for age and period effects (Levenson, Aldwin, & Spiro, 1998). Mortality, however, is high among people with substance use disorders; and among those still alive, substance use declines with age. Rates are higher in the teens and early twenties and decline as people enter their thirties (see review by Patterson & Jeste, 1999). Still, as the Baby Boomers age, the number of older adults with substance use problems is expected to double from its current rate of 2.5 million to 5 million (Gfroerer, Penne, Pemberton, & Folsom, 2003).

Schizophrenia.   Schizophrenia affects only 1.3% of people between the ages of 18 and 54 and approximately .6% of people over the age of 55 (U.S. Department of Health and Human Services, 1999). Although relatively uncommon, schizophrenia is often associated with a chronic, unremitting course, severe symptoms, and high rates of suicide, all of which make it one of the most challenging mental disorders to treat. When inferring cohort trends from cross-sectional studies, the excessive mortality rates among people with schizophrenia relative to people with other disorders also raise particular concern regarding biases from attrition (Keith, Regier, & Rae, 1991; Martin, Cloninger, Guze, & Clayton, 1985).

Despite concerns that attrition biases may yield inflated cohort effects for this disorder relative to others, cohort trends are less consistent for schizophrenia than the aforementioned disorders (see Table 5.5). Some researchers find increasing prevalence rates in successively born cohorts (e.g., Keith et al.,

TABLE 5.4

Summary of Studies Examining Substance Abuse Disorders

Study	N	Ages Examined (approx.)	Birth Cohorts or Years Examined^ (approx.)	Peak Age(s) (approx.)	Peak Cohort(s) (approx.)	Trend	Assess.	Sex	Country
ALCOHOL ABUSE & DEPENDENCE									
Lifetime Prevalence/Risk									
Canino et al. (1987)	1,513	18–64	1920–1966	45–64	1920–1939	Decrease	I	M/F	P.R.
One-Year Prevalence									
Grant & Harford (1994)	42,862	18–65+	pre 1927–1974	18–29	1963–1974	Increase	SR	M/F	U.S.
Six-Month Prevalence									
Bland et al. (1988)	3,258	18–65+	pre 1919–1966	18–24	1960–1966	Increase	I	M	Canada
				18–24	1960–1966	Stable (25–65)	I	F	Canada
Canino et al. (1987)	1,513	18–64	1920–1966	45–64	1920–1939	Stable	I	M/F	P.R.
One-Month Prevalence									
Regier et al. (1988)	18,571*	18–65+	pre 1905–1964	18–24	1957–1964	Increase	I	M/F	U.S.
SUBSTANCE USE DISORDERS									
Lifetime Prevalence/Risk									
Bland et al. (1988)	3,258	18–65+	pre 1919–1966	18–34	1950–1966	Increase	I	M/F	Canada
Kessler et al. (1994)	8,098**	15–54	1936–1976	25–34	1957–1966	Quadratic	I	M/F	U.S.
Kessler et al. (2005)	9,282	18–60+	pre 1940–1985	30–44	1955–1969	Quadratic	I	M/F	U.S.
One-Year Prevalence									
Kessler et al. (1994)	8,098**	15–54	1936–1976	15–24	1967–1976	Increase	I	M/F	U.S.
Offord et al. (1996)	8,116	15–64	1926–1975	15–24	1966–1975	Increase	I	M/F	Canada
ALCOHOL-RELATED PROBLEMS									
Lifetime & One-Year Prevalence									
Hasin et al. (1990)	—	22–59	1967, 1969, 1979, 1984^	—	—	Increase	I	M/F	U.S.

(Continued)

123

TABLE 5.4
Summary of Studies Examining Substance Abuse Disorders (*Continued*)

Study	N	Ages Examined (approx.)	Birth Cohorts or Years Examined^ (approx.)	Peak Age(s) (approx.)	Peak Cohort(s) (approx.)	Trend	Assess.	Sex	Country
ALCOHOLISM									
Lifetime Prevalence/Risk									
Reich et al. (1988)	956	17–65+	1928–1963λ	17–25	1955–1963	Increase	I,HR,FH	M/F	U.S.
ALCOHOL DEPENDENCE									
Lifetime Prevalence/Risk									
Rice et al. (2003)	5,153	18–65+	1910–1979	15–44	1950–1979	Increase	I	M/F	U.S.
Prevalence									
Hilton (1988)	6,993	18–60+	1979–1984^	—	—	Increase	I	M	U.S.
				—	—	Stable	I	F	U.S.
DRUG ABUSE/DEPENDENCE									
Lifetime Prevalence/Risk									
Robins et al. (1984)	9,543*	18–65+	pre 1905–1964	18–24	1957–1964	Increase	I	M/F	U.S.
Six-Month Prevalence									
Bland et al. (1988)	3,258	18–65+	pre 1919–1966	18–24	1960–1966	Increase	I	M/F	Canada

^ Years Examined
* Data derived from the Epidemiologic Catchment Area (ECA) Program
** Data derived from the National Comorbidity Survey (NCS)
I: Interview
SR: Self-Report
HR: Hospital Records
FH: Family History Data
P.R.: Puerto Rico
λ: combined pre 1928 and post 1963 cohorts

TABLE 5.5

Summary of Studies Examining Schizophrenia

Study	N	Ages Examined (approx.)	Birth Cohorts or Years Examined^ (approx.)	Peak Age(s) (approx.)	Peak Cohort(s) (approx.)	Trend	Assess.	Sex	Country
SCHIZOPHRENIA									
Lifetime Prevalence/Risk									
Canino et al. (1987)	1,513	18–64	1920–1966	25–44	1940–1959	Quadratic	I	M/F	P.R.
Keith et al. (1991)	18,571*	18–65+	pre 1905–1964	18–44	1937–1964	Increase	I	M/F	U.S.
Robins et al. (1984)	9,543*	18–65+	pre 1905–1964	25–44	1937–1956	Quadratic	I	M/F	U.S.
Six-Month Prevalence									
Canino et al. (1987)	1,513	18–64	1920–1966	—	—	Stable	I	M/F	P.R.
One-Month Prevalence									
Regier et al. (1988)	18,571*	18–65+	pre 1905–1964	—	—	Stable§	I	M	U.S.
				18–44	1937–1964	Increase	I	F	U.S.
Incidence									
Boydell et al. (2003)	1,055	—	1965–1997^	—	—	Increase	HR	M/F	U.K.
Folnegovic et al. (1990)	—	—	1965–1984^	—	—	Stable	HA	M/F	Croatia
Kendell et al. (1993)	—	—	1971–1989^	—	—	Decrease	HA	M/F	Scotland
Suvisaari et al. (1999)	5,645	16–26	1954–1965	20–21	1954–1955	Decrease	HR	M/F	Finland

(Continued)

TABLE 5.5
Summary of Studies Examining Schizophrenia (Continued)

Study	N	Ages Examined (approx.)	Birth Cohorts or Years Examined^ (approx.)	Peak Age(s) (approx.)	Peak Cohort(s) (approx.)	Trend	Assess.	Sex	Country
SCHIZOPHRENIA (cont.)									
Current Prevalence									
Cavanagh & Shajahan (1999)	—	—	1980–1995^	—	—	Stable	HR	M	Scotland
						Decrease	HR	F	Scotland
Eagles et al. (1988)	—	—	1969–1984^	—	—	Decrease	PCR	M/F	Scotland
Eagles & Whalley (1985)	—	—	1969–1978^	—	—	Decrease	HD	M/F	Scotland
Joyce (1987)	—	<20–55+	1974–1984^	—	—	Decrease	HA	M/F	N.Z.
Munk-Jorgensen & Mortensen (1992)	8,500	—	1971–1987^	—	—	Decrease	HR	M/F	Denmrk
Stoll et al. (1993)	—	—	1972–1988^	—	—	Decrease	HD	M/F	N.A.

^ Years Examined
* Data derived from the Epidemiologic Catchment Area (ECA) Program
§ Stable until the age of 65, then a significant decline
I: Interview
HR: Hospital Records
HA: Hospital Admissions
PCR: Psychiatric Case Register
HD: Hospital Discharge Data
N.A: North America
P.R.: Puerto Rico
N.Z.: New Zealand

1991; Regier et al., 1988), whereas others find stable or decreasing rates (e.g., Cavanagh & Shajahan, 1999). One difficulty in assessing cohort effects for schizophrenia is that researchers typically examine changes that occur in the population between two points in time, but do not break down prevalence rates by cohort (e.g., Bamrah, Freeman, & Goldberg, 1991; Eagles & Whalley, 1985). Thus, although it is possible to determine if rates have increased or decreased between two time points, it is impossible to know which cohort is driving the directional shift.

Another challenge is that hospital admission rates are most often used to calculate prevalence rates. Several problems arise with this method including changing diagnostic criteria for admission, difficulties in determining first versus repeat admission, changes in outpatient treatments, and efficacy of medication therapy (Kendell, Malcolm, & Adams, 1993). Taking these concerns into consideration, results are mixed. For example, between 1971 and 1987, hospital admission rates of schizophrenia decreased in Denmark (Munk-Jorgensen & Mortensen, 1992), whereas rates in Scotland remained stable for men and slightly decreased for women between 1980 and 1995 (Cavanagh & Shajahan, 1999). In a study including all psychiatric and hospital records, as opposed to hospital admission rates alone, cases of schizophrenia in London increased between 1965 and 1977 (Boydell et al., 2003).

With the caveat of the methodological limitations mentioned above, the literature on incidence rates is less ambiguous than the literature on prevalence rates. This research suggests that the age of onset for schizophrenia has decreased among more recently born cohorts. A review of medical records from a Normandy psychiatric hospital indicated that individuals diagnosed for the first time with schizophrenia between 1904 and 1944 averaged 25.3 years of age. For individuals born between 1945 and 1964 (i.e., the Baby Boomers), the mean age of onset dropped to 23.3, and was still younger for people born between 1965 and 1984, who averaged 20.4 years at initial diagnosis (Di Maggio, Martinez, Menard, Petit, & Thibaut, 2001). Prior to drawing any conclusions, however, more research must be conducted.

Dementia. Dementia comprises a group of disorders most dependent on age, and one that poses perhaps the greatest challenge in the face of an aging population. The Baby Boomers have higher levels of education, which is a protective factor against the most common dementing illness, Alzheimer's disease (e.g., Mortimer & Graves, 1993). However, the large number of Baby Boomers coupled with their greater overall life expectancy could lead to an unprecedented increase in rates of dementia in the upcoming years. A one-year prevalence rate of severe cognitive impairment is 1.2% in adults between the ages of 18 and 54. That number rises sharply to 6.6% in individuals over the age of 55, and continues to increase exponentially over the late adult life span (U.S. Department of Health and Human Services, 1999). In fact, rates of Alzheimer's disease are believed to double every five years after age 65 (Jorm, Korten, & Henderson, 1987), with estimates of 25% among those aged 85 years and older for Alzheimer's disease, and 42% for those with minor cognitive impairment (Yesavage, 2002). Slightly lower, but comparable, statistics have been reported by Kawas, Gray, Brookmeyer, Fozard, and Zonderman (2000). They estimate that the incidence rate of Alzheimer's disease increases .08% each year between the ages of 60 and 65, but increases 6.5% each year after the age of 85. As the oldest Baby Boomers begin to enter into old age, dementing conditions, particularly Alzheimer's disease, will present a new mental health challenge for this generation.

METHODOLOGICAL ISSUES

The cross-sectional nature of the majority of the existing data reviewed previously raises methodological concerns. Two studies form the basis of much of the research on age and cohort effects in the rates of mental disorders: the Epidemiological Catchment Area Survey (Robins & Regier, 1991) and the National Comorbidity Survey (Kessler et al., 1994). Both studies, completed in the United States, examine age and cohort effects using a cross-sectional design and self-reported interviews. Other studies contribute to the question of cohort, age, and period effects in rates of disorders, but they too are predominantly cross-sectional in design (e.g., Lewinsohn et al., 1993).

Cohort, Age, and Period Effects

Cross-sectional designs make it particularly difficult to disentangle cohort, age, and period effects. Birth cohort effects, most germane to the current chapter, refer to changes in illness rates that can be attributed to the year or time period in which an individual is born (Klerman & Weissman, 1989). Whether people born in 1950 are more likely than those born in 1960 to contract a particular illness is an example of a birth cohort effect. Age effects, in contrast, refer to changes in illness rates that occur when the likelihood of being diagnosed with a disorder varies with age. The positive association between age and certain diseases such as dementia, cancer, and heart disease are examples of age effects (Klerman, 1993). Finally, period effects refer to changes in illness rates that are not linked with year of birth, but are instead tied to a particular period of time (Klerman & Weissman, 1989), such as the surge in HIV cases during the late 1980s and early 1990s. Although advanced statistical techniques have allowed for a more precise separation of cohort, age, and period effects (Heimberg et al., 2000; Rice et al., 2003), distinguishing among the three is still complicated, as some degree of overlap will almost always occur (for review, see Rice, Moldin, & Neuman, 1991).

Why Comparing Age Groups Raises Concerns.   Other methodological concerns have also been raised when inferring age or cohort differences using cross-sectional analyses. Biased recall, mortality, institutionalization, selective migration, and societal mores are factors that may bias community-based survey data when comparing across age groups (Lasch et al., 1990). Perhaps the most disconcerting aspect of these biases is that they all have the tendency to skew results in the same direction. Moreover, this direction—where reports are higher among younger adults—is precisely the one substantiated in the literature.

The relation between bias and age is compounded by the nature of psychological disorder. Incidence of disorder is not uniform across the life span, but is more likely to occur at younger ages. Over 90% of people who report a mental disorder have had their first symptoms by the age of 38 (Lewinsohn, Duncan, Stanton, & Hautzinger, 1986). As a result, the number of years between the onset of first symptoms and the time of report is much greater for older adults than it is for younger adults. Thus, older adults are faced with a much more difficult task, a fact made worse by findings suggesting that memory performance declines with age (Salthouse, 2004). Using depression as an example, the age of onset has varied across studies, with peak incidence rates ranging from the teens and early 20s (Burke, Burke, Regier, & Rae, 1990) to early middle age (Lewinsohn et al., 1986). In either case, an initial diagnosis is fairly rare in old age, and longer time intervals between an episode and its report may result in underreporting the disorder (Lewinsohn et al., 1993). Indeed, researchers have found that even a small rate of forgetting can produce large cohort effects that mimic those observed in the literature (Giuffra & Risch, 1994).

In addition to faulty memory processes, sample attrition is more of a problem for older adults than it is for younger adults. People with severe symptoms earlier in life may not live to old age. In addition, a greater number of older adults as compared to younger adults may be institutionalized or have a greater likelihood of living in less accessible areas as a result of a cascade of accumulated hardships due to their disorders. All of these factors may cause the available pool of older community residents to be a more biased, healthier sample compared to the available pool of younger adults.

Period effects, defined as social changes that influence people of all ages, may also obscure cohort comparisons. People born earlier in the twentieth century may frame symptoms of distress as less serious, or may be more reluctant to report symptoms of psychological distress when compared to more recently born cohorts. As society has grown more accepting and aware of mental health issues, younger cohorts may be more likely to report their symptoms, whereas older cohorts, who may not readily characterize past mental distress as having been problematic, may underreport previous episodes (Hasin & Link, 1988). An example from a study of depression presents findings that fuel these concerns. A secular rise in reports of mild to moderate symptoms of depression is documented when comparing incidence rates between 1947 and 1972, but rates of severe depression display no such pattern (Hagnell et al., 1982). Assuming that severe depression is less susceptible to report bias and harder to deny, its diagnosis may be less susceptible to bias than mild and moderate levels of depression. In addition, younger cohorts may be more susceptible to shifts in social norms, which may make them more likely to engage in certain behaviors, such as alcohol consumption or participation in psychotherapy. These period effects may alter age patterns that are not easily interpreted without longitudinal data (cf., Levenson et al., 1998).

Addressing Methodological Concerns

Researchers acknowledge these methodological concerns, but state that the observed cohort effects are too consistent and robust to be an artifact of sampling and report bias (Kessler et al., 1994). Researchers contend that differential mortality and memory biases cannot account for the magnitude of the cohort effect found in their data (Klerman et al., 1985). In addition, studies using 30-day prevalence rates, where memory bias is not as great of a concern as it is when using lifetime prevalence, demonstrate that younger adults still report higher rates of mental illness when compared to older adults (e.g., Blazer, Kessler, McGonagle, & Swartz, 1994; Lasch et al., 1990; Regier et al., 1988).

They further maintain that linear increases occurring over periods as short as five years indicate that societal acceptance and awareness of mental health problems are not sufficient to account for the findings. In large cross-sectional studies, researchers find patterns of increased prevalence and incidence rates for depression in more recently born cohorts even after controlling for social desirability (Lewinsohn et al., 1993). They also argue that objective indicators, such as increased rates of suicides among adolescents since World War II, parallel the results found in studies that have used self-report data to examine temporal trends of psychiatric disorders (Klerman, 1993). Lastly, the variability in the strength of the cohort effects, and the lack of cohort effects among certain samples, indicate that methodological limitations are not completely responsible for the findings (Klerman et al., 1985).

Multiple-cohort sequential studies, querying different cohorts as they move throughout time, would address many of these methodological concerns, but such data are rare. Although one such study found increases in mental disorders with successively younger cohorts at different time points (Hagnell et al., 1982), converging evidence from more than one source is needed to address this question successfully. For now, we are limited to the available information when comparing Baby Boomers to previous generations. Although the findings are suggestive of cohort effects, we must interpret them with these methodological concerns in mind.

PSYCHOSOCIAL CORRELATES OF MENTAL DISTRESS

The Diathesis/Stress Model of Mental Health

Identifying the individual and interactive effects of mental health determinants is difficult, but charting changes in these influences across cohorts poses an even greater challenge. The diathesis/stress model provides a framework for understanding how the multiple determinants of mental disorder encompassing genetic, physiological, environmental, and psychosocial processes work together in the pathogenesis of mental illness. According to this model, people vary in their vulnerability—or diathesis—to illness. In its most narrow definition, diathesis refers to genetic predisposition to illness. Social scientists, however, often use a broader definition for diathesis that encompasses personal characteristics, including genetic as well as psychosocial processes. Mental health is determined not only by the strength of these predisposing qualities, but also the stress individuals experience in their lives. When stressors exceed a person's ability to maintain his or her current state, or homeostasis, the likelihood of illness increases. Thus, the extent to which a stressor taxes an individual's ability to cope depends on both the severity of the stressor and individual characteristics (Monroe & Simons, 1991).

Evidence for genetic vulnerability to mental illness stems from a number of sources, including studies comparing families and family members on diagnosed conditions. Certain conditions such as depression (Klein, Lewinsohn, Rohde, Seeley, & Durbin, 2002) and dementia (Hedera & Turner, 2002) cluster within families, and higher concordance rates have been found among identical twins compared to fraternal twins for depression (Kendler, Kessler, Neale, Heath, & Eaves, 1993), bipolar disorder (McGuffin et al., 2003), and schizophrenia (Gottesman & Shields, 1971). Clearly, certain people are more at risk than others as a result of biological factors. Consistent with the diathesis/stress model of illness, stressors may activate these latent vulnerabilities and transform predispositions into psychopathology (e.g., Monroe & Simons, 1991). Schizophrenia, for example, has a higher likelihood of occurrence in an individual who has a family history of the disease and encounters stressful life events compared to an individual with only one of these risk factors (van Os et al., 1994).

Explaining shifts in disorders across time using a purely genetic argument would be difficult. Changes in prevalence rates have been documented across short periods of time, during which different cohorts do not represent successive generations. Dramatic changes in the genetic composition of the population, particularly given this short time frame and consistent and gradual linear increase, are implausible (Monroe & Simons, 1991). Interactions between genetic and environmental influences can change over these short time periods, but such change would most likely result from shifts in environmental effects, not genetic composition. To understand changing rates of mental illness without assuming shifts in the genetic composition of the population, psychologists have focused on psychological and environmental factors within the diathesis/stress model.

People vary in their social, economic, and psychological resources (Lazarus, 1995). For example, cognitive appraisals developed over time are strongly linked to psychological health and distress (Beck, Brown, Steer, & Eidelson, 1987; Lazarus, 1991). Life circumstances, such as bereavement or physical disability, may also leave some people more vulnerable (Kemp & Krause, 1999; Thompson, Gallagher-Thompson, Futterman, Gilewski, & Peterson, 1991). In addition, the physical environment may contribute to changes in mental health over time (see reviews by van Os & Sham, 2003; Tarter, 2000). Increases in environmental toxins, such as overexposure to chemicals, for example, have been associated with a number of behavioral and cognitive problems (Brown, 2002).

The scope and complexity of these issues limit the current discussion to psychological and sociological influences, and only to several processes within these large categories. Psychological and sociological influences include cognitions, behavior, and social and cultural circumstances that define both the person and the environment. Potential influences from these categories are many; therefore, we restrict our discussion to intragroup competition, increases in consumer consumption, and perceived alienation and personal threat.

Intragroup Competition

The size of the Baby-Boomer cohort gave this generation their name and shaped their economic lives. According to economist Richard Easterlin, the Baby Boomers experienced a phenomenon that occurs for any larger cohort that follows a smaller one: greater intragroup competition (Easterlin, 1987; Easterlin & Crimmins, 1985). Easterlin observes that after World War II, economic prosperity created job opportunities within the United States. This economic prosperity continued as the first Baby Boomers entered a workforce filled with opportunity. The number of new workers entering the workplace, however, soon outpaced job growth, and the later Baby Boomers faced more competition and more rejection on the job market. Greater competition drove demand down and job advancement began to slow (Cornman & Kingson, 1996). As more Baby Boomers entered the workforce, intragroup competition increased (Easterlin, 1987). These changes in economic indicators did not bode well for the Baby Boomers, as economic downturns are related to psychological distress and substance use (Dooley & Prause, 2004; Hagnell, Lanke, Rorsman, & Oejesjoe, 1982; Kop, 1976). Cycles of unemployment, for example, have been related to increases in depression (Hagnell et al., 1982) and suicide (Kessing, Agerbo, & Mortensen, 2003). Indeed, researchers have attributed the higher rates of suicide in cohorts born after World War II to psychological distress caused, in part, by greater intragroup competition (Easterlin, Schaeffer, & Macunovich, 1993; McIntosh, 1994).

Increased Consumerism

Despite intragroup competition, Baby Boomers have higher standards of living compared to the previous generation (Easterbrook, 2003). At every stage of their lives, Baby Boomers have been more prosperous than their parents (Keister & Deeb-Sossa, 2001) and will enter retirement with more assets (Easterlin et al., 1993). Their opinions concerning their economic status, however, suggest otherwise. They report more concerns and failures regarding their economic situations (Levy, 1987) and greater concern regarding the economic future of society (Russell, 2001) compared to preceding generations.

Economist Juliet Schor (1998) offers an explanation for the apparent discrepancy between the Baby Boomers objective standard of living and their reports of relative deprivation when they compare themselves to their peers and their parents. She states that the twentieth century is marked by a widening income gap across the population (Schor, 1998). As a result, people feel less successful when engaging in peer comparisons. Regardless of income, people who compare themselves to their peers on economic indices tend to have a lower amount of personal savings and report lower levels of happiness than those who do not engage in such comparisons (Schor, 1998). Schor further states that social comparison has been exacerbated by increased exposure to people of much higher socioeconomic status. Previously, people compared themselves to their next-door neighbors in attempts to "keep up with the Joneses." Because people lived in economically homogeneous neighborhoods, this comparison was not as deleterious as the current practice, where people now compare themselves to images portrayed in the media.

In addition, her research indicates that luxury items that were once the domain of the rich have increasingly entered the middle and lower classes. As examples, she discusses the need for "McMansions" and professional-grade cooking equipment for people too busy to spend leisure time at home, much less to cook (Schor, 1992; Schor, 1998). Over a quarter of people who earn $100,000 or more a year state they earn less than they need (Schor, 1998). People who look back and wonder why they need two incomes to continue the middle class life style that their parents had enjoyed on only one income often fail to recall that their parents lived with one car, a watch purchased at the local drug store, and clothes that were not identified by designer labeling. People view television shows and read magazine advertisements touting luxury cars and other accoutrements of a lifestyle that they need, and buy into this vision. Schor states that the emphasis on and need to obtain more expensive private consumption goods has resulted in greater hours at work, less leisure time, and lower levels of happiness (Schor, 1992; Schor, 1998).

Is There an Upside?

Despite the problems involved with intragroup competition, one positive consequence may have resulted from this greater competition. Muller (1997) posits that less economic opportunity has caused more recently born cohorts to turn to other areas of their lives for fulfillment, and that this shift is reflected in their reported values. The first of the Baby Boomers, those born in the 1940s and 1950s, rank personal issues such as self-respect and a sense of accomplishment as highest in their order of priorities, whereas later-born Boomers rank relationships with others as most important (Muller, 1997). Schor (1998) also reports that a minority of people surveyed in the United States report that they have actively changed their lifestyle to downsize their needs. Apparently, as marketing campaigns for consumer products continue to inundate society with messages of increased consumerism, a minority of people are questioning this value system.

Alienation and Personal Threat

In addition to this surge in consumerism, other aspects of society also shifted in the years following World War II. Elder (1993) has argued that the impact of historical change on an individual depends on the age at which that change is experienced. The Baby Boomers reached their formative years at a time when the face of society was changing (Light, 1988). During their lifetimes, trust in institutions declined and was replaced by an increased emphasis on individualism (Fukuyama, 1999). This individualism is not the self-reliance integral to the ideals of Western culture, but instead describes feelings of isolation, or alienation from others. At the same time, increased crime rates and a proliferation of information from the media regarding these environmental dangers resulted in a more knowledgeable, albeit more fearful, population (Easterbrook, 2003; Twenge, 2000).

In the years preceding and immediately following World War II, United States citizens expressed high levels of trust in both the government and in each other (Fukuyama, 1999). They had experienced life-altering events such as the Great Depression, the bombing of Pearl Harbor, and World War II (Elder, 1998), and they had worked through these difficult times together. The Baby Boomers were also witnesses to war, but the responses to Vietnam created division as opposed to unification. National pride that brought the nation together during World War II fell by the wayside during Vietnam. Protests replaced flags and views of the military drastically changed. A growing distrust in governmental institutions ensued with the Civil Rights Movement, Watergate, the Kent State Massacre, and the energy crisis (Light, 1988). Whereas the majority of United States citizens expressed trust in their fellow citizens and in governmental institutions in the 1950s, only a fraction of people expressed the same sentiments in the 1990s (Fukuyama, 1999). Demonstrating that the decline in trust is not solely a period effect, Robinson and Jackson (2003) found that levels of trust are highest in cohorts born before the 1940s and decline with each consecutive cohort born throughout the second half of the twentieth century.

As a consequence of the breakdown in societal trust, people began to turn inward and a rise in feelings of isolation was ignited (Furedi, 2002). Because people have an intrinsic need to belong, to feel embedded in a community and tied to each other (Baumeister & Leary, 1995), social isolation, or a lack of belonging to a community, is associated with multiple negative outcomes, including increased anxiety and depression (Baumeister & Tice, 1990; Seligman, 1990). Indeed, sociocultural decreases in social embeddedness have been linked to higher rates of anxiety among college students throughout the second half of the twentieth century (Twenge, 2000). Throughout the Baby Boomers' lifetimes, societal changes occurred that have decreased social embeddedness, including higher divorce rates (Kreider & Fields, 2002), fewer connections with the surrounding community (Fukuyama, 1999; Furedi, 2002), and greater social mobility (Klerman & Weissman, 1989).

This greater alienation has been defined as not only a decrease in strong interpersonal ties in the family, but also to decreases in ties to the larger community. For example, religious participation, a practice that represented to many Americans in the 1950s a show of patriotism as well as religious fealty (see review by Herberg, 1955), has decreased among more recent cohorts (Hoge & Hoge, 1992). Belief systems reflect this shift in community, with the Baby Boomers reporting greater feelings of cynicism toward the seemingly good intentions of others overall, and less confidence in national leaders in multiple realms, including politics, science, industry, and medicine (e.g., Riggs & Turner, 2000; Russell, 2001).

Feeling unsupported by social network members as well as the broader community may also exacerbate feelings of personal danger. Although crime rates have been decreasing since the early 1990s, national crime rates surged from 1963 to the 1990s (Fukuyama, 1999; United States Department of Justice, 2003). In addition, the second half of the twentieth century was witness to a massive proliferation of information from the media. Reports of random acts of violence, along with the occurrence of all types of risk, regardless of how small, may also have exacerbated feelings of apprehension about personal safety (Wakshlag, Vial, & Tamborini, 1983), which in turn may have contributed to higher rates of anxiety and other forms of mental distress for the Baby Boomers.

MENTAL HEALTH ACROSS ADULTHOOD

The cohort who once popularized the adage "never trust anyone over 30" now represents the middle-aged adults in the United States, with the oldest beginning to reach retirement age. Twenty-five years from now, the Baby Boomers will represent the majority of older adults, an age group which will comprise 20% of the population. Symptoms of clinical disorders often change with age, leaving researchers to question the applicability of the same diagnostic criteria for people of all ages (Hybels, Blazer, & Pieper, 2001). For mental health professionals, treating the clinical problems of the Baby Boomers will require an understanding of developmental trajectories of psychological health.

Age represents more than just a chronological marker; it is tied to one's sense of self and serves as an organizing framework for thoughts and behavior (Herzog & Markus, 1999; Whitbourne, 2002). Age is also related to life events that are deleterious to mental health. Bereavement is more common among the older adult population and is associated with decreases in well-being (Thompson et al., 1991). Although symptoms decline over time among bereaved individuals (Reich, Zautra, & Guarnaccia, 1989), those with additional vulnerabilities may not recover as easily. For example, symptoms of posttraumatic stress can re-emerge with age-associated losses such as retirement, declines in health, or the death of a loved one (Clipp & Elder, 1996).

Older age is also associated with worse physical health and a greater number of physical disabilities (Reich et al., 1989), which in turn threatens wellbeing (e.g., Wrosch, Schulz, & Heckhausen, 2004). In the second half of the twentieth century, rates of degenerative disorders and chronic diseases have increased as the mortality rate of acute diseases has decreased (Barsky, 1988). A longer projected life expectancy (Stahl, 1990) coupled with increasing physical disabilities may raise quality-of-life issues for some aging Baby Boomers.

Despite negative social and physical changes that occur in old age, trajectories of psychological disorder, with the exception of the dementias, do not show this increasing trend. For people who have been diagnosed with a mental disorder earlier in life, symptoms often improve with age. For example, the positive symptoms of schizophrenia, such as agitation and disorganized thinking, decrease over time (Lawton, 1972) and older adults exhibit less positive symptomatology than younger adults (Ciompi, 1985). Although decreased functional mobility and pain is reported more often among middleaged and older adults with schizophrenia compared to people without the disease (Sciolla, Patterson, Wetherell, McAdams, & Jeste, 2003), coping style among people with schizophrenia improves with age (Solano & Whitbourne, 2001), and differences in quality of life between schizophrenics living in the community and nonpsychotic controls are small (Cohen et al., 2003). In addition, emotions of high surgency, or high energy, are reported less often among older adults (Lawton, Kleban, Rajagopal, & Dean, 1992), which may play a role in fewer symptoms of impulsivity and lower levels of antisocial behavior among older people with personality disorders compared to their younger counterparts (Molinari, Kunik, Snow-Turek, Deleon, & Williams, 1999).

For people without a diagnosed psychological disorder, aging is also associated with certain benefits in the mental health domain. The onset of most disorders, with the exception of the dementias, is rare (Fisher, Zeiss, & Carstensen, 2001). In addition, rates of psychological distress decrease over time. When querying people of all ages about their levels of overall well-being, older adults report similar levels of positive affect and lower levels of negative affect over time (Charles, Reynolds, & Gatz, 2001), as well as increases in life satisfaction (Mroczek & Spiro, 2003).

Given the social and physical health-related losses that accompany old age, findings of gains in well-being may seem counterintuitive. Recent theories, however, suggest that growing older is associated with changes in perspective that lead to improvements in well-being (Carstensen, Fung, & Charles, 2003). For example, older adults are as or more adept at analyzing highly emotional material compared to younger adults, which may help them in their daily problem solving (Blanchard-Fields, 1998). Time perspective is another explanation for increases in emotion regulation, such that older adults recognize the ephemeral nature of life and, as a result, structure their time and priorities to enhance their well-being (Carstensen, Isaacowitz, & Charles, 1999). These age-related changes are posited to follow developmental trajectories, helping all Baby Boomers as they age.

Of course, there are exceptions to a trend of improved or stable well-being over time, and this trend does not continue throughout the entire life span. Researchers have noticed increased rates in depressive symptoms in very old age, particularly among those aged 85 years and older (Gatz & Hurwicz, 1990). Although part of this increase may arise from the overlap between depressive symptoms and physical health problems (Roberts, Kaplan, Shema, & Strawbridge, 1997), physical health status alone cannot explain the increase (Gatz & Hurwicz, 1990; Haynie, Berg, Johansson, Gatz, & Zarit, 2001). Researchers have thus proposed that a new type of depression, termed minor depression, may be necessary to define this phenomenon among older adults (e.g., Hybels et al., 2001).

The age-related trajectory of mental health may vary for the Baby Boomers compared to previous generations. They have access to social and medical advances unavailable to previous generations. In addition, the Baby Boomers have attained higher levels of education than past cohorts (Russell, 2001) and are more knowledgeable about health promotion and risk than were previous cohorts (MacNeil, 2001; Russell, 2001). Moreover, the Baby Boomers are not as hesitant as the current cohort of older adults to utilize mental health services, which may make them less reluctant to seek help as they age (Silverstone, 1996). For proactive, educated Baby Boomers, underutilization of mental health services should not be a problem. The growing number of culturally diverse, low SES older adults, however, raises the concern that these advances will not benefit all people equally as they age (e.g., Hough et al., 1987; Lopez, 2002). It is estimated that one in four Baby Boomers in the United States is an ethnic or racial minority (Russell, 2001); consequently, as Baby Boomers in the United States age, older adults will be a much more diverse group than preceding generations. Research targeted at understanding the needs of ethnically diverse older adults will be crucial throughout the next few decades.

CONCLUSION

The Baby Boomers face both benefits and challenges as they look to the future. Their experience of aging will be shaped by their life experiences and the biological and social changes related to age. In their examination of aging and cohort effects, Elder and his colleagues emphasize the importance of examining not only current circumstances, but the entire life story of an individual (e.g., Clipp & Elder, 1996; Crosnoe & Elder, 2002). The lives of the Baby Boomers have been marked by societal advancement. They are the largest cohort to reach older adulthood and will continue to influence societal views and expectations as they age (MacNeil, 2001). They have survived tumultuous times but also have higher prevalence rates of certain psychological disorders than previous generations. They represent an aging population more diverse and larger than any other in history. Just as their size may have inadvertently led to psychological stressors through greater intragroup competition, their numbers may also generate a greater awareness and focus of the mental health needs of older adults. This increased awareness of mental health issues for an aging generation will benefit not only the Baby Boomers, but those following in their footsteps.

REFERENCES

American Psychiatric Association. (1994). *Diagnostic and statistical manual of mental disorders* (4th ed.). Washington, DC: Author.
Angst, J. (1985). Switch from depression to mania: A record study over decades between 1920 and 1982. *Psychopathology, 18*, 140–154.
Bamrah, J. S., Freeman, H. L., & Goldberg, D. P. (1991). Epidemiology of schizophrenia in Salford, 1974–84: Changes in an urban community over ten years. *British Journal of Psychiatry, 159*, 802–810.
Barsky, A. J. (1988). The paradox of health. *New England Journal of Medicine, 318*, 414–418.
Baumeister, R. F., & Leary, M. R. (1995). The need to belong: Desire for interpersonal attachments as a fundamental human motivation. *Psychological Bulletin, 117*(3), 497–529.
Baumeister, R. F., & Tice, D. M. (1990). Anxiety and social exclusion. *Journal of Social & Clinical Psychology, 9*(2), 165–195.

Beck, A. T., Brown, G., Steer, R. A., & Eidelson, J. I. (1987). Differentiating anxiety and depression: A test of the cognitive content-specificity hypothesis. *Journal of Abnormal Psychology, 96*(3), 179–183.

Blanchard-Fields, F. (1998). The role of emotion in social cognition across the adult life span. In K. W. Schaie & M. P. Lawton (Eds.), *Annual review of gerontology and geriatrics: Vol. 17. Focus on emotion and adult development* (pp. 238–265). New York: Springer.

Bland, R. C., Newman, S. C., & Orn, H. (1988). Period prevalence of psychiatric disorders in Edmonton. *Acta Psychiatrica Scandinavica, 77*(Suppl. 338), 33–42.

Blazer, D. G., Kessler, R. C., McGonagle, K. A., & Swartz, M. S. (1994). The prevalence and distribution of major depression in a national community sample: The National Comorbidity Survey. *American Journal of Psychiatry, 151*(7), 979–986.

Boydell, J., Van Os, J., Lambri, M., Castle, D., Allardyce, J., McCreadie, R. G., & Murray, R. M. (2003). Incidence of schizophrenia in south-east London between 1965 and 1997. *British Journal of Psychiatry, 182*(1), 45–49.

Brown, J. S. (2002). *Environmental and chemical toxins and psychiatric illness* (1st ed.). Washington, DC: American Psychiatric Publishing.

Burke, K. C., Burke, J. D., Rae, D. S., & Regier, D. A. (1991). Comparing age at onset of major depression and other psychiatric disorders by birth cohorts in five US community populations. *Archives of General Psychiatry, 48*(9), 789–795.

Burke, K. C., Burke, J. D., Regier, D. A., & Rae, D. S. (1990). Age at onset of selected mental disorders in five community populations. *Archives of General Psychiatry, 47*(6), 511–518.

Canino, G. J., Bird, H. R., Shroute, P. E., Rubio-Stipec, M., Bravo, M., Martinez, R., et al. (1987). The prevalence of specific psychiatric disorders in Puerto Rico. *Archives of General Psychiatry, 44*, 727–735.

Carstensen, L. L., & Charles, S. T. (1998). Emotion in the second half of life. *Current Directions in Psychological Science, 7*(5), 144–149.

Carstensen, L. L., Fung, H. H., & Charles, S. T. (2003). Socioemotional selectivity theory and the regulation of emotion in the second half of life. *Motivation & Emotion, 27*(2), 103–123.

Carstensen, L. L., Isaacowitz, D. M., & Charles, S. T. (1999). Taking time seriously: A theory of socioemotional selectivity. *American Psychologist, 54*(3), 165–181.

Carstensen, L. L., Pasupathi, M., Mayr, U., & Nesselroade, J. R. (2000). Emotional experience in everyday life across the adult life span. *Journal of Personality & Social Psychology, 79*(4), 644–655.

Cavanagh, J. T. O., & Shajahan, P. M. (1999). Increasing rates of hospital admission for men with major mental illnesses: Data from Scottish mental health units, 1980–1995. *Acta Psychiatrica Scandinavica, 99*(5), 353–359.

Charles, S. T., Reynolds, C. A., & Gatz, M. (2001). Age-related differences and change in positive and negative affect over 23 years. *Journal of Personality and Social Psychology, 80*(1), 136–151.

Ciompi, L. (1985). Aging and schizophrenic psychosis. *Acta Psychiatrica Scandinavica, 71*, 93–105.

Clipp, E. C., & Elder, G. H. (1996). The aging veteran of World War II: Psychiatric and life course insights. In P. E. Ruskin & J. A. Talbott (Eds.), *Aging and posttraumatic stress disorder* (pp. 19–51). Washington, DC: American Psychological Association.

Cohen, C. I., Ramirez, P. M., Kehn, M., Magai, C., Eimicke, J., & Brenner, R. (2003). Assessing quality of life in older persons with schizophrenia. *American Journal of Geriatric Psychiatry. Special Issue: Schizophrenia in Late Life, 11*, 658–666.

Cornman, J. M., & Kingson, E. R. (1996). Trends, issues, perspectives, and values for the aging of the Baby Boom cohorts. *Gerontologist, 36*(1), 15–26.

Coryell, W., Endicott, J., & Keller, M. (1992). Major depression in a nonclinical sample. *Archives of General Psychiatry, 49*, 117–124.

Crosnoe, R., & Elder, G. H. (2002). Successful adaptation in the later years: A life course approach to aging. *Social Psychology Quarterly, 65*, 309–328.

Cross-National Collaborative Group. (1992). The changing rate of major depression: Cross-national comparisons. *The Journal of the American Medical Association, 268,* 3098–3105.

Diener, E., Suh, E. M., Lucas, R. E., & Smith, H. L. (1999). Subjective well-being: Three decades of progress. *Psychological Bulletin, 125*(2), 276–302.

Di Maggio, C., Martinez, M., Menard, J. F., Petit, M., & Thibaut, F. (2001). Evidence of a cohort effect for age at onset of schizophrenia. *American Journal of Psychiatry, 158*(3), 489–492.

Dooley, D., & Prause, J. (2004). *The social costs of underemployment.* New York: Cambridge.

Eagles, J. M., & Whalley, L. J. (1985). Decline in the diagnosis of schizophrenia among first admissions to Scottish mental hospitals from 1969–78. *British Journal of Psychiatry, 146,* 151–154.

Easterbrook, G. (2003). *The progress paradox: How life gets better while people feel worse* (1st ed.). New York: Random House.

Easterlin, R. A. (1987). *Birth and fortune: The impact of numbers on personal welfare* (2nd ed.). Chicago: University of Chicago Press.

Easterlin, R. A., & Crimmins, E. M. (1985). *The fertility revolution: A supply–demand analysis.* Chicago: University of Chicago Press.

Easterlin, R. A., Schaeffer, C. M., & Macunovich, D. J. (1993). Will the Baby Boomers be less well off than their parents? Income, wealth, and family circumstances over the life cycle in the United States. *Population and Development Review, 19,* 497–522.

Elder, G. H. (1993). *Children in time and place: Developmental and historical insights.* New York: Cambridge.

Elder, G. H. (1998). The life course as developmental theory. *Child Development, 69*(1), 1–12.

Fisher, J. E., Zeiss, A. M., & Carstensen, L. L. (2001). Psychopathology in the aged. In P. B. Sutker & H. E. Adams (Eds.), *Comprehensive handbook of psychopathology* (3rd ed., pp. 921–951). New York: Kluwer.

Folnegovic, Z., Folnegovic-Smalc, V., & Kulcar, Z. (1990). The incidence of schizophrenia in Croatia. *British Journal of Psychiatry, 156,* 363–365.

Fukuyama, F. (1999). *The great disruption.* New York: Free Press.

Furedi, F. (2002). *Culture of fear* (Rev. ed.). London: Continuum.

Gatz, M., & Hurwicz, M. (1990). Are old people more depressed? Cross-sectional data on Center for Epidemiological Studies Depression Scale factors. *Psychology & Aging, 5,* 284–290.

Gatz, M., Kasl-Godley, J. E., & Karel, M. J. (1996). Aging and mental disorders. In J. E. Birren & K. W. Schaie (Eds.), *Handbook of the psychology of aging* (4th ed., pp. 365–382). San Diego: Academic Press.

Gershon, E. S., Hamovit, J. H., Guroff, J. J., & Nurnberger, J. I. (1987). Birth-cohort changes in manic and depressive disorders in relatives of bipolar and schizoaffective patients. *Archives of General Psychiatry, 44*(4), 314–319.

Gfroerer, J., Penne, M., Pemberton, M., & Folsom, R. (2003). Substance abuse treatment need among older adults in 2020: The impact of the aging baby-boom cohort. *Drug and Alcohol Dependence, 69*(2), 127–135.

Giuffra, L. A., & Risch, N. (1994). Diminished recall and the cohort effect of major depression: A simulation study. *Psychological Medicine, 24*(2), 375–383.

Gottesman, I. I., & Shields, J. (1971). Schizophrenia: Geneticism and environmentalism. *Human Heredity, 21,* 517–522.

Grant, B. F., & Harford, T. C. (1994). Prevalence of DSM–IV alcohol abuse and dependence, United States, 1992. *Alcohol Health & Research World, 18*(3), 243–248.

Hagnell, O., Lanke, J., Rorsman, B., & Oejesjoe, L. (1982). Are we entering an age of melancholy? Depressive illnesses in a prospective epidemiological study over 25 years: The Lundby Study, Sweden. *Psychological Medicine, 12*(2), 279–289.

Hasin, D., Grant, B., Harford, T., Hilton, M., & Endicott, J. (1990). Multiple alcohol-related problems in the United States: On the rise? *Journal of Studies on Alcohol, 51*(6), 485–493.

Hasin, D., & Link, B. (1988). Age and recognition of depression: Implications for a cohort effect in major depression. *Psychological Medicine, 18*(3), 683–688.

Haynie, D. A., Berg, S., Johansson, B., Gatz, M., & Zarit, S. H. (2001). Symptoms of depression in the oldest old: A longitudinal study. *Journals of Gerontology, 56,* P111–P118.

Hedera, P., & Turner, R. S. (2002). Inherited dementias. *Neurologic Clinics, 20*(3), 779–808.

Heimberg, R. G., Stein, M. B., Hiripi, E., & Kessler, R. C. (2000). Trends in the prevalence of social phobia in the United States: A synthetic cohort analysis of changes over four decades. *European Psychiatry, 15*(1), 29–37.

Helzer, J. E., Burnam, A., & McEvoy, L. T. (1991). Alcohol abuse and dependence. In L. N. Robins & D. A. Regier (Eds.), *Psychiatric disorders in America: The Epidemiologic Catchment Area Study* (pp. 81–115). New York: The Free Press.

Herberg, W. (1955). *Protestant, Catholic, Jew.* Chicago: University of Chicago Press.

Herzog, A. R., & Markus, H. R. (1999). The self-concept in life span and aging research. In V. L. Bengtson & K. W. Schaie (Eds.), *Handbook of theories of aging* (pp. 227–252). New York: Springer.

Hilton, M. E. (1988). Trends in drinking problems and attitudes in the United States: 1979–1984. *British Journal of Addiction, 83,* 1421–1427.

Hoge, D. R., & Hoge, J. L. (1992). The return of the fifties? Value trends at the University of Michigan, 1952–1989. *Sociological Quarterly, 33*(4), 611–623.

Hough, R. L., Landsverk, J. A., Karno, M., Burnam, M. A., Timbers, D. M., Escobar, J. I., & Regier, D. A. (1987). Utilization of health and mental health services by Los Angeles Mexican Americans and non-Hispanic Whites. *Archives of General Psychiatry, 44*(8), 702–709.

Hybels, C. F., Blazer, D. G., & Pieper, C. F. (2001). Toward a threshold for subthreshold depression: An analysis of correlates of depression by severity of symptoms using data from an elderly community sample. *Gerontologist, 41,* 357–365.

Jorm, A. F., Korten, A. E., & Henderson, A. S. (1987). The prevalence of dementia: A quantitative integration of the literature. *Acta Psychiatrica Scandinavica, 76*(5), 465–479.

Joyce, P. R. (1987). Changing trends in first admissions and readmissions for mania and schizophrenia in New Zealand 1974–1984. *Australian and New Zealand Journal of Psychiatry, 21,* 82–86.

Karno, M., Hough, R. L., Burnam, M. A., Escobar, J. I., Timbers, D. M., Santana, F., & Boyd, J. H. (1987). Lifetime prevalence of specific psychiatric disorders among Mexican Americans and non-Hispanic Whites in Los Angeles. *Archives of General Psychiatry, 44,* 695–701.

Kawas, C., Gray, S., Brookmeyer, R., Fozard, J., & Zonderman, A. (2000). Age-specific incidence rates of Alzheimer's disease: The Baltimore longitudinal study of aging. *Neurology, 54*(11), 2072–2077.

Keister, L. A., & Deeb-Sossa, N. (2001). Are Baby Boomers richer than their parents? Intergenerational patterns of wealth ownership in the United States. *Journal of Marriage and the Family, 63*(2), 569–579.

Keith, S. J., Regier, D. A., & Rae, D. S. (1991). Schizophrenic disorders. In D. A. Regier & L. N. Robins (Eds.), *Psychiatric disorders in America: The Epidemiologic Catchment Area Study* (pp. 33–52). New York: Free Press.

Kemp, B. J., & Krause, J. S. (1999). Depression and life satisfaction among people ageing with post-polio and spinal cord injury. *Disability & Rehabilitation: An International Multidisciplinary Journal. Special Issue: Ageing and Disability, 21*(5–6), 241–249.

Kendell, R. E., Malcolm, D. E., & Adams, W. (1993). The problem of detecting changes in the incidence of schizophrenia. *British Journal of Psychiatry, 162,* 212–218.

Kendler, K. S., Kessler, R. C., Neale, M. C., Heath, A. C., & Eaves, L. J. (1993). The prediction of major depression in women: Toward an integrated etiologic model. *American Journal of Psychiatry, 150,* 1139–1148.

Kessing, L. V., Agerbo, E., & Mortensen, P. B. (2003). Does the impact of major stressful life events on the risk of developing depression change throughout life? *Psychological Medicine, 33*(7), 1177–1184.

Kessler, R. C., Berglund, P., Demler, O., Jin, R., Koretz, D., Merikangas, K. R., Rush, A. J., Walters, E. E., & Wang, P. S. (2003). The epidemiology of major depressive disorder: Results from the National Comorbidity Survey Replication (NCS–R). *Journal of the American Medical Association, 289*, 3095–3105.

Kessler, R. C., Berglund, P., Demler, O., Jin, R., Merikangas, K. R., & Walters, E. E. (2005). Lifetime prevalence and age-of-onset distributions of DSM–IV disorders in the National Comorbidity Survey Replication. *Archives of General Psychiatry, 62*, 593–602.

Kessler, R. C., McGonagle, K. A., Zhao, S., Nelson, C. B., Hughes, M., Eshleman, S., Wittchen, H. U., & Kendler, K. S. (1994). Lifetime and 12-month prevalence of DSM–III–R psychiatric disorders in the United States: Results from the National Comorbidity Study. *Archives of General Psychiatry, 51*, 8–19.

Keyes, C. L. M., & Ryff, C. D. (1999). Psychological well-being in midlife. In S. L. Willis & J. D. Reid (Eds.), *Life in the middle: Psychological and social development in middle age* (pp. 161–180). San Diego: Academic Press.

Klein, D. N., Lewinsohn, P. M., Rohde, P., Seeley, J. R., & Durbin, C. E. (2002). Clinical features of major depressive disorder in adolescents and their relatives: Impact on familial aggregation, implications for phenotype definition, and specificity of transmission. *Journal of Abnormal Psychology, 111*(1), 98–106.

Klerman, G. L. (1976). Age and clinical depression: Today's youth in the twenty-first century. *Journal of Gerontology, 31*, 318–323.

Klerman, G. L. (1993). The postwar generation and depression. In A. A. Ghadirian & H. E. Lehmann (Eds.), *Environment and psychopathology* (pp. 73–86). New York: Springer.

Klerman, G. L., Lavori, P. W., Rice, J., Reich, T., Endicott, J., Andreasen, N. C., Keller, M. B., & Hirschfield, R. M. (1985). Birth-cohort trends in rates of major depressive disorder among relatives of patients with affective disorder. *Archives of General Psychiatry, 42*, 689–693.

Klerman, G. L., & Weissman, M. M. (1989). Increasing rates of depression. *Journal of the American Medical Association, 261*, 2229–2234.

Kop, P. P. (1976). Age of marriage and divorce trends in Amsterdam during the period 1911–71. *Journal of Biosocial Science, 8*, 137–143.

Kreider, R. M., & Fields, J. M. (2002). *Number, timing, and duration of marriages and divorces: 1996*. U.S. Census Bureau [Electronic Version]. Retrieved November 2, 2003, from http://www.census.gov/prod/2002pubs/p70-80.pdf

Lachman, M. E., & Weaver, S. L. (1998). Sociodemographic variations in the sense of control by domain: Findings from the MacArthur studies of midlife. *Psychology & Aging, 13*, 553–562.

Lasch, K., Weissman, M., Wickramaratne, P., & Bruce, M. L. (1990). Birth-cohort changes in the rates of mania. *Psychiatry Research, 33*(1), 31–37.

Lavori, P. W., Klerman, G. L., Keller, M. B., Reich, T., Rice, J., & Endicott, J. (1987). Age–period–cohort analysis of secular trends in onset of major depression: Findings in siblings of patients with major affective disorder. *Journal of Psychiatric Research, 21*(1), 23–35.

Lawton, P. (1972). Schizophrenia forty-five years later. *Journal of Genetic Psychology, 121*, 133–143.

Lawton, M. P., Kleban, M. H., Rajagopal, D., & Dean, J. (1992). The dimensions of affective experience in three age groups. *Psychology and Aging, 7*, 171–184.

Lazarus, R. S. (1991). *Emotion and adaptation*. London: Oxford University Press.

Lazarus, R. S. (1995). Psychosocial factors play a role in health, but we have to tackle them with more sophisticated research and thought. *Advances, 11*, 14–18.

Lee, K. C., Kovak, Y. S., & Rhee, H. (1987). The national epidemiological study of mental disorders in Korea. *Journal of Korean Medical Science, 2*, 19–34.

Levenson, M. R., Aldwin, C. M., & Spiro, A. (1998). Age, cohort and period effects on alcohol consumption and problem drinking: Findings from the Normative Aging Study. *Journal of Studies on Alcohol, 59*(6), 712–722.

Levy, F. (1987). *Dollars and dreams: The changing American income distribution.* New York: Russell Sage Foundation.

Lewinsohn, P. M., Duncan, E. M., Stanton, A. K., & Hautzinger, M. (1986). Age at first onset for nonbipolar depression. *Journal of Abnormal Psychology, 95,* 378–383.

Lewinsohn, P. M., Rohde, P., Seeley, J. R., & Fischer, S. A. (1993). Age-cohort changes in the lifetime occurrence of depression and other mental disorders. *Journal of Abnormal Psychology, 102*(1), 110–120.

Light, P. C. (1988). *Baby Boomers* (1st ed.). New York: Norton.

Lopez, S. R. (2002). Mental health care for Latinos: A research agenda to improve the accessibility and quality of mental health care for Latinos. *Psychiatric Services, 53*(12), 1569–1573.

MacNeil, R. D. (2001). Bob Dylan and the Baby Boom generation: The times they are a-changin'—again. *Activities, Adaptation & Aging, 25*(3–4), 45–58.

Martin, R. L., Cloninger, C. R., Guze, S. B., & Clayton, P. J. (1985). Frequency and differential diagnosis of depressive syndromes in schizophrenia. *Journal of Clinical Psychiatry, 46*(11, Sect. 2), 9–13.

McGuffin, P., Rijsdijk, F., Andrew, M., Sham, P., Katz, R., & Cardno, A. (2003). The heritability of bipolar affective disorder and the genetic relationship to unipolar depression. *Archives of General Psychiatry, 60,* 497–502.

McIntosh, J. L. (1994). Generational analyses of suicide: Baby Boomers and 13ers. *Suicide & Life-Threatening Behavior, 24*(4), 334–342.

Molinari, V., Kunik, M. E., Snow-Turek, A. L., Deleon, H., & Williams, W. (1999). Age-related personality differences in inpatients with personality disorder: A cross-sectional study. *Journal of Clinical Geropsychology, 5*(3), 191–202.

Monroe, S. M., & Simons, A. D. (1991). Diathesis stress theories in the context of life stress research: Implication for depressive disorders. *Psychological Bulletin, 110*(3), 406–425.

Mortimer, J. A., & Graves, A. B. (1993). Education and other socioeconomic determinants of dementia and Alzheimer's disease. *Neurology, 43*(Suppl. 4), S39–S44.

Mroczek, D. K., & Kolarz, C. M. (1998). The effect of age on positive and negative affect: A developmental perspective on happiness. *Journal of Personality & Social Psychology, 75*(5), 1333–1349.

Mroczek, D. K., & Spiro, A. (2003, November). *Life satisfaction increases over 20 years: Findings from the Normative Aging Study.* Poster presented at the 56th Annual Scientific Meeting of the Gerontological Society of America, San Diego, CA.

Muller, T. E. (1997). The benevolent society: Value and lifestyle changes among middle-aged Baby Boomers. In L. R. Kahle & L. Chiagouris (Eds.), *Values, lifestyles, and psychographics* (pp. 299–316). Mahwah, NJ: Lawrence Erlbaum Associates.

Munk-Jorgensen, P., & Mortensen, P. B. (1992). Incidence and other aspects of the epidemiology of schizophrenia in Denmark, 1971–87. *British Journal of Psychiatry, 161,* 489–495.

Murphy, J. M., Laird, N. M., Monson, R. R., Sobol, A. M., & Leighton, A. H. (2000). A 40-year perspective on the prevalence of depression. *Archives of General Psychiatry, 57,* 209–215.

Murphy, J. M., Sobol, A. M., Neff, R. K., Olivier, D. C., & Leighton, A. H. (1984). Stability of prevalence, depression and anxiety disorders. *Archives of General Psychiatry, 41,* 990–997.

Offord, D. R., Boyle, M. H., Campbell, D., Goering, P., Lin, E., Wong, M., & Racine, Y. A. (1996). One-year prevalence of psychiatric disorder in Ontarians 15 to 64 years of age. *Canadian Journal of Psychiatry, 41,* 559–561.

Patterson, T. L., & Jeste, D. V. (1999). The potential impact of the baby-boom generation on substance abuse among elderly persons. *Psychiatric Services, 50*(9), 1184–1188.

Regier, D. A., Boyd, J. H., Burke, J. D., Rae, D. S., Myers, J. K., Kramer, M., et al. (1988). One-month prevalence of mental disorders in the United States: Based on five Epidemiologic Catchment Area sites. *Archives of General Psychiatry, 45,* 977–986.

Regier, D. A., Rae, D. S., Narrow, W. E., Kaelber, C. T., & Schatzberg, A. F. (1988). Prevalence of anxiety disorders and their comorbidity with mood and addictive disorders. *British Journal of Psychiatry. Special Issue: Recognition and Management of Anxiety Syndromes, 173*, 24–28.

Reich, J. W., Zautra, A. J., & Guarnaccia, C. A. (1989). Effects of disability and bereavement on the mental health and recovery of older adults. *Psychology & Aging, 4*(1), 57–65.

Reich, T., Cloninger, R., Van Eerdewegh, P., Rice, J. P., & Mullaney, J. (1988). Secular trends in the familial transmission of alcoholism. *Alcoholism: Clinical and Experimental Research, 12*, 458–464.

Rice, J. P., Moldin, S. O., & Neuman, R. (1991). Age, period, and cohort effects on rates of mental disorders. In M. T. Tsuang & K. S. Kendler (Eds.), *Genetic issues in psychosocial epidemiology: Vol. 8. Series in psychosocial epidemiology* (pp. 94–115). New Brunswick, NJ: Rutgers University Press.

Rice, J. P., Neuman, R. J., Saccone, N. L., Corbett, J., Rochberg, N., Hesselbrock, V., Hirschfeld, R. M., & Klerman, G. L. (2003). Age and birth cohort effects on rates of alcohol dependence. *Alcoholism: Clinical and Experimental Research, 27*(1), 93–99.

Rice, J., Reich, T., Andreasen, N. C., Endicott, J., Van Eerdewegh, M., Fishman, R., Hirschfeld, R. M., & Klerman, G. L. (1987). The familial transmission of bipolar illness. *Archives of General Psychiatry, 44*(5), 441–447.

Riggs, A., & Turner, B. S. (2000). Pie-eyed optimists: Baby Boomers the optimistic generation? *Social Indicators Research, 52*(1), 73–93.

Roberts, R. E., Kaplan, G. A., Shema, S. J., & Strawbridge, W. J. (1997). Prevalence and correlates of depression in an aging cohort: The Alameda County Study. *Journals of Gerontology: Series B. Psychological Sciences & Social Sciences, 52*, S252–S258.

Robins, L. N., Helzer, J. E., Weissman, M. M., Orvaschel, H., Gruenberg, E., & Burke, J. D. (1984). Lifetime prevalence of specific psychiatric disorders in three sites. *Archives of General Psychiatry, 41*, 949–958.

Robins, L. N., & Regier, D. A. (1991). *Psychiatric disorders in America: The Epidemiologic Catchment Area Study.* New York: Free Press.

Robinson, R. V., & Jackson, E. F. (2003). Is trust in others declining in America? An age–period–cohort analysis. *Social Science Research, 30*, 117–145.

Russell, C. (2001). *The Baby Boom: Americans aged 35–54.* Ithaca, NY: New Strategist Publications.

Salthouse, T. A. (2004). What and when of cognitive aging. *Current Directions in Psychological Science, 13*(4), 140–144.

Schor, J. (1992). *The overworked American: The unexpected decline of leisure.* New York: Basic Books.

Schor, J. (1998). *The overspent American: Upscaling, downshifting and the new consumer.* New York: Basic Books.

Sciolla, A., Patterson, T. L., Wetherell, J. L., McAdams, L. A., & Jeste, D. V. (2003). Functioning and well-being of middle-aged and older patients with schizophrenia: Measurement with the 36-item short-form (SF–36) health survey. *American Journal of Geriatric Psychiatry. Special Issue: Schizophrenia in Late Life, 11*, 629–637.

Seligman, M. E. P. (1990). Why is there so much depression today? The waxing of the individual and the waning of the commons. In R. E. Ingram (Ed.), *Contemporary psychological approaches to depression: Theory, research, and treatment* (pp. 1–9). New York: Plenum.

Silverstone, B. (1996). Older people of tomorrow: A psychosocial profile. *Gerontologist, 36*(1), 27–32.

Simon, G. E., Vonkorff, M., Ustun, B., Gater, R., Gureje, O., & Sartorius, N. (1995). Is the lifetime risk of depression actually increasing? *Journal of Clinical Epidemiology, 48*(9), 1109–1118.

Solano, N. H., & Whitbourne, S. K. (2001). Coping with schizophrenia: Patterns in later adulthood. *International Journal of Aging & Human Development, 53*(1), 1–10.

Stahl, S. M. (1990). *The legacy of longevity: Health and health care in later life.* Thousand Oaks, CA: Sage.

Stoll, A. L., Tohen, M., Baldessarini, R. J., Goodwin, D. C., Stein, S., Katz, S., Geenens, D., Swinson, R. P., Goethe, J. W., & McGlashan, T. (1993). Shifts in diagnostic frequencies of schizophrenia and major affective disorders at six North American psychiatric hospitals, 1972–1988. *American Journal of Psychiatry, 150*(11), 1668–1673.

Sturt, E., Kumakura, N., & Der, G. (1984). How depressing life is—Life-long morbidity risk for depressive disorder in the general population. *Journal of Affective Disorders, 7,* 109–122.

Suvisaari, J. M., Haukka, J. K., Tanskanen, A. J., & Lonnqvist, J. K. (1999). Decline in the incidence of schizophrenia in Finnish cohorts born from 1954 to 1965. *Archives of General Psychiatry, 56,* 733–740.

Tarter, R. E. (2000). Considerations of culture for understanding the neuropsychological sequelae of medical disorders. In E. Fletcher-Janzen & T. L. Strickland (Eds.), *Handbook of cross-cultural neuropsychology. Critical issues in neuropsychology* (pp. 205–213). Dordrecht, Netherlands: Kluwer.

Thompson, L. W., Gallagher-Thompson, D., Futterman, A., Gilewski, M. J., & Peterson, J. (1991). The effects of late-life spousal bereavement over a 30-month interval. *Psychology & Aging, 6,* 434–441.

Twenge, J. M. (2000). The age of anxiety? The birth cohort change in anxiety and neuroticism, 1952–1993. *Journal of Personality & Social Psychology, 79*(6), 1007–1021.

United States Department of Justice. (2003, April 14). *Bureau of Justice Statistics: Reported Crime in United States—Total.* Retrieved January 20, 2004, from http://bjsdata.ojp.usdoj.gov/dataonline/Search/Crime/State/statebystaterun.cfm?stateid=52

U.S. Department of Health and Human Services. (1999). *Mental Health: A Report of the Surgeon General—Executive Summary.* Rockville, MD: National Institutes of Health, National Institute of Mental Health. Retrieved June 21, 2003, from http://www.surgeongeneral.gov/library/mentalhealth/home.html

van Os, J., Fahy, T. A., Bebbington, P., Jones, P., Wilkins, S., Sham, P., Russell, A., Gilvarry, K., Lewis, S., & Toone, B. (1994). The influence of life events on the subsequent course of psychotic illness: A prospective follow-up of the Camberwell Collaborative Psychosis Study. *Psychological Medicine, 24*(2), 503–513.

van Os, J. V., & Sham, P. (2003). Gene–environment correlation and interaction in schizophrenia. In R. M. Murray & P. B. Jones (Eds.), *The epidemiology of schizophrenia* (pp. 235–253). New York: Cambridge University Press.

Wakshlag, J., Vial, V., & Tamborini, R. (1983). Selecting crime drama and apprehension about crime. *Human Communication Research, 10,* 227–242.

Weissman, M. M., Bruce, M. L., Leaf, P. J., Florio, L. P., & Holzer, C. I. (1991). Affective disorders. In L. N. Robins & D. A. Regier (Eds.), *Psychiatric disorders in America: The Epidemiologic Catchment Area Study* (pp. 53–80). New York: The Free Press.

Weissman, M. M., Gershon, E. S., Kidd, K. K., Prusoff, B. A., Leckman, J. F., Dibble, E., Hamovit, J., Thompson, W. D., Pauls, D. L., & Guroff, J. J. (1984). Psychiatric disorders in the relatives of probands with affective disorders. *Archives of General Psychiatry, 41,* 13–21.

Weissman, M. M., Leaf, P. J., Bruce, M. L., & Florio, L. (1988). The epidemiology of dysthymia in five communities: Rates, risks, comorbidity, and treatment. *American Journal of Psychiatry, 145*(7), 815–819.

Weissman, M. M., & Myers, J. K. (1978). Affective disorders in a US urban community: The use of research diagnostic criteria in an epidemiological survey. *Archives of General Psychiatry, 35,* 1304–1311.

Whitbourne, S. K. (2002). *The aging individual: Physical and psychological perspectives* (2nd ed.). New York: Springer.

Wickramaratne, P. J., Weissman, M. M., Leaf, P. L., & Holford, T. R. (1989). Age, period and cohort effects on the risk of major depression: Results from five United States communities. *Journal of Clinical Epidemiology, 42*(4), 333–343.

Wittchen, H. U., Knaeuper, B., & Kessler, R. C. (1994). Lifetime risk of depression. *British Journal of Psychiatry, 165*(Suppl. 26), 16–22.

Wrosch, C., Schulz, R., & Heckhausen, J. (2004). Health stresses and depressive symptomatology in the elderly: A control-process approach. *Current Directions in Psychological Science, 13*(1), 17–20.

Yesavage, J. A. (2002). Functioning and well-being of middle-aged and older patients with schizophrenia: Measurement with the 36-item short-form (SF–36) health survey. *Journal of Psychiatric Research, 36*, 281–286.

PART THREE

Psychosocial Issues

Identity Processes and the Transition to Midlife Among Baby Boomers

Kelly M. Jones
Susan Krauss Whitbourne
University of Massachusetts Amherst

Karyn M. Skultety
Stanford University and the Veterans Administration Palo Alto Healthcare

The aging process affects the individual across a broad range of physical, psychological, and social functions. Therefore, an understanding of individuals as they develop through the midlife period requires the integrative perspective provided by a biopsychosocial framework. The aging process presents a number of challenges to the midlife adult's sense of self, or identity. Although these challenges can be difficult, the Baby Boomers in particular may be more likely to struggle with the changes experienced as a result of the aging process. Baby Boomers must reckon with the fact that they have now become middle aged, and have therefore become like the parents they very likely rebelled against as part of the establishment of their own identity during their adolescent and early young adult years.

In this chapter, we begin by presenting Identity Process Theory (IPT), a model of identity development in adulthood based on Eriksonian and Piagetian theories. After outlining this theoretical approach, we examine the empirical evidence to support IPT as a framework for understanding the changes of midlife that confront the identities of Baby Boomers as they age.

MODELS OF IDENTITY AND DEVELOPMENT

Erikson's Theory

Erikson's (1963) theory forms an important backdrop for exploring the issue of identity in midlife. In Erikson's model, identity refers to the individual's sense of self over time. It is conceptualized as incorporating the domains of physical functioning, cognition, social relationships, and experiences in the world. According to Erikson, after the initial search for identity in adolescence, adults pass through three psychosocial crisis stages. Each psychosocial crisis is theorized to offer an opportunity for the development of a new function or facet of the ego. However, the crisis involving identity has special significance as it establishes the most important functions of the ego: self-definition and self-awareness.

The stages corresponding to the early and middle adult years focus on the establishment of close interpersonal relationships (intimacy vs. isolation), and the passing on to the future of one's creative products (generativity vs. stagnation). In the final stage (ego integrity vs. despair), the individual must resolve conflicted feelings about the past, adapt to the changes associated with the aging process, and come to grips with the inevitability of death. Erikson's ideas, although difficult to operationalize, have provided a major intellectual inspiration to workers in the field of personality development studying middle and later adulthood.

Marcia's Approach

A major step forward in testing Erikson's theory of identity development was the work of James Marcia (1966), who defined four *identity statuses*, or styles of resolving the identity versus identity diffusion psychosocial crisis of adolescence. Marcia provided the important insight that it was possible for an adolescent to achieve an identity without undergoing a period of evaluating alternatives. The identity statuses are defined along the dimensions of crisis and commitment. The crisis dimension refers to evaluation of alternatives; the commitment dimension characterizes the adolescent's strength or certainty of adhering to a particular choice. The four identity statuses represent the following combinations: identity achievement (+ crisis, + commitment), foreclosed (− crisis, + commitment), moratorium (in crisis, − commitment), and diffuse (+/− crisis, − commitment).

Although both diffuse and moratorium statuses share the criterion of being defined by a lack commitment, they can be distinguished from each other. The moratorium status is characterized by a high level of effort to arrive at commitments; individuals in the diffuse status do not attempt to commit to an identity. The distinction between the foreclosed and achieved statuses is that although both have arrived at a set of commitments, the foreclosed have done so without evaluating alternatives to decisions made prior to adolescence, often reflecting the wishes of parents. From the identity statuses the notion of foreclosure has become an important basis for examining the possibility that individuals can have a firm sense of identity without necessarily having examined alternative self-definitions.

The identity statuses were defined in the areas of occupation (career choice and college major) and ideology (religion and politics). Although a global identity status can be assigned, there are advantages to conceptualizing individuals as potentially having different identity statuses in different areas. The identity statuses thus occupy a unique position in personality development theory because, unlike typological approaches, they take into account variations within the individual rather than attempting to place individuals into global categories.

Identity Process Theory

The concepts introduced by Marcia led directly to the proposal that adults can approach issues relevant to identity along dimensions of crisis (exploration of alternatives) and commitment (solidity; Whitbourne, 1986). The identity statuses were first applied to the Baby Boomers when they were in college in the mid-1960s, when identities were challenged by new social orders and a questioning of traditional values. In middle adulthood, the members of the baby-boom generation face a new and equally compelling set of issues. However, Marcia's framework does not map directly onto midlife issues. Since the midlife period has a less discrete beginning and end point than does adolescence, it is difficult to pinpoint the period during which identity change would be expected to occur. Would middle aged adults who had questioned their identities when they were in college still be considered *identity achieved* even though this questioning took place thirty years ago? Would it not be stretching the definition of moratorium to apply this category to midlife adults still questioning their identities? The identity status framework, which requires there to be a period of expected questioning of commitments, therefore is not a viable one for understanding identity in midlife. Instead, a process approach is warranted. Identity Process Theory (IPT) draws from the identity status framework but moves away from the status approach to examining identity in terms of a more continuous set of processes.

According to IPT, identity is conceptualized as a biopsychosocial entity that encompasses the individual's self-representations and experiences encountered in the realms of physical, psychological, and social functioning. Examples of the self-schemas that compose identity might be physical (able to run up a flight of stairs), cognitive (able to remember people's names), and social (valued by others in the family). These self-representations are cognitive and affectively loaded based on previous experience and self-perceived competencies, values, and personality dispositions. The cognitive components of these schemas are the perceived characteristics that the individual possesses, most typically thought of as self-concept. The affective component of these schemas is the positive valence that psychologically healthy individuals tend to place on their self-assessment of their own qualities, most typically thought of in terms of self-esteem. To recognize unacceptable aspects of the self can be troubling and anxiety provoking.

IPT proposes that individual development in adulthood can be best understood according to the relative use of three identity processes: identity assimilation, identity accommodation, and identity balance. Although individuals rely on all three sets of processes, they do so to differing degrees. Before examining the empirical data to support IPT, we describe, based on theory, how individuals who use one process to a greater extent than the others would behave with regard to aging during the midlife years.

Identity Assimilation.   Identity assimilation refers to the interpretation of identity salient experiences in terms of previously established cognitive and affective schemas about the self. According to IPT, identity assimilation is a process that individuals use to maintain a sense of self-consistency even in the face of discrepant experiences or information about the self. When individuals use identity assimilation, they tend to minimize the impact of identity discrepant experiences. Such experiences would include, for example, the perception that one's physical abilities are failing or that cognitive functions are on the decline.

Because identity assimilation serves to protect the individual from potentially negative feedback about the self, it has some decided advantages from an affective perspective (Whitbourne, 1996). Individuals who rely on this process can feel healthy and remain optimistic and confident. However, there may be a cost to that emotional benefit. People who use assimilative processes to an excessive degree approach new experiences in a fixed and formulaic way and seek out information that is consistent with their current identity schemas. Moreover, the excessive use of this identity process when inappropriate can lead to social isolation as well as psychological and physical overexertion. For example, individuals who rely exclusively on using identity assimilation may harm themselves by continuing to participate in former activities that are no longer in their range of competence. Overuse of identity assimilation can also lead an individual to appear ridiculous. A line in the musical Sunset Boulevard sums this up well: "Nothing's wrong with being 50, as long as you're not acting 20!"

Identity Accommodation.   An individual using the process of identity accommodation adapts to new experiences and feedback from others by changing his or her thoughts and behaviors about the self. There is a positive component to this process in that the individual remains in touch with experiences, showing a sort of depressive realism. They can change as circumstances demand, and in terms of aging, are not subject to the risk of appearing as if they are holding on to their youth. However, there are decided disadvantages for individuals who rely heavily on identity accommodation as an approach to the aging process. There is the risk that they will overreact to small signs of aging and see themselves as old before this conclusion is justified, such as the first gray hair or a momentary memory lapse (humorously referred to as a senior moment). The problem is that they then become discouraged from exercising or using other forms of prevention and compensation. Another possibility is that they adopt the identity of an old person and become preoccupied with their own aging and health problems. These reactions to experiences may lead these individuals to feel hopeless; eventually discouraging them from taking what would otherwise be beneficial preventive and compensatory measures. On the other hand, they may become so panic-stricken at the prospects that time will bring that they seek unnecessary medical interventions or rely heavily on anti-aging supplements.

Ironically, people who primarily use identity accommodation in confronting age related changes may actually begin to show premature declines. Their fear of appearing or having become old may lead them to avoid situations and tasks in which they are otherwise capable of participating. Consequently, these individuals become anxious, insecure, and unpredictable. As they begin to view themselves in an unduly negative light, they can develop low self-esteem, self-doubt, and a need for outside approval. Because the excessive use of accommodation is also associated with being easily influenced by negative evaluations from others, the identities of these individuals lack internal consistency. They will accept negative evaluations from others more readily because these evaluations are consistent with their own inner confusion and fears about their level of competence.

Identity Balance. Individuals who use identity balance manage to maintain a stable sense of self while nevertheless adjusting their self-schemas to incorporate the consequences of the effects of aging on their bodies and minds. Based on the negative consequences associated with the overuse of either identity assimilation or accommodation, it follows that identity balance or the dynamic balance between the two processes has been found to be the optimal approach to aging (Whitbourne & Connolly, 1999). Individuals who use identity balance are in the best position to age successfully because they can adapt and integrate age-related changes while maintaining a relatively consistent self-concept. They are concerned primarily with acquiring accurate self-knowledge, thus enabling them to approach age-related changes realistically. For example balanced individuals who in the past were active in sports such as soccer, football, or wrestling may successfully seek sports with less contact such as swimming or golf, when they can no longer participate in contact sports. This adaptation permits individuals to continue to identify themselves as athletes without ignoring important physical limitations, such as the normal decrease in muscle tissue associated with the aging process (Whitbourne, 2005).

The realistic approach represented by the identity balanced individual in middle and later life can be extremely beneficial when used in relation to manageable situations; however, many age-related changes are out of the individual's control. Consequently, individuals who feel that self-control and efficacy are of great importance may become negatively affected or anxious when confronted by uncontrollable events (Diehl, 1999; Shapiro, Schwartz, & Astin, 1996), Nevertheless, it has been theorized that when balanced individuals cannot psychologically or physically adjust to biological, social, and psychological age-related changes on their own, they are most likely to seek out the appropriate medical or psychological interventions. For example, balanced individuals would be more likely to interpret having a heart attack as a reason to change their unhealthy habits than would be the case for individuals who predominately use identity assimilation (Whitbourne, Sneed, & Skultety, 2002).

Empirical Tests of IPT

Questionnaire measures of identity assimilation, accommodation, and balance have been developed to test empirically identity process theory. These questionnaires have been used to study identity processes in relation to self-esteem, physical changes, defense mechanisms, and memory controllability, as well as examining the relations among the identity processes themselves. Two questionnaires have been developed: the Identity and Experience Scale–General (IES–G), a 33-item scale assessing the relative use of each of the three identity processes, and the Identity Experience Scale–Specific Aging (IES–SA), a 21-item scale in which the three processes are applied to the physical changes that are most salient to the individual. Both questionnaires were initially derived from responses to the Adult Identity Interview, a semistructured instrument based on Marcia's identity status interview for college students. The Adult Identity Interview was used to evaluate crisis and commitment in adulthood in the areas of aging, work, family, and gender (Whitbourne, 1986).

Age, Cohort and Gender Considerations in IPT

The relationship between age and identity processes has been investigated in a number of studies on middle aged and older individuals. Although there is mixed support for predicted patterns involving identity accommodation and balance, there does seem to be an emerging pattern of results to support predictions involving identity assimilation. Some of the earliest research examining the differences between the two types of identity scales (i.e., the IES–SA and IES–G) found that with regard to adapting to specific age-related changes, midlife adults are more likely than older adults to use identity assimilation. On the other hand, midlife adults are the most likely to use identity accommodation when identity processes are examined with regard to general personality style rather than particular areas of change.

Sneed and Whitbourne (2001) examined identity processes in middle and later life and found that adults between the ages of 36 and 52 were more likely to use identity balance and less likely to use assimilation than individuals 53 and older. A more recent study also found that middle-aged individuals (ages 40–55) reported greater use of accommodation and less use of assimilation than did older adults (ages 56 to 91) (Skultety & Whitbourne, 2004). There were no significant differences between age groups on scores of identity balance. In other words, middle-aged individuals in these samples tended to accommodate or change as a result of age-related changes more often than was true for older adults.

In addition to age being a factor in the use of identity processes, it is likely that cohort also influences how individuals respond to the challenges to identity presented by the aging process. The Baby Boomers are reaching middle adulthood at a time in history when youth and beauty are revered more than ever. Furthermore, this generation has dominated the social and cultural landscape since their coming of age in the 1960s. Having defined social standards of the desirability of youth, it may be particularly hard for this generation to accept the fact that changes happen within their bodies due to forces outside their own control. On the other hand, current cohorts of middle-aged individuals, at least those with higher levels of education, have embraced the values of exercise and dietary control. Therefore, they may actually be less likely to experience the challenges to identity presented by changes observed among historically less fit older cohorts. Another observation emerging from these studies of identity processes is that different patterns exist for men and women (Skultety & Whitbourne, 2004). Women are more likely than men to use identity accommodation both in middle and late life to adapt to age related changes. Men and women have been found to be equally likely to use identity balance and assimilation; however, women tend to use identity assimilation more in later life whereas men appear to use identity assimilation both in middle and older age. Thus, the way in which individuals approach and respond to aging may differ based on gender, which we may assume is related to their adherence to gender roles. Further studies would benefit by examining specifically how gender role and gender interact to influence identity processes in midlife adults.

Self-Esteem, Self-Complexity, and IPT

Studies of IPT have focused on self-esteem as a correlate of the affective component of the identity processes. It is thought that identity and the changes made in identity over time are likely to affect an individual's self-esteem during the aging process. Self-esteem refers to an individual's global sense of overall worthiness or goodness. Broadly speaking, self-esteem can be conceptualized as incorporating objective and subjective components of the self as well as the processes that people engage in when they are interpreting experiences relevant to the self (Kunda, 1999). For the purposes of IPT, the focus is on the result of these self-relevant interpretations of experiences. There is also evidence that self-esteem is related to self-clarity. People who have a high self-esteem tend to have a clearer sense of self (Baumeister, 1998; Campbell & Lavallee, 1993). Baumgardner (1990) found that individuals with low self-esteem were less clear about their own sense of self but nevertheless able to understand the self-concepts of other people. It seems that individuals with low self-esteem may organize and integrate knowledge about themselves differently from knowledge about others.

What is the advantage of having a clear sense of self? Linville (1985, 1987) noted that college students with highly complex self-schemas (i.e. self-concepts that may include many distinct aspects) were better able to withstand the impact of stressful events. In other words, those individuals who were higher in self-complexity (i.e. had different and distinct aspects of the self) were less negatively affected by failure because these failures remained solely in the area in which the setback occurred. In contrast, failure had a more pervasively negative effect on young adults who lacked self-concept clarity. We can take these findings to suggest that for middle-aged and older adults whose sense of self is not clearly articulated, they would be more negatively affected by aging than people who have a highly complex identity. For example, an individual with a complex and well-defined sense of self may not make a connection between changes in mobility and decreases in cognitive functioning; however, people with low self-complexity and an unstable sense of self may interpret changes in appearance as the first of many signs that their overall youth is deteriorating.

The characterization of individuals with low self-esteem and low self-complexity as people who lack certainty, stability, confidence and coherence can be seen as applying to individuals using the identity process of accommodation. Individuals with high scores on accommodation are low in self-esteem. Middle-aged individuals as a group tend to use higher levels of accommodation and less assimilation compared to older adults. Sneed and Whitbourne (2001) found that individuals using the other two identity processes of assimilation and balance, i.e. individuals with a more coherent sense of self, had higher levels of self-esteem.

The relationship between identity assimilation and higher levels of self-esteem has been described as the *Identity Assimilation Effect* (IAE). This effect refers to the fact that middle aged and older adults are able to maintain normal functioning later in life by ignoring or at least minimizing age-related changes.

In a study of adults spanning young to later adulthood on reactions to specific age-related changes, identity assimilation was found to be used more by a middle-aged adults (individuals from 40 to 65 years of age) to maintain self-esteem in the specific domains of appearance and cognition (Whitbourne & Collins, 1998). The IAE is consistent with theories of the self that suggest accurate perception, to a certain degree, of the self and one's social environment is not essential for psychological health. Taylor and Brown (Taylor & Brown, 1988) argue that "positive illusions" that is, people's unrealistic optimism, positive self-views, and exaggerated perceptions of control can have beneficial and protective effects on an individual's self-esteem or self-concept. Thus, midlife individuals using some degree of assimilation or denial may combat negative stereotypes and changes associated with getting older. In addition, it also appears that the use of assimilation may be more beneficial for aging women than for men (Skultety & Whitbourne, 2004). As discussed earlier, given that women are more likely to engage in accommodation, and the fact that women face a number of negative societal stereotypes, the use of assimilation may be particularly powerful in protecting women's self-esteem as they move through middle and later adulthood.

Older adults tend to use identity assimilation more than do middle-aged adults. Perhaps middle-aged individuals, transitioning into late adulthood, use less assimilation and more accommodation, but later in life overcompensate with the extreme use of assimilation. Another possibility is that the IAE is a product of cohort effects. For example older adults may be more inclined to use denial when confronted by negative age-related changes than middle-aged individuals, perhaps as result of growing up in the generation accepting hardship. In comparison, Baby Boomers may be more likely to vocalize their complaints and issues with old age since they grew up in a time where speaking out against injustices was more accepted; thus future research should employ cohort sequential designs to investigate this possible cohort effect.

MIDLIFE CHANGES AND IDENTITY

In the process of developing and testing the identity process scales, ideas have emerged about the nature of identity among the Baby Boomers and how they are coping with the changes involved in the aging process during midlife. Below, we discuss some of the challenges of midlife that may be most difficult for the Baby Boomers and then address how identity may be changed or maintained as these changes occur. Specifically, we address psychological changes in the form of aging self-stereotypes, physical changes of aging, cognitive changes and how these changes relate to the identity process model.

Psychological Changes: Aging Self-Stereotypes and Identity

Aging stereotypes are thought to originate in early childhood and be maintained and reinforced throughout adulthood until they are transformed into aging self-stereotypes. Levy and colleagues (2000) define aging self-stereotypes as "older individuals' internalized beliefs about elderly people" (p. 205).

Aging self-stereotypes are theorized to be acquired by older individuals through a two stage process. In the first stage, individuals reach an age that is defined as old, either formally by an institution or informally by other individuals. For example, upon entering their 40s and 50s, individuals may begin to accept their own self-stereotypes because they are now eligible for benefits based on age (i.e. AARP) or because their friends start to define them as old. Being given a fortieth birthday card with an "over-the-hill" theme may provide a signal that, at least in the eyes of friends, decrements are likely to begin to occur soon. In this stage, the aging self-stereotype is imposed on people because they are being recategorized by others into this age-defined group. However, people may not perceive themselves as getting older simply because others do. It is only in the second stage of developing aging self-stereotypes that individuals begin to internalize their identities as "aging."

Levy (2003) suggests that aging self-stereotypes are reinforced because cognitive resources are limited and therefore individuals continue to rely on stereotypes to increase efficient and fast processing when interpreting new or overwhelming amounts of information. As the Baby Boomers deal with changes in their physical and cognitive functioning, they may be faced with confronting their own aging self-stereotypes.

Although aging self-stereotypes have not been studied in terms of identity processes, it would seem reasonable to propose that individual differences in the acceptance of aging self-stereotypes would vary according to the predominant identity process that the individual uses. IPT would predict that individuals who rely heavily on identity accommodation would be most vulnerable to aging self-stereotypes because they are so easily influenced by the views of others, including the stereotypical beliefs about aging held by the population in general. For example, an individual who tends to use identity accommodation might apply an aging stereotype that older workers are less productive than younger workers when making a small mistake on the job or forgetting to complete a workload assignment. Such individuals may more readily start to see themselves as old even when there is very little objective data to support such a conclusion. Although it had been observed that, in general, individuals are more likely to use identity accommodation, stereotypes associated with midlife may have a particularly pronounced impact on individuals whose predominant identity process has been accommodation.

Conversely, individuals in midlife who tend to use identity assimilation would be less likely to incorporate into their sense of self the negative stereotypes about aging. They may be able to defend their youthful identities by differentiating themselves from their age peers by seeing their peers as old but themselves as young. People who use identity assimilation to an extreme may tend to ignore their aging self-stereotypes through the process of denial; however, unless they are extremely lucky in terms of their health and general functioning, they will eventually be forced to confront their own aging. Such a process may result in a particularly devastating coming to terms with reality that, ironically, can be more harmful then the early adoption of negative self-stereotypes by individuals who use identity accommodation.

By contrast, balanced individuals are aware of negative self-stereotypes but would seem more likely to avoid incorporating these negative self-beliefs into their identities. This ability to resist negative self-stereotyping may reflect a stronger sense of self, built up over a lifetime of flexibly adapting to change. Incorporating into their identities the view of themselves as middle-aged or aging would not, therefore, have a devastating impact.

Physical Changes

Changes in appearance and mobility are the first changes that adults tend to notice, perhaps even early in adulthood when muscle strength first starts to show an impact of the aging process. Furthermore, an individual's outside appearance serves as a social cue of age, leading many people in this society to be sensitive to even small age-related changes. Changes in bodily systems that contribute to appearance may also have more significance in terms of general health and susceptibility to illness. For example, increases in body fat in the middle years have ramifications for health and disease as well as for appearance. Alterations in the structures that contribute to mobility may also lead to more general problems for the individual, such as the weakening of bones that may contribute to a heightened risk of falling or development of postural changes. Baby Boomers are also more likely to complain about changes in vision, even though vision losses are far more prevalent in adults 65 and older (Whitbourne & Collins, 1998).

The effect of social context on the individual's aging during the years of middle adulthood is particularly salient in the discussion of appearance. Individuals in Western society face social rejection and discrimination when their appearance starts to change in middle age. In a society where age rather than youth is considered beautiful, people would aspire to look older than their years. They would not consider dyeing their hair, and they would try to accentuate rather than cover up the bags and sags that develop around their face. Unfortuantely, in Western society, people (especially women) find the aging of appearance to represent a significant threat to their positive feelings about themselves as well as potentially their opportunities for employment.

Their sensitivity to becoming like their parents may lead Baby Boomers in general to be more sensitive than previous cohorts were to negative cultural stereotypes of old age. Research based on IPT using the Identity and Experiences Scale has demonstrated that Baby Boomers are in fact concerned about age-related changes at a younger age than would be expected on the basis of what is known about the aging process. Compared to their elders, the Baby Boomers are more likely to complain about the effects of aging on such features of appearance as gray hair, wrinkling, and body fat (Whitbourne & Collins, 1998). Beginning in their 40s, they express concerns about their physical functioning in general, and by the 50s their concerns include loss of muscle strength, loss of mobility, joint pain, shortness of breath, and inability to carry out physical activities.

Individuals using identity accommodation in particular are more likely to ruminate excessively about these changes and become more self-conscious about the effects of aging on physical appearance and health. They may be expected to regard with fear and despair decreases in health, appearance, and physical abilities earlier in life than would otherwise be expected (Hooker & Kaus, 1994). By contrast, individuals who rely on identity assimilation as their predominant identity process would be far less likely to express outward concern about the impact of aging on their bodies even though, underneath their armor of defensiveness, they are inwardly frightened by the prospects that await them as they age. Tragically, they may also be the people who are likely to die of a heart attack by overexerting themselves on a task which their bodies are ill prepared to handle.

Cognitive Changes

Cognitive changes in midlife for the Baby Boomers are occurring against a social backdrop in the 2000s of heightened concern, if not nearly paranoia, about the prevalence of disabling cognitive disorders such as Alzheimer's disease. With the media constantly presenting inflated estimates of the prevalence of this and other forms of dementia, it is no wonder that midlife adults express concern about the impact of aging on cognition far before, statistically speaking, any change could be detected (Whitbourne & Collins, 1998).

Accurate estimates of the prevalence of Alzheimer's disease place the number afflicted at 2 to 2.5 million in the United States, which is approximately 5 to 7% of the overall population (Brookmeyer & Kawas, 1998; Hy & Keller, 2000). These percentages vary by age group with figures of 1% for ages 65 to 74, 7% for ages 75 to 84, and 25% for those 85 or older. Clearly, individuals between the ages of 40 to 64 are not at great risk for suffering from the disease. However, as the popularity of the term senior moment indicates, Baby Boomers are vigilant for changes in their cognitive functioning far earlier than would be warranted.

Ironically, memory loss may in fact be related to the tendency of individuals to approach their own memory functioning in midlife with undue pessimism. Those who hold negative stereotypes concerning self-efficacy and ability to control memory in later life may be particularly ill-equipped to handle the changes in cognition that do occur in middle to later adulthood. There is evidence to suggest that that negative stereotypes surrounding the cognitive capabilities of older adults have been found to contribute to memory loss in old age perhaps through decreases in self-efficacy and motivation (Levy, 1996). The perceptions by Baby Boomers of who they are and what they can do may be threatened by long held stereotypical beliefs about what it means to be old, particularly in terms of cognitive functioning.

As we have seen elsewhere, those who use identity accommodation are particularly at risk for such consequences. The conclusions they generate about their memory may place them at risk for further declines. According to Bandura (1989), individuals who regard memory as an innate ability that declines due to genetic programming will have little reason to challenge this belief and thus will not attempt to improve their memory functioning. This may lead individuals with low memory self-efficacy to underutilize their actual cognitive abilities and even prevent them from using exercises and techniques that could improve their memory skills. Therefore it could be harmful for middle aged individuals using identity accommodation to develop low memory self-efficacy. These individuals will most likely stop using preventive and compensatory strategies when faced with normal aging changes such as cognitive slowing or decreases in working memory.

Stereotype Threat

Steele's (1997) theory of *stereotype threat* and the notion of the disidentification that follows may explain why and how individuals might develop negative aging self-stereotypes. Stereotype threat refers to the tendency for people to perform more poorly on a task when a relevant stereotype or stigmatized social identity is made more salient. According to Steele's theory of stereotype threat, situational influences increase the likelihood of being stereotyped, which may trigger an internalized weak sense of self-efficacy within the individual. In other words, how threatening the stereotype becomes depends on the person's identification with the stereotype-relevant domain. Some individuals, in response to stereotype threat about memory, disidentify or reconceptualize their identities as cognitively skilled individuals as a way to prevent the domain from negatively affecting their self-images. Therefore, these individuals may no longer care or desire to improve their memory functioning, which once again may lead to decreases in actual cognitive performance. Although disidentification attempts serve an adaptive and protective function of self-esteem and identity, the consequences may be damaging and maladaptive.

Incorporating the notion of stereotype threat to conceptualizations of self-efficacy and identity adds an important dimension to our understanding of the transition of the Baby Boomers from midlife to later adulthood. We can learn important principles of development as well as gain specific understanding of this cohort's experience by investigating the ways in which stereotypes become incorporated into the individual's sense of self and ultimately into behavior.

SUMMARY

Early views of midlife in the field of adult development characterized the years of 30 to 65 as a period of quiescence and stability. The themes of midlife were acceptance and, with increasing age, preparation for the years of retirement and grandparenthood. However, with the entry of the Baby Boomers into the midlife period, these notions of middle age are changing rapidly. Midlife adults are portrayed throughout the media as active, youth-oriented, and in search of changes and challenges. Not every middle aged Baby Boomer, to be sure, shows an unwillingness to grow up compared to the parent generation of the Baby Boomers, yet consumer behavior echoes the media stereotypes. The Baby Boomers who can afford luxuries are embracing Botox, anti-aging facial treatments, plastic surgery, and youth-oriented designer clothing and accessories.

Although the notion of the midlife crisis popularized in the late 1970s was clearly an exaggeration not consistent with data, the Baby Boomers reaching midlife at the turn of the century have reacted to the prospect of growing older with a refusal to "go gently into that good night." As we have seen in this chapter, there is an overall tendency for the Baby Boomers at midlife to use the identity process of accommodation in which small age-related changes and experiences are exaggerated. However, not all Baby Boomers take this potentially maladaptive approach and, indeed, those who use identity assimilation may place themselves at an equal risk for future problems. The flexible use of identity balance, in which individuals acknowledge the fact that they are aging without becoming panic-stricken, is clearly the optimal strategy.

Twenty years ago, we might have predicted that societal values would track the baby-boom generation as they reached midlife with the effect that the accoutrements of age would in fact be regarded as acceptable, if not stylish. To a certain extent, media figures such as Harrison Ford and Meg Ryan, for example, have helped to bolster the view that a person can be middle-aged and attractive, if not downright sexy. However, for every middle-aged media role model, there are probably at least three or four budding celebrities who are barely out of their teens, and the numbers do not seem to be dwindling. The Baby Boomers, having contributed to the culture of youth when they were in their 20s, now find themselves ironically in the position of being the victims of their own youth-oriented values.

As we have pointed out repeatedly in this chapter, not every middle-aged person becomes obsessed with aging or despondent at the thought of what will happen to their aging bodies and minds. Furthermore, those who steadfastly refuse to admit to the fact that they are growing older may run quite a different risk, as they fail to take advantage of the preventative and compensatory strategies that can in fact preserve their functioning.

With increasing research on adults in the midlife years, we can hope that the variations in approaches to the aging process will continue to be a focus of investigation. It is unfortunate when an entire cohort is given a label, as indeed has happened to the Baby Boomers, because the notion becomes lodged in public consciousness that everyone of a certain age can be considered to share a given psychological characteristic. In this chapter, we set forth a model that we believe has great heuristic value. It may help us understand the variations among this large and fascinating cohort and the ways they approach developmental challenges in the middle years.

REFERENCES

Bandura, A. (1989). Regulation of cognitive processes through perceived self-efficacy. *Development Psychology, 25*, 729–735.

Baumeister, R. F. (1998). The self. In D. T. Gilbert, S. T. Fiske, & G. Lindzey (Eds.), *Handbook of social psychology* (4th ed., Vol. 1, pp. 680–740). New York: McGraw-Hill.

Baumgardner, A. H. (1990). To know oneself is to like oneself: Self-certainty and self-affect. *Journal of Personality and Social Psychology, 58*, 1062–1072.

Brookmeyer, R., & Kawas, C. (1998). Projections of Alzheimer's disease in the United States and the public health impact of delaying disease onset. *American Journal of Public Health, 88*, 1337–1342.

Campbell, J. D., & Lavallee, L. F. (1993). Who am I? The role of self-concept confusion in understanding the behavior of people with low self-esteem. In R. F. Baumeister (Ed.), *Self-esteem: The puzzle of low self-regard* (pp. 3–20). New York: Plenum.

Diehl, M. (1999). Self-development in adulthood and aging: The role of critical life events. In C. D. Ryff & V. W. Marshall (Eds.), *The self and society in aging processes* (pp. 150–183). New York: Springer.

Erikson, E. H. (1963). *Childhood and society* (2nd ed.). New York: Norton.

Hooker, K., & Kaus, C. R. (1994). Health-related possible selves in young and middle adulthood. *Psychology and Aging, 9*, 126–133.

Hy, L. X., & Keller, D. M. (2000). Prevalence of AD among whites: A summary by levels of severity. *Neurology, 55*, 198–204.

Kunda, Z. (1999). *Social cognition: Making sense of people*. Cambridge: Bradford.

Levy, B. (1996). Improving memory in old age through implicit self-stereotyping. *Journal of Personality and Social Psychology, 71*, 1092–1107.

Levy, B. R. (2003). Mind matters: Cognitive and physical effects of aging self-stereotypes. *Journal of Gerontology Series B: Psychological and Social Sciences, 58,* P203–111.

Levy, B. R., Hausdorff, J., Hencke, R., & Wei, J. Y. (2000). Reducing cardiovascular stress with positive self-stereotypes of aging. *Journal of Gerontology: Psychological Sciences, 55B,* P205–213.

Linville, P. W. (1985). Self-complexity and affective extremity: Don't put all your eggs in one cognitive basket. *Social Cognition, 3,* 94–120.

Linville, P. W. (1987). Self-complexity as a cognitive buffer against stress-related illness and depression. *Journal of Personality and Social Psychology, 52,* 663–676.

Marcia, J. E. (1966). Development and validation of ego-identity status. *Journal of Personality and Social Psychology, 3,* 551–558.

Shapiro, D. H., Schwartz, C. E., & Astin, J. A. (1996). Controlling ourselves, controlling our world: Psychology's role in understanding positive and negative consequences of seeking and gaining control. *American Psychologist, 51,* 1213–1230.

Skultety, K., & Whitbourne, S. K. (2004). Gender differences in identity processes. *Journal of Women and Aging, 16,* 175–188.

Sneed, J. R., & Whitbourne, S. K. (2001). Identity processing styles and the need for self-esteem in middle-aged and older adults. *International Journal of Aging & Human Development, 52,* 311–321.

Steele, C. M. (1997). A threat in the air: How stereotypes shape intellectual identity and performance. *American Psychologist, 52,* 613–629.

Taylor, S. E., & Brown, J. D. (1988). Illusion and well-being: A social psychological perspective on mental health. *Psychological Bulletin, 103,* 193–210.

Whitbourne, S. K. (1986). *The me I know: A study of adult identity.* New York: Springer-Verlag.

Whitbourne, S. K. (1996). Psychosocial perspectives on emotions: The role of identity in the aging process. In C. Magai & S. H. McFadden (Eds.), *Handbook of emotion, adult development, and aging* (pp. 83–98). San Diego, CA: Academic Press.

Whitbourne, S. K. (2005). *Adult development and aging: Biopsychosocial perspectives* (2nd ed.). New York: Wiley.

Whitbourne, S. K., & Collins, K. C. (1998). Identity and physical changes in later adulthood: Theoretical and clinical implications. *Psychotherapy, 35,* 519–530.

Whitbourne, S. K., & Connolly, L. A. (1999). The developing self in midlife. In S. L. Willis & J. D. Reid (Eds.), *Life in the middle: Psychological and social development in middle age* (pp. 25–45). San Diego, CA: Academic Press.

Whitbourne, S. K., Sneed, J. R., & Skultety, K. M. (2002). Identity processes in adulthood: Theoretical and methodological challenges. *Identity, 2,* 29–45.

CHAPTER SEVEN

Daily Life Stressors of Early and Late Baby Boomers

David M. Almeida
Pennsylvania State University

Joyce Serido
Cornell University

Daniel McDonald
University of Arizona

The landscape of the baby-boom generation has typically been viewed through a wide-angle lens of sociodemographic shifts in the workplace and family roles. Indeed, as other chapters in this volume will attest, the Baby Boom differs from other generations in their educational attainment, workplace opportunities, and timing as well as the size of families. Although such descriptive information is helpful in defining this generation, we believe that much can be learned by taking a more close-up portrait of Baby Boomers themselves. There are three major aims of this chapter. First, we provide a detailed look at the daily experiences of Baby Boomers. In particular we are interested in the frequency and types of daily stressors Baby Boomers face and the meaning Boomers ascribe to such stressors. Second, we explore possible differences among the Baby Boomers based on when they were born. We contend that historical factors may have influenced the sociodemographic profile of individuals born early in the Baby Boom differently than individuals born later. In this chapter we consider how birth year (i.e., early vs. late entry year into the Baby Boom) may translate into potential historic effects (i.e., educational opportunities) and family life-course differences (i.e., having young children in the home). Third, we assess how such sociodemographic differences within the Baby Boom are associated with exposure and reactivity to daily stressors.

DAILY STRESS AMONG BABY BOOMERS

The first aim of this chapter focuses primarily on the daily stressors that Baby Boomers encounter. The distinctiveness of the Baby Boomers has typically been based on the experience and timing of major life events such as marriage, birth of a child, retirement, and death of a family member. Although studying life events is critical to charting major transitions in life, we believe that daily stressors tap into those more frequent experiences that often go unrecognized by researchers, but are still meaningful to individuals. Daily stressors are defined as minor events arising out of day-to-day living, such as the everyday concerns of work, caring for others, and commuting between work and home. They may also refer to small, more unexpected events that disrupt daily life, little life events such as arguments with children, unexpected work deadlines, and malfunctioning computers. Daily stressors may be less severe than life events; they nevertheless serve as personally significant and distinct events that represent attention-getting experiences in the ongoing lives of people.

In terms of their physiological and psychological effects, reports of life events may be associated with prolonged arousal whereas reports of daily hassles may be associated with spikes in arousal or psychological distress that day. In addition, minor daily stressors exert their influence not only by having separate and immediate direct effects on emotional and physical functioning, but also by piling up over a series of days to create persistent irritations, frustrations, and overloads that may result in more serious stress reactions such as anxiety and depression. Indeed, an emerging literature has shown that daily stressors, such as spousal conflicts, home overloads, and work deadlines play an important part in health and emotional adjustment (Almeida & Kessler, 1998; Larsen & Kasimatis, 1991; Lazarus & DeLongis, 1983; Lazarus & Folkman, 1984; Mallers, Almeida, & Neupert, 2005; Stone, 1992).

Little is known, however, about the meaning and nature of day-to-day stressors among Baby Boomers. One way to better understand the significance that daily stressors play in the lives of individuals is to explore the characteristics that make stressors unique—to take a detailed look at the types and dimensions of stressors that people experience. In this chapter, we consider the nature of daily stressors from two perspectives. First, we assess specific characteristics of stressors using an investigator-based approach (e.g., Brown & Harris, 1978; Wethington, Almeida, Brown, Frank, & Kessler, 2001). Independent coders analyzed open-ended descriptions of daily stressors provided by the respondents who identified several characteristics of stressors, including type of stressor (e.g., arguments, overloads) and focus (i.e., who was involved in the stressor). Second, the appraised meaning of stressors was assessed through respondents' descriptions and subjective ratings of severity of stressors and what was at stake for them as a result of daily stressors. We believe the combination of investigator-rated characteristics and respondents' subjective meaning provides a more robust account of the daily stressors experienced by individuals in the Baby Boom.

Heterogeneity Within the Baby-Boom Generation

The second aim of this chapter is to explore if the stressors experienced by individuals depends, to a certain extent, on when they entered the boomer generation. Although there is some agreement that the baby-boom generation refers to individuals born between 1946 and 1964, there may be substantial heterogeneity within this generation based, at least in part, on when Boomers were born (Alwin, 1999). There are many different ways to group Baby Boomers. For example, Easterlin and colleagues (1990) identify four categories of Baby Boomers based on five-year intervals by birth year (i.e., 1945–1949; 1950–1954; 1955–1959; 1960–1964). For his analyses, Eggebeen (see chap. 1, this volume) selects three groups from the baby-boom generation (i.e., leading edge, 1947–1949; intermediate, 1953–1955; and trailing edge, 1960–1962). In this chapter, we categorize Baby Boomers into two groups: early Baby Boomers, those born between 1946 and 1954, and late Baby Boomers as those born between 1955 and 1964. The early Boomers entered adulthood during a time of unprecedented economic growth and prosperity, when the torch was passed to a new generation, engulfed in tumultuous change marked by war, assassinations, and civil unrest. In contrast, the later Boomers were welcomed into adulthood by recessions, gas shortages, high unemployment, and a nation recovering from defeat.

Historic Effects

We contend that significant historic changes associated with birth year would have altered the life course of Boomers in distinct ways. The first and foremost historic event involved the war in Vietnam and how the reenactment of the selective service system influenced attendance in higher education. Draft for the Vietnam War was at its height in the late 1960s and early 1970s and so too was draft evasion. The avoidance of Selective Service contributed to the rise in college enrollment for males in the 1960s and was the main factor explaining the spike in college enrollment and completion among men born between 1945 and 1950 (Card & Lemieux, 2001). Throughout the 1960s, early male Baby Boomers entered college in record numbers, resulting in a corresponding increase in conferred degrees. In past military conflicts, such as World War II and Korea, men returning to civilian life took advantage of the GI Bill, but that trend was not as evident for Vietnam era veterans (Heale, 2001). Although the overall number of college students remained high in the 1970s, the trend to attend college tapered off and the actual number of bachelor's degrees conferred dropped in comparison to the pool of college-aged young people. At the same time, the number of women enrolling in college and obtaining degrees increased substantially, so that by the late 1980s a higher proportion of bachelor's degrees were bestowed on women as compared to men (Snyder, 1993). Later in this chapter we will assess differences in educational and employment opportunities between early and late Baby Boomers and whether these differences translate into differences in daily stress processes.

Another historic factor we contend may have altered the life course differently for early and late Baby Boomers is the economic situation they encountered as they transitioned from adolescence to adulthood and entered the workforce. One indicator of particular note is the unemployment rate. The unemployment rate hovered around 4% during the latter part of the 1960s when early Boomers were starting their careers. Gradually, the unemployment rate increased to 6% as the decade of the 70s commenced, climbing to 9% by the mid-70s. By the early 80s, when trailing edge Boomers were entering the labor market, the unemployment rate climbed precipitously to a high of 11% (Snyder, 1993).

It is clear that numerous events and trends occurring throughout the lives of both early and late boomers might have presented quite different life experiences depending on one's exposure to those events and the salience they held. As Elder and Rockwell (1979) have shown in their research on two cohorts of men born during the Depression era, historic and economic experiences can significantly influence future life experiences and alter the trajectory of the timing and decisions made throughout the life course.

Timing in the Life cycle

Our portrait of daily life among Baby Boomers is framed not only by historic features of their birth cohort but also by their placement in the life cycle. Currently Baby Boomers are at midlife. This life stage may be a time of change in stressful experiences due to role changes in the family and work domains (Sales, 1978). These role changes may be precipitated by one's grown children leaving home (Lowenthal & Chiriboga, 1972), career transitions, such as reentry into the occupational domain, or declining career opportunities (Ackerman, 1990; Etaugh, 1993), and renegotiating of family relationships (Blatter & Jacobsen, 1993; Rollins, 1989). In addition, Lachman and James (1997) point out that "being in the middle" often entails expanding and managing multiple responsibilities, such as caretaking for one's aging parents and children. During midlife individuals are entering and exiting such roles and such role transitions may also contribute to the frequency and types of daily stressors Baby Boomers experience.

Exposure and Reactivity to Daily Stressors

The final aim of this paper is to assess differences in exposure and reactivity to daily stressors among early and late Baby Boomers. *Stressor Exposure* is the likelihood that an individual will experience a daily stressor. Although some daily stressors do occur randomly (Wheaton, 1999), experiencing most stressors is not simply a matter of chance or bad luck (Kendler, Neale, Kessler, Heath, & Eaves, 1993). In this paper we assess if sociodemographic characteristics play a role in the types of stressors individuals experience as well as how they appraise these stressors. Differential exposure corresponds to a mediational model in path-analytic terms. *Stressor Reactivity* is the likelihood that an individual will show emotional or physical reactions to daily stressors (Bolger & Zuckerman, 1995). Reactivity represents the degree to which similar stressors evoke different emotional and physical reactions. Thus, stressor reactivity is not defined as well-being, but is operationalized as the within-person slope between stressors and well-being over time. Reactivity, therefore, is a dynamic process that links stressors and well-being over time. Differences in reactivity depend on the resources of individuals and their environments (e.g., education, income, children in the household) that limit or enhance the possibilities and choices for coping with daily experiences (Lazarus, 1999). Being an early or late Baby Boomer may be related to allocation of such resources. In this paper we assess if sociodemographic characteristics associated with birth year modify how daily stressors affect daily well-being.

THE NATIONAL STUDY OF DAILY EXPERIENCES

A recent project called the National Study of Daily Experiences (NSDE) seeks to investigate the sources of exposure and reactivity to daily stressors. The NSDE is a telephone diary study of a U.S. national sample of 1,483 adults ranging in age from 25 to 74 years. Interviews occurred over 8 consecutive nights resulting in 11,578 days of information.

For the present analyses, only those respondents who were born between 1946 and 1964 (herein referred to as the baby-boom subsample) are included. This resulted in a total of 475 respondents, who were further divided into 237 early Baby Boomers (those born between 1946 and 1954) and 238 late Baby Boomers (those born between 1955 and 1964). The NSDE subsample and the MIDUS sample from which it was drawn had similar distributions across demographic characteristics.

Daily Stressors

The content and appraisal of daily stressors were assessed through a semi-structured Daily Inventory of Stressful Events (DISE; Almeida, Wethington, & Kessler, 2002). The inventory consisted of a series of stem questions asking whether certain types of daily stressors had occurred in the past 24 hours, along with a set of interviewer guidelines for probing affirmative responses and a series of structured questions that measured respondents' appraisal of the stressors. The aim of the interviewing technique was to acquire a short narrative of each stressor that included descriptive information (e.g., topic or content of the stress, who was involved, how long the stressor lasted) as well as what was at stake for the respondent. Open-ended information for each reported stressor was tape recorded, transcribed and coded for several characteristics. This investigator-based approach allowed us to distinguish between a stressful event (e.g., conflict with spouse) and the affective response to the stressor (e.g., crying or feeling sad). Another benefit of this approach was our ability to identify overlapping reports of stressors. In the present study, approximately 5% of the reported stressors were discarded because they were either solely affective responses or they were identical to a stressor that was previously described on that day.

Description of Daily Stressor Measures

Table 7.1 presents the description and inter-rater reliability of the DISE measures. For each stressor expert coders rated: (a) content classification of the stressor (e.g., work overload, argument with spouse, traffic problem); (b) focus of who was involved in event; and (c) severity of stress. In addition respondents provided reports of (d) degree of severity and (e) primary appraisal domains (i.e., areas of life that were at risk because of the stressor).

The first two measures in Table 7.1 assess the objective nature of the stressor. Each stressor was initially placed into a content classification that combined the broad type (e.g., argument) with specific content or topic of the stressor (e.g., housework). A pilot study of a national sample of 1,006 adults was initially conducted to generate the content classification list of daily stressors common to adults in the United States. The initial list included 8 broad types and 39 specific classifications. This list was then lengthened to incorporate 10 additional specific classifications of arguments and tensions and 5 other miscellaneous classifications. In the present analyses we examined six of the broad content types: interpersonal tensions, work/education overloads, home overloads, health events, network events, and other miscellaneous stressors. Interpersonal tensions included stressors involving disagreements and verbal arguments, as well as nonconflictual but tense interactions with others. Overloads referred to stressors that involved having too much work at home or the workplace. Health stressors refer to health or accident events that happened to the respondent. Network stressors were events that happened to close friends or relatives that were stressful for the respondent (e.g., sick friend). Another characteristic of daily stressors we measured was focus of involvement that assessed whether other individuals were involved in the stressors and, if so, what their relation was to the respondent (Brown & Harris, 1978). Contextual threat refers to an independent rating of the degree of disruption or unpleasantness for the average person. Coders were trained to evaluate the narrative information about the circumstances of the event ob-

TABLE 7.1

Description and Inter-Rater Coding Reliability of DISE Measures

Coding Category	Description	Codes	Inter-Rater Reliability
Content Classification	Stressful events are categorized into one of seven broad types organized by interpersonal tensions, life domains, network events and miscellaneous events. Next they are placed in one of 54 specific classifications. Broad types are listed in the cell to the right, followed by the number of specific classifications associated with each heading.	Interpersonal Tensions (21) Work/Education (9) Home (9) Health/Accident (5) Network (7) Miscellaneous (9)	Broad Types .90 Specific Classification .66
Focus of Involvement	Focus of involvement refers to who was involved in the event.	Respondent Other Joint	.88
Investigator-rated Contextual Threat	The contextual threat of an event refers to the degree and duration of disruption and/or unpleasantness created for the respondent. Ratings range from '1': a minor or trivial annoyance, to '4': a severely disruptive event.	Low Severity Events Medium Severity Events High Severity Events Extreme Severity Events	.75
Subjective Severity	The subjective assessment of severity is the respondent's assessment of the degree of stressfulness involved in the event.	Not at all Stressful Not Very Stressful Somewhat Stressful Very Stressful	*Not coded by raters*
Primary Appraisal Domains	Primary appraisal domains refer to the respondent's report of how much the following areas were at risk or at stake in the situation: (1) disruption routine; (2) finances; (3) how respondent feels about self; (4) how others feel about respondent; (5) health or safety; (6) well-being of one close to respondent; (7) future plans.	Not At All A Little Some A Lot	*Not coded by raters*

tained from the respondents during the telephone interview to independently rate contextual threat. Contextual threat ranged from 1 (disruption or discomfort lasting less than one hour for the average person) to 4 (expected to generate unpleasant emotions lasting more than a day for an average person). The remaining measures in Table 7.1 assess the meaning of the stressor for the respondent. These included the respondents' perceived or subjective severity of stressor and reports on seven primary appraisal domains (i.e., the degree of risk the stressor posed in various areas of life).

The documentation and guidelines for all of these ratings is provided in an interview and coding manual (Almeida, 1998). In addition, all of the transcribed descriptions of daily stressors and their corresponding ratings are contained in an electronic dictionary stored in a computer spreadsheet. This dictionary consists of over 4,000 rated daily stressors and can be searched and cross-referenced by any of the DISE measures.

Daily Psychological Distress

Most researchers interested in psychological distress have relied on respondents' global reports of distress typically recalled over months and even years. However, global reports are largely correlated with personality traits and seem to be relatively stable (Costa, Somerfield, & McCrae, 1996). In addition, the length of recall period systematically influences how people recall emotions. A general pattern seems to be that longer reference periods are prone to a systematic bias for recall of more intense emotional experiences. For example, weekly retrospective reports overestimate the intensity of both positive and negative affect as compared to daily reports of affect averaged across a week (Thomas & Diener, 1990).

Using an inventory of 10 emotions from the Non-Specific Psychological Distress Scale (Mroczek & Kolarz, 1998), NSDE respondents indicated how much of the time that day they experienced each emotion on a 5-point scale from 0 (none of the time) to 45 (all of the time). The inventory includes emotions such as sadness, hopelessness, anxiety, and restlessness. Psychological distress was calculated as the sum of the responses on each day, leading to a possible range of 0–40. Cronbach's alpha for the scale in this sample was .85.

EDUCATION AND FAMILY LIFE DIFFERENCES WITHIN THE BABY BOOM

Our analyses began with an assessment of sociodemographic differences between early Baby Boomers and late Baby Boomers (see Table 7.2). Both groups had similar distributions for gender, marital status, family size and current working status. Two main differences emerged between the two groups:

TABLE 7.2

Sociodemographic Comparison of Early and Late Baby Boomers

	Early Baby Boom 1946–1954 n = 237	Late Baby Boom 1955–1964 n = 238	df	χ^2
Gender:			1	1.53
Men	.53	.47		
Women	.50	.50		
College educated	.55	.24	1	9.81**
Married	.72	.66	1	.51
Working now	.70	.79	1	2.24
Children under 18	.48	.71	1	21.65***
Family size	1.91	1.59	1	3.09

Note. Early Baby Boom: Age Range 41–49, Average age 45
Late Baby Boom: Age Range 31–40, Average age 36
**$p < .01$. ***$p < .001$.

compared to later Boomers, early Boomers were more likely to have gradu-ated from college and less likely to have children in the household.

Given the historical differences outlined earlier, it is possible that these historical factors may have influenced the educational differences between early and late Boomers. When early Baby Boomers graduated from high school, in addition to continuing their education or entering the workforce, many had to consider a third option: whether or not to join the armed forces. Young adults who could afford an education may have decided to continue their education to avoid military service. By the time the late Baby Boomers were making a similar life decision, the specter of military service was no longer present. If these factors influenced early and late Boomers differently, we should see a gender difference in college education between these two groups. Additional analyses examined rates of college education differences for men and for women. For women, there were no significant differences in college education between early and late Boomers. However, compared to late Baby Boomers, more early Baby Boomer men had college degrees $(t(215) = 2.75, p < .01)$.

Family size in the household refers to the number of children under the age of 18 residing in the household. Such a cutoff reflects an assumption that the parental role and associated responsibilities change once a child turns 18. A family life course perspective may explain why late Baby Boomers have more children in the home. Given the average age of the late Baby Boomers ($m = 36$) compared to the early Baby Boomers ($m = 45$) and the age range of each co-hort (31 to 40 vs. 41 to 49) this difference is not surprising.

DAILY STRESSORS DIFFERENCES WITHIN THE BABY BOOM

Our next set of analyses assessed if early and late Baby Boomers differed in their daily stressful experiences. Table 7.3 presents the comparison of stressor characteristics and appraised meaning between both groups.

Frequency of Daily Stressors

The first two rows show the percentage of days that respondents reported experiencing any stressors or multiple stressors. Later Boomers experienced a stressor on approximately 46% of the diary days, or 3.7 days out of the eight day period, and multiple stressors on approximately 14% of the diary days, or one day out of the eight-day period. Early Boomers experienced slightly fewer stressor days. The contextual threat experienced by both early and late Boom-

TABLE 7.3
Description of Daily Stressors Variables Among Early and Late Baby Boomers

	Early baby boom M(SD)	Late baby boom M(SD)	t-ratio
Stressor Characteristics:[1]			
Any Stressors	42 (26)	46 (28)	−1.80
Multiple Stressors	13 (17)	14 (20)	−0.85
Self-focused	28 (30)	26 (30)	0.68
Other focused	10 (19)	06 (13)	2.17*
Joint focused	62 (33)	67 (32)	−1.58
Type of Stressor:[1]			
Tensions	24 (20)	28 (24)	−2.31*
Work	11 (16)	11 (16)	0.39
Home	05 (11)	07 (12)	−1.39
Health	10 (04)	01 (04)	0.30
Network	09 (13)	08 (13)	0.32
Miscellaneous	02 (07)	02 (06)	0.37
Contextual threat[2]	1.82 (.65)	1.81 (.66)	0.04
Appraisal Dimensions:[2]			
Perceived stressfulness	2.71 (.65)	2.74 (.66)	−0.50
Disrupt routine	2.30 (.77)	2.44 (.77)	−1.73
Finance	1.26 (.52)	1.39 (.65)	−2.20*
Self-concept	1.49 (.65)	1.49 (.69)	−0.00
Other's view of self	1.41 (.59)	1.50 (.56)	−1.47
Personal health	1.29 (.53)	1.27 (.46)	0.42
Other's health	1.49 (.68)	1.48 (.65)	0.20
Plans for future	1.35 (.61)	1.45 (.61)	−1.59
Daily Distress[2]	11.62 (3.10)	11.94 (3.50)	−2.79**

[1]Percentage of stressor days. [2]Average rating across all stressors.
*p < .05. **p < .01.

ers was rated as medium, suggesting that these experiences immediately disrupt or potentially disrupt an aspect of the respondent's life that may last up to an hour or two for the average person. Focus (who else was involved in the experience) was calculated as the proportion of stressors that involved the respondent only (self-focused), the respondent and another person (joint focused), or happened to someone other than the respondent (other focused). For both groups, over 60% of the stressors involved another person, and almost 30% of stressors involved only the respondent. Early Baby Boomers reported experiencing significantly more other-focused stressors (i.e., stressors that happened to another person but impacted the respondent) than did late Baby Boomers. It may be that older Baby Boomers are exposed to more stressors that happen to close others, such as aging parents or adult children, whereas younger Baby Boomers are more directly impacted by stressors that involve others, such as younger children.

Types of Daily Stressors

The next set of measures examined the types of daily stressors that respondents were most likely to experience. The type of stressor was calculated as a percentage of study days during which respondents experienced each type of stressor. For both early and late Baby Boomers, tensions were the most frequently experienced type of stressor. Late Baby Boomers, however, reported experiencing significantly more tensions than did early Baby Boomers. There were no other differences between the cohorts across all other types of stressors.

Meaning of Daily Stressors

The final set of measures assessed the appraisal or the personal meaning of the stressor. Both early and late Baby Boomers rated the perceived stressfulness or severity of the stressor with respect to his/her current life situation as somewhat stressful. Respondents also reported on the degree of risk the stressor posed to specific areas of the respondent's personal life. The only significant difference between early and late Baby Boomers was found in appraisal of risk to finances; with late Baby Boomers reporting that stressors presented more of a risk to finances than did early Baby Boomers. This may be because early Baby Boomers are more stable financially than the late Baby Boomers (e.g., own their home, are at a higher status position in their career). In addition, it may be that having younger children in the home stretches the individual's financial resources so that there are fewer resources available to handle unexpected expenses. The last row in the table shows that late Baby Boomers reported experiencing significantly higher levels of psychological distress than early Baby Boomers. Given the higher reported risk to finances and more children in the household, this finding is not surprising.

Exposure and Reactivity to Daily Stressors

Our analyses thus far indicate that the time when an individual was born may play a role in Baby Boomers' sociodemographic characteristics as well their daily experiences. The next set of analyses attempt to bring these findings together by investigating whether sociodemographic factors associated with birth year increase exposure to daily stressors. Based on findings presented in Tables 7.2 and 7.3 we tested whether differences in education and having younger children in the household accounted for birth year differences in daily experiences. A series of five hierarchical multiple regressions were estimated to examine the associations between birth year and both education and children in the household on each of the following stressor outcomes: frequency, other focus, finances, tensions, and distress. In the first step of the hierarchical regression, birth year (i.e., early vs. late Baby Boomer) was entered. In the second step, education and children in household were entered. Table 7.4 shows the results from these analyses. There was some evidence for mediating effects of education and having children in the household, though the pattern varied by outcome measure. First, having younger children in the household ac-

TABLE 7.4
Multiple Regressions of Birth Year, Education, and Children
in the Household Predicting Aspects of Daily Stressors

Stressor Variables		Step 1 B (SE B)	Potential Mediator	Step 2 B (SE B)	Final R^2
Any Stress	Timing	0.02 (.01)	Timing	0.02 (.01)	
			Education	0.04 (.01)**	
			Children	0.06 (.03)*	
					.04
Other Focus	Timing	−0.02 (.01)*	Timing	−0.02 (.01)*	
			Education	−0.02 (.01)	
			Children	0.01 (.02)	
					.03
Tensions	Timing	0.04 (.01)*	Timing	0.02 (.01)	
			Education	0.02 (.01)	
			Children	2.62 (.02)**	
					.03
Finances	Timing	0.07 (.03)*	Timing	0.05 (.03)	
			Education	−0.01 (.04)	
			Children	0.06 (.07)	
					.01
Distress	Timing	0.03 (.01)*	Timing	0.02 (.01)	
			Education	−0.04 (.01)**	
			Children	−0.00 (.03)	
					.03

*$p < .05$. **$p < .01$.

counted for the effect of timing on frequency of daily interpersonal tensions. Thus, late Baby Boomers experiencing more daily tensions compared to early Baby Boomers may be due to the presence of children in the household. Second, education mediated the effect of timing on psychological distress, suggesting that the higher educational levels of early versus late Baby Boomers may explain the lower levels of reported distress in that cohort. Though birth year did not significantly predict differences in stressor frequency, both level of education and children in the household were significant predictors of experiencing any stressors. Finally, neither education nor children in the household accounted for the difference in early Baby Boomers experiencing more other-focused stressors than later Baby Boomers.

The final set of analyses examined the question of birth year and reactivity to stressors. Previous analyses revealed that education accounted for the effect of birth year on daily psychological distress. We extend these findings by assessing whether education affects how early versus late Baby Boomers react to stressors. For these analyses SAS PROC MIXED was used to simultaneously examine both between-person differences and within-person variation in distress over the diary period. The mixed model was estimated separately for early and late Baby Boomers. The results of this analysis are presented in Table 7.5.[1]

In the first step of the model, there were significant main effects for stressors on distress for both groups of Baby Boomers. On days when respondents experienced a stressor, they reported higher levels of distress than on non-stressor days. For late Baby Boomers, there was also a significant main effect for education on distress. The effect was not significant for early Baby Boomers. In the second step of the model, there was a significant interaction for late Baby Boomers with education buffering the effects of stressor days on psychological distress. There was no interaction effect for early Baby Boomers. The difference in this interaction was investigated by plotting levels of distress for respondents with a college degree and respondents without a college degree

---

[1]The following within-person model was estimated:

$$\text{Distress}_{it} = \gamma_{00} + \gamma_{10}\text{Stressor}_{it} + \gamma_{20}\text{Education}_i + \gamma_{30}\text{Stressor}_{it} \times \text{Education}_i + u_{0i} + e_{it} \quad (1)$$

where Distress_{it} represents the reported psychological distress for respondent i for event t, Stressor_{it} identifies whether or not the respondent experienced a stressor on that day, Education_i is the level of education for respondent i, $\text{Stressor}_{it} \times \text{Education}_i$ is respondent i's score for the interaction effect of Stressor and level of Education, γ_{00} is the intercept defined as the respondent's average level of distress after controlling for effects of any stressors, and education, γ_{10} through γ_{30} are coefficients defining the effects of any stressor, education, and the interaction of any stressor and education, u_{0i} is the residual between-person variation, and e_{it} is the residual within-person variation in distress after controlling for the set of predictors. The model was run twice, once for early Baby Boomers and a second time for late Baby Boomers.

TABLE 7.5

Hierarchical Linear Models: Stressors and Education Predicting Distress

	Step 1		Step 2	
Variables	B	SE B	B	SE B
Early Baby Boomer:				
Stressor	1.18***	.13	1.15***	.14
Education	−0.22	.14	−0.16	.16
Stressor × Education			−0.13	.14
Late Baby Boomer:				
Stressor	1.53***	.14	1.35***	.17
Education	−0.70***	.19	−0.53*	.21
Stressor × Education			−0.37*	.17

*$p < .05$. ***$p < .001$.

for each baby-boom group. Figure 7.1 presents the results. For late Baby Boomers, a college education appears to buffer the effects of the stressor on psychological distress. On days when late Boomers experienced a stressor, those with a college degree reported lower levels of distress than late Boomers without a college degree.

CONCLUSIONS

The goal of this chapter is to provide an up-close portrait of Baby Boomers by charting the daily stressful experience those Boomers most often encounter. In addition we explored whether the sociodemographic characteristics and daily stressors differ by when a person entered the Baby Boom, an effect we have labeled birth year. Previous research has argued that the developmental consequences of birth year are due to a combination of the types of historic events a person experiences as well as where a person is in the adult life cycle (see chap. 3, this volume). The primary purpose of our chapter is to illustrate how birth year may have consequences for daily stress processes.

In our sample we found that early Baby Boomers (those born between 1946 and 1954) and late Baby Boomers (those born between 1954 and 1964) were similar in terms of employment and marital status as well as family size. Early Baby Boomers, however, were more likely to have graduated from college and less likely to have young children at home. We contend that the education difference stems from historic effects, whereas having a child in the household difference is most likely the result of position in the life cycle. It is important to mention that these educational differences may also be due to distinctive characteristics of our sample. Our later Baby Boomers were in their early thirties when they participated in the study and may not have completed their formal

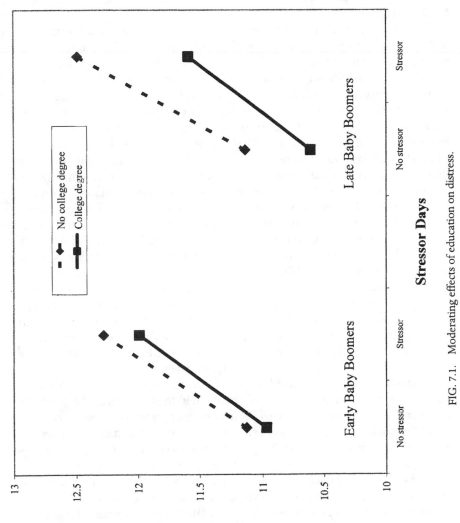

FIG. 7.1.   Moderating effects of education on distress.

education. Furthermore lower socioeconomic status individuals may not be as well represented in the NSDE as in other larger national samples. Indeed Eggebeen's analysis of the Current Population Surveys (chap. 1, this volume) showed a lower prevalence of college educated individuals compared to NSDE participants.

Similarities and differences were also evident in exposure and reactivity to stressful experiences at the daily level. Overall early and late Baby Boomers experienced the same frequency and severity of daily stressors. In addition, both experienced a similar number of work, home, and health related stressors. However, there were some important differences in exposure and meaning of stressors in the daily life of early and late Boomers. Early Boomers were more likely to experience stressors that focused on another person (e.g., a sick family member). Late Boomers on the other hand reported more interpersonal tensions. Further, late Boomers perceived their stressors as more likely to disrupt finances compared to early Boomers. Additional analyses showed that having children in the household accounted for differences in interpersonal tensions. Late Boomers also experienced higher levels of daily psychological distress compared to early Baby Boomers. Further analyses showed that level of education accounted for differences in daily distress. Perhaps the difference in overall educational levels between early and late Boomers contributes to the differences in reactivity to daily stressors. Higher levels of education are often associated with higher status careers and higher levels of income. Thus, when stressors arise in everyday life, these additional resources may buffer individuals who possess them from their ill-effects. A comparison of education levels within each cohort shows that respondents without a college degree report higher levels of distress on both stressor and nonstressor days. Among late Boomers, that effect is exacerbated on stressor days.

To appreciate how the combination of fewer resources and the additional demands of children in the household play out in the daily life of the late Baby Boomers, it may be helpful to examine the descriptions of experiences provided by NSDE participants. As part of our assessment of daily stressors, we asked respondents to describe the stressful events that occurred over the preceding 24 hour period. These brief narratives provide us with a snapshot of the day-to-day experiences of Boomers, and enable us to frame the picture so as to reveal the interdependency of resources and demands of daily life. One illustration of this interweave comes from a late Boomer describing the argument he had with his wife: "It has to do with finances and how we're spending money and that kind of thing. I work three jobs. She doesn't work. She's home with the kids. There should be some cutbacks. She feels it's not possible. There's a conflict right there. No matter how many hours I work, you don't seem to get over that mountain. There's so many bills . . . and I worry about it. There's nothing we can do. It's a lot on my shoulders. . . . It's just frustrating arguing about it. I wish I could make a little more. I blame myself sometimes."

In another example a late Boomer relates a stressful situation involving his boss that disrupted the flow of the day after the episode: "It was just a conflict of interest. You know, he is the boss, you do what they say. I am a mechanic and make decisions on most things, but when there is more money involved, you got to involve the boss and sometimes they just don't do things right, they don't want to spend the money to do things right and I like to do things right. Knowing I should do things right and not cut corners."

Of course early Boomers are not immune from daily stressors. Recall that early Boomers' stressors are more likely to revolve around stressors of others. One rather touching example involves an early Boomer who tells of her concern for the health of her aging mother, and the fear she has for her husband's health as well: "Calling my mom and talking to her . . . knowing she's not doing well. She's had two major surgeries in six months and the last one was to remove a cancerous tumor. And, she's getting back on her feet, God love her. I don't know how she does it. But I can hear the age in her voice, where I couldn't hear it before. This last six months has taken a lot out of her. She's a neat lady. . . . It's very stressful. It's like the same fear as my husband's health problems. I'm not ready to lose my mom or my husband to health problems. You know, I want them to take vitamins and run. They're both having a tough time. I crack jokes and make them laugh and that kind of gets everyone through it."

Finally, an early Boomer tells of her concern for her adult son who has recently left the nest: "He has gone to New York, and he had lost a lens out of his glasses. We were worried how he was going to get it replaced, and how he was going to get the money. He has a credit card and he's going to use that. This is the first real job away from home."

These are just a few of the stories that illustrate differences in the daily experiences of early and late Baby Boomers. These differences remind us once again that historical effects and life stage are important influences on individual well-being, even at the level of daily experiences. Although the design of our study can not disentangle age and historic effects we hope that we have illustrated the value of assessing a more detailed look at the daily life of Baby Boomers. As future research continues to define the landscape of this generation in terms of who the Baby Boomers are and what makes them different from other generations, we should also pay attention to how this landscape serves as a background for individual portraits of daily life.

ACKNOWLEDGMENTS

The research reported in this chapter was supported by the MacArthur Foundation Research Network on Successful Midlife Development and the National Institute on Aging Grant AG19239.

REFERENCES

Ackerman, R. J. (1990). Career developments and transitions of middle-aged women. *Psychology of Women Quarterly, 14,* 513–530.

Almeida, D. M., & Kessler, R. C. (1998). Everyday stressors and gender differences in daily distress. *Journal of Personality and Social Psychology, 75,* 1–11.

Almeida, D. M., Wethington, E., & Kessler, R. C. (2002). The Daily Inventory of Stressful Events: An interview-based approach for measuring daily stressors. *Assessment, 9,* 41–55.

Alwin, D. F. (1999). Aging and errors of measurement: Implications for the study of life-span development. In N. Schwarz & D. C. Park (Eds.), *Cognition, aging, and self-reports* (pp. 365–385). Hove, England: Psychology Press/Erlbaum.

Blatter, C. W., & Jacobsen, J. J. (1993). Older women coping with divorce: Peer support groups. *Women and Therapy, 14,* 141–155.

Bolger, N., & Zuckerman, A. (1995). A framework for studying personality in the stress process. *Journal of Personality and Social Psychology, 69,* 890–902.

Brown, G. W., & Harris, T. O. (1978). *Social origins of depression: A study of psychiatric disorder in women.* London: Tavistock.

Card, D., & Lemieux, T. (2001). Going to college to avoid the draft: The unintended legacy of the Vietnam War. *American Economic Review, 91,* 97–102.

Costa, P. T., Jr., Somerfield, M. R., & McCrae, R. R. (1996). Personality and coping: A reconceptualization. In M. Zeidner & N. S. Endler (Eds.), *Handbook of coping: Theory, research, applications* (pp. 44–61). New York: Wiley.

Easterlin, R. A., Macdonald, C., & Macunovich, D. J. (1990). Retirement prospects of the Baby Boom generation: A different perspective. *The Gerontologist, 30,* 776.

Elder, G. H., & Rockwell, R. C. (1979). The life-course and human development: An ecological perspective. *International Journal of Behavioral Development, 2,* 1–21.

Etaugh, C. (1993). Women in the middle and later years. In F. L. Denmark & M. A. Paludi (Eds.), *Psychology of women: A handbook of issues and theories* (pp. 213–246). Westport, CT: Greenwood Publishing Group.

Heale, M. J. (2001). *The sixties in America: History, politics, and protest.* Edinburgh: Edinburgh University Press.

Kendler, K., Neale, M., Kessler, R., Heath, A., & Eaves, L. (1993). A longitudinal twin study of personality and major depression in women. *Archives of General Psychiatry, 50,* 853–862.

Lachman, M. E., & James, J. B. (Eds.). (1997). *Multiple paths of midlife development.* Chicago: University of Chicago Press.

Larsen, R. J., & Kasimatis, M. (1991). Day-to-day physical symptoms: Individual differences in the occurrence, duration, and emotional concomitants of minor daily illnesses. *Journal of Personality, 59,* 388–423.

Lazarus, R. S. (1999). *Stress and emotion: A new synthesis.* New York: Springer.

Lazarus, R. S., & DeLongis, A. (1983). Psychological stress and coping in aging. *American Psychologist, 38,* 245–254.

Lazarus, R. S., & Folkman, S. (1984). *Stress, appraisal, and coping.* New York: Springer.

Lowenthal, M. F., & Chiriboga, D. A. (1972). Transition to the empty nest: Crisis, change, or relief? *Archives of General Psychiatry, 26,* 8–14.

Mallers, M. C., Almeida, D. M., & Neupert, S. D. (2005). Women's daily physical health symptoms and stressful experiences across adulthood. *Psychology and Health, 20,* 389–403.

Mroczek, D. K., & Kolarz, C. M. (1998). The effect of age on positive and negative affect: A developmental perspective on happiness. *Journal of Personality and Social Psychology, 75,* 1333–1349.

Rollins, B. C. (1989). Marital quality at midlife. In S. Hunter & M. Sundel (Eds.), *Midlife myths: Issues, findings, and practice implications* (pp. 184–194). Newbury Park, CA: Sage.

Sales, E. (1978). Women's adult development. In I. H. Frieze, J. E. Parsons, P. B. Johnson, D. N. Ruble, & G. L. Zellman (Eds.), *Women and sex roles: A social psychological perspective* (pp. 157–190). New York: W. W. Norton.

Snyder, T. D. (1993). *120 years of American education: A statistical portrait.* Washington, DC: U.S. Department of Education, Office of Educational Research and Improvement.

Stone, A. A. (1992). Selected methodological concepts: Mediation and moderation, individual differences, aggregation strategies, and variability of replicates. In P. McCabe, N. Schneiderman, & A. Baum (Eds.), *Stress and disease process* (pp. 55–71). Hillsdale, NJ: Lawrence Erlbaum Associates.

Thomas, D. L., & Diener, E. (1990). Memory accuracy in the recall of emotions. *Journal of Personality & Social Psychology, 59,* 291–297.

Wethington, E., Almeida, D. M., Brown, G. W., Frank, E., & Kessler, R. C. (2001). The assessment of stress exposure. In A. Vingerhoets (Ed.), *Assessment in behavioral medicine* (pp. 113–134). New York: Taylor & Francis.

Wheaton, B. (1999). Social stress. In C. S. Aneshensel & J. C. Phelan (Eds.), *Handbook of sociology of mental health. Handbook of sociology and social research* (pp. 277–300). Dordrecht, Netherlands: Kluwer Academic.

CHAPTER EIGHT

The View From the Driver's Seat: Sense of Control in the Baby Boomers at Midlife

Marilyn McKean Skaff
University of California, San Francisco

> *Each generation has a collective personality, shaped by its moment in history. Both of my parents endured the lean and fearful times of the Great Depression and then the tensions of World War II, and they understandably became obsessed with security—physical, political, and social. Their children, on the other hand, were born into relative affluence, our freedom and physical well being somewhat assured and our range of opportunities expanding rapidly.*
>
> *America was the world's new superpower superstar, and my birthright, along with that of many other white middle-class boomers, seemed to include the possibility of pursuing any career and achieving any amount of wealth, success, or fame.*
>
> —Nisker (2004, p. 11)

Based on this description of the social climate of the late 1940s, one might predict that the baby-boom generation, at least those persons similar to Mr. Nisker, would grow up believing that their destinies rested in their own hands and that they could achieve whatever their goals might be. This chapter examines the beliefs among individuals in this cohort regarding the degree to which they have control over what happens in their lives, by integrating three perspectives: the theoretical and empirical literature on sense of control, the historical and contextual factors that might distinguish this cohort from others on issues relevant to control beliefs, and the contributions of life span developmental theory regarding sense of control in midlife. Specifically, the goal is to describe and explain sense of control in this cohort at this stage of their lives.

A caveat is needed here regarding intracohort variability. This cohort is defined by the birth years between 1946 and 1964, and the implicit focus is on

Americans. However, it is essential to acknowledge from the outset the variability due to age, gender, SES, race/ethnicity, and nationality, as well as the non-normative experiences of individuals (Baltes, 1987) within this cohort. Although we will seek to describe normative trends for the cohort, we must remain constantly aware of how variability in these characteristics can affect intracohort variation in control beliefs.

DEFINING SENSE OF CONTROL

A primary challenge to the task at hand is to define what is meant by control. It is important to note at the outset that it is perceived control, or control beliefs, that we are talking about, not actual control. Constructs describing control beliefs have grown out of diverse disciplinary and theoretical traditions and, thus, vary in a number of important ways. As Baltes and Baltes (1986) suggested, "psychological control refers to a field of study rather than to a singular construct" (p. xviii). Two common differences in control constructs involve whether the focus is on outcome contingencies or on the capacity of the individual to take the actions necessary to exert control (Skinner, 1995). More specifically, some constructs focus on beliefs about whether control is contingent on one's behavior or whether control resides in the hands of an external source. Others assume that it is beliefs about the capacity to effect outcomes that determine the individual's control beliefs.

Skinner (1996) has provided a more elaborate description of factors differentiating constructs of control. These include the agents of control, the means and mechanisms of control, and the ends or targets of control. These are useful not only for distinguishing among control constructs, but as a means of understanding the development of control across the life span. The agent of control refers to the individual or group who exercises control. Control beliefs may also vary according to the means or mechanisms by which control is exercised, involving behavior or cognition. In some instances the means may involve calling upon powerful others who are seen as being in control. Finally, control beliefs may differ in the targets or ends toward which control efforts may be directed, that is, toward the environment or toward the self. Skinner also differentiates between control over the occurrence of events and control over one's reactions to the repercussions of the events.

Another aspect of control that has important implications for a life span perspective is the distinction between global sense of control and control in specific domains. Increasingly, research on control has distinguished between general or global control beliefs and domain specific control. The importance of distinguishing between these two perspectives is now clear. Although related, global control beliefs and domain specific control are distinguishable and both provide independent information about individuals' sense of control (Abeles, 1991; Lachman, 1986; Skinner, 1996; Skaff, Mullan, Fisher, & Chesla,

2003). Although global control may represent a weighted average across domains, the salience of such domains as health, interpersonal relations, work, and intellectual functioning, may vary across the life span as well as across individuals and across diverse groups (Fung, Abeles, & Carstensen, 1999; Lachman, 1986; Lachman & Weaver, 1998b).

With these distinctions in mind we now discuss three of the most commonly used constructs of control beliefs: locus of control, self-efficacy, and sense of control. Having its origins in social learning theory, *locus of control* (LOC) theory differentiates between internal and external control over outcomes (Rotter, 1973). LOC reflects the degree to which people believe that their outcomes are due to internal or personal influence or to influences external to the self, such as powerful others or luck, chance, or fate. Thus, locus of control focuses on who or what is in control. It has traditionally been measured as a general or global set of beliefs and often dichotomizes people into *internals* and *externals*, although the measures used generally reflect a continuum from extreme external to extreme internal. Although often operationalized as a global construct, there has been some work looking at domain specific LOC, such as in the area of health (Wallston, Wallston, Kaplan, & Maides, 1976).

Self-efficacy theory proposes that people's beliefs about their own abilities to take certain courses of action will have an influence on their outcome expectancies and subsequently on their actions (Bandura, 1997). Thus, beliefs about whether one possesses the competence, and therefore has access to the means to achieve a desired end, determines which goals the individual will pursue and how much effort he or she will put into that pursuit. Although self-efficacy was originally operationalized as a domain-specific construct, more recently it has been used as a global measure of the beliefs held by individuals about their overall competence.

Sense of control includes beliefs about both the self and the environment. In Skinner's (1996) definition, "A sense of control includes a view of the self as competent and efficacious and a view of the world as structured and responsive" (p. 559). It is akin to such general constructs as personal control, mastery, and perceived control (Abeles, 1990; Fung, Abeles, & Carstensen, 1999; Pearlin & Schooler, 1978; Rodin, 1990; Skinner, 1996). Sense of control has roots in both psychology and sociology and reflects assessments that individuals make about the amount of control they have over what happens in life. Sense of control is often measured as a global assessment, much in the same way self-esteem is considered a general assessment of one's worth as a person. However, sense of control encourages domain-specific control beliefs as well.

Another important contribution to a dynamic, comprehensive model of control has been made by Abeles and colleagues (Abeles, 1990; Abeles, 1991; Fung et al., 1999). The Abeles model provides a useful framework for the consideration of variations in control across the life span and across diverse social and historical contexts. They speak of sense of control as an "umbrella term," incorporating beliefs and expectations about the self and the environment. This model also emphasizes both domain-specific components and a global or general sense of control.

The model described by Fung & colleagues (1999) has four components that allow a much broader conceptualization of control than many previous constructs of control, such as LOC or self-efficacy. First, they emphasize that sense of control involves subjective experience, that is, internal cognitive processes and structures. The relationship between objective and subjective control is seen as a topic worthy of consideration, particularly across diverse groups and across the life span. Second, they encourage us to think of control not as a unitary concept, but as a collection of beliefs about the self and the environment. This comprehensive definition allows for inclusion of such constructs as LOC, personal efficacy, and learned helplessness. Using the concept of schema, defined as a subjective theory about how the world operates, Fung & colleagues (1999) describe the ways in which context might influence subjective experience of the environment and beliefs about the self in relationship to the environment. This could potentially encompass not only current sociocultural environments, but historical and life span considerations as well. Third, they describe the dynamic and dialectical nature of control beliefs, with feedback from experience changing those beliefs as individuals move across the life span. This dynamic relationship is an important key to understanding how control beliefs both influence and are influenced by life experiences. Finally, they point to what they believe is the greatest gap in the study of control beliefs: an understanding of the antecedents of control.

In summary, sense of control refers to a set of beliefs held by individuals regarding the amount of control they have over what happens in their lives. Control is generally seen as a global belief, but also includes domain-specific beliefs. These beliefs encompass both individuals and the environment in which they live. The four-component model of control seems particularly useful for examining both historical context and developmental change in control. However, as we shall see, the majority of research on control has utilized either locus of control or self-efficacy.

HISTORICAL CONTEXT: BABY BOOMERS AND CONTROL

Historical period and social context exert powerful influences on individuals and their development, including their beliefs about the world and their place in it, at least in part by shaping the opportunity structures to which they have access (Staudinger & Bluck, 2001). In the case of Baby Boomers in the United States, this cohort has grown up and is living their lives in an increasingly diverse society. Before examining this social diversity, we shall first concentrate on social forces that may have affected this cohort as a whole.

Which historical events and social trends have influenced the sense of control among those born between 1946 and 1964? As noted throughout this book, the world into which the leading edge of the Baby Boom cohort was born is considerably different from that which greeted the trailing edge. The interaction of developmental stage and historical climate can result in very different outcomes (Baltes & Baltes, 1986; Elder, 1974). Therefore, the political and social climate of the 1960s will have had a very different influence on those who were in their teens and early 20s during that time, compared to those who were infants or young children.

Clark-Plaskie and Lachman (1999) describe the cohort entering midlife in 1986 as one with high expectations. They were more hopeful, born into a period of affluence, with more education, carrying the message put forth by John F. Kennedy that they could have an impact on their world. One of the first influences mentioned when talking about Baby Boomers is the relative affluence of the postwar period. As the quote by Nisker (2004) at the opening of the chapter suggests, at least for middle class European Americans, this was a period of abundance and optimism about future possibilities. For the baby-boom generation, increased opportunity in both income and education were important influences; these two factors are frequently related to higher sense of control over life (Lachman & Weaver, 1998a; Lachman & Weaver, 1998b; Ross & Sastry, 1999).

Other social trends that could be expected to influence sense of control in this cohort include the youth culture of the 60s, the women's movement, and changes in the traditional family (Moen & Wethington, 1999). The political activism and youth culture of the 60s might be expected to increase the degree to which young adults at that time felt they could have some influence on the political process as well as on their lives in general. On the other hand, as Nisker (2004) pointed out, the atomic bomb could have left that same generation feeling that much was out of their hands. It remains to be seen whether the Baby Boomers carry the positive and/or negative implications of these opposing social influences on their sense of control as they move through middle adulthood.

The availability of the birth control pill and the growth of the women's movement had very real effects on the degree to which women could control their fertility and, potentially, their lives. Increased education and entry into the work force might be expected to have positive effects on women's sense of control over their lives. However, in a study using longitudinal data from four large national samples, Doherty and Baldwin (1985) reported an increase in external locus of control among women beginning in the mid-1970s, with no such change for men. They attribute these differences to a cultural shift in women's awareness of the constraints on their lives, an awareness brought about by the women's movement, as well as women's experience with inequality in their own lives.

Major changes have also taken place during the life span of the Baby Boomers in the form and functioning of the family. Although birth control gave women much more control over the number of children they had, there have also been increases in the number of dual income couples, increasing divorce rates, and changes in the definition of family. Clydesdale (1997) studied a group of adults who had graduated from college in 1965. He described their childhoods as characterized by relative affluence and their families of origin as traditional. However, although their income tended to be higher in adulthood than that of their parents, so also was their divorce rate, especially for those of higher income. These conflicting influences are factors that could potentially affect sense of control. For example, higher incomes and more education are factors usually associated with higher sense of control. On the other hand, the stressors associated with increasing rates of divorce, single parenthood, and dual income couples would suggest challenges to sense of control in this group.

Riggs and Turner (2000) studied a group of Baby Boomers in Australia born between 1945 and 1950, asking whether this cohort could be described as "pie-eyed optimists," having been born in a period of economic growth and social change. They described them as a privileged group in terms of education, employment, and social changes such as contraceptive choice and women's rights. However, they found that many of them expressed feelings of powerlessness as individuals, while at the same time expressing beliefs in collective or group power. That is, they acknowledged a sense of empowerment as a generation, which the authors attributed to 60s activism. This collective power did not seem to translate into individuals' sense of control over their own lives.

The question remains as to whether these historical and social trends resulted in greater sense of control and for whom. An AARP report (1999) on the Baby Boomers who are now approaching retirement found high levels of self-reliance and optimism among a significant portion of them. However, the report also emphasized the significant diversity in this cohort and large disparities in economic resources. Schooler (1990) also has emphasized the differences within cohorts as well as between. The span of 20 years separating the leading edge from the trailing edge of the baby-boom generation alone is sufficient to result in considerable variation. When variations in sex, ethnicity, geographical location, and socioeconomic status are added, it is clear that it is necessary to be cautious when generalizing about this large and varied group. For example, Clark-Plaskie and Lachman (1999) point out that the economic climate into which the younger Baby Boomers were born and developed might result in individuals having fewer expectations, and, they propose, lower sense of control. However, they also question what might happen to older Baby Boomers with high expectations who find those expectations unfulfilled in middle adulthood. They also suggest that we might expect differences among the Baby Boomers related to where they are now in their life span, with the older group nearing the end of middle age and the younger ones just beginning middle age.

LIFE SPAN DEVELOPMENT AND CONTROL

Beyond the challenges presented by a lack of agreement on what control is and how to measure it, there are several other obstacles to describing control at midlife, including the lack of comprehensive, dynamic life span theories of sense of control. One exception is a theory of control strategies described by Schulz and Heckhausen (1996). Primary control, which involves acting directly on the environment, is viewed as increasing throughout childhood and adolescence, remaining somewhat stable through middle adulthood, and decreasing in late life. Secondary control is defined as the control strategies individuals direct toward their own responses to challenges. This latter type of control strategy is present throughout life, but gains relative importance in later life, when less actual control may be exercised over some domains. This theory has been compared to assimilative and accommodative control. Midlife is viewed as a time when individuals begin to focus and invest in selected domains that are controllable (Schulz, Heckhausen, & Locher, 1991).

Primary and secondary control theory has raised some important issues regarding control across the life span. However, there are some important limitations to this theory. First, primary and secondary control refer to control strategies, that is, what people do to retain or regain control when it is challenged, more closely akin to coping than to control beliefs (Skinner, 1996; Lockenhoff & Carstensen, 2003). Although beliefs and behavior are closely related, progress in this field requires greater specificity of constructs.

Second, this theory has been questioned regarding its relevance across varied cultures and ethnic groups. Gould (1999) points out that there is an underlying assumption that primary control is superior to secondary control. Yet, in non-European American cultures, secondary control is often viewed as a preferred way of interacting with the world. This may be an important consideration in late life as well. A realistic appraisal of one's influence on various domains and an adaptive response to that reality need not be considered an inferior strategy. Furthermore, as Gould suggests, secondary control may be favored as people age when they have more time to contemplate their choices. Schooler (1990) stated "I think it is clear that the varied cultural, social-structural, and institutional processes brought about by different historical circumstances lead to differences in the emphases placed on the importance of self-direction and efficacy for the individual" (p. 19). According to this view, it is necessary to use caution in generalizing across diverse members of a cohort. Indeed, as Schooler continues: "Furthermore, such differences in emphasis may exist not only between cultures, but may also exist within societies, particularly those that are not homogenous socially or culturally" (p. 19). Schooler's comments underscore the importance of being sensitive to sociocultural variations in the meaning and manifestations of control beliefs and to resist making value judgments about those variations, based on a European American (and perhaps middle class) model.

Development in Midlife

In the literature, midlife has been largely ignored compared to childhood and late life. Lachman and Bertrand (2001) suggest that this is due to several factors. First, there has been the assumption that midlife is a period in which little development takes place. Second, the markers for this life stage are less definitive than for other stages, i.e., the transition from young to middle adulthood remains relatively unexplored. Finally, a pragmatic reason for the lack of research on midlife is the very role engagement that characterizes this period: middle aged people are often too busy to participate in research.

There is relatively little in developmental theory to suggest what the implications of development are for sense of control during midlife. Erikson (1950) described midlife as a period in which the psychosocial crisis of "generativity versus stagnation" is central. Generativity is a feeling of concern for future generations that leads to commitment and productivity. Because this is expressed in work and relationships in midlife, one might expect that sense of control in midlife is also influenced by competence in major roles such as work, marriage/partnership, and family.

Heckhausen (2001) described midlife as a time of both growth and decline, when adults may be reaching their peak level of performance in some areas, but are also beginning to experience physical decline and a change in time perspective. She suggests that there is a reality shift in midlife, in which people move from believing anything is possible to gaining a more realistic perspective on whether their aspirations will be met. Staudinger and Bluck (2001) also talk about midlife as a time when there is a "tie" between gains and losses.

Clark-Plaskie and Lachman (1999) describe midlife as a time when adults are at their peak in competence, productivity, responsibility, and ability to handle stress. However, sense of responsibility for others and the importance of work could also place individuals in midlife in a position of vulnerability. Therefore, as was discussed in the section on social influences on this cohort, midlife development also presents a somewhat mixed picture. On the one hand, individuals may be at their peak in performance and earnings, and in some sense, truly more in control of their lives. On the other hand, responsibilities and stressors in major domains may challenge the midlife person's sense of control. Youthful idealism may yield to a more realistic perspective on what can and cannot be controlled, including the physical changes that gradually take place. When these opposing forces are also considered within a changing sociopolitical context, it is difficult to predict what we will find regarding sense of control in the Baby Boomers as they move through midlife. Thus, on the one hand, having more actual control over work, family, and finances might mean higher sense of control during midlife. On the other hand, because of the number of roles individuals are likely to occupy, we may find that stressors in major life domains diminish sense of control during this life stage. Thus, both in terms of social trends and developmental tasks, one might predict both higher and lower sense of control for this cohort at midlife. Perhaps, the resolution to this conundrum lies in intra cohort variations in gender, year of birth, SES, and ethnicity, as well as in the number and quality of roles occupied. We now turn to an examination of the empirical evidence on sense of control during midlife.

Sense of Control in Midlife

Given the limited research on midlife in general, it is not surprising that there is even less research on the sense of control at midlife. In addition, what does exist regarding control does little to resolve the conundrum raised previously; that is, some evidence indicates that during middle adulthood control is lower, some indicates that it is higher, and some indicates that there are no age differences. There are a number of reasons for these discrepancies (Lachman & Bertrand, 2001; Grob, Little, & Wanner, 1999). The samples are often nonrepresentative, include wide age ranges or do not include people in midlife, or there is no consideration given to gender differences. Most study designs are cross-sectional, confusing cohort with life stage. A major source of discrepancy is the confusion in the definition of sense of control, as discussed previously. Most research has used global constructs, some of which, such as LOC, are not really developmental constructs (Skinner & Connell, 1986). It is possible that the constructs that have been studied may vary in their trajectories across the life span. It is also likely that the salience of specific domains and their relationship with global control change across time. We know very little about the means or mechanisms by which sense of control is lost, maintained, or increased by life experiences.

Because much of life in middle adulthood is organized by the roles or domains individuals occupy, we start with an examination of the impact of role quality on sense of control. Freud identified love and work as the major tasks of adulthood. Although there is no evidence on the "love" part of the Freudian equation for adulthood, if we accept marriage or partnership as a proxy, marriage does appear to have an impact on sense of control, although in opposite directions for women and men. For men, marriage appears to increase sense of control, but for women, marriage is accompanied by a decreased sense of control. Ross (1991) reported that, adjusting for income, unmarried women had higher control than men and married women. Only by increasing income does marriage improve control for women.

Family responsibilities are likely to have an influence on control in midlife. Although parenthood is an important role for most adults, there appears to be little evidence on how parenting affects sense of control. One could surmise that its relationship to control should vary by the age of the children, with greater control likely when children are young. This might be offset, however, by parental stress or complicated by role overload. In addition to parenting, midlife adults are often faced with increasing responsibility for aging parents. The vast caregiving literature includes evidence of a negative effect on adult children of caring for frail elderly parents (Skaff, Pearlin, & Mullan, 1996).

In regard to work, research examining locus of control demonstrates that the characteristics of an individual's work life do have an impact on control beliefs. Hoff and Hohner (1986) report that people engaged in professional jobs had high levels of internal control, whereas those with low education and in nonsupervisory jobs had higher external control. A study by Kivett, Watson, and Busch (1977) also examined the relationship between locus of control and occupation. They found that professional workers were higher in internal control than laborers or clerical workers. Heavy machine operators were, in turn, higher in internal control than the laborers or clerical workers. Kivett and colleagues interpreted these patterns of findings to mean that actual control over either people or machines seemed to generalize to the rest of life in terms of control beliefs.

Among Baby Boomers, increasing numbers of women have entered the work force and it seems reasonable to expect that they would consequently have a greater sense of control, whereas, Ross and Sastry (1999) suggest that occupying the traditional housewife role should contribute to lower sense of control due to economic dependency, restricted opportunities, and the routine nature of most household tasks. However, Ross and Sastry report that women who are mothers and who work full-time show increased powerlessness. It appears that the role overload, or the feeling of having too many things to do and not being able to do any of them well, can lead to decreased sense of control. More specifically, Ross and Mirowsky (1992) demonstrated that it was the combination of quality of work life and responsibility for chores at home that had an effect on sense of control. Highest in control were those who were employed in jobs with high autonomy and earnings, but had low responsibility for household chores. Control was lowest in women who were employed in jobs with low autonomy and earnings and had high responsibility for household chores. This group was even lower in control than those women who were unemployed.

In summary, the work cited above would suggest that it is both the quality of roles (e.g., the amount of autonomy and rewards) and the potential for role overload in the situation of multiple roles that have an impact on women's (and presumably, men's) sense of control (Ross, 1991; Skaff, et al., 1996). There is evidence that multiple roles are not always detrimental to well-being and potentially to sense of mastery. For example, the work of Stephens and colleagues (e.g., Christensen, Stephens, & Townsend, 1998; Stephens, Frank, & Townsend, 1994) provide support both for detrimental and positive effects of multiple roles. In an analysis examining mastery in women who occupied four roles—wife, mother, worker, and caregiver for an impaired elderly parent—Christensen et al. (1998) found that women reported highest mastery in their work roles, but mastery in all four roles contributed to the women's life satisfaction and, negatively, to depression.

One domain that is likely to present an increasing challenge to control beliefs as the baby-boom generation moves toward later life is that of health. The inevitable changes that occur with aging become increasingly difficult to accommodate into beliefs about control over one's health. In their study of what people most feared becoming (in the future possible selves), Hooker and Krause (1994) found that middle aged participants had more health related possible selves, perhaps in anticipation of later health problems. However, Lachman and Weaver (1998a) found no significant age differences in control over health. Although Gatz and Karel (1993) found perceived health to be a significant predictor of locus of control; health did not account for age and cohort differences in control.

We now turn to the evidence for sense of control in midlife, based largely on cross-sectional data comparing it to other life stages. Although there is little evidence on control across the life span, most work has suggested that the trajectory of control might follow an inverted U shape, with midlife as a period of relative stability. Reker, Peacock, and Wong (1987) examined control in a sample aged 16 to 75, predicting that control would gradually increase across childhood and adolescence, peak and remain stable in adulthood, and show a decline in late life. Looking at a global construct they called *life control*, what they found was "stability" across five developmental stages. Nurmi, Pulliainen, and Salmela-Aro (1992) examined domain specific locus of control in a sample aged 19 to 71. They described increases with age in external locus of control in health, self, and property. They attributed this finding to an increase with age in realistic evaluation of control.

A major contribution to our understanding of the trajectory of sense of control in adulthood, and specifically in the baby-boom generation, comes from the MacArthur Study of Midlife. Lachman and Weaver (1998b) examined both global sense of control (mastery and personal constraints) and domain specific control. The domains they examined included health, work, finances, contribution to the welfare of others, relationship with children, marriage, and sex. The sample included adults in three age groups: 25 to 39, 40 to 59, and 60 to 75. The midlife (40 to 59) sample includes early Baby Boomers, and the younger adult group includes the late Baby Boomers. Of the two measures of global control, mastery showed no age differences across the groups. Personal constraints were highest in the oldest group. The midlife group showed no differences in control from the younger adult group in the areas of work, marriage, and life overall. They reported lower control regarding sex life and children (the latter perhaps reflecting the presence of teenagers in the home), but higher control over finances, reflecting higher earnings in midlife.

Another study that examined Baby Boomers in middle adulthood is that of Grob, Little, and Wanner (1999). They predicted that domain specific control should vary over the life span as the relevance of specific domains changes. They suggested that such changes could reflect actual changes in opportunities to exercise influence within domains or the possibility that people become more accurate in their appraisals of control as they age. Grob and colleagues examined three domains of control: physical appearance, social, and societal. They also looked at four conceptualizations of control: control expectancy (self-efficacy), goal importance, control striving, and comparative control (relative to their peers). Their participants were ages 14 to 85, including three midlife groups: ages 30 to 39, 40 to 49, and 50 to 59. The group 30 to 39 included individuals who were born at the trailing edge of the baby-boom generation; those in the middle group (40 to 49) were born at the height of the Baby Boom, and the oldest group in middle adulthood (50 to 59) included individuals from the early years within this cohort. Domains were examined within each of the control conceptualizations and differences were observed across the three age groups. Within control expectancy, personal and social control appeared to be highest in the 30s, but lower in the two older groups. There was a linear decrease in societal control expectancies across the age groups, but this domain was also lower than the other two overall.

Grob & colleagues (1999) found that goal importance varied across the three domains. Social control was equally important across age groups, whereas importance of personal control decreased across age groups until 65, when it became stable. Age differences were also found in the importance of societal control, with older groups valuing societal control more than younger groups. Around age 55, social control surpassed societal control in importance. There was a linear decrease across age groups in control striving in the personal domain, but no differences were observed in social control striving. Control striving in the societal domain was high in adolescence, low in young adulthood, high in later adulthood, and low in old age. Finally, looking at comparative control, individuals reported feeling more control than peers generally, except in adolescence and old age. Based on these results, the authors suggest a modified life-task perspective on control. According to this perspective, developmental tasks may change over the life span, but the importance of domains within which the tasks reside remains constant. Grob and colleagues emphasize that control striving remains constant across the life span, but life tasks are affected both by age differences and by societal changes. Although cross-sectional, this study suggests that control is important across the adult life span, but that the specific targets of control may vary with age and cohort.

Although most of the above research was cross-sectional, in a cross-sequential study looking at both age differences and change over time, Lachman (1986) reported stability over a four-year period. She also found a pattern of lower personal efficacy in early middle age, with stability in the 40s and 50s. Personal efficacy was highest in the oldest group, age 60 to 67. She attributed the lower levels of efficacy in the middle adult years to the overload of roles and demands from family and work. It appears likely that the apparent shift downward at the beginning of middle adulthood may also reflect greater realism. The heightened sense of control in children, adolescents, and young adults may reflect an unrealistic assessment of their own power as well as youthful optimism.

One of the major contributions to disentangling the effects of aging, cohort, and time of measurement comes from the work by Gatz and Karel (1993). They examined changes in locus of control over a 20-year period in three generations. The three generations were followed up four times over the 20-year period, including 1971, 1985, 1988, and 1991. Included within this study is one cohort especially relevant to this book, the grandchildren of the original sample, who were born between the years 1941 and 1956, thus including leading edge Baby Boomers. In the entire sample, locus of control remained stable, with an average correlation of .33 over the 20 years. The lowest stability was among granddaughters (Baby Boomers). The primary developmental change that was observed was an increase in internality between adolescence and middle age. In cross-sectional analyses at Time 1, age differences were observed between grandparents and grandchildren who were both more external than the parents who were in midlife.

Gatz and Karel (1993) observed several cohort effects. The oldest women in the study were most likely to have high external locus of control. Sequential analyses revealed that the women who were 55 to 70 in 1971 were more external than women in that age range in 1991. Also, the age group who were 35 to 50 in 1971 had more external beliefs than the Baby Boomers who were 35 to 50 in 1991. Time of measurement effects on control may have been reflected in the increased internality over time. The authors attributed the increased internality in the younger cohorts to the self-improvement and autonomy movements that were popular in the late 70s and early 80s. They suggest both cohort and gender differences, such as the ones they observed, could help explain some of the contradictory findings about age differences in control. This leads us back to a consideration of intracohort variations in sense of control.

INTRACOHORT DIFFERENCES

As discussed at the beginning of this chapter, even though the baby-boomer cohort is often treated as one large group, it is imperative to recognize the variability within the group on such factors as gender, age, SES, and race/ethnicity—factors that can have a major impact on sense of control. The research cited previously (Ross & Mirowsky, 1992; Ross & Sastry, 1999) provides a good example of the effects gender might have on the control beliefs of this cohort. There still remain major differences in sex roles, in t'.c workplace as well as in the home. The advances by women in education, employment, and reproductive choice have not consistently resulted in increases in the sense of control they feel over their lives. Multiple roles, while they are sometimes advantageous (Stephens, Franks, & Townsend, 1994) can also lead to role overload (Pearlin, 1983; Varghese & Medinger, 1979).

We have seen examples of how the early members of the baby-boom cohort differ in important ways from the later members. These differences are due not only to age and life stage differences, but also to historical and social differences. Further research is clearly needed to help disentangle age, cohort, and historical period effects on control.

Socioeconomic status has repeatedly been found to predict sense of control such that lower socioeconomic status is related to lower sense of control. This is because people with low levels of income and education have less access to resources that allow one to control the environment (Varghese & Medinger, 1979). Likewise, researchers have demonstrated a relationship between autonomy on the job and the individual's sense of control (Hoff & Hohner, 1986; Kohn & Schooler, 1982; Lewis, Ross, & Mirowsky, 1999). In addition to their relationship to SES, race and ethnicity often are associated with lifetime experiences of racism and discrimination, which in themselves can deny individuals access to control over their lives (Kessler & Neighbors, 1986; Mirowsky & Ross, 1984; Ross & Sastry, 1999; Skinner, 1995). Especially when opportunities for access to control are denied on the basis of ascribed characteristics such as race, rather than on the basis of ability, the repercussions for the sense of control are considerable (Varghese & Medinger, 1979; Hoff & Hohner, 1986). However, evidence for racial/ethnic differences in control beliefs provides many of the conflicting results found in age differences.

BABY BOOMERS AT MIDLIFE: MORE OR LESS CONTROL?

We are left with two questions. First, what can we say about sense of control in the Baby Boomers at midlife? And second, where do we go from here? Taking into account both cohort and life span development it would appear that Baby Boomers should be a group with a strong sense of control over their lives. They started out in a historical period with greater financial and educational opportunities, as well as sociopolitical messages about taking things in their own hands. Now they are at the period in their development when it is likely that they have the greatest actual control over their lives. However, what evidence there is does not necessarily provide support for greater control among the members of this cohort. Indeed, the research presented is wrought with equivocal evidence. Perhaps the best summary statement would be "it depends." As was suggested earlier in this chapter, the variations in sense of control observed among members of this cohort at midlife may reflect the influences of gender, age, SES, and ethnicity, as well as individual life experiences.

Thus, looking at both the life span and historical influences on this cohort, the picture is paradoxical. The increasing affluence of the late 1940s and early 1950s, which might be expected to contribute to greater sense of control, may have been tempered by the advent of The Bomb, reminding individuals of their lack of control. Social movements in the 60s, 70s, and 80s encouraged a sense of personal empowerment, at least for some, but may also have resulted in a lower sense of control in those who failed to realize their expectations or for those who became more aware of their relative powerlessness. From a life stage perspective, many Baby Boomers are now at their height of actual control in terms of personal finances. However, experiences within the work place, marriage, and family appear to have a major impact on feelings of control, and therefore control beliefs may vary with the amount of control within those domains, as well as with competition between roles. The women's movement provided women with newfound freedom in relation to their own bodies as well as in education and occupation. At the same time, it also made them more aware of the inequalities in their lives. In addition, for many women, working outside the home, which might offer opportunities for greater control (i.e., more income, responsibility), has not been accompanied by a decrease in responsibilities for home and family. If multiple role responsibilities exceed individuals' resources, they may be left feeling that they are not doing justice to any of the roles and subsequently feel little mastery over any individual role or over their life in general. On the other hand, feeling in control in one role, especially if it is particularly salient, might offset negative self-assessments in another role.

TAKING A LIFE SPAN PERSPECTIVE ON CONTROL

The picture that has emerged is that neither cohort nor life stage can adequately predict sense of control. Both cohort and life stage may help us to identify some of the larger social forces at work and the ways in which lives are more likely to be organized at a particular life stage for a particular cohort. What does seem clear at this point is that we need a more comprehensive, dynamic, contextual model of control across the life span, similar to what has been suggested by both Skinner (1991; Skinner & Connell, 1986) and Abeles and colleagues (Abeles, 1990; Abeles, 1991; Fung, et al., 1999).

A comprehensive theory of life span development of control must be multidimensional, considering both global and domain-specific control, but also acknowledging variations in the agents, means, and targets of control. Such a model must include the antecedents of sense of control as well as those factors that influence change and stability in control beliefs throughout the life span. It is essential that we consider sense of control both as a resource that directs behavior and as an outcome of life experience.

A contextualized view of subjective beliefs about control acknowledges that factors such as income, education, occupation, gender, and race/ethnicity are likely to be more powerful predictors of sense of control than are age, cohort, or life stage. There are at least two reasons why this is true. First, the social-structural characteristics of people's lives determine to a large extent the resources they have as well as the challenges to which they are exposed. In addition, these characteristics influence the beliefs and expectations with which individuals grow up and traverse the life course. These expectations include beliefs about who is in control, what is controllable, and how control might be achieved, not to mention the degree to which control is valued and the very meaning of control. As Skinner (1995) put it, "Perceptions of control are constructed from an individual's history of experiences interacting with the social and physical context" (p. 5). When considering the mechanisms by which control is exerted, it is essential to consider the objective realities of the environment in which the individual resides, that is, the degree to which individuals or groups have access to means of control as well as the barriers that may block control efforts (Lachman & Weaver, 1998b).

A dynamic view of the relationship between global sense of control and domain specific control beliefs is essential to a life span view of sense of control. Skinner (1995) has suggested that age differences in control beliefs involve both changing concern about control in different domains as well as age differences in the strategies used to exert control. Similarly, Grob & colleagues (1999) recommend a modified life task perspective to understand age differences in control, taking into account the domains that are likely to be more or less salient at different life stages. The salience of some domains will be chosen by the individual, but others may be thrust into importance by unexpected life events or chronic stressors.

The changing salience of various domains across the life span may be due to both changes in the opportunity to influence these domains as well as in the developing understanding of what is and is not controllable (Grob et al., 1999). Likewise, it is likely that beliefs may vary across the life span and across diverse groups regarding the degree to which control is directed toward the self or toward the environment (Schulz, Heckhausen, & Locher, 1991). As people age, there may be more areas in their life over which they have less control, for example, health, changing family relationships, or finances (Pearlin & Skaff, 1996), and perhaps the wise person is the one who is more realistic about what is controllable and how control can be maintained.

One perspective that has been largely ignored in models of control is the stress process model. As Pearlin and Skaff (1996) suggest, stress models have a natural relationship to life span development, including the interactive role played by sense of control. Patterns of stressors tend to be organized by life stage and, as we have seen, stress within important roles can present a major challenge to sense of control (Pearlin, Lieberman, Menaghan, & Mullan, 1981; Medinger & Varghese, 1981). Medinger and Varghese (1981) suggest that some of the stress experienced in midlife results from the attempt to integrate life experiences into existing values and beliefs, a process they believe can be facilitated by an internal locus of control. Control beliefs are made more salient when the individual is challenged by life stressors. Understanding the dynamic relationship between stressors and sense of control could contribute to a life span model of control.

Likewise, drawing from developmental theories, the dynamic processes of assimilation and accommodation may help us to understand changes in sense of control across the life span. For example, developmental models such as identity theory (Whitbourne, 1986), which describe the individual differences in salience of domains and the processes used to adapt to changes and life experiences, can inform the understanding of the changing salience of control within specific domains and their relationship to global sense of control.

SUMMARY

In summary, a life span theory of control, within which to frame control at midlife or any other life stage, would involve identifying those factors that distinguish each stage of development, but also linking the experiences across the life span that contribute to or challenge sense of control. This would have to be a dynamic theory recognizing both continuity and discontinuity and one that could incorporate the changing salience of specific domains of control and their relationship to global sense of control. Developing and testing such a theory of control will require longitudinal data, as well as research focused on specific life stages. It will also require a commitment to identify the antecedents of and influences on sense of control across the life span and across diverse groups, including examining how individuals manage to maintain control in seemingly uncontrollable circumstances (Skinner, 1995). It will require suspending judgments about different means of control, considering instead the match between environmental challenges and beliefs. It may require new constructs or reevaluation of old ones beneath the umbrella of control beliefs. There is considerable evidence that control beliefs are important, but we need to ask whether we can continue to take a "one size fits all" approach to the measurement of control and to our assumptions about whether control beliefs have the same meaning and manifestations across diverse groups (Skaff & Gardiner, 2003).

In relation to control in midlife among the Baby Boomers, the challenge remains to examine the intracohort variation in antecedents, consequences, and meaning of control, especially as this cohort begins to enter late life. Chances are that many of the Baby Boomers will continue to be at an advantage in relation to previous cohorts and that this advantage will be reflected in their sense of control in late life. However, this transition will also provide a rich opportunity to continue to examine how control beliefs both affect and are affected by increasing challenges experienced with aging.

REFERENCES

AARP Research. (1999). *Baby Boomers envision their retirement: An AARP segmentation analysis.* Retrieved February 28, 2004, from http://research.aarp.org/econ/boomer_seg_prn.html

Abeles, R. P. (1990). Schemas, sense of control, and aging. In J. Rodin, C. Schooler, & K. W. Schaie (Eds.), *Self-directedness: Cause and effects throughout the life course* (pp. 85–94). Hillsdale, NJ: Lawrence Erlbaum Associates.

Abeles, R. P. (1991). Sense of control, quality of life, and frail older people. In J. E. Birren & J. E. Lubbin (Eds.), *The concept and measurement of quality of life in the frail elderly* (pp. 297–314). San Diego, CA: Academic Press.

Baltes, M. M., & Baltes, P. B. (Eds.). (1986). *The psychology of control and ageing.* Hillsdale, NJ: Lawrence Erlbaum Associates.

Baltes, P. B. (1987). Theoretical propositions of life-span developmental psychology: On the dynamics between growth and decline. *Developmental Psychology, 23,* 611–626.

Bandura, A. (1997). *Self-efficacy: The exercise of control.* New York: W. H. Freeman.

Christensen, K. A., Stephens, M. A. P., & Townsend, A. L. (1998). Mastery in women's multiple roles and well-being: Adult daughters providing care to impaired parents. *Health Psychology, 172,* 163–171.

Clark-Plaskie, M., & Lachman, M. E. (1999). The sense of control in midlife. In S. L. Willis & J. D. Reid (Eds.), *Life in the middle: Psychological and social development in middle age* (pp. 181–208). San Diego, CA: Academic Press.

Clydesdale, T. T. (1997). Family behaviors among early U.S. Baby Boomers: Exploring the effects of religion and income change, 1965–1982. *Social Forces, 722,* 605–636.

Doherty, W. J., & Baldwin, C. (1985). Shifts and stability in locus of control during the 1970s: Divergence of the sexes. *Journal of Personality and Social Psychology, 484,* 1048–1053.

Elder, G. H. J. (1974). *Children of the Great Depression.* Chicago: University of Chicago Press.

Erikson, E. H. (1950). *Childhood and society.* New York: W. W. Norton.

Fung, H. H., Abeles, R. P., & Carstensen, L. L. (1999). Psychological control in later life: Implications for life-span development. In J. Brandtstadter & R. M. Lerner (Eds.), *Action and self-development: Theory and research through the life-span* (pp. 345–372). Thousand Oaks, CA: Sage.

Gatz, M., & Karel, M. J. (1993). Individual change in perceived control over 20 years. *International Journal of Behavioral Development, 162,* 305–322.

Gould, S. J. (1999). A critique of Heckhausen and Schulz's (1995) life span theory of control from a cross-cultural perspective. *Psychological Review, 1063,* 597–604.

Grob, A., Little, T. D., & Wanner, B. (1999). Control judgments across the life span. *International Journal of Behavioral Development, 234*, 833–854.

Heckhausen, J. (2001). Adaptation and resilience in midlife. In M. E. Lachman (Ed.), *Handbook of midlife development* (pp. 345–394). New York: Wiley.

Hoff, E., & Hohner, H. (1986). Occupational careers, work, and control. In M. M. Baltes & P. B. Baltes (Eds.), *The psychology of control and aging* (pp. 345–371). Hillsdale, NJ: Lawrence Erlbaum Associates.

Hooker, K., & Krause, C. R. (1994). Health-related possible selves in young and middle adulthood. *Psychology and Aging, 91*, 126–133.

Kessler, R. C., & Neighbors, H. W. (1986). A new perspective on the relationships among race, social class, and psychological distress. *Journal of Health and Social Behavior, 27*, 107–115.

Kivett, V. R., Watson, J. A., & Busch, J. C. (1977). The relative importance of physical, psychological, and social variables to locus of control orientation in middle age. *Journal of Gerontology, 322*, 203–210.

Kohn, M. L., & Schooler, C. (1982). Job conditions and personality: A longitudinal assessment of their reciprocal effects. *American Journal of Sociology, 876*, 1257–1286.

Lachman, M. E. (1986). Locus of control in aging research: A case for multidimensional and domain-specific assessment. *Journal of Psychology and Aging, 11*, 34–40.

Lachman, M. E., & Bertrand, R. M. (2001). Personality and the self in midlife. In M. E. Lachman (Ed.), *Handbook of midlife development* (pp. 279–309). New York: Wiley.

Lachman, M. E., & Weaver, S. L. (1998a). The sense of control as a moderator of social class differences in health and well-being. *Journal of Personality and Social Psychology, 743*, 763–773.

Lachman, M. E., & Weaver, S. L. (1998b). Sociodemographic variations in the sense of control by domain: Findings from the MacArthur Studies of Midlife. *Psychology and Aging, 134*, 553–562.

Lewis, S. K., Ross, C. E., & Mirowsky, J. (1999). Establishing a sense of personal control in the transition to adulthood. *Social Forces, 774*, 1573–1587.

Lockenhoff, C. E., & Carstensen, L. L. (2003). Is the life span theory of control a theory of development or a theory of coping? In S. H. Zarit, L. I. Pearlin, & K. W. Schaie (Eds.), *Personal control in social and life course contexts* (pp. 263–280). New York: Springer.

Medinger, F., & Varghese, R. (1981). Psychological growth and the impact of stress in middle age. *International Journal of Aging and Human Development, 134*, 247–263.

Mirowsky, J., & Ross, C. E. (1984). Mexican culture and its emotional contradictions. *Journal of Health and Social Behavior, 25*, 2–13.

Moen, P., & Wethington, E. (1999). Midlife development in a life course context. In S. L. Willis & J. D. Reid (Eds.), *Life in the middle: Psychological and social development in middle age* (pp. 3–23). San Diego, CA: Academic Press.

Nisker, W. (2004). *The big bang, the buddha, and the Baby Boom.* San Francisco: Harper.

Nurmi, J., Pulliainen, H., & Salmela-Aro, K. (1992). Age differences in adults' control beliefs related to life goals and concerns. *Psychology and Aging, 72*, 194–196.

Pearlin, L. I. (1983). Role strains and personal stress. In H. B. Kaplan (Ed.), *Psychosocial stress: Trends in theory and research* (pp. 3–32). New York: Academic Press.

Pearlin, L. I., Lieberman, M. A., Menaghan, E. G., & Mullan, J. T. (1981). The stress process. *Journal of Health and Social Behavior, 22*, 337–356.

Pearlin, L. I., & Schooler, C. (1978). The measure of coping. *Journal of Health and Social Behavior, 19*, 2–21.

Pearlin, L. I., & Skaff, M. M. (1996). Stress and the life course: A paradigmatic alliance. *The Gerontologist, 362*, 239–247.

Reker, G. T., Peacock, E. J., & Wong, P. T. P. (1987). Meaning and purpose in life and well-being: A life-span perspective. *Journal of Gerontology, 421*, 44–49.

Riggs, A., & Turner, B. S. (2000). Pie-eyed optimists: Baby Boomers the optimistic generation? *Social Indicators Research, 52,* 73–93.

Rodin, J. (1990). Control by any other name: Definitions, concepts, and processes. In J. Rodin, C. Schooler, & K. W. Schaie (Eds.), *Self-directedness: Cause and effects throughout the life course* (pp. 1–17). Hillsdale, NJ: Lawrence Erlbaum Associates.

Ross, C. E. (1991). Marriage and the sense of control. *Journal of Marriage and the Family, 534,* 831–838.

Ross, C. E., & Mirowsky, J. (1992). Households, employment, and the sense of control. *Social Psychology Quarterly, 553,* 217–235.

Ross, C. E., & Sastry, J. (1999). The sense of personal control: Social-structural causes and emotional consequences. In C. S. Aneshensel & J. C. Phelan (Eds.), *Handbook of the sociology of mental health* (pp. 369–394). New York: Kluwer Academic/Plenum.

Rotter, J. B. (1973). *Social learning and clinical psychology.* New York: Johnson Reprint Corporation.

Schooler, C. (1990). Individualism and the historical and social-structural determinants of people's concerns over self-directedness and efficacy. In J. Rodin, C. Schooler, & K. W. Schaie (Eds.), *Self-directedness: Causes and effects throughout the life course* (pp. 19–49). Hillsdale, NJ: Lawrence Erlbaum Associates.

Schulz, R., & Heckhausen, J. (1996). A life span model of successful aging. *American Psychologist, 517,* 702–714.

Schulz, R., Heckhausen, J., & Locher, J. L. (1991). Adult development, control, and adaptive functioning. *Journal of Social Issues, 474,* 177–196.

Skaff, M. M., Mullan, J. T., Fisher, L., & Chesla, C. (2003). Control, behavior, and health: A biopsychosocial view of type 2 diabetes. *Psychology and Health, 183,* 295–312.

Skaff, M. M., Pearlin, L. I., & Mullan, J. T. (1996). Transitions in the caregiving career: Effects on sense of mastery. *Psychology and Aging, 112,* 247–257.

Skinner, E. A. (1991). Development and perceived control: A dynamic model of action in context. In M. R. Gunnar & L. A. Sroufe (Eds.), *Self processes and development* (pp. 167–216). Hillsdale, NJ: Lawrence Erlbaum Associates.

Skinner, E. A. (1995). *Perceived control, motivation, and coping.* Thousand Oaks, CA: Sage.

Skinner, E. A. (1996). A guide to constructs of control. *Journal of Personality and Social Psychology, 713,* 549–570.

Skinner, E. A., & Connell, J. P. (1986). Control understanding: Suggestions for a developmental framework. In M. M. Baltes & P. B. Baltes (Eds.), *The psychology of control and aging* (pp. 35–69). Hillsdale, NJ: Lawrence Erlbaum Associates.

Staudinger, U. M., & Bluck, S. (2001). A view of midlife development from life-span theory. In M. E. Lachman (Ed.), *Handbook of midlife development* (pp. 3–39). New York: Wiley.

Stephens, M. A. P., Franks, M. M., & Townsend, A. L. (1994). Stress and rewards in women's multiple roles: The case of women in the middle. *Psychology and Aging, 91,* 45–52.

Varghese, R., & Medinger, F. (1979). Fatalism in response to stress among the minority aged. In D. E. Gelfand & A. J. Kutzik (Eds.), *Ethnicity and aging: Theory, research, and policy* (pp. 96–116). New York: Springer.

Wallston, B. S., Wallston, K. A., Kaplan, G. D., & Maides, S. A. (1976). Development and validation of the health locus of control (HLC) scale. *Journal of Consulting and Clinical Psychology, 444,* 580–585.

Whitbourne, S. (1986). *Adult development* (2nd ed.). New York: Praeger.

CHAPTER NINE

Cognitive Functioning in the Baby Boomers: Longitudinal and Cohort Effects

Sherry L. Willis
K. Warner Schaie
Pennsylvania State University

SIGNIFICANCE OF COGNITIVE FUNCTIONING IN BABY BOOMER COHORTS

Middle age is a particularly important developmental period currently in our society given that the baby-boomer cohorts (b1946–1964), the largest birth cohort in U.S. history, are now in midlife. The boomer cohorts represent approximately one third of the total U.S. population, approximately 76 million people (U.S. Bureau of Census, 2002). Baby-boomer families account for approximately 48% of U.S. families (MetLife Mature Market Institute, 2003). A portion of these cohorts will be in middle age through the first quarter of this century (2024). The leading edge baby-boomer cohorts (1946–1955) will enter old age in 2011.

Recent policy debates have focused on whether Social Security and health coverage programs such as Medicare will remain viable when the Baby Boomers reach retirement ages (Kotlikoff & Burns, 2004). The age at which full Social Security benefits are paid has been raised and further increases in age eligibility are being discussed (Crystal & Shea, 2002). For example, raising the retirement age by three years would reduce benefit costs and increase taxes paid by workers such that concern regarding looming deficits in Social Security would be erased over the next 75 years. Such a fix depends in part on the assumption that the next generation is able to work to later ages than prior cohorts due to the slowing of the rate of aging, including cognitive aging (Schaie, 2005).

As these huge baby-boomer cohorts reach old age, it will be critical from both an individual and societal perspective for this generation to maintain an independent lifestyle. Maintenance of mental competence and prevention or delay of cognitive deficits are critical to independent functioning. The prevalence of dementias, such as Alzheimer's disease (AD) vary by age group, but increase with age, and the percentage of persons affected by AD doubles every decade beyond age 65 (Arking, 1998). Thus understanding the early antecedents in midlife of cognitive decline and dementia has important public health implications. Public health data indicate that if the onset of AD, for example, could be delayed in the population by 5 years, the prevalence of the disease would decline by one half (Brookmeyer, Gray, & Kawas, 1998).

The focus of this chapter is on cognitive functioning in midlife of the boomer cohorts. In the first part of the chapter, we briefly review prior research on cognition in midlife, noting the limitations in research, including the emphasis on normative or average levels of functioning with little attention to individual differences in developmental trajectories in middle age. We also briefly review the debate in the literature on cohort differences in human intelligence over the past thirty years, with special consideration of the *Flynn effect* (Flynn, 1984, 1987, 1999). Flynn and colleagues have argued that "massive IQ" gains on the order of 5 to 25 points have occurred in the post World War II cohorts—which in the U.S. represents the Boomers. Although data from 14 nations have been cited in support of this position, the U.S. data focus on the 1950s cohorts. In the second part of the chapter we present data from the Seattle Longitudinal Study (SLS; Schaie, 2005; Willis & Schaie, 2005) regarding both cohort differences and longitudinal developmental trajectories for the boomer cohorts. In the third part of the chapter, we review literature on possible factors associated with longitudinal change and cohort differences in cognitive functioning in the boomer cohorts. Particular attention is given to historical events impacting the boomer cohorts directly or indirectly through their parents' generation. We present a model adapted from Bronfenbrenner (1986; Bronfenbrenner & Crouter, 1983) for the study of domains of influence on cognitive functioning, illustrated by findings relevant to the boomer cohorts.

PRIOR RESEARCH ON MIDLIFE COGNITION AND ON BOOMERS IN YOUNG ADULTHOOD

Limitations of Prior Midlife Cognitive Research

It is ironic that currently there may be a greater variety of theories or conceptual models of midlife development (Staudinger & Bluck, 2001; Moen & Wethington, 1999; Whitbourne & Connolly, 1999; Rosenberg, Rosenberg, & Farrell, 1999) than there are longitudinal data sets against which to evaluate such theories. The paucity of literature on midlife cognition, for example, was illustrated by a literature search for studies of memory in middle age, conducted by Dixon and colleagues (Dixon, de Frias, & Maitland, 2001) for the first handbook on midlife development (Lachman, 2001). The authors reported that an average of 5 articles containing midlife participants were published annually during the past 20 years. However, virtually none of these studies was focused primarily on midlife, but were identified because they included a middle age group. Moreover, the vast majority of studies were cross-sectional in design (Bachman & Nilsson, 1985). The authors concluded that there is little evidence of programmatic research on memory in midlife with different authors employing alternative sets of tasks as well as utilizing diverse definitions of middle age.

The paucity of longitudinal data specifically targeting middle age is due in part to limitations in the design of many past aging studies (Dixon et al., 2001). The traditional extreme age group comparative design (young adults compared with old adults) of many cognitive aging studies in the past few decades (A. D. Smith & Earles, 1996) has resulted in serious design limitations for building a life-span perspective of adult cognitive development. Comparison of only two age groups implies the assumption of a linear trajectory of change, with performance in midlife assumed to fall midway between young adulthood and old age. Given only two data points, nonlinear forms of developmental trajectories could not be tested. Moreover, the assumption that the extreme groups differed primarily as a function of age was problematic, since the old and young also differed on other variables related to cognition, such as in health, job status, sensory deficits, and educational attainment.

More recent studies (Craik & Jennings, 1992) have involved research designs that included a group in middle age. However, often the age range for the midlife group has been considerably larger than the age ranges for the young or older groups, since later adulthood is now segmented into young-old, old-old, and very old age. Moreover, cohort comparisons of midlife adults when at the same chronological age may be particularly important. A number of life-span developmentalists (Baltes, 1987; Schaie, 1984; Staudinger & Bluck, 2001) have proposed that midlife is the period most heavily impacted by sociocultural events, rather than biological events, given that puberty is past and the biological decline of old age is only at an early stage.

Focus on Cognitive Stability and Normative Performance in Midlife

Trait theories such as those concerned with personality (Costa & McCrae, 1980, 1993; McCrae & Costa, 1984) or intelligence (Schaie, 1996, 2005) have depicted midlife as a period of considerable stability with relatively little intra-individual change occurring, at least when studied at the aggregate level (see also Martin & Zimprich, 2005).

Ability performance has been reported in longitudinal studies of psychometric intelligence as representing a flat plateau with little change in slope in midlife. These findings have been interpreted to indicate that there is considerable intra-individual stability in the middle years (Dixon, de Frias, & Maitland, 2001; Schaie, 1984, 1996; Willis & Schaie, 1999). With the exception of perceptual speed which exhibits early age-related decline, longitudinal studies have reported that normative decline on most abilities does not occur until the mid-sixties, which is considered young-old age and beyond midlife. The study of stability in personality or ability traits has focused primarily on possible change in the level of functioning with less examination or concern regarding slope.

Recently, however, there has been increasing interest in studying individual differences in both level and slope. An aggregate or mean level approach to study of cognition is likely to mask the subgroups of individuals that exhibit either positive or negative slope trajectories in midlife. In this chapter we utilize data from the Seattle Longitudinal Study to explore individual differences in trajectories of cognitive change during midlife and discuss possible factors associated with variability in change trajectories.

The Debate on Cohort Gains in Post World War II Cohorts in Early Life

There has been extensive debate on cohort differences in human intelligence over the past century and the interpretation of these differences, in both psychological and sociological literatures. While negative changes in cohort functioning have been supported by evidence on SAT declines and reports of negative cohort differences in verbal ability performance (Alwin, 1991; Glenn, 1994), the majority of evidence has focused on positive cohort changes (Flynn, 1984; Wilson & Gove, 1999). An extensive literature largely stimulated by the analyses of Flynn (1984, 1987, 1999; Dickens & Flynn, 2001) has argued that massive IQ gains on the order of 5 to 25 points have occurred in a single generation. Data from fourteen nations have been cited in support of this position (Flynn, 1987).

These assertions, however, have been based almost exclusively on differences found between two particular cohorts differing approximately thirty years in age—the massive cohort gains are reported for the post World War II cohort with most data cited for those born in the 1950s. From a U.S. perspective, it is immediately evident that these cohorts represent the Baby Boomers and their parent generation, sometime referred to as the Depression cohorts. Although data from a number of developed countries including Japan are cited, the data are largely limited to these two U.S. birth cohorts.

Flynn and colleagues have reported that the largest cohort differences in intellectual functioning have been found for what are commonly known as fluid abilities. Less or no cohort gains have been found for acculturated skills acquired through schooling and commonly known as crystallized intelligence.

The positive cohort trends reported by Flynn and colleagues are in contrast to reports of decline in scholastic aptitude test (SAT) scores. A number of explanations for declining SAT scores have been suggested, including a marked increase in the proportion of students taking the SAT (Hanford, 1991) and increases in social diversity and perturbations. In support of the SAT data, Alwin (1991) reported a decline in education-adjusted verbal test performance from the General Social Surveys that "confirms systematic declines in verbal test scores in cohorts born in the post World War II era, but reveals a trend beginning much earlier" (p. 635). Glenn (1994) further supported the negative cohort trends for verbal ability. Although negative changes in cohort functioning have been supported by evidence on SAT declines and reports of negative cohort differences in verbal ability performance (Alwin, 1991; Glenn, 1994), the majority of evidence has focused on positive cohort changes (Flynn, 1987; Wilson & Gove, 1999).

From a life-span perspective, the question arises as to whether these findings of "massive IQ gains" represent a phenomenon unique to a specific historical period and to the post World War II boomer cohorts or whether they are indicative of a long-term societal or evolutionary change. The data reported by Flynn and others are insufficient to address this question given the limited range of cohorts examined. In addition, the data reported are limited in that each cohort was studied at only a limited chronological period, typically in adolescence or young adulthood; it is unclear from the data cited by Flynn at what age or developmental period these cohort differences arose or whether these cohort differences persisted into middle and later adulthood.

At the same time the Flynn effect findings are of particular interest in studying cognition in the boomer cohorts. Consideration of the historical and cultural factors that may be associated with such cohort gains across successive generations is needed. From a life-span perspective, it is important to consider how these advantaged cohorts are functioning at later stages in the life course, such as midlife, compared to prior cohorts. There has been an ongoing debate in research on cognitive aging about whether individuals functioning at higher levels suffer less decline or whether cognitive decline occurs later in life.

COHORT AND LONGITUDINAL EFFECTS IN THE BABY BOOMERS AT MIDLIFE: FINDINGS FROM THE SEATTLE LONGITUDINAL STUDY (SLS)

In this section we present data from the Seattle Longitudinal Study on the baby-boomer cohorts. We first consider cohort trends for the Boomers. We examine cohort differences between the Boomers and earlier cohorts born in the twentieth century. In addition, we consider the magnitude of cohort differences within the Boomer cohorts (1946–1964), which spans a twenty-year period. Second, we consider longitudinal or intraindividual change in boomer cohorts in midlife. Individual differences in developmental trajectories are shown, suggesting that although for most Boomers in midlife there is cognitive stability, there are subgroups of Boomers experiencing decline or growth in cognitive performance in middle age.

Cohort Differences in Level of Performance: Boomers Versus Prior Cohorts

Because of the sequential design of data collections in the Seattle Longitudinal Study (SLS), we have repeatedly recruited samples randomly drawn from successive birth cohorts and we test them at comparable ages (Schaie, 1996, 2005). Hence, it has been possible to compute cohort differences in performance level of successive cohorts averaged over several ages and thus to determine cumulative cohort trends for various mental abilities. In this section, we will summarize our findings on cohort differences in intelligence.

It is possible from data such as ours to estimate cohort differences in level of performance between any two cohorts by comparing the performance of successive cohorts over the age ranges for which both cohorts have been observed. The cohort effects estimated in this manner will, of course, be confounded with period effects, but if series of cohort differences are computed across the same time period, each estimate will be equally affected. In our case it is possible to generate twelve cohort differences for thirteen 7-year birth cohorts with mean birth years from 1889 to 1973. To obtain the most stable estimates available, the average level difference between any two cohorts is defined as the average of unweighted mean differences at all ages where observations are available for these two cohorts.

Partial Support for "Flynn Effect" Within SLS Data. The resulting findings are charted in Fig. 9.1. The vertical bars indicate the boomer cohorts (1946–1964) in the SLS. The post World War II cohorts relevant to Flynn effect data are the SLS birth cohorts 1945 and 1952 (Flynn, 1987). The earlier cohorts to whom the post World War II cohorts are compared would include the SLS birth cohorts of 1931 and 1938.

With respect to the purest measures of both fluid and crystallized intelligence, the trends in the SLS data broadly support the Flynn effect. There is an increase on the order of approximately one half a standard deviation (5.0 T-Score points) for fluid intelligence as measured by inductive reasoning from birth cohort 1931 to birth cohort 1952. Indeed inductive reasoning shows the strongest positive linear trend of any ability examined within the SLS study for

Cumulative Mean T-Score Differences

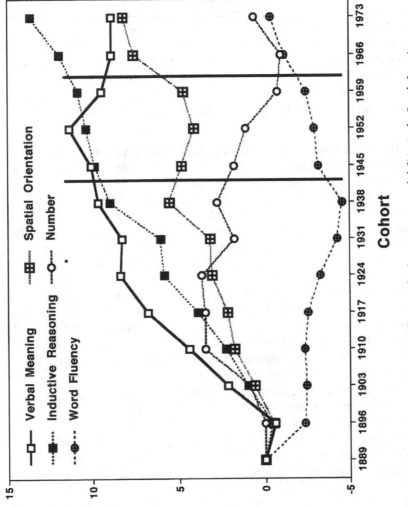

FIG. 9.1.   Cumulative cohort differences for the primary mental abilities in the Seattle Longitudinal Study (from Schaie, 2005). Vertical lines indicate baby-boom cohorts.

these cohorts. The positive cohort trend for inductive reasoning continues in postboomer cohorts born in the 1970s, although the magnitude of cohort differences is reduced. In contrast, cohort differences over the same cohorts are more modest for the two crystallized abilities of verbal and number ability; magnitude of cohort differences between the 1931 and 1952 cohorts is 2.9 T-Score points for verbal. There is a significant negative cohort trend from the 1931 to 1959 cohorts for number ability of approximately 2.6 T-score points. For the fluid ability of spatial orientation, the cohort difference between the 1931 and 1952 cohorts is minimal although there is some evidence of increasing cohort differences between the 1931 cohort and cohorts born in the 1960s and 1970s. Thus, positive linear cohort trends from the 1931 to 1952 cohorts are only shown for inductive reasoning and verbal ability with a negative cohort trend for verbal ability in cohorts subsequent to 1952.

The Flynn Effect Compared With Earlier Cohort Gain.   Flynn (1987) describes the differences between the 1930 and 1950 cohorts as representing massive cohort gains. However, when five distinct cognitive abilities are examined across thirteen rather than four cohorts, a much more complex picture of cohort differences is evident (Fig. 9.1). In contrast to the conclusions that would be drawn from data cited for the Flynn effect these SLS data indicate that there are systematic and substantial positive advances in cohort level for both crystallized ability (verbal meaning) and for fluid abilities (spatial orientation and inductive reasoning). Indeed, the cohort differences (1910–1931) for verbal ability over a comparable 21-year period are of almost equivalent magnitude to that for inductive reasoning. Moreover, although considerable attention has been given to the "massive IQ gains" for the post World War II 1950 cohorts, the SLS data suggest that the magnitude of cohort gains (at least for verbal and inductive reasoning) were greater for the cohorts born in the early 1900s than for the cohorts cited in the Flynn effect.

On the other hand, quite different patterns of cohort differences are observed for number and word fluency. Number ability shows positive cohort differences up to about the 1910 cohort. But then there is first a plateau and then a negative shift to a successive lowering of performance level. The 1924 cohort exceeds both earlier- and later-born cohorts on number ability; the boomer cohorts are therefore currently at a disadvantage in number ability when compared with the earlier cohorts. The 1950 cohorts (1952, 1959) are functioning one third to one half standard deviation below the 1924 cohort on number ability. Word fluency, by contrast, shows a concave pattern. A negative cohort trend prevails until the 1938 cohort, but improvement occurs for subsequent cohorts. For this ability, then, earlier cohorts have a slight advantage over the later-born ones; but beginning with the cohort born in 1945 there are successive positive cohort differences for this ability also.

Longitudinal Change in Midlife: Variability in Developmental Trajectories

In our prior research on midlife cognition within the SLS, we have focused on normative change in ability performance in middle age (Schaie, 2005; Willis, 1987, 1989; Willis & Schaie, 1999). That is, we have presented average estimates of cognitive change for all SLS participants studied over a given age range.

Figure 9.2 presents the typical finding of stability in cognitive performance in midlife (age 39 to 60 years) when data are aggregated across all SLS participants studied longitudinally over this age range. Performance is shown for six abilities: verbal meaning, spatial orientation, inductive reasoning, number, word fluency, delayed recall (Schaie, 1996, 2005). For these six mental abilities, the magnitude of change across the 14-year period is less than 0.2 standard deviation (SD) units. No statistically reliable age-related change is shown for any ability. Cognitive functioning at the aggregate level thus supports the position of life-span developmental theory that since both gains and loss occur in

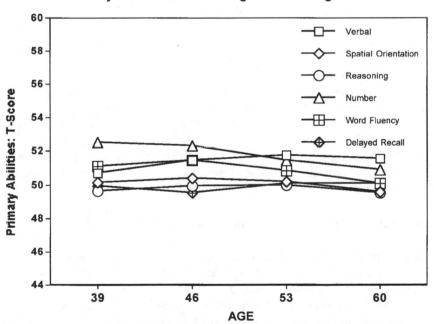

FIG. 9.2.   Mean-level longitudinal change in midlife on primary mental abilities in the Seattle Longitudinal Study: all SLS cohorts with midlife data.

midlife, the relative balance of gains and losses in middle age may create the illusion of stability.

Different Trajectories of Cognitive Change in Midlife

Life-span developmental theories, however, also maintain that there are individual differences in the experience of middle age (Martin & Zimprich, 2005; Schaie, 1989a, 1989b; Willis & Schaie, 2005). Individuals vary in the relative amount of gains and losses experienced in midlife. Variability in patterns of gains and losses becomes evident when subgroups of individuals varying in cognitive change trajectories are studied, rather than focusing on the mean or aggregate level (Schaie & Willis, 1993).

In this section we present new findings from the SLS, examining different patterns or trajectories of cognitive change across midlife for the Baby Boomer birth cohorts (1942–1948). We focus on three cognitive abilities studied in the SLS: number ability, memory recall, and word fluency (Thurstone & Thurstone, 1949). As shown in Fig. 9.2, all three abilities exhibit patterns of stability in midlife when examined at the aggregate or mean level. These abilities represent distinct domains of cognition. Number ability represents the crystallized intelligence domain, which in cross-sectional studies appears to be maintained into old age because of negative cohort differences, but which in longitudinal studies shows decline beginning in early old age (Schaie, 2005). Episodic memory, as represented by list learning recall (immediate and delayed) is one of the most widely studied abilities in cognitive aging (Hultsch, Hertzog, Dixon, & Small, 1998), showing age-related decline in the sixties; changes in this ability are most commonly associated with early stages of cognitive impairment and dementia (Albert & Killiany, 2001; Petersen, 2003). Word fluency is a measure of executive functioning representing higher order cognitive skills required for executing complex tasks of daily living (Lezak, 1995). In the SLS we have found midlife performance on both memory recall and word fluency to be predictive of neuropsychologists' ratings of cognitive impairment in old age (Willis & Schaie, 2005).

Development of Cognitive Change Trajectories

Midlife change in these abilities was studied over a 14-year interval, involving two 7-year intervals and three data points (ages 39, 46, 53). Ability change was examined at the individual level. Defining cognitive change trajectories required consideration of: level of performance at baseline (age 39, intercept) and rate of change over the 14-year period (slope). For each of the three abilities, participants were classified as having reliably declined (decliners), improved (gainers), or remained stable (stable) over the 14-year interval. The statistical criterion for the definition of individual decline or gain was one standard error of measurement or greater over the 14-year period. Subjects were classified by defining a one standard error of measurement confidence interval about their baseline score (age 39; Dudek, 1979; Schaie & Willis, 1986; Willis & Schaie, 1986). If their score at age 53 fell below or above this interval, they were classified as having declined or gained, respectively. Standard errors of measurement (T-score units) for the three abilities were: number = 6; memory recall = 6; word fluency = 6. The proportions of participants classified as stable for number, memory recall, and word fluency were: 81%, 71%, 68%, respectively. The proportions classified as having declined or gained were: decline: 13%, 17%, 16%; gain: 6%, 12%, 16%, respectively. Thus, although Fig. 9.2 presents a normative pattern of stability across midlife, the above procedure indicates that 13 to 17% of individuals have declined on at least one of the three abilities from age 39 to age 53. Word fluency was the ability exhibiting the greatest proportion of individuals showing either decline (16%) or gain (16%).

Memory Ability: Cognitive Change Trajectories

Figure 9.3 presents age-related change for the memory recall ability for the three groups. At age 39, the group of decliners did not differ in performance level from the stable group but did differ from the performance of gainers; the stables

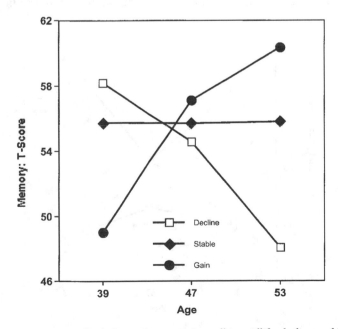

FIG. 9.3.   Longitudinal change in memory recall in midlife: decline, stable, and gain subgroups.

also differed from the gainers. By age 46, the three groups did not differ significantly in level of performance. By age 53, the decline group exhibited 1 SD of change over the 14-year period, while the gain group showed 1.1 SD of gain.

Word Fluency: Cognitive Change Trajectories

Figure 9.4 presents age-related change for the word fluency ability for the three groups. The decline group differed from both the stable and gain group at age 39. The three groups did not differ in performance level at age 46. By age 53, the decline group had dropped over the 14-year period by over 1 SD unit, while the gain group had increased by 1 SD unit.

Number Ability: Cognitive Change Trajectories

Figure 9.5 presents age-related change in number ability for individuals classified as having remained stable, declined, or increased over the 14-year interval. At age 39, the decline and gain groups differed significantly in level; but neither group differed from the stable group. The groups did not differ at age 46. However, by age 53 the decliners had declined 1 SD over the 14-year period and the gain group had increased by 1 SD.

In summary, these data indicate that while there is indeed considerable stability in cognitive functioning when studied at the aggregate level, there are

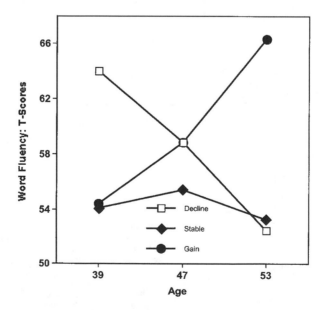

FIG. 9.4.   Longitudinal change in word fluency in midlife: decline, stable, and gain subgroups.

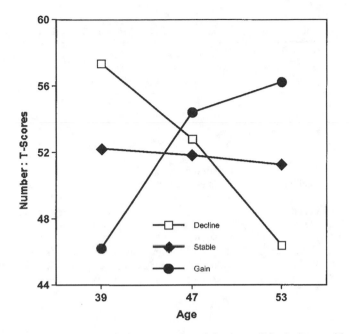

FIG. 9.5. Longitudinal change in number ability in midlife: decline, stable, and gain subgroups.

wide individual differences in patterns of cognitive change for subgroups of Boomers in midlife. For all three abilities examined, both decline and gain groups exhibited a change over the 14-year period of 1 SD or greater. These findings are limited by the fact that only the leading-edge Boomers have reached the 50s by 1998, the last wave of SLS data. Whether these patterns of individual differences in trajectories are manifest for all cohorts of Boomers must await further study as these individuals reach late middle age.

INFLUENCES ON COGNITION IN THE BABY BOOMERS: A CONCEPTUAL FRAMEWORK

From the point of view of life-span developmental psychology, we are interested in identifying those influences in the historical cultural context that might impact cohort differences, particularly for the boomer cohorts, in both the mean level and differential trajectories of mental abilities across adulthood. In Table 9.1 we propose a conceptual framework, adapted from Bronfenbrenner (1986; Bronfenbrenner & Crouter, 1983) for studying the major domains of influence that would provide possible mechanisms for cohort differences in intellectual performance. Although the Bronfenbrenner model is typically presented as a series of concentric circles, our framework is pre-

TABLE 9.1
Conceptual Framework for the Study of Development in Historical Context

Developmental Phase	Mesosystem Contexts of the Individual	Exosystem Contexts of Significant Others	Chronosystem Single-Domain Transitions & Life Course on Cumulative Events
Childhood	1) Family 2) Academic 3) Leisure/Social 4) Media	1) Parents 2) Extended family & friends	1) Single domain transitions, normative & non-normative 2) Life course/cumulative events (economic, political, social, etc.)
Adolescence	1) Family 2) Academic 3) Work 4) Leisure/Social 5) Media	1) Parents 2) Extended family, friends & colleagues	1) Single domain transitions, normative & non-normative 2) Life course/cumulative events (economic, political, social, etc.)
Young Adulthood	1) Family 2) Academic 3) Work 4) Leisure/Social 5) Media	1) Parents 2) Spouse or significant other 3) Extended family, friends & colleagues	1) Single domain transitions, normative & non-normative 2) Life course/cumulative events (economic, political, social, etc.)
Middle Age	1) Family 2) Academic 3) Work 4) Leisure/Social 5) Media	1) Parents 2) Spouse or significant other 3) Extended family, friends & colleagues	1) Single domain transitions, normative & non-normative 2) Life course/cumulative events (economic, political, social, etc.)
Young-Old Age	1) Family 2) Academic 3) Work 4) Leisure/Social 5) Media	1) Parents 2) Spouse or significant other 3) Extended family, friends & colleagues	1) Single domain transitions, normative & non-normative 2) Life course/cumulative events (economic, political, social, etc.)
Old-Old Age	1) Family 2) Academic 3) Work 4) Leisure/Social 5) Media	1) Spouse or significant other 2) Extended family, friends & colleagues	1) Single domain transitions, normative & non-normative 2) Life course/cumulative events (economic, political, social, etc.)

sented as a matrix (Schaie, Willis, & Pennak, 2005). This conceptual structure is necessary to make explicit multiple systems of influence at different developmental phases (childhood, adolescence, young adulthood, middle age, and old age) across the life span.

Three Environmental Systems

The framework (Table 9.1) includes three systems of influence at each developmental phase: Mesosystem, Exosystem, and Chronosystem. In the Bronfenbrenner model, after the family, the nearest and most direct environmental system, the Mesosystem, is given first and primary consideration among the extrafamilial systems. However, given our primary concern with the impact of broad sociocultural events on cohort differences, equal or greater consideration is given to the Exosystem and the Chronosystem.

Mesosystem.   The Mesosystem involves the principal contexts or environments in which individual development takes place. Given the focus on childhood, the family is considered the primary context of development in the Bronfenbrenner model. However, in our framework with a focus on adult development, we include the family as one of the facets of the environments within the mesosystem. Other environments experienced directly by the individual include work, leisure / social context, and more recently media or technology-based contexts. The relative impact of these various environments is expected to vary across the life course and to interact with the personal characteristics of the individual (Schaie & Achenbaum, 1993).

Exosystem.   The Exosystem deals with environments that are not directly experienced by the target individual (i.e., external to the individual), but that represent important environments for significant others.

As the Kahn and Antonucci (1980) model of convoys of social support would suggest, the significant others in the individual's life would be expected to change across the life course, progressing from parents, to spouses and extended family, friends, and work colleagues. The external environments in the exosystem that impact individual development would thus vary across the life course as the significant others change. In the child literature, the parents' work environment has been shown to impact childrearing practices (Kohn & Schooler, 1983), occupational aspirations of the adolescent (Mortimer & Kumka, 1982), and curricular activities (Morgan, Alwin, & Griffin, 1979).

In the Bronfenbrenner model, the exosystem appears to focus primarily on the concurrent environments of significant others (e.g., parent's work environment) that may impact the developing individual. However, in our framework, we will also include transitions occurring across the adult lives of significant others that may influence the individual. For example, the father's educational or occupational experiences as a young adult that occur in a particular historical period have been studied as influences on subsequent intellectual functioning of the offspring (Hauser & Featherman, 1976).

Chronosystem.   The Chronosystem is concerned with the changes and continuities over time in environments that impact the individual's development. Two dimensions of the chronosystem are considered. First, the simplest form of chronosystem focuses on domain-specific life transitions. Two types of transitions have been distinguished in the psychological and sociological literatures (Baltes, 1979; Riley, Johnson, & Foner, 1972): normative (school entry, puberty, work entry, marriage, child bearing, retirement) and non-normative (off-time death or severe illness, winning the lottery). These transitions are usually specific to a particular life domain (e.g., marriage, work) although there may be spillover to other domains. Also. these transitions are usually defined by a circumscribed relatively brief time period during which they occur.

In contrast, a second dimension of the chronosystem deals with cumulative effects of an entire sequence of transitions or events occurring over a more extended time period in the individual's life (e.g., war, depression, technological advances). The impact of such historical or sociocultural life course events on individual development have been an important focus of the work of social psychologists such as Elder (1974), Stewart (2003), and to some extent Helson and Moane (1987). However, the developmental outcomes of interest in the prior work have primarily been factors such as well-being, and stability and success in work and marriage, rather than intellectual performance. Of critical importance is the expectation that the relative impact of these long-term historical or sociocultural events will vary depending on the developmental phase of the individual. Thus, the same historical event may result in very different outcomes for different cohorts experiencing the event at different developmental phases. For example, leading-edge Boomers experienced events such as the Vietnam War and Watergate as young adults, but experienced the 9/11 event in middle age.

It is assumed that long-term cumulative events primarily impact individual development indirectly as mediated by environmental factors in the mesosystem and exosystem and interact with the personal characteristics (e.g., personality, attitudes, life styles) of the individual who is a member of the cohort under investigation.

Influences on Cognition in Boomer Cohorts: Mesosystem, Exosystem, Chronosystem

Clearly, there is a wide range of contexts that impact intellectual functioning and possible cohort differences in intellectual performance. In a recent review of factors associated with cognitive change in 34 longitudinal studies, Anstey and Christensen (2000) concluded that education, hypertension, objective health status, cardiovascular disease and APO-E gene are the factors consistently related to cognitive change across adulthood. Although risk factors (e.g., disease, biomarkers) for cognitive decline have received far greater attention, there is growing recognition of the role of protective factors in cognitive maintenance and plasticity (Kramer & Willis, 2003). Protective factors are important not only as suggesting mechanisms for preventive interventions, but also are of interest due to the dramatic increase in the level of protective factors such as education and occupational status that have been experienced by recent cohorts such as the Baby Boomers, compared to earlier-born cohorts. In this section, we will focus on factors, such as education, occupation, and technology that are said to play a protective or enhancing role in development and maintenance of intelligence across adulthood.

Mesosystem: Educational and Occupational Influences

Education. Education has been shown to be the most consistent non-biological correlate of both cognitive level and rate of change (Anstey & Christensen, 2000; Katzman, 1993). Educational level is associated with cognitive change not only in old age, but throughout adulthood (Farmer, Kittner, Rae, Barko, & Regier, 1995; Lyketsos, Chen, & Anthony, 1999). Education most often predicts change in crystallized abilities, memory and mental status, and is less consistently predictive of change in fluid abilities and speed. In the MacArthur study of successful aging, education was the best predictor of change in cognition (Albert et al., 1995). The effects of education on cognitive change remain when controlling for factors such as age, gender, race, and health.

Several explanations for the effect of education on cognitive change have been proposed (Albert et al., 1995; Katzman, 1993). One explanation maintains that education may serve as a proxy for factors such as health behavior, socioeconomic status, occupational hazards, or nutrition that affect cognitive change and covary with education. Alternatively, education may produce direct effects on brain structure, through an increase in number of synapses or vascularization (Greenough, Larson, & Withers, 1985).

It has also been hypothesized that education does not alter vulnerability to disease but rather delays the appearance of clinical symptoms by postponing the point at which a sufficient number of abnormalities have accumulated. Moreover, education's impact on brain structure may continue throughout life by instilling lifelong habits of mental stimulation that produce neurochemical or structural alternations in the brain that are themselves protective. Thus, although formal education is acquired early in life, the effects of education on brain function would be mediated by habits that are maintained throughout life.

A third proposition is that education may protect and preserve learning acquired through schooling, but does not affect the rate of biological decline. Greater expertise in crystallized knowledge would compensate for or disguise the rate of biological aging in the well educated. Since crystallized intelligence increases through most of adulthood and declines only in late life, the positive effects of education would be expected to increase progressively into midlife and old age (Christensen et al., 1997).

Some investigators have argued that the most parsimonious explanation for cohort differences in intelligence might be found in profound changes in educational processes and structures that have occurred over the past century (e.g., Alwin & McCammon, 2001). Hauser and Featherman (1976) report a total increase in the average length of schooling of about 4 years from birth years 1897 to 1951 based on 1973 OCG Survey data; they note that a gain of 4 years is likely an underestimate since the youngest cohort (birth cohort 1951) had probably not completed their education in 1973. Intergenerational differences between successive generations, approximately 20 to 30 years apart, range from 2 to 4 years. Hauser and Featherman (1976) note that intergenerational differences in schooling peaked among men born shortly after World War I (parents of the Boomers) and a deceleration has occurred across more recent cohorts.

The proportion of 17-year-olds in the U.S. who were high school graduates was highest (greater than 75%) during the 1960s and 1970s when Boomers were in elementary and secondary education, compared to 70% in 2000. The number of individuals enrolled in a degree granting institution of higher education grew from less than 3 million in 1949 to over 8 million in 1969. As noted by Eggebeen and Sturgeon (chap. 1, this volume), level of education of boomer cohorts by middle age far exceeds prior cohorts. In 2000, over 80% of boomers had completed high school, almost 60% had some college, over 25% had a college degree and 12% had advanced degrees (U.S. Bureau of the Census, 2004). Leading edge boomers were more likely to have continued their education immediately after high school (over 50%), whereas later Boomers were more likely to have entered work immediately after high school (50–60%). The incentive of a college deferment during the Vietnam War may have contributed to college enrollment among leading-edge Boomers. Those attending college immediately after high school were more likely to attain a college degree than those working immediately after high school. There are however, significant ethnic differences in educational attainment among the Boomers with Whites more than twice as likely to have college degrees than African Americans, at least for leading-edge Boomers. There is some evidence that ethnic differences in educational attainment diminished somewhat for trailing-edge Boomers.

Although Boomers were children during a period of high optimism, expectations, and dramatic economic expansion, the sheer size of the post World War II cohorts caused them to experience crowding throughout their lives. Enrollments in elementary and secondary schools increased by 41% between 1955 and 1975 (U.S. Bureau of the Census, 1991). They attended overcrowded elementary schools and suffered stiff competition for entry into college and afterward into the labor force (Easterlin, 1987). Interestingly, when midlife Boomers were interviewed regarding their high school experiences, they reported lack of computers and technology and racial/gender discrimination as the major problems rather than overcrowded classrooms (AARP, 2003). Light (1988) and others have suggested that the experience of long-term social crowding has fueled the Boomers' desire for individualism. Faced with crowded schools, colleges and labor markets, Boomers have been portrayed as placing high value on individual recognition and distinction.

The Boomers, particularly the early Boomers, are also unique in being the first U.S. cohort to have access to television and subsequent electronic media from childhood onward. Boomers as children and adolescence experienced via television and in real time events such as the entry into space, presidential assassinations, and the civil rights movement. They were the first generations to encounter educational programming, such as *Sesame Street*, via electronic media. The entry of personal computers during the mid-1980s (when Boomers were in young adulthood) made them the first generation to experience computers and electronic communication in the workplace throughout their careers and adult lives.

Educational attainment early in life appears to have long-term outcomes for Boomers now in middle age—at least in terms of midlife Boomers' attitudes toward the future as old age approaches (AARP, 2002). Less educated middle-age Boomers express greater concern regarding finances and physical and mental health than college graduates; they also feel less empowered, and have a less positive outlook for the near-term future. Boomers without a college degree (27%) are more likely to feel there is little they can do to change important things in their lives than those with a college degree (10%). More Boomers without a college degree use words like "boring," "anxious," "uncertain" and "stressful" to describe their feelings about the near future, as compared to Boomers with college degrees who are more likely to use the term "fulfilling" to describe their feelings.

Occupation and Retirement. Given the higher educational attainment of the Boomers, it follows that Boomers are likely to attain higher occupational status in their work lives. Over 70% of male Boomers are employed full-time in midlife, compared to approximately 50% of female Boomers; somewhat more female Boomers are employed full-time in the trailing-edge cohorts (U.S. Bureau of the Census, 1991). In 2000, approximately 30% of Boomers were in managerial or professional positions, and 30% were in technical jobs. In contrast, approximately 10% were in service, 13% in craft, and 15% in operator/labor jobs.

For the past two generations of older Americans, retirement has been characterized as the golden years—a time of leisure and financial security, an endless vacation that begins in the early sixties. Median age of retirement currently is 62 years. However, for the boomer cohorts, work life is likely to continue to a later age, and retirement may well involve full-time or part-time employment. The sheer size of the boomer cohorts is a strain on both Social Security and Medicare; moreover, employers are less likely to provide workers with traditional fixed-benefit pensions, and instead offer plans that depend on workers' own savings, like 401(k) accounts and give no guarantees. The rethinking of retirement is driven by both necessity and by changing attitudes. Surveys by AARP (AARP, 2002, 2003b) are finding that up to 80% of Boomers plan to do some sort of paid work into their 70s. They see continued participation in the work force as a way to help them stay mentally sharp and socially engaged, as well as financially more secure. The golden years concept of retirement no longer works economically or socially. Given these societal conditions and changing attitudes, an important issue is whether the workers are cognitively competent to work past the age of 62 and whether complex work environments can foster continue cognitive competence in the workers.

Schooler and colleagues have examined the effects of environmental demand, particularly in the work context, on adult cognition and have considered whether the work environment can continue to impact cognition in late middle age (Schooler, 1990, 1998; see also DeFrias & Schaie, 2001). Recent findings are particularly relevant to midlife cognition. The reciprocal relationship between substantively complex activities (work, leisure) and cognition has been examined longitudinally over three decades. Job conditions involving self-directed, substantively complex work increase intellectual flexibility and self-direction. Recent findings indicate that the reciprocal relation between substantively complex work and cognition are even stronger for men in late midlife than was found previously in younger men (Schooler, Mulatu, & Oates, 1999, 2004). Since professional/managerial and technical positions are most likely to involve cognitively complex work, it should be expected that a greater proportion of Boomers are in challenging work environments than experienced in prior cohorts. Schooler's work does suggest that there are age/cohort differences in work complexity; older age/cohort workers were found to do less substantively complex work.

Schooler and colleagues (Schooler, 1987; Schooler, Mulatu, & Oates, 2004) suggest that if technical and economic development in a society leads to more complex environments, including intellectually demanding work conditions, such increased environmental complexity should result in higher levels of intellectual functioning. Environmental complexity is defined by stimulus and demand characteristics; the more diverse the stimuli, the greater the number of decisions required, and the greater the number of factors to be taken into account in making decisions, the more complex the environment. Cognitively demanding complex environments stimulate higher intellectual functioning, and also greater valuation of self-direction and autonomy (Schooler, 1990). A self-directed, substantively complex environment impacts cognitive functioning, not only in young adulthood, but also in midlife and old age (Attwell, 1987; Schooler et al., 2004).

ExoSystem: Educational Influences of Parent Cohort

We now turn briefly to the exosystem to illustrate its importance in understanding boomer cohort differences in intellectual functioning. We will focus on educational experiences and attainment among parents of the Boomers, as this may impact educational aspirations and achievement of the Boomers.

Fathers' Background and Educational Attainment of the Children.
There have been a number of studies examining key social background variables associated with final educational attainment (cf. Alwin & Thornton, 1984). Of relevance for this article is the fact that a number of these social background variables pertain to the parent's characteristics and thus would be considered in our framework in exosystem models.

The GI Bill.
In several historical periods, federal funding was provided and targeted to select groups in the U.S. Since these targeted groups often represented particular birth cohorts, the cohort differences in educational attainment can be shown to be partially due to these economic interventions in educational funding. One of the most prominent examples is the postwar rehabilitation programs for veterans, known as the GI Bills (Laub & Sampson, 2005; Nam, 1964; Sampson & Laub, 1996). The fathers of the Boomers were members of the cohorts benefiting from the GI Bill and the expansion of higher education in the U.S. following World War II. Boomers were the first generation whose parents achieved some level of post secondary education. As a consequence, parental expectations that their children achieve some form of post secondary education first became normative in the boomer cohorts.

Further educational training was provided through GI Bills for veterans of World War II, the Korean War, and the Vietnam War. Study of the effects of the GI Bills on World War II veterans is of particular interest, because a greater proportion of the U.S. male population was involved in World War II than in the Korean or Vietnam wars. Parents of the Boomers would have been particularly affected by the GI Bill associated with World War II.

The effects of the GI Bill on post-secondary education were pronounced (Nam, 1964; Sampson & Laub, 1996). Almost half of all veterans of World War II and the Korean conflict used the benefits for education and training, and 82% of those veterans who had attended college before the war made use of GI benefits to continue their education. Approximately one third of veterans whose college work was interrupted by military service finished college or went on to graduate or professional school. For veterans who had just completed high school or had barely started college, one fifth went on to get a college degree and a larger proportion took at least some college work. In comparison, only 10% of those who were working at the time of military service acquired at least an academic year of schooling after the war. Sampson and Laub (1996) report that GI Bill training as well as in service schooling enhanced subsequent occupational status, job stability, and economic well-being, independent of childhood differences and socioeconomic background.

Moreover, the dramatic numbers of veterans on college campuses after World War II and the Korean War significantly altered academic protocol and curriculum in higher education. In 1947 7 out of 10 men enrolled in college or universities were veterans of World War II. Similarly, in 1956 one fourth of all male college students were veterans of the Korean conflict (Nam, 1964). These veterans not only challenged prewar assumptions of who could benefit from a college education, but also challenged the very definition of what higher education should offer. Feeling as though the war had delayed their entry into adult life, veterans demanded streamlined education and wanted the curriculum to be geared to real life, in contrast to the more traditional emphasis in higher education on liberal arts and humanities. These veterans pressed academia with the view that the main duty of the university was to train individuals for adult participation in the modern world and to be the vehicle toward a secure job in a large corporation (Vinocour, 1947).

In contrast, the impact on young women of World War II, the GI Bill, and associated trends in consumerism and heightened societal expectation is mixed and continues to stir debate. The image of Rosie the Riveter is seen as legitimatizing women's role in the workforce. Moreover, during the war women's enrollment in colleges increased and in some cases daughters received the college funds that would have been allocated for their brothers. However, as veterans, partly due to the GI Bill, flooded higher education, many colleges after the war sharply curtailed the number of women allowed into college in order to accommodate the veterans. Although the absolute number of women in higher education continued to increase, their numbers in relation to men declined (Clarke, Smith, Jobst, Refsum, Sutton, & Ueland, 1998). More importantly, there was a cultural trend toward urging women to devote themselves to domestic life upon the return of their soldier husbands. As noted by Eggebeen and Sturgeon (chap. 1, this volume), 96% of women born between 1920 and 1930 married, compared to 87% of women born between 1945 and 1949. Although debates on women's choices between marriage, career and college were common themes in the 1940s and 1950s, college typically was seen as taking a backseat to marriage and family. Hence, women who were young adults in the post World War II period began to produce what is now known as the baby-boom generations.

ChronoSystem: Historical Changes
in the Educational System

The changes in educational structures and processes are embedded in historical events and sociocultural transformations. Hence, we will now turn to describing the historical framework that we hope will enrich our understanding of cohort differences in intelligence. Major shifts in performance level across cohorts are likely to lag societal transitions, such as changes in access to the educational system, and dramatic changes following major societal upheaval (cf. Schaie & Elder, 2005). Although it is convenient to define cohorts in relatively brief time intervals, it may be necessary to examine differences between cohorts that are separated in time for longer periods, particularly where the separation includes major societal shifts.

In Table 9.1, the chronosystem component includes both single-domain transitions and cumulative life course transitions and events; we will provide illustrations primarily from the latter since these are most likely to reflect historical change. The most common measure of educational attainment is quantitative—the total number of years of schooling; however education involves both quantitative and qualitative aspects. Quantitative measures reflected in total years of schooling include the age range over which schooling is experienced and the density of the educational experience (school days / school year). Qualitative indicators focus on educational practice, including curriculum and pedagogy. We will begin by discussing the impact of historical changes in legislation and in public funding of education on quantitative indices of educational attainment.

Legislation on Compulsory Schooling.   Two major forms of legislation originating in the early 1900s contributed to significant differences in educational attainment for cohorts born at various decades in the twentieth century. State legislation on the length of the school year and compulsory school attendance enacted during the early 1900s impacted not only the proportion of children in school, but also the intensity of the educational experience. The average length of the school year has increased by almost two months from cohorts born at the beginning of the twentieth century to the 1950 cohorts (U.S. Department of Education, 2002). The average length of the school year for cohorts at the beginning of the twentieth century was 140 days, compared to 170 days and 180 days for parents of the Boomers and Boomers, respectively. Moreover, compulsory school attendance legislation increased the average daily attendance of various cohorts. Daily attendance was approximately 65% among early twentieth century cohorts compared with 85% and 90% for Boomers' parents and Boomers themselves (U.S. Department of Education, 2002).

Time-Specific Federal Funding for Education

National Defense Education Act.   In 1957 the Soviet Union launched Sputnik. The national panic generated by this event resulted in Congress passing a federal-aid-to-education bill, known as The National Defense Education Act of 1958. A major provision of the law involved a $15 million grant with the provision of funds to identify talented students and encourage them to pursue higher education. In the 1957–1958 term alone, Congress proposed over eighty laws to establish programs that would seek out bright students and provide them with financial support for schooling. This focus on talented youth and the provision of educational funds to the gifted would have impacted primarily the Boomer cohorts.

Historical Change in the Educational Curriculum.   Further support for extensive historical changes in curricula taught at different ages is shown in the recent work of Blair and colleagues (Blair, Gamson, Thorne, & Baker, 2005). Findings of this research are particularly relevant to the prior discussion of Flynn IQ effects, where the claim is made that IQ gain for the post World War II cohorts has been primarily in the fluid abilities. Blair and colleagues have documented cohort differences in the age at which students were introduced to visuo-spatial skills such as those traditionally taught in geometry. An 1894 college textbook included a problem that required the student to draw and cut out a two-dimensional triangle and to fold the triangle to develop a three-dimensional polyhedron. By 1955, this type of problem was included in seventh-grade textbook. By 1971 the same concept was being taught to third graders, and by 1991 a first-grade textbook included a simplified version of the concept.

SUMMARY

In this chapter we discussed the salience of cognitive functioning in the baby-boomer cohorts. These are the largest birth cohorts in U.S. history now members of the workforce who will soon enter retirement. Maintenance of cognitive competence in these cohorts is of individual and societal importance. Boomers report that they plan to continue in some form of paid work into their 60s and even 70s in contrast to prior generations that embraced the concept of the golden years. The Boomers report interest in continued work not only due to economic necessity but because they also recognize the need to remain mentally sharp.

The Boomers are also of interest in terms of their cognitive functioning since they represent the key cohorts described in the Flynn effect. Flynn and colleagues maintain that the post World War II cohorts showed massive cohort gain in IQ in adolescence and young adulthood compared to immediately-prior cohorts. Data from cohort-sequential studies such as the SLS provide partial support for the Flynn effect, but also show that equally large cohort gains in IQ were apparent earlier in the twentieth century; however, gain in the earlier birth cohorts involved crystallized as well as fluid intelligence. The boomer cohort functions at a higher aggregate level than any prior cohort based on fluid abilities. The question for the future is whether these cognitive advantages in early life serve as a form of cognitive reserve as these cohorts reach midlife and enter old age, typically a time of cognitive decline (Wilson, Mendes de Leon, Barnes, Scheider, Bienias, Evans, & Bennett, 2002). Findings are mixed on the debate about whether aging is kinder to the initially more able.

Study of cognitive functioning in midlife has received relatively little attention within the adult development and aging literature. This is partially due to the common finding of stability in cognitive functioning in midlife, when studied at the aggregate level. There is, however, increasing recent interest and attention to study of variability in cognitive trajectories at various stages of the life span, including midlife. In this chapter we present preliminary data regarding cognitive trajectories of leading-edge boomer cohorts in midlife. Indeed, the majority of these cohorts show remarkable stability in cognitive functioning in the 40s and 50s, yet there is a small but important minority who exhibit dramatic change over at least 14 years in midlife. One group exhibits abnormally early decline in midlife on the magnitude of one standard deviation—a greater magnitude of decline than has been reported to occur normatively a decade later in the 60s. In contrast, another group exhibits remarkable plasticity in midlife, showing significant cognitive gain of almost a standard deviation. Further study of these groups who deviated from the normative pattern of cognitive stability in midlife is merited. There is growing evidence that preclinical cognitive impairment may begin in midlife for some individuals; future research should examine whether early behavioral or pharmaceutical interventions would be of benefit. Equally interesting are the individuals who continue to exhibit reliable gain in cognitive functioning into the 50s in midlife. The lifestyles of these individuals require further examination of factors that foster continued growth.

In the last section of this chapter we present a conceptual framework for studying three levels of influence on cognitive development—with particular focus on factors in midlife and of historical relevance to the boomer cohorts. Although the initial Bronfenbrenner model focused largely on the Mesosystem, we propose that in studies of adult development and cohort differences, the Exosystem and Chronosystem are of particular interest. We briefly review historical events in the childhood and young adulthood of the Boomers associated with educational opportunities and trends that may have impacted their cognitive development. Further study of such events is needed.

In summary, the boomer cohorts offer a unique opportunity to advance the study of cognitive functioning in adulthood and in midlife in particular. Given their historical and societal significance, much has and is being written on the unique sociocultural context in which they developed. This affords a special opportunity for social scientists to extend our understanding of the nature of cohort differences and their impact on individual development.

REFERENCES

AARP. (2002). *Boomers at midlife: The AARP Life Stage Study* (Vol. 1). Washington, DC: AARP.

AARP. (2003a). *Back to the future: Baby Boomers keeping the faith in public education*. Washington, DC: AARP.

AARP. (2003b). *Staying ahead of the curve 2003: The AARP Working in Retirement Study*. Washington, DC: AARP.

Albert, M. S., Jones, K., Savage, C. R., Berkman, L., Seeman, T., Blazer, D., & Rowe, J. W. (1995). Predictors of cognitive change in older persons: MacArthur Studies of Successful Aging. *Psychology and Aging, 10*, 578–589.

Albert, M., & Killiany, R. (2001). Age-related cognitive change and brain–behavior relationships. In J. E. Birren & K. W. Schaie (Eds.), *Handbook of the psychology of aging* (5th ed., pp. 161–185). San Diego, CA: Academic Press.

Alwin, D. F. (1991). Family of origin and cohort differences in verbal ability. *American Sociological Review, 56*, 625–638.

Alwin, D. F., & McCammon, R. J. (2001). Aging, cohorts, and verbal ability. *Journals of Gerontology: Social Sciences, 56B*, S151–S161.

Alwin, D. F., & Thornton, A. (1984). Family origins and the schooling process: Early versus late influence of parental characteristics. *American Sociological Review, 49*, 784–802.

Anstey, K., & Christensen, H. (2000). Education, activity, health, blood pressure and Apolipoprotein E as predictors of cognitive change in old age: A review. *Gerontology, 46*, 163–177.

Arking, R. (1998). *Biology of aging: Observations and principles* (2nd ed.). Sunderland, MA: Sinauer Associates.

Attwell, P. (1987). The deskilling controversy. *Work and Occupation, 14*, 323–346.

Bachman, L., & Nilsson, L. G. (1985). The avoidance of age differences in single-trial free recall. *Annals of the New York Academy of Science, 444*, 523–524.

Baltes, P. B. (1979). Life-span developmental psychology: Some converging observations on history and theory. In P. B. Baltes & O. G. Brim, Jr. (Eds.), *Life-span development and behavior* (Vol. 2). New York: Academic Press.

Baltes, P. B. (1987). Theoretical propositions of life-span developmental psychology: On the dynamics between growth and decline. *Developmental Psychology, 23*, 611–626.

Blair, C., Gamson, D. A., Thorne, S., & Baker, D. P. (2005). Rising mean IQ: Cognitive demand of mathematics education for young children, population exposure to formal schooling, and the neurobiology of the prefrontal cortex. *Intelligence.*

Brookmeyer, R., Gray, S., & Kawas, S. (1998). Projections of Alzheimer's disease in the United States and the public health impact of delaying disease onset. *American Journal of Public Health, 88*, 1337–1342.

Bronfenbrenner, U. (1986). Ecology of the family as a context for human development research perspectives. *Developmental Psychology, 22*, 723–742.

Bronfenbrenner, U., & Crouter, A. (1983). The evolution of environmental models in developmental research. In P. H. Mussen (Series Ed.) & W. Kessen (Vol. Ed.), *Handbook of child psychology: Vol. 1. History, theory, and methods* (4th ed., pp. 357–414). New York: Wiley.

Christensen, H., Korten, A. E., Jorn, A. F., Henderson, A. S., Jacomb, P. A., Rodgers, B., & Mackinnon, A. J. (1997). Education and decline in cognitive performance: Compensatory but not protective. *International Journal of Geriatric Psychiatry, 12*, 323–330.

Clarke, R., Smith, A. D., Jobst, K. A., Refsum, H., Sutton, L., & Ueland, P. M. (1998). Folate, vitamin B22 and serum total homocysteine levels in confirmed Alzheimer disease. *Archives of Neurology, 55*, 1449–1455.

Costa, P. T., Jr., & McCrae, R. R. (1980). Still stable after all these years: Personality as a key to some issues in adulthood and old age. In P. Baltes & O. G. Brim, Jr. (Eds.), *Life span development and behavior* (Vol. 3, pp. 65–102). New York: Academic Press.

Costa, P. T., Jr., & McCrae, R. R. (1993). Stability and change in personality from adolescence through adulthood. In C. A. Halverson, G. A. Kohnstamm, & R. P. Martin (Eds.), *The developing structure of temperament and personality from infancy to adulthood* (pp. 235–252). Hillsdale, NJ: Lawrence Erlbaum Associates.

Craik, F. I. M., & Jennings, J. M. (1992). Human memory. In F. I. M. Craik & T. A. Salhouse (Eds.), *The handbook of aging and cognition*. Hillsdale, NJ: Lawrence Erlbaum Associates.

Crystal, S., & Shea, D. (Eds.). (2002). *Economic outcomes in later life: Public policy, health and cumulative advantage: Vol. 22. Annual Review of Gerontology and Geriatrics*. New York: Springer.

DeFrias, C., & Schaie, K. W. (2001). Perceptions of work environment and cognitive performance. *Experimental Aging Research, 27,* 67–81.

Dickens, W. T., & Flynn, J. R. (2001). Heritability estimates versus large environmental effects: The IQ paradox resolved. *Psychological Review, 108,* 346–369.

Dixon, R. A., de Frias, C. M., & Maitland, S. B. (2001). Memory in midlife. In M. E. Lachman (Ed.), *Handbook of midlife development* (pp. 248–278). New York: Wiley.

Dudek, F. J. (1979). The continuing misinterpretation of the standard error of measurement. *Psychological Bulletin, 86,* 335–337.

Easterlin, R. A. (1987). *Birth and fortune: The impact of numbers on personal welfare* (2nd ed.). Chicago: University of Chicago Press.

Elder, G. H., Jr. (1974). *Children of the Great Depression*. Chicago: University of Chicago Press.

Farmer, M. E., Kittner, S. J., Rae, D. S., Barko, J. J., & Regier, D. A. (1995). Education and change in cognitive function: The Epidemiologic Catchment Area Study. *Annals of Epidemiology, 5,* 1–7.

Flynn, J. R. (1984). The mean IQ of Americans: Massive gains, 1932 to 1978. *Psychological Bulletin, 95,* 29–51.

Flynn, J. R. (1987). Massive IQ gains in 14 nations: What IQ tests really measure. *Psychological Bulletin, 101,* 171–191.

Flynn, J. R. (1999). Searching for justice: The discovery of IQ gains over time. *American Psychologist, 54,* 5–20.

Glenn, N. D. (1994). Television watching, newspaper reading, and cohort differences in verbal ability. *Sociology of Education, 67,* 216–230.

Greenough, W. T., Larson, J. R., & Withers, G. S. (1985). Effects of unilateral and bilateral training in a reaching task on dendritic branching of neurons in the rat motor-sensitivity forelimb cortex. *Behavioral Neural Biology, 44,* 301–314.

Hanford, G. H. (1991). *Life with the SAT*. New York: College Entrance Examination Board.

Hauser, R. M., & Featherman, D. L. (1976). Equality of schooling: Trends and prospects. *Sociology of Education, 49,* 99–120.

Helson, R., & Moane, G. (1987). Personality change in women from college to midlife. *Journal of Personality and Social Psychology, 53,* 176–186.

Hultsch, D. F., Hertzog, C., Dixon, R. A., & Small, B. J. (1998). *Memory change in the aged*. Cambridge: Cambridge University Press.

Kahn, R. L., & Antonucci, T. C. (1980). Convoys over the life course: Attachment, roles and social support. *Life Span Development, 3,* 253–286.

Katzman, R. (1993). Education and the prevalence of dementia and Alzheimer's disease. *Neurology, 43,* 13–20.

Kohn, M. L., & Schooler, C. (1983). *Work and personality: An inquiry into the impact of social stratification*. Norwood, NJ: Ablex.

Kotlikoff, L. J., & Burns, S. (2005). *The coming generational storm*. Boston, MA: MIT Press.

Kramer, A. F., & Willis, S. L. (2003). Cognitive plasticity and aging. In B. H. Ross (Ed.), *The psychology of learning and motivation: Advances in research and theory* (Vol. 43, pp. 267–302). Amsterdam: Academic Press.

Lachman, M. E. (Ed.). (2001). *Handbook of midlife development*. New York: Wiley.

Laub, J. H., & Sampson, R. J. (2005). Coming of age in wartime: How World War II and the Korean War changed lives. In K. W. Schaie & G. Elder (Eds.), *Historical influences on lives and aging*. New York: Springer.

Light, P. C. (1988). *Baby Boomers*. New York: W. W. Norton.

Lyketsos, C. G., Chen, L. S., & Anthony, J. C. (1999). Cognitive decline in adulthood: An 11.5-year follow-up of the Baltimore Epidemiologic Catchment Area Study. *American Journal of Psychiatry, 156*, 58–65.

Morgan, W. R., Alwin, D. F., & Griffin, L. J. (1979). Social origins, parental values and the transmission of inequality. *American Journal of Sociology, 85*, 156–166.

Mortimer, J. T., & Kumka, D. (1982). A further examination of the "occupational link hypothesis." *Sociological Quarterly, 23*, 3–16.

Nam, C. B. (1964). Impact of the "GI Bills" on the educational level of the male population. *Social Forces, 43*, 26–32.

Lezak, M. D. (1995). *Neuropsychological assessment* (3rd ed.). New York: Oxford University Press.

Martin, M., & Zimprich, D. (2005). Cognitive development in midlife. In S. L. Willis & M. Martin (Eds.), *Middle adulthood: A lifespan perspective*. Thousand Oaks, CA: Sage.

McCrae, R. R., & Costa, P. T. (1984). *Emerging lives, enduring dispositions: Personality in adulthood*. Boston: Little, Brown.

Metlife Mature Market Institute. (2003). *Demographic profile: American Baby Boomers*. New York: Metropolitan Life Insurance.

Moen, P., & Wethington, E. (1999). Midlife development in a life course context. In S. L. Willis & J. Reid (Eds.), *Life in the middle: Psychological and social development in middle age*. San Diego, CA: Academic.

Petersen, R. C. (Ed.). (2003). *Mild cognitive impairment: Aging to Alzheimer's disease*. Oxford: Oxford University Press.

Riley, M. W., Johnson, M. J., & Foner, A. (1972). *Aging and society: Vol. 3. A sociology of age stratification*. New York: Sage.

Rosenberg, S. D., Rosenberg, H. J., & Farrell, M. P. (1999). The midlife crisis revisited. In S. L. Willis & J. Reid (Eds.), *Life in the middle: Psychological and social development in middle age*. San Diego, CA: Academic.

Sampson, R. J., & Laub, J. H. (1996). Socioeconomic achievement in the life course of disadvantaged men: Military service as a turning point, circa 1940–1965. *American Sociological Review, 61*, 347–367.

Schaie, K. W. (1984). Midlife influences upon intellectual functioning in old age. *International Journal of Behavioral Development, 7*, 463–478.

Schaie, K. W. (1989a). The hazards of cognitive aging. *Gerontologist, 29*, 484–493.

Schaie, K. W. (1989b). Individual differences in rate of cognitive change. In V. L. Bengtson & K. W. Schaie (Eds.), *The course of later life: Research and reflections* (pp. 65–85). New York: Springer.

Schaie, K. W. (1996). *Intellectual development in adulthood: The Seattle Longitudinal Study*. New York: Cambridge University Press.

Schaie, K. W. (2005). *Developmental influences on adult intelligence: The Seattle Longitudinal Study*. London: Oxford Press.

Schaie, K. W., & Achenbaum, W. A. (Eds.). (1993). *Societal impact on aging: Historical perspectives*. New York: Springer.

Schaie, K. W., & Elder, G. H., Jr. (Eds.). (2005). *Historical influences on lives and aging*. New York: Springer.

Schaie, K. W., & Willis, S. L. (1986). Can intellectual decline in the elderly be reversed? *Developmental Psychology, 22*, 223–232.

Schaie, K. W., & Willis, S. L. (1993). Age difference patterns of psychometric intelligence in adulthood: Generalizability within and across ability domains. *Psychology and Aging, 8,* 44–55.

Schaie, K. W., Willis, S. L., & Pennak, S. (2005). A historical framework for cohort differences in intelligence. *Research in Human Development, 2*(1&2), 43–67.

Schooler, C. (1987). Cognitive effects of complex environments during the life span: A review and theory. In C. Schooler & K. W. Schaie (Eds.), *Cognitive functioning and social structure over the life course* (pp. 24–49). Norwood, NJ: Ablex.

Schooler, C. (1990). Psychosocial factors and effective cognitive functioning in adulthood. In J. E. Birren & K. W. Schaie (Eds.), *Handbook of the psychology of aging* (3rd ed., pp. 347–358). San Diego, CA: Academic Press.

Schooler, C. (1998). Environmental complexity and the Flynn effect. In U. Neisser (Ed.), *The rising curve: Long-term gains in IQ and related measures* (pp. 67–79). Washington, DC: American Psychological Association.

Schooler, C., Mulatu, M. S., & Oates, G. (1999). The continuing effects of substantively complex work on the intellectual functioning of older workers. *Psychology and Aging, 14,* 483–506.

Schooler, C., Mulatu, M. S., & Oates, G. (2004). Occupational self-direction, intellectual functioning and self-directed orientation in older workers: Findings and implications for individuals and societies. *American Journal of Sociology, 110,* 161–197.

Smith, A. D., & Earles, J. L. K. (1996). Memory changes in normal aging. In F. Blanchard-Fields & T. M. Hess (Eds.), *Perspectives on cognitive change in adulthood and aging* (pp. 192–220). New York: McGraw-Hill.

Stewart, A. J. (2003). Gender, race and generation in a Midwest high school: Using ethnographically informed methods in psychology. *Psychology of Women Quarterly, 27,* 1–11.

Staudinger, U. M., & Bluck, S. (2001). A view of midlife development from life-span theory. In M. E. Lachman (Ed.), *Handbook of midlife development* (pp. 3–39). New York: Wiley.

Thurstone, L. L., & Thurstone, T. G. (1949). *Examiner Manual for the SRA Primary Mental Abilities Test* (Form 10-14). Chicago: Science Research Associates.

U.S. Bureau of the Census. (1991). *Statistical Abstract of the United States: 1991* (111th ed.). Washington, DC: Author.

U.S. Bureau of the Census. (2002). *Current Population Survey, March 1989 Technical Documentation.* Washington, DC: Administrative and Publications Services Division, Microdata Access Branch.

U.S. Bureau of the Census. (2004). *Educational attainment.* (http://www.census.gov/population/www/socdemo/educ-attn.html)

U.S. Department of Education, National Center for Education Statistics. (2002, August). *Statistics of public elementary and secondary school systems: Common core of data survey and projections of education statistics to 2012* (Report No. 200412). Washington, DC: Government Printing Office.

Vinocour, S. M. (1947, November). The veteran and college. *Newsweek, 80,* 140.

Whitbourne, S. K., & Connolly, L. A. (1999). The developing self in midlife. In S. L. Willis & J. Reid (Eds.), *Life in the middle: Psychological and social development in middle age.* San Diego, CA: Academic.

Willis, S. L. (1987). Adult intelligence. In S. Hunter & M. Sundel (Eds.), *Midlife myths: Issues, findings, and practice applications* (pp. 97–111). Newbury Park, CA: Sage.

Willis, S. L. (1989). Cohort differences in cognitive aging: A sample case. In K. W. Schaie & C. Schooler (Eds.), *Social structure and aging: Psychological processes* (pp. 94–112). Hillsdale, NJ: Lawrence Erlbaum Associates.

Willis, S. L. (1996). Everyday problem solving. In J. E. Birren & K. W. Schaie (Eds.), *Handbook of the psychology of aging* (4th ed., pp. 287–307). San Diego, CA: Academic Press.

Willis, S. L., & Schaie, K. W. (1986). Training the elderly on the ability factors of spatial orientation and inductive reasoning. *Psychology and Aging, 1,* 239–247.

Willis, S. L., & Schaie, K. W. (1999). Intellectual functioning in midlife. In S. Willis & J. Reid (Eds.), *Life in the middle* (pp. 233–247). San Diego, CA: Academic Press.

Willis, S. L., & Schaie, K. W. (2005). Cognitive trajectories in midlife and cognitive functioning in old age. In S. L. Willis & M. Martin (Eds.), *Middle adulthood: A lifespan perspective* (pp. 243–276). Thousand Oaks, CA: Sage.

Wilson, R. S., Mendes de Leon, Carlos, F., Barnes, L. L., Scheider, J. A., Bienias, J. L., Evans, D. A., & Bennett, D. A. (2002). Participation in cognitively stimulating activities and risk of incident Alzheimer Disease. *Journal of the American Medical Association, 287,* 742–748.

Wilson, J. A., & Gove, W. R. (1999). The intercohort decline in verbal ability: Does it exist? *American Sociological Review, 64,* 253–266.

PART FOUR

Functioning in Context

The Baby Boomers and Their Parents: Cohort Influences and Intergenerational Ties

Karen Fingerman
Purdue University

Megan Dolbin-MacNab
Virginia Polytechnic Institute and State University

INTRODUCTION

The term Baby Boom conveys the swell in the population that occurred because a group of mothers and fathers were so prolific. Birth rates in industrialized nations have declined steadily over the past two centuries (Alwin, McCammon, & Hofer, 2005), yet parents born between 1910 and 1945 produced a plethora of children between 1946 and 1964. These children have been the focus of scholarly studies, marketing, and social interest since they first entered the world. The Baby Boom became a social phenomenon as a result. In early life, when the Baby Boomers were children, their parents were necessarily partners in the phenomenalization of the cohort. As the Baby Boomers are ensconced in midlife, their parents are growing old and dying. Recent documentaries and books focus attention on the Baby Boomers' parents as the Greatest Generation, emphasizing their role in World War II and subsequent leadership (e.g., Brokaw, 1998). Yet, marketing efforts, scholarship, and general interest in the Baby Boomers' aging parents are not as pervasive as was the interest in the Baby Boomers' own childhood. There are fewer movies, television images, or icons of relationships between middle-aged Baby Boomers and their parents than was the case when the Baby Boomers were children. As such, relationships between middle aged adults and their parents today are more personalized and less publicly defined than the early relationships between Baby Boomers and their parents.

THE BROAD AND NARROW HISTORY
OF PARENT–OFFSPRING TIES

Understanding relationships between middle-aged Baby Boomers and their parents requires both a broad and a narrow focus on time and history. As life course theory suggests, current relationships between Baby Boomers and their parents stem from their shared personal past as well as from the cultural and political historical settings in which they have been embedded (Elder, 1998). The combination of these early experiences and cultural settings contribute to the ties middle aged Baby Boomers experience with their parents today.

As we discuss in this chapter, many of the period effects observed in relationships between Baby Boomers and their parents appear to be an extension of changes the parents experienced when they were younger. These experiences may in turn have shaped their subsequent intergenerational ties with their progeny. In many respects, the lives of the parent generation represent a paradigm shift relative to the family patterns of prior cohorts. Many of the parents have lived longer and experienced a greater number of distinct life stages (e.g., childhood, adolescence, young adulthood) as compared to prior cohorts. Of course, the parents also produced a greater number of children than the cohorts immediately before them (Eggebeen, 1992). This chapter addresses the ways in which the life patterns of the parents shaped their relationships with their baby-boomer children.

As other chapters in this volume document, the Baby Boom actually involves multiple cohorts; individuals born from 1946 to 1964 have experienced a wide range of historical events. The earliest Baby Boomers were born during a period of relative economic stability, domestic political tranquility, and a tenuous post World War II atmosphere of competing superpowers. These early Baby Boomers encountered tumultuous social changes of the 1960s and 1970s during their adolescence or early adulthood: Women entered the work world in increasing numbers, racial discrimination began to dissipate, sexual mores loosened considerably, fashion became more casual, and college enrollments increased dramatically. In contrast, Baby Boomers born at the end of the cohort arrived at the start of the social upheavals of the 1960s and experienced widespread technological advances through young adulthood, i.e. personal computers, electronic mail, cable television, and compact disc players, that provided them with access to information, education, and entertainment unavailable to prior generations. In concert with the life course perspective, relationships between the Baby Boomers and their parents were embedded in these historical phenomena.

Investment in Children

Although the Baby Boomers involve multiple cohorts, these cohorts experienced a common shift towards increased investment by their parents of emotion, time, and financial resources in the parent–child tie. The early Baby Boom was accompanied by a groundswell of interest in children and family, as an outgrowth of a nation returned home from war triumphant. Industry and communities focused on these cherished progeny. For example, toy companies generated trinkets to amuse them, and communities built schools to educate them. Moreover, childrearing experts offered the parents of the Baby Boomers bountiful advice on how to raise their children. It is perhaps no coincidence that Benjamin Spock's 1946 book, *The Common Sense Book of Child and Baby Care* sold 3 million volumes in the first year it was published (Hulbert, 2003). Thus, the earliest years of the Baby Boomers were accompanied by a cultural focus on childhood and relationships between parents and children.

Of course, relationships between Baby Boomers and their parents pre-date 1946. The parents of the Baby Boomers brought a mentality to parenting that stemmed from their own experiences as children. Hulbert's (2003) history of childrearing attitudes suggests that the parents were themselves among the first cohorts to be raised by parents who attended to the advice of experts. From 1910 to the 1940s, when the parents were themselves children, American culture underwent economic shifts that facilitated the presence of a mother in the household whose primary focus was on the children (Coontz, 2000). Childrearing experts focused advice on this mother. In the early part of the century, mothers were subject to rigid ideas about scheduling and caring for children that were later relaxed when these children became mothers and raised their own baby-boomer children under the tutelage of experts such as Drs. Spock and Brazelton (Hulbert, 2003). Therefore, due to these cultural influences, many of the parents were self-consciously aware of the act of parenting.

Building on this child-focused parenting, during their childhoods, marketing and social institutions also contributed to a child-focused milieu for the baby-boomer children. For example, advertising for children's items in the late 1950s led to the success of companies such as Wham-O selling 10 million Hula Hoops. The successful marketing of this trivial children's toy depended in large part on the willingness of parents to indulge their children in leisure and play.

Freedom in Adolescence

The indulgence of leisure and play experienced by the Baby Boomers is also evident in the extended length of time the Baby Boomers spent in the years of adolescence. The early twentieth century ushered in modern adolescence as a distinct stage of life prior to adult work. Many of the parents experienced the first phase of freedom when they themselves were adolescents during the 1920s. Indeed, the wide scale concept of adolescence as a time of training and preparation for adulthood came into being from 1890 to 1920, a period when many more high schools were built and child labor laws took hold in the U.S. (Hine, 1999).

In this sense, the childhood and adolescence experienced by the Baby Boomers appears along a trajectory towards increased freedom from work for children and adolescents that started when their parents were young. The term teenager came into the lexicon when the earliest Baby Boomers entered adolescence in the 1950s, conveying that these youth were free to focus on dating, entertainment, dress, and after school jobs (Fasick, 1994; Greenberger & Steinberg, 1986; Hine, 1999). Although the Great Depression and World War II served as interruptions in this process, the parents experienced a period of training during their own adolescence and a freedom from work unknown to their own parents. Once they had their own children during a period of relative prosperity, the parents of the Baby Boomers encouraged them to remain free from work demands and responsibilities into young adulthood, and to enjoy a period of life as a teenager.

PRESENT TIES BETWEEN BABY BOOMERS AND PARENTS

Vestiges of cultural shifts beginning in the early to mid twentieth century are evident today in relationships between middle aged Baby Boomers and their parents. For example, the emphasis on the maternal bond has persisted; intergenerational ties between adults and their mothers tend to be closer and warmer than relationships between adults and their fathers (Fingerman, 2001a; Rossi & Rossi, 1990). Similarly, the child-focused nature of the relationship has persisted long after the Baby Boomers were grown. Parents continue to provide more material, instrumental and emotional support for offspring than the reverse until the very final stages of life (Zarit & Eggebeen, 2002). At the same time, certain features of relationships between Baby Boomers and their parents may transcend culture and period. Parental investment in launching offspring into adulthood has persisted for centuries, as has some offspring's concerns about parental aging.

Indeed, theoretical perspectives on intergenerational ties suggest that relationships between adults and their parents are often characterized by emotional and cognitive features that generate feelings of connection. Solidarity theory, which focuses on intergenerational connections, has held a dominant role in guiding research on the Baby Boomers and their parents (e.g., Atkinson, Kivett, & Campbell, 1986; Rossi & Rossi, 1990). Solidarity theory, like attachment theory in infancy, is based on the premise of universal patterns underlying strong bonds between parents and offspring. Attachment is a biologically based series of behaviors that emerges in infancy (Bowlby, 1969/ 1982). As individuals grow older they are susceptible to increasing diversity of experience that also shapes these ties. Behavioral manifestations of attachment, per se, may be less clear, but feelings of emotional closeness may persist.

Solidarity theory suggests that affection, patterns of association, consensus of values, and exchanges of assistance contribute to feelings of connection between adults and their parents (Rossi & Rossi, 1990; Silverstein & Bengtson, 1997).

Scholars applied solidarity theory to address intergenerational ties during the post World War II period, as society continued to shift from multigenerational agrarian farms to a manufacturing economy (e.g., Homans, 1950). Social scientists at the time argued that the nuclear family would become the primary family unit (Parsons, 1943). Gerontologists continued to believe older adults were integral to family life, and that adults valued their extended family members. As such, scholars who studied solidarity theory were interested in questions about the strength of intergenerational bonds. Solidarity theory arose when the parents of the Baby Boomers were adults and establishing intergenerational patterns with their own parents. The mechanisms have been more widely examined as the Baby Boomers passed through adulthood (e.g., Atkinson, Kivett, & Campbell, 1986; Rossi & Rossi, 1990; Silverstein & Bengtson, 1997). The solidarity model suggests that emotional connections formed in early life persist into feelings of unity between adults and their parents.

More recently, scholars have suggested that middle-aged Baby Boomers and their parents also experience ambivalence in their relationships (Connidis & McMullin, 2002; Fingerman, Hay, & Birditt, 2004; Luescher & Pillemer, 1998). The intergenerational ambivalence model is premised on the assumption that social structures may generate conflicting norms about interactions with parents and grown offspring, and as a result, adults may experience ambivalent feelings or beliefs about the tie. It is notable that this theory arose only as the Baby Boomers were ensconced in midlife and their parents faced old age. Certainly, the theoretical emphasis on conflicting norms reflects the personalized nature of this intergenerational relationship and the heterogeneity of the baby-boomer cohort.

In this chapter, we attempt to delineate features of relationships between middle-aged Baby Boomers and their parents that: (a) reflect historical period, (b) stem from their early relationships, and (c) involve current demands in the tie. We also consider how social changes of the past 60 years have rendered relationships between Baby Boomers and their parents distinct in comparison to previous or future cohorts. We also address what may be more universal features of these ties such as love, solidarity, and ambivalence.

As a note of caution, it would be easy to oversimplify the complexities of relationships between Baby Boomers and their parents by taking a monolithic view of these ties with regard to historical setting. As other chapters in this volume point out, the experiences of historical events among the Baby Boomers varied considerably, as did the experiences of their parents. The Baby Boomers include individuals who are currently aged 40 to 60, representing a large age span and multiple subcohorts. Diversity of macrolevel social structures goes without saying; these individuals come from a wide array of racial and ethnic groups, and the full range of socioeconomic classes. Cultural images of the childhood of the Baby Boomers (such as the nuclear family) tend to be those images associated primarily with a European American middle class, however, rather than the broader population of the U.S. at that time (Coontz, 2000).

Ties between Baby Boomers and parents vary along a variety of dimensions at midlife including work status, sexual orientation, and marital status, among others. For example, relationships between Baby Boomers and their parents may vary as a function of their own work status (Zarit & Eggebeen, 2002). Some Baby Boomers work for pay, some are retired, some are homemakers, and some have scraped by in marginalized economic positions throughout their lives. Similarly, Baby Boomers also vary in sexual orientation and marital status. As such, it is difficult to discuss one social structure (e.g., employment) without considering another social structure (e.g., marital status). Moreover, the political beliefs, social values, and strength of religiosity vary considerably among the Baby Boomers. Scholars have suggested that deep cultural rifts have arisen between those who are culturally conservative and those who are culturally progressive (Clydesdale, 1997). Add to this the variability in parent–offspring relationships as a function of gender, and consideration of cohort is mired in complexity. For example, is the relationship between a married 60-year-old woman caring for her widowed frail mother comparable to a divorced 42-year-old woman who turns to her healthy parents for assistance with her own children? Pillemer and Suitor (1998) suggest that current social structures present so many choices, options, juxtapositions, and contradictions, that Baby Boomers and their parents are in a considerable state of turmoil. Despite this heterogeneity, however, it is still possible to consider some commonalities and global aspects of the cohort.

TIES TO PARENTS AND SOCIAL HISTORICAL CHANGES

A myriad of social, cultural, political, and technological changes have occurred during the lives of the Baby Boomers as well as the lives of their parents. We face distinct challenges in attempting to look at intergenerational relationships in the context of historical changes. Clearly, the Baby Boomers experienced historical changes in different ways than did their parents. For example, over the past 30 years, baby-boom women were able to take advantage of increased opportunities in traditionally male fields such as law, medicine, and business. Their mothers, were less able to do so because by the time these changes occurred, they already had children to care for in the home. Further, it is not possible to discuss specific historical events as they affected the Baby Boomers at large and their parents at large. Many of the parents of the tail end

Baby Boomers (born 1959–1964) were born in the 1930s or 1940s. These parents overlap more with the early Baby Boomers (born 1946–1950) than with their parents, particularly if the early Baby Boomer was a youngest child and the tail end Baby Boomer an oldest child.

Nonetheless, societal changes in the latter half of the twentieth century and early twenty-first century have shaped intergenerational ties between the Baby Boomers and their parents. Here, we focus specifically on four areas of cultural, political, or economic change that have influenced relationships between Baby Boomers and their parents: (1) increased life expectancy, (2) the economy, education, and mobility, (3) family structure, and (4) gender and sexuality. In each section below, we address an area of social change and consider how it has affected relationships between Baby Boomers and their parents.

How Life Expectancy Affects Baby Boomers and Their Parents

Increases in life expectancy in industrialized countries over the past 100 years may be the most important factor that shapes ties between Baby Boomers and their parents. Average life expectancy in the U.S. currently hovers around age 76, compared to age 41 in the year 1900. The notion of a midlife period from ages 40 to 60 only arose in the past century (Moen & Wethington, 1999). Relationships between the Baby Boomers and their parents have been broadly shaped by these shifts in life expectancy and concurrent shifts in conceptualization of the life course. Relationships between parents and offspring are one of the few ties that last from birth through childhood, young adulthood and into midlife with such strong intensity (ties between siblings tend to become less intense in young adulthood (Connidis & Campbell, 1995).

Although life expectancy has increased, it is still finite. As the Baby Boomers traverse midlife, their parents are either aging or have passed away. It is beyond the scope of this chapter to discuss bereavement, but most of the older Baby Boomers have lost at least one parent (particularly their fathers). It is also notable that some elderly parents have lost a baby-boom child (Johnson & Barer, 1997). For the remaining Baby Boomers, the aging of their parents may be upon them, and the sense that their relationships will soon end. Increases in life expectancy have also contributed to the huge numbers of aging parents who have survived into old age.

Before their parents reached old age, however, the Baby Boomers and their parents may have possessed a sense that time was expansive. The parents (who were born between approximately 1910 and 1945) were among the first cohorts to see increases in life expectancy and great numbers of individuals surviving into old age. Watching grandparents or parents grow old, individuals began to plan their lives around the idea of a wide stretching future. In other words, the parents are among the first cohort of individuals to think about old age as a normal aspect of life. Most of the parents entered the work world after 1935 when Social Security began and thus, had an expectation of retirement from the onset of their working careers. These parents gave birth to the Baby Boomers with the assumption that their relationships would endure long after the children were adults.

Ties Between Baby Boomers and Their Parents in Young Adulthood

The sense that time was expansive appeared to transcend many other historical counter forces during the youth of the Baby Boomers. Part of the optimism of the 1950s reflected the sense among Americans that the future was available to them. This is notable because the Baby Boomers grew up during the first period in human history during which countries held the capacity to annihilate the human species. The nuclear bombs of Hiroshima and Nagasaki exploded just before the earliest Baby Boomers were born. The early Baby Boomers were aware of the Cold War, arms races, and "duck and cover" campaigns during their childhood. Despite the global ramifications of these threats, however, it is not clear whether most Baby Boomers themselves grew up with a sense of vulnerability. Indeed, David Elkind developed a well known theory of social cognition during their adolescence and young adulthood; the "personal fable" describes the ways in which adolescent egocentrism leads to a sense of immunity (Elkind, 1967, 1978). Thus, most Baby Boomers may have been more attuned to the idea of a long life than to the idea that the Soviet Union might end their lives early.

The sense that relationships between parents and offspring would endure for decades colored that relationship throughout the lives of the Baby Boomers. When the earliest Baby Boomers entered adolescence and young adulthood in the 1960s societal challenges were ripe for intergenerational conflicts. Disputes over the American engagement in the Vietnam War, increased sexual permissiveness, a decline in formal manners, casual clothing styles, and a relaxing of social mores provided fodder for such disputes. Yet, the Baby Boomers entered young adulthood with a sense that they had 20 or 30 years of ties with their parents ahead of them. Scholars have suggested that, as a result, the Baby Boomers were more likely to align their values with members of their cohort than with their parents (Stewart, 2003; Stewart & Healey, 1989). Intergenerational strife during young adulthood would be in keeping with a prolonged time horizon associated with increased life expectancy. According to socioemotional selectivity theory, individuals who foresee a curtailed future value their relationships more than individuals who view the future as open (Carstensen, Isaacowitz, & Charles, 1999). The ability to break away may partly reflect the belief held by the Baby Boomers that their parents would still be alive for several decades. When parental death seems imminent, offspring shift their behaviors to protect their parents instead (Fingerman, 2001a).

Yet, it would be overstating the case to assert that Baby Boomers and their parents' relationships were strife-ridden, even for early Baby Boomers who experienced the greatest social upheavals relative to their parents. Studies pursuing a "generation gap" between the early Baby Boomers and their parents found scant disputes (Bengtson & Kuypers, 1971; Troll, 1971). In fact, tensions between Baby Boomers and their parents were no greater than intergenerational tensions documented in other historical periods (Haber, 1983; Hareven, 1995). For example, during the 1920s, the parents of the Baby Boomers who were adolescents and young adults experienced increased sexual liberation relative to the Victorian era, and as a result, traditional moorings to family, church, and community groups loosened. Technological advances such as the radio and automobile also gave the parents a wider range of societal information than that provided by their families, again providing ample opportunity for intergenerational strife (Brumberg, 1997). More recent research (Graber & Brooks-Gunn, 1999; Laursen, Coy, & Collins, 1998; Smetana, 1995) concerning the Baby Boomers as parents and their adolescent children revealed similar intergenerational conflicts. Most conflicts between adolescents and their parents continue to revolve around everyday issues such as hair styles, curfews, and household chores rather than core values such as educational aspirations or religion (Smetana, 1995). Therefore, regardless of cohort, shifting societal expectations involving day-to-day clothing, household chores, and societal mores may generate tensions for adolescents and their parents. However, the manifestation of those conflicts may vary by cohort. For example, shifts in mores pertaining to filial obedience may have allowed the Baby Boomers to vocalize their dissent with their parents more openly than prior generations.

In sum, increases in life expectancy may have contributed to the nature of the relationships between Baby Boomers and their parents in young adulthood by lending the sense of an expansive future. Relationships between Baby Boomers and their parents may have also involved pressures for the Baby Boomers to differentiate themselves from parents, particularly during the turbulent 1960s and 1970s. It is unclear, however, that their ties were more strife ridden than prior or subsequent cohorts. The effects of increased longevity appear to be more evident in Baby Boomers' current ties to elderly parents.

Ties Between Baby Boomers and Their Aging Parents

Increases in longevity have been accompanied by improvements in health among older adults (Schoeni, Freedman, & Wallace, 2001), but as the parents of the Baby Boomers confront late life, they experience inevitable declines. Indeed, improvements in the treatment of acute disease and infection have resulted in the domination of prolonged chronic diseases at the end of life (Zarit, in press). Although life expectancy trajectories reveal consistent increases in the number of older adults over the past century, parents of the Baby Boomers are among the first cohorts to survive into advanced old age (their 80s and 90s), a period in which frailty and dependence may increase dramatically (Femia, Zarit, & Johansson, 2001). As a result, parental health problems are a central focus of ties between middle-aged Baby Boomers and their parents. Additionally, the centrality of parental health to the tie may precipitate midlife. Studies reveal that younger adults worry about their parents' aging before those parents show any signs of aging (Cicirelli, 1988; Hay, 2004).

As their parents age and encounter true health problems, the Baby Boomers confront caregiving demands and unchartered territory with little clear guidance. For example, it is unclear whether adults should intervene with regard to their parents' medical and day-to-day decisions, particularly when the parents remain in relatively good health (Fingerman, 2001b). Zarit (in press) reports a history of research on caregiving for elderly parents and notes:

> By the 1970s, the increase in the number of people providing help to an elderly relative was sufficient to get attention in the media. The term "sandwich generation" was applied to the dilemma of a middle aged woman who simultaneously rears adolescent children while assisting a disabled parent. Caregiving, however, had not yet become the focus of research or practice.

Groups interested in the public good and family caregiving, such as the Alzheimer's Association, were formed in the late 1970s. Thus, the Baby Boomers have greater resources to address their parents' needs today than was the case 25 years ago. Yet, even the tail end Baby Boomers may feel that they receive inadequate guidance with regard to the health problems their parents confront, given the complexities of the issues involved.

Women in the baby-boomer cohorts have been most likely to provide care for their parents when they become frail or ill (Zarit, in press). These baby-boom women have the advantage of multiple siblings to assist with decisions pertaining to the parental aging process. At the same time, relationships with siblings can become strained when parents are in need (Brody et al., 1989; Fingerman & Bermann, 2000). It is notable that a society that focused full attention on the Baby Boomers as children has been less able to rally a consistent and useful plan for them with regard to their aging parents.

As mentioned previously, scholars have suggested that middle aged adults today find their relationships with their parents characterized by feelings of ambivalence (Connidis & McMullin, 2002; Luescher & Pillemer, 1998). Social structures do not provide clear guidance for assisting older adults. Even when societal changes help Baby Boomers to assist aging parents, the implications of these changes remain unclear. For example, the Family and Medical Leave

Act (FMLA; U.S. Department of Labor, 1993) allows workers to take time off to help care for an aging parent, but work place structures and norms generate counter pressures for doing so (Gerstel & McGonagle, 1999; Hendrix, 2001). Furthermore, 60% of employees in the U.S. work in jobs not covered by the FMLA, and this is especially true for women (Trzcinski, 1994). Even individuals who are covered by the FMLA must navigate medical systems, seek formal care providers, or provide hands-on care as parental health declines.

Of course, we might ask whether the issues the Baby Boomers confront are truly distinct to their cohort. Do the concerns and challenges of aging parents simply receive more attention because there are so many Baby Boomers, so many aging parents, and such widespread media for publicizing their concerns? It is clear that some aspects to this issue are cohort specific, including the large numbers of older adults in need of care, the lack of facilities, policies, or economic and social mores for dealing with aging parents. Other features, such as the concern for aging parents, may transcend these period effects.

ECONOMIC AND EDUCATIONAL CHANGES, MOBILITY PATTERNS, AND SHIFTS IN GENDER ROLES AND SEXUALITY

The Baby Boomers and their parents have encountered unprecedented shifts in the nature of the overall economy in the United States. The parents were born as the Industrial Revolution of 1700 to the late 1880s came to a close. Changes in manufacturing and residential patterns had strong effects on their lives, effects that carried over into the lives of their children. Furthermore, the expansion of higher education that began with the role of the GI Bill in educating the fathers extended to baby-boom men and women alike. These changes have shaped the nature of contact between the Baby Boomers and their parents.

Shifts Away From the Agrarian Life

During their lifetimes, parents of the Baby Boomers experienced strong shifts in lifestyle as the U.S. economy moved from agrarian life towards a manufacturing base. Further, the Baby Boomers were much less likely to grow up in agrarian settings than were their parents. For example, from 1940 and 1964, the farm population declined from 30 million to 13 million, and there were 40% fewer farms overall (Roark et al., 1998).

Furthermore, historians have documented shifts in the residential patterns of nonagrarian families during the early Baby Boomers' youth:

> Suburbs were not new in the United States, but they entered a period of unparalleled growth in that decade [1950s]. Of the 13 million new homes built in 1950s, 11 million were in the suburbs. While cities failed to grow, the number of

people living just outside cities increased by 45 percent, as more than one million Americans moved to suburban areas every year. By 1960, one in every four Americans lived in the suburbs. (Roark et al., 1998, p. 1075)

These changes in living patterns reflect broader shifts in the nature of the American economy and in family life. Although present day agrarian families remain closely linked through economic interdependence (King & Elder, 1995), most Baby Boomers are no longer linked to their parents economically or residentially.

Today, most intergenerational ties appear to be driven by emotional bonds. This is not to say that the parents have abandoned offspring economically. McGarry and Schoeni (1997) looked at intergenerational exchanges using the AHEAD study, involving a national sample of nearly 7,000 adults over the age of 70. They found that these aging parents continued to provide financial and instrumental support for many of their baby-boom children. Yet, parents provided the most aid to offspring who had the fewest resources. In other words, shifts from an agrarian to a manufacturing and technology economy may have led to greater diversity in the nature of intergenerational exchanges during the lives of the Baby Boomers; children and their parents do not work side-by-side on the family farm, but the parents continue to provide finances, advice, child care, and other types of assistance. As such, intergenerational exchanges appear to be more individualized and driven by need rather than by a shared economic motivation.

The Expansion of Educational Opportunity

The Baby Boom began at a time when the GI bill enabled many of the fathers to return to college in the United States, precipitating an expansion of higher education that extends into the present. The fathers were more likely to attend college after World War II than were cohorts before them, and the Baby Boomers of both genders were considerably more likely to attend college than were their parents. In fact, statistics from the United States Census Bureau (2004) indicate that rates of college completion have increased steadily since 1940. Indeed, when Sputnik was launched by the Russians in 1957, Americans worried about being in second place and Congress pointed to the weakness of higher education (Center for Higher Education Support Services, 2004). By the 1960s, as the Baby Boomers came of college age, scholarship, work–study programs, and the current Pell Grant Program provided opportunities for students to fund their college educations.

The implications of these shifts in educational attainment for relationships between Baby Boomers and their parents vary. When parents were familiar with the types of goals the Baby Boomers pursued, their relationships appear to have benefited from these accomplishments. Suitor (1987) conducted a study of baby-boom women who were born during the 1950s and early 1960s who had not attended college when they were 18 to 22 and their mothers. These Baby Boomers were now returning to higher education later than their peers. Mothers who had higher education were supportive of their daughters' efforts to obtain education. When the parents were less familiar with the Baby Boomers' goals and achievements, they were less supportive of these aims, and their relationships included a greater degree of strife and less support as a result.

In keeping with shifts in higher education, parallel shifts in the nature of work have evolved during the lives of the Baby Boomers. The shift from an industrialized economy to an information and service economy has presented distinct challenges to the Baby Boomers as they have entered and pursued careers (for a review, see chap. 12, this volume). Interestingly, a study examining middle-aged Baby Boomers and their children revealed that when offspring outperformed their parents, the parents sometimes felt worse about themselves (Ryff, Lee, Essex, & Schmutte, 1994). It is not clear whether the Baby Boomers' parents also felt this way when their offspring surpassed their achievements.

Geographic Separation of Baby Boomers and Their Parents

Scholars have attended to a key consequence of expanded higher education, the nonagrarian economy, and job mobility—namely geographic separation of Baby Boomers and their parents (Crimmins & Ingegneri, 1990; Moss, Moss, & Moles, 1985). Indeed, the first studies of geographic distance between adults and their parents began when the earliest Baby Boomers were in their 30s (e.g., Shanas, 1979). These Baby Boomers were among the first adults for whom geographic distance played a key role in shaping the qualities of their relationships with parents.

Geographic distance between adults and their parents grew more variable during the lives of the Baby Boomers. For example, during their young adulthood, the pursuit of education drew many Baby Boomers away from their families to college campuses. Furthermore, many individuals remain at a distance to pursue more prestigious jobs after completing their education (Fingerman, Chen, Hay, Cichy, & Lefkowitz, 2004). At the same time, nearly half of Baby Boomers reside within 50 miles of their parents (Lin & Rogerson, 1995). Geographic distance has an impact on Baby Boomers and their parents, though individuals can still feel emotionally close to their parents when they are geographically separated. Nonetheless, Baby Boomers who reside near their parents are more likely to provide instrumental support and care for their parents than their siblings who reside far away (Brody et al., 1989). Indeed, a recent study of adults who live far from their parents suggests that, as a result of geographic separation, the ability to enjoy companionship suffers more than other facets of the relationship (Fingerman et al., 2004).

In sum, shifts in higher education and the economy affect ties between Baby Boomers and their parents. Education has drawn Baby Boomers away from their parents physically and emotionally when the parents themselves have little education. Although little is known about the ways in which changing economic structures affect this tie, artifacts of those structures such as geographic distance affect exchanges of aid. Nonetheless, Baby Boomers who reside far from their parents have been able to retain feelings of emotional closeness, suggesting that societal shifts resulting in physical separation from parents have not undermined these ties.

In sum, educational opportunities and career patterns clearly do affect intergenerational ties. The heterogeneity of the Baby Boomers' career patterns makes it difficult to generalize about the exact effects of their career choices on their relationships with their parents. In general, however, when Baby Boomers and their parents share experiences or attitudes about work, they also have stronger relationships.

Family Structures and Investment in Intergenerational Ties

The defining feature of the baby-boom cohorts, of course, is that they are all members of larger families of origin than individuals in prior or subsequent cohorts. Family size for the Baby Boomers appears to be negatively associated with parental investment; parents report lower investment in any given child the more offspring they have (Fingerman, 2001a). Therefore, although the parents of the Baby Boomers invested considerable energy in the work of parenting them on the whole, their reported emotional investment in a given child may be lower than a parent with fewer progeny.

The issue of family and parental investment may carry over into the present ties. As described previously, socioemotional selectivity theory suggests that individuals become increasingly emotionally invested in their family ties as they enter late life and approach death (Carstensen et al., 1999; Troll, 1988). Yet, the strength of their parents' emotional investment may not be reciprocated by Baby Boomers who encounter competing demands from their own spouse, children, work, and leisure demands. Indeed, middle aged Baby Boomers describe tensions with their parents over the parameters of the relationship, frequency of contact, and how much time and energy they can give to this tie (Fingerman, 2001a).

Further, connections to extended family and commitment to family decreased during the lives of the Baby Boomers. For example, nearly 50 years ago, Bardis (1959) developed a widely used scale to assess *familialism*, or commitment to the broader family network. The items in this scale seem quaint in the twenty-first century. For example, "A person should always support his aunts and uncles if they are in need," "Children below 18 should always obey their parents," and "A person should always help his parents with support of his younger brothers and sisters if necessary." The scale presumes family forms and norms that are out of date.

Further, not all Baby Boomers grew up in households with nuclear families (Coontz, 2000). Divorce rates began to increase after World War II. Indeed, despite visions of Ozzie and Harriett with their loving children on the television during the 1950s and early 1960s, the Baby Boomers were more likely to experience divorce of their parents than were prior cohorts of individuals. Although the Baby Boomers themselves are more likely to divorce than were their parents, their parents divorced at greater rates than the grandparents of the Baby Boomers (Krieder & Fields, 2002). Again, a trajectory of declining sentiment for obligatory family ties appears to have begun with the parents of the Baby Boomers, and truly taken hold among the Baby Boomers.

Despite harbingers that the family is on the decline, however, data show that most Baby Boomers are invested in family and list family members as the people in the world to whom they feel closest (Fingerman & Birditt, 2003). Baby Boomers have described their ties to their parents as close and important throughout their lives (Atkinson, Kivett, & Campbell, 1986; Rossi & Rossi, 1990).

The fundamental shifts in relationships between Baby Boomers and their parents may reflect the nature of family forms rather than the emotional feelings in their relationships. As stated, the family members of the Baby Boomers are not arranged in neat bundles of married couples with children. Also, the Baby Boomers have established a wider range of family types than did cohorts before them (Pillemer & Suitor, 1998). Compared to their parents, Baby Boomers married later, experienced higher rates of divorce, and higher rates of remarriage (Krieder & Fields, 2002). Additionally, when compared to the cohort of their parents, a larger proportion of Baby Boomers remained single (Krieder & Fields, 2002).

It is not clear that these variations in family form have affected ties between the Baby Boomers and their parents in negative ways, however. For example, in some cases, ties to parents have been strengthened by their own divorce. Single baby-boom mothers often found their parents a source of support as they navigated their way out of unsuccessful marriages (Johnson, 1998). As such, these Baby Boomers benefit from ties to their own parents, whereas their relationships with their progeny may be more tenuous. Thus, the ties the Baby Boomers have to their own parents seem to have transcended the decline in commitment to extended family and the reformation of family forms.

At the same time, our prior research suggests that discrepancies in family forms can generate tensions for middle aged Baby Boomers and their parents (Fingerman, 2001a). The majority of middle-aged Baby Boomers' ties to parents involve ties to a widowed or unmarried parent, particularly for leading-edge boomers. The Baby Boomers themselves, however, are likely to have a romantic partner and/or adolescent and young adult children who occupy much of their time (Fingerman, Nussbaum, & Birditt, 2004). These differences in family structures can result in feelings of time pressure and guilt for Baby Boomers. It can also generate resentments if the parent wants more time and help than they receive.

Nonetheless, as the prior sections discussed, the parents of the Baby Boomers have retained a high degree of independence and supported the Baby Boomers in a variety of domains throughout their lives. Their relationships generally seem to be strong and close, across familial structures.

Gender and Sexuality

During the lives of the Baby Boomers, gender roles have been transformed dramatically. The earliest Baby Boomers began life during a historical period when women who could afford to do so often left the work force to stay home with their children. The trailing-edge Baby Boomers were more likely to have mothers who worked during their childhood than the early Baby Boomers; 33.9% of women worked full-time in 1950 compared to 45.9% in 1975 (Fullerton, 1999; Hayghe, 1997). Furthermore, during the early lives of the Baby Boomers, mores and values changed with regard to women's roles at home, clothing styles, and relationships between the genders (Duncan & Stewart, 2000). Yet, the effects of these shifts on ties between the Baby Boomers and their parents are unclear.

Gender Roles and Mother/Daughter Ties.   Although many of the mothers of the early and mid Baby Boomers entered the workforce at least briefly during World War II, they were more likely to define themselves as wives and mothers than as workers (Duncan & Stewart, 2000). In comparison to their mothers, women born between 1946 and 1964 are more likely to have pursued higher education and to have an identity that includes an idea of career (Duncan & Stewart, 2000; U.S. Census Bureau, 2004b). As noted at the start of this chapter, the idea of motherhood as a primary role is relatively unique in human history (Coontz, 2000; Hulbert, 2003). As such, it is unclear whether the Baby Boomers' mothers or the baby-boom women are the more unique cohort.

In any case, vicissitudes in gender roles do not seem to have disrupted relationships between most baby-boom women and their parents. Women experienced greater changes in their lifestyle and work status roles than did men during this period. Given these social upheavals for women, scholars hypothesized that baby-boom women and their mothers might experience considerable ambivalence (e.g., Connidis & McMullin, 2002). Yet, a number of studies have found that early and later born baby-boom women have reported strong and enduring bonds with their parents throughout adulthood, despite these shifting gender roles (Fingerman, 2001a; Rossi & Rossi, 1990; Troll, 1984; Walker & Thompson, 1983). Moen and colleagues (1997) examined gender attitude changes among mothers who were interviewed in 1956 and 1986. Their daughters, born between 1929 and 1964, were interviewed in 1988. The analyses do not permit examination specifically of the Baby Boomers among those daughters, but the findings suggest that gender role ideologies of daughters in 1988 were closely aligned with the gender role ideologies of their mothers in 1956, and that congruence grew even stronger when comparing their beliefs in the 1980s. As mentioned previously, relationships between Baby Boomers and their mothers do vary as a function of the educational attainment of the mother and her beliefs about what her daughter should achieve (e.g., Suitor, 1987), but most mothers and daughters align their beliefs, and strong filial bonds persist despite societal changes.

Sexuality and Sexual Identity. Sexuality and sexual openness varied considerably from the time when the earliest Baby Boomers grew up to the period when the latter Baby Boomers grew up. During the 1960s, when leading edge Baby Boomers were in young adulthood, the advent of successful and easy-to-use birth control was accompanied by increasing acceptance of sexual behavior outside of marriage. Baby Boomers in both subcohorts were able to take advantage of these changes in societal mores in ways that most of their parents did not.

Rates of cohabitation began increasing starting around 1940, and truly increased dramatically as the Baby Boomers reached adulthood (Cherlin, 1992). For individuals born between 1938 and 1942, 3% to 11% reported cohabiting with a partner before the age of 25 (Bumpass, Sweet, & Cherlin, 1991). In contrast, for individuals born between 1958 and 1962, 21% to 46% reported cohabiting with a partner before the age of 25 (Bumpass et al., 1991). It was one thing for the Baby Boomers to clandestinely engage in premarital sex without their parents' knowledge, and another thing to do so in a way that advertised this fact to the general public! When asked to describe the most conflicted time in their relationship, Baby Boomers and their parents often refer to a period when the offspring was living with a partner outside of marriage (Fingerman, 2001a). In these cases, however, the long-term effects of cohabitation on relationships with parents do not appear to be grave. Baby Boomers who resided with a partner have either gone on to marry the partner, disbanded the partnership, or remained in a partnership the parents accepted. Also, the Baby Boomers' parents seem less irritated by their cohabitation (Fingerman, 2001a). The barrage of sexuality in the mass media over the past three decades may have partially inured the parents to their offspring's behaviors. Further, by 2005, the youngest of the Baby Boomers have entered midlife, and the concerns their parents had about their early sexuality may have diminished. Nonetheless, Baby Boomers who continued to cohabitate with a partner in the late 1990s engaged in fewer exchanges or interactions with their parents than other members of their cohort (Eggebeen, 2003).

Society also saw increased openness concerning sexual identity throughout the Baby Boomers' lives. Although headlines in the year 2004 concerning gay marriage indicate considerable prejudice against gay couples, this issue would not have been discussed in public before the Baby Boomers were born. As such, society on the whole is more open about sexual identity than in the past. Cohler (2004) described tensions that parents have faced when their gay or lesbian offspring disclose their sexuality. These disclosures may threaten parental expectations of role transitions such as their offspring's marriage or their own grandparenthood. Further, parents may worry about the stigma their offspring might suffer. At the same time, sensitive parents are often relieved to know their child has a means of finding a loving and satisfying relationship. Indeed, Cohler suggested that shifts in openness concerning sexuality are a prime example of a setting for intergenerational ambivalence (Savin-Williams, 2001). Nonetheless, most parents continue to love their offspring, despite ambivalent feelings about the disclosure.

In sum, shifts in gender roles have not undermined ties between parents and offspring. Although baby-boom women have entered the work world in increasing numbers, they also endorsed strong ties to their mothers and families of origin (Moen et al., 1997; Rossi & Rossi, 1990). As shifts in sexuality and value structures occur at the larger societal level, parents and offspring within families appear to align their values and beliefs in ways that foster strong intergenerational bonds.

WHAT THE BABY BOOMERS TELL US ABOUT INTERGENERATIONAL TIES

In this chapter, we have described the ways in which key social changes have affected relationships between the Baby Boomers and their parents. Clearly, social changes over the past 60 years have had a large impact on intergenerational relationships. In concluding this chapter, we look at how experiences of the Baby Boomers interface with theories of intergenerational ties.

As their parents have grown old, the incredible heterogeneity of the family structures and experiences of the Baby Boomers has led to diversity in the nature of their ties to their parents. Overall, studies employing solidarity theory to examine the heterogeneity of the experiences of the Baby Boomers suggest that most intergenerational ties endure through a range of experiences including geographic separation and periods of turmoil. Although the vast majority of Baby Boomers have reported strong ties to their parents in adulthood (e.g., Rossi & Rossi, 1990; Umberson, 1989), a small proportion of Baby Boomers have disbanded ties to their parents or retain very weak ties (Silverstein & Bengtson, 1997). As such, there is variability in the quality of relationships between adults and their parents.

As mentioned previously, although the Baby Boomers have crossed midlife, scholars have introduced additional theoretical perspectives on their ties to their parents, including a model of sociological and psychological ambivalence (e.g., Connidis & McMullin, 2002; Luescher & Pillemer, 1998). According to scholars who use this model, ambiguous norms and roles generate intergenerational ambivalence. As described, middle-aged Baby Boomers are often at a loss with regard to appropriate interactions with aging parents, suggesting their relationships should be marred with ambivalence. Yet, our prior research on psychological ambivalence or mixed emotions indicated that only about one third of Baby Boomers viewed their relationships with their parents as primarily ambivalent in nature. Indeed, ratings of ambivalence towards parents was highest for individuals who were in their 20s at the time, namely the generation after the Baby Boomers. Most Baby Boomers viewed their ties to their parents as primarily close and positive (Fingerman, Hay, & Birditt, 2004). These findings suggest that, despite the ambiguous situations Baby Boomers and their parents confront, positive sentiments in this tie prevail for the majority of individuals.

Indeed, social changes may have had the greatest effects in early adulthood, when Baby Boomers and their parents anticipated that they still had 20 or 30 years to enjoy their relationships. As the Baby Boomers reach midlife and their parents grow old and die, their relationships appear to hit a stride, even in the face of the social and physical demands of aging. Past grievances no longer dominate, parents and offspring appear to reach a state of acceptance, and the disruptions of youth are behind both parties.

In sum, the Baby Boomers are among the first individuals to expect normatively to live to old–old age, and to do so in the context of increased opportunities, shifting social values, and changes in economic structures. The general strength of intergenerational ties in these cohorts suggests processes of mutual closeness into late life. The changes and upheavals the Baby Boomers experienced may not have been so distinct from those that their parents experienced with their parents. The rapid paced changes of a technological society may render societal change a normal aspect of the life course. Of course, the parents were not able to take advantage of some of the social changes from which the Baby Boomers themselves benefited, but these parents seem to have adjusted their own expectations and attitudes in ways that generally benefited the tie. Thus, the Baby Boomers and their parents have laid the groundwork for future cohorts who hope to navigate 40 to 60 years of intergenerational relationships.

ACKNOWLEDGMENTS

Research reported here was supported by grants to the first author from the National Institute on Aging (AG14484A and AG17916). The authors are grateful to Danielle Swiontek for consultation pertaining to twentieth-century history.

REFERENCES

Alwin, D. F., McCammon, R. J., & Hofer, S. M. (2005). Baby Boom cohorts within a demographic and developmental context: Conceptual and methodological issues. In S. K. Whitbourne & S. Willis (Eds.), *The Baby Boomers grow up: Contemporary perspectives on midlife*. New York: Lawrence Erlbaum Associates.

Atkinson, M. P., Kivett, V. R., & Campbell, R. T. (1986). Intergenerational solidarity: An examination of a theoretical model. *Journal of Gerontology, 41*, 408–416.

Bardis, P. D. (1959). A familism scale. *Marriage and Family Living, 21*, 340–341.

Bengtson, V. L., & Kuypers, J. A. (1971). Generational difference and the developmental stake. *Aging and Human Development, 2*, 249–260.

Bowlby, J. (1969/1982). *Attachment and loss: Vol. 1. Attachment*. New York: Basic Books.

Brody, E. M., Hoffman, C., Kleban, M. H., & Schoonover, C. B. (1989). Caregiving daughters and their local siblings: Perceptions, strains, and interactions. *Gerontologist, 29*, 529–538.

Brokaw, T. (1998). *The greatest generation*. New York: Random House.

Brumberg, J. J. (1997). *The body project: An intimate history of American girls*. New York: Random House.

Bumpass, L. L., Sweet, J. A., & Cherlin, A. (1991). The role of cohabitation in declining rates of marriage. *Journal of Marriage and the Family, 53*, 913–927.

Carstensen, L. L., Isaacowitz, D. M., & Charles, S. T. (1999). Taking time seriously: A theory of socioemotional selectivity. *American Psychologist, 54*, 165–181.

Center for Higher Education Support Services (2004). *The history of financial aid*. Retrieved March 6, 2004 from http://www.chessconsulting.org/financialaid/history.htm

Cherlin, A. J. (1992). *Marriage, divorce, remarriage*. Cambridge, MA: Harvard University Press.

Cicirelli, V. G. (1988). A measure of filial anxiety regarding anticipated care of elderly parents. *Gerontologist, 28*, 478–482.

Clydesdale, T. T. (1997). Family behaviors among early U. S. Baby Boomers: Exploring the effects of religion and income change, 1965–1982. *Social Forces, 76*, 605–635.

Cohler, B. J. (2004). The experience of ambivalence within the family: Young adults "coming out" gay or lesbian and their parents. In K. Lüscher & K. Pillemer (Eds.), *Intergenerational ambivalence* (pp. 255–284). Amsterdam: Elsevier.

Connidis, I. A., & Campbell, L. D. (1995). Closeness, confiding, and contact among siblings in middle and late adulthood. *Journal of Family Issues, 16*, 722–745.

Connidis, I. A., & McMullin, J. A. (2002). Sociological ambivalence and family ties: A critical perspective. *Journal of Marriage and Family, 64*, 558–567.

Coontz, S. (2000). Historical perspectives on family studies. *Journal of Marriage and the Family, 62*, 283–297.

Crimmins, E., & Ingegneri, D. G. (1990). Interaction and living arrangements of older parents and their adult children. *Research on Aging, 10,* 56–80.

Duncan, L. E., & Stewart, A. J. (2000). A generational analysis of women's rights activists. *Psychology of Women Quarterly, 24,* 297–308.

Eggebeen, D. J. (1992). Changes in sibling configurations for American preschool children. *Social Biology, 39,* 27–44.

Eggebeen, D. J. (2003, May). *Cohabitation and exchanges of support.* Paper presented at the Annual Meeting of the Population Association of America, Minneapolis, MN.

Elder, G. H., Jr. (1998). The life course as developmental theory. *Child Development, 69,* 1–12.

Elkind, D. (1967). Egocentrism in adolescence. *Child Development, 38,* 1025–1034.

Elkind, D. (1978). Understanding the young adolescent. *Adolescence, 13,* 127–134.

Fasick, F. (1994). On the "invention" of adolescence. *Journal of Early Adolescence, 14,* 6–23.

Femia, E. E., Zarit, S. H., & Johansson, B. (2001). The disablement in very late life: A study of the oldest–old in Sweden. *Journals of Gerontology: Psychological Sciences, 56,* 12–23.

Fingerman, K. L. (2001a). *Aging mothers and their adult daughters: A study in mixed emotions.* New York: Springer.

Fingerman, K. L. (2001b). The paradox of a distant closeness: Intimacy in parent/child ties. *Generations, 25,* 26–33.

Fingerman, K. L., & Bermann, E. (2000). Applications of family systems theory to the study of adulthood. *International Journal of Aging and Human Development, 51,* 5–29.

Fingerman, K. L., & Birditt, K. S. (2003). Do age differences in close and problematic family ties reflect the pool of available relatives? *Journals of Gerontology Series B–Psychological Sciences and Social Sciences, 58,* P80–P87.

Fingerman, K. L., Chen, P. C., Hay, E. L. Cichy, K. E, & Lefkowitz, E. S. (2004). *Close ties with distant parents: Geographic separation and intergenerational relationships.* Unpublished manuscript, Purdue University, West Lafayette, IN.

Fingerman, K. L., Hay, E. L., & Birditt, K. S. (2004). The best of ties, the worst of ties: Close, problematic, and ambivalent relationships across the lifespan. *Journal of Marriage and Family, 66,* 792–808.

Fingerman, K. L., Nussbaum, J., & Birditt, K. S. (2004). Keeping all five balls in the air: Juggling family communication at midlife. In A. L. Vangelisti (Ed.), *Handbook of family communication* (pp. 135–152). Hillsdale, NJ: Lawrence Erlbaum Associates.

Fullerton, H. N. (1999). Labor force participation: 75 years of change, 1950–98 and 1998–2025. Retrieved March 6, 2004 from http://www.bls.gov/opub/mlr/1999/12/art1full.pdf

Graber, J. A., & Brooks-Gunn, J. (1999). "Sometimes I think that you don't like me". How mothers and daughters negotiate the transition into adolescence. In M. J. Cox & J. Brooks-Gunn (Eds.), *Conflict and cohesion in families* (pp. 207–242). Mahwah, NJ: Lawrence Erlbaum Associates.

Greenberger, E., & Steinberg, L. (1986). *When teenagers work: The psychological and social costs of adolescent employment.* New York: Basic Books.

Haber, C. (1983). Aging in colonial America. In C. Haber (Ed.), *Beyond sixty-five: The dilemma of old age in America's past* (pp. 8–46). Cambridge, England: Cambridge University Press.

Hareven, T. K. (1995). Historical perspectives on the family and aging. In R. Blieszner & V. H. Bedford (Eds.), *Handbook of aging and the family* (pp. 13–31). Westport, CT: Greenwood Press.

Hay, E. (2004). *The experience of worry in relationships between adults and their parents.* Unpublished doctoral thesis, Pennsylvania State University.

Hayghe, H. V. (1997). Developments in women's labor force participation. *Monthly Labor Review,* 41–46.

Hine, T. (1999). *The rise and fall of the American teenager.* New York: Bard Books.

Homans, G. F. (1950). *The human group.* New York: Harcourt, Brace, & World.

Hulbert, A. (2003). *Raising America: Experts, parents, and a century of advice about children.* New York: Alfred A. Knopf.

Johnson, C. L. (1998). Effects of adult children's divorce on grandparenthood. In M. E. Szinovacz (Ed.), *Handbook of grandparenthood* (pp. 184–199). Westport, CT: Greenwood Press.

Johnson, C., & Barer, B. (1997). *Life beyond 85 years: The aura of survivorship.* New York: Springer.

King, V., & Elder, G. H. (1995). American children view their grandparents: Linked lives across three rural generations. *Journal of Marriage and the Family, 57,* 165–178.

Krieder, R. M., & Fields, J. M. (2002). *Number, timing, and duration of marriages and divorces: 1996.* Retrieved March 6, 2004 from http://www.census.gov/prod/2002pubs/p70-80.pdf

Laursen, B., Coy, K. C., & Collins, W. A. (1998). Reconsidering changes in parent–child conflict across adolescence: A meta-analysis. *Child Development, 69,* 817–832.

Lin, G., & Rogerson, P. A. (1995). Elderly parents and the geographic availability of their adult children. *Research on Aging, 17,* 303–331.

Luescher, K., & Pillemer, K. (1998). Intergenerational ambivalence: A new approach to the study of parent–child relations in later life. *Journal of Marriage and the Family, 60,* 413–425.

McGarry, K., & Schoeni, R. F. (1997). Transfer behavior within the family: Results from the asset and health dynamics study. *Journals of Gerontology, 52B,* 83–92.

Moen, P. (1997). Their mothers' daughters? The intergenerational transmission of gender attitudes in a world of changing roles. *Journal of Marriage and Family, 59,* 281–293.

Moen, P., & Wethington, E. (1999). Midlife development in a life course context. In S. L. Willis & J. D. Reid (Eds.), *Life in the middle: Psychological and social development in middle age* (pp. 3–23). New York: Academic Press.

Moss, M. S., Moss, S. Z., & Moles, E. L. (1985). The quality of relationships between elderly parents and their out-of-town children. *The Gerontologist, 25,* 134–140.

Parsons, T. (1943). The kinship system of the contemporary United States. *American Anthropologist, 45,* 22–28.

Roark, J. L., Johnson, M. P., Cohen, P. C., Stage, S., Lawson, A., & Hartmann, S. M. (1998). *The American promise: A history of the United States from 1865* (Vol. 2). Boston: Bedford Books.

Rossi, A. S., & Rossi, P. H. (1990). *Of human bonding: Parent–child relations across the life course.* New York: Aldine de Gruyter.

Ryff, C. D., Lee, Y. H., Essex, M. J., & Schmutte, P. S. (1994). My children and me: Midlife evaluations of grown children and of self. *Psychology & Aging, 9,* 195–205.

Savin-Williams, R. C. (2001). *Mom, dad. I'm gay. How families negotiate coming out.* Washington, DC: American Psychological Association.

Schoeni, R. F., Freedman, V. A., & Wallace, R. B. (2001). Persistent, consistent, widespread, and robust? Another look at recent trends in old-age disability. *Journals of Gerontology: Social Sciences, 56,* S206–S218.

Shanas, E. (1979). Social myth as hypothesis: The case of the family relations of old people. *Gerontologist, 19,* 3–9.

Silverstein, M., & Bengtson, V. L. (1997). Intergenerational solidarity and the structure of adult child–parent relationships in American families. *American Journal of Sociology, 103,* 429–460.

Smetana, J. G. (1995). Parenting styles and conceptions of parental authority during adolescence. *Child Development, 66,* 299–316.

Stewart, A. J. (2003). Gender, race, and generation in a midwest high school: Using ethnographically informed methods in psychology. *Psychology of Women Quarterly, 27,* 1–11.

Stewart, A. J., & Healey, J. M. (1989). Linking individual development and social changes. *American Psychologist, 44,* 30–42.

Suitor, J. J. (1987). Mother–daughter relations when married daughters return to school: Effects of status similarity. *Journal of Marriage and the Family, 49,* 435–444.

Troll, L. E. (1971). The "generation gap" in later life. *Sociological Focus, 5,* 18–28.

Trzcinski, E. (1994). Family and medical leave, contingent employment, and flexibility: A feminist critique of the U.S. approach to work and family policy. *Journal of Applied Social Sciences, 18*, 71–87.

Umberson, D. (1989). Relationships with children: Explaining parents' psychological well-being. *Journal of Marriage and the Family, 51*, 999–1012.

United States Census Bureau. (2004a). *20th century statistics.* Retrieved March 28, 2004 from http://www.census.gov/prod/99pubs/99statab/sec31.pdf.

United States Census Bureau. (2004b). *Percent of people 25 years and older who have completed high school or college, by race, Hispanic origin, and sex: Selected years 1940 to 2002.* Retrieved March 5, 2004 from http://www.census.gov/population/socdemo/education/tabA-2.pdf

United States Department of Labor (2004). *Fact sheet #28: The Family Medical Leave Act of 1993.* Retrieved March 5, 2004 from http://www.dol.gov/esa/regs/compliance/whd/whdfs28.htm

Walker, A. J., & Thompson, L. (1983). Intimacy and aid and contact among mothers and daughters. *Journal of Marriage and the Family, 45*, 841–848.

Zarit, S. H., & Eggebeen, D. J. (2002). Parent–child relationships in adulthood and later years. In M. H. Bornstein (Ed.), *Handbook of parenting: Vol. 1. Children and parenting* (2nd ed., pp. 135–161). Mahwah, NJ: Lawrence Erlbaum Associates.

Zarit, S. H. (in press). History of caregiving. In S. M. LoboPrabhu, J. W. Lomax, & V. Molinari (Eds.), *Caregiving in dementia: A guide for health care providers and caregivers.* Baltimore, MD: Johns Hopkins University Press.

CHAPTER ELEVEN

Perspectives on Close Relationships Among the Baby Boomers

Rosemary Blieszner
Karen A. Roberto
Virginia Polytechnic Institute and State University

THE BABY BOOM COHORT AND CLOSE RELATIONSHIPS

We begin our discussion of close relationships in the lives of Baby Boomers at midlife by taking a life-span developmental perspective. We suggest the importance of looking at developmental antecedents that could affect relationships at this stage of life, as well as describing current relationships. Key influences begin as early as infancy when attachment bonding sets the stage for close relationships both then and later on (Main, Kaplan, & Cassidy, 1985; Möller & Stattin, 2001). For antecedents of midlife relationships we focus in particular on adolescence and young adulthood when key developmental challenges associated with close relationships emerge. This is based on Erikson's (1950) theory of psychosocial development.

Members of the baby-boom cohort were born between the late 1940s and the middle 1960s. This group actually encompasses two subcohorts. Leading-edge Baby Boomers experienced the formative years of adolescence in the 1960s, when optimism and exuberance born of success in launching space satellites, the pop art movement, discovery of DNA by Watson, Wilkins, and Crick, and the election of John F. Kennedy were contrasted with Civil Rights protests and marches, Kennedy's assassination, and demonstrations against the Vietnam war. They witnessed the passage of the Civil Rights Act, the rising popularity of the Beatles rock band, and the race riots in the Watts section of Los Angeles. This cohort experienced young adulthood during the 1970s, when numerous popular books about human sexuality were published, President Richard Nixon visited the People's Republic of China, and anti-Vietnam war protests were increasingly common. In the 1970s, unemployment and inflation were rising, Nixon resigned from office after confessing that he had impeded investigation of the burglary at the Democratic Party headquarters, and the Vietnam war finally ended (Carruth, 1993).

In contrast, the trailing-edge Baby Boomers experienced adolescence in the 1980s, when Ronald Reagan was President, personal computer ownership was on the rise, Sandra Day O'Connor became the first female Supreme Court Justice, inflation reached 14% then dropped as the recession receded and the economy grew, the Equal Rights Amendment was not ratified, and U.S. embassies abroad were bombed by terrorists. They experienced young adulthood during the 1990s, when the World Wide Web was made broadly accessible and both music on CDs and films on DVDs became ubiquitous, lawsuits against cigarette manufacturers were launched, Princess Diana of England died, teenagers in Littleton, Colorado, and elsewhere killed schoolmates, Bill Clinton served as President, and the movie *Titanic* was a box-office hit. Also during this decade, Cambodia and Vietnam became integrated into the international community, immigration into the U.S. increased, the human genome project began, and genetic experimentation advanced (Carruth, 1993).

Now as we write this in 2005, the leading-edge Baby Boomers are in their middle to late 50s, typically focusing their attention on emancipation of children, needs of aging parents, and their own plans for transitioning into retirement. In contrast, the trailing-edge Baby Boomers are in their late 30s and early 40s, just entering the middle years, and more likely concerned with rearing young children and teenagers, advancing their own career prospects, and finding their place in civic engagement roles. According to life span and life course perspectives of influences on personal development (Settersten, 1999) and theory about the emergence of historical generations (Rogler, 2002), the social, cultural, and historical events described previously have had a profound impact on the formation of attitudes, values, and behavioral choices of people in these two birth cohorts (Stewart & Healy, 1989). Their pursuit of close relationships is affected both by their developmental stage and by the particular eras in which they lived. Therefore, we reviewed the literature for adolescent and young adult antecedents of subsequent social interactions. We scanned publications on adolescent development and teenagers' family, dating, and friend relationships published from 1960 to the mid-1980s, and likewise we searched for research on young adult development and relationships published from 1970 to 1990. We used these writings to analyze perceptions of the personal characteristics and relationship issues prevalent in earlier life development that might affect close relationships in the middle years.

Relationships of Baby Boomers in Adolescence

Research on relationships in adolescence published in the 1960s and 1970s focused on a range of parent–child, grandparent–grandchild, sibling, dating, and friendship interactions. Early in this period, investigators of families were concerned about what they saw as increasing alienation and rebelliousness over the years of adolescence and they questioned whether such turbulence affected teens' mental health. They studied parental authority patterns as sources of influence on personality development in childhood and adolescence, showing, for example, that parental aggression is associated with adolescent aggression. Single-parent homes were assumed to be headed by mothers, so researchers inquired about the effects of father absence on adolescent development and critiqued the lack of literature on father–adolescent relationships. Much of the research in the 1960s assumed a unidirectional causal influence from parent to child; this perspective was corrected in the 1970s when it became apparent that parent–child ties are dynamic and reciprocally influential on the development of both generations (Peterson, 1988; Walters & Stinnett, 1971; Walters & Walters, 1980). Later research also showed a curvilinear trend in identity and closeness with parents; it was higher among teenagers in the 1960s and 1980s but relatively lower in the highly turbulent 1970s. The overall conclusion was that earlier descriptions of adolescence as a time of "storm and stress" had been based on studies of clinical populations and depicted exaggerated levels of parent–adolescent conflict (Gecas & Seff, 1990). Nevertheless, it is not unusual for adolescence to be often marked by mild bickering, disagreements, and conflicts over everyday issues as teenagers and parents negotiate their roles and the evolution of their relationship. The tension in these relationships typically dissipates with the child's transition to young adulthood. Structural factors (e.g., gender, race, socioeconomic status), family characteristics (e.g., size, composition, norms), and life events (e.g., employment, marriage, parenthood) affect interaction patterns between the generations and can have long-term influences on their relationships.

Descriptions by grandparents of their relationships with young and adolescent grandchildren suggest that, although these relationships are important to them, grandchildren are often peripheral to their everyday lives. Their direct involvement with their grandchildren depends on the interplay among environmental, individual, and familial variables. Geographic distance from grandchildren influences the frequency of association and exchange of assistance (Kivett, 1991), but not necessarily the quality of the relationships (Kennedy, 1989; Roberto & Stroes, 1992). As both grandchildren and grandparents grow older, some researchers report that interactions and perceived closeness between the generations decline (Clingempeel, Coylar, Brand, & Hetherington, 1992), whereas others report the development of close and satisfying relationships (Hodgson, 1998; Silverstein & Long, 1998). Family-related variables influencing grandparent–grandchild interactions include the nature of relationships between grandparents and parents (Lawton, Silverstein, & Bengtson, 1994; Thompson, & Walker, 1987) and divorce in the parent generation (Johnson, 1998). The power of parents to mediate cross-generational relationships appears to remains strong throughout the life cycle.

When the Baby Boomers were children, researchers examined their sibling relationships with respect to birth order, temperament, gender mix, and parental interactions (Dunn, 1993). Interactions among siblings in their formative years were found to contribute to their social development, providing the opportunity to learn skills of engagement that could enhance or impede the success of future relationships. Findings from cross-sectional studies suggest that as these individuals moved into adolescence and young adulthood, their relationships with siblings continued to develop (Cicirelli, 1995; White & Riedmann, 1992), but often changed as other roles and relationships took precedence. Interactions with siblings declined as college and career moves resulted in geographic separation and family circles expanded with the inclusion of new members.

With respect to romantic relationships, researchers inquired about the meaning of premarital sexual relationships and their impact on later marriage, in light of the "sexual revolution" evidenced by increasing proportions of young adults admitting to having had such encounters. Dating became viewed as a part of the continuum of courtship behaviors leading to marriage, and attention was given to dating frequency and conflict, mate selection, and processes leading to early marriage (Cannon & Long, 1971; Clayton & Bokemeier, 1980; Moss, Apolonio, & Jensen, 1971). Studies on the causes and consequences of adolescent childbearing became prominent in the 1970s, but the work resulted largely in atheoretical lists of correlates with little attention to multiple intersecting influences on behavior, an inordinate focus on young women but not their male partners, and mistaken causal assumptions about the antecedents of poor teen parent or child outcomes. Though it was clear that teenagers and college students were sexually active, the implications were not well understood (Chilman, 1980). Later studies addressed antecedents of adolescent sexual intercourse and contraceptive use; the extent to which pregnancy was resolved by marriage, abortion, or adoption; and the characteristics of adolescent parents. The research tended to acknowledge diversity in both predictors and outcomes of these behaviors as well as diversity across subgroups of society, lending a more balanced picture to the understanding of behaviors in youthful romantic relationships (Miller & Moore, 1990).

Relatively fewer studies were conducted on nonromantic peer relations, but the general assumptions stated in textbooks and articles were that friend influences became stronger than parent influences during the teenage years and could, indeed, influence youths' developmental outcomes (e.g., Tokuno, 1986). Compared to childhood, friend networks were larger, more complex, and more intimate as a result of both cognitive development and increases in social competence (Petersen, 1988). Concern arose with respect to the potential for peers to influence youth to engage in problematic behaviors such as smoking and delinquency (Jessor & Jessor, 1977). In general, research showed that peers influence one another in both positive and negative ways, with the influence based more on respect and admiration than on coercion. The extent of peer influence varied across individuals and diminished with increasing maturity (Steinburg & Morris, 2001).

Relationships of Baby Boomers in Young Adulthood

Research on relationship issues during the transition to adulthood among Baby Boomers is scarcer than studies covering their adolescent years. The literature that does exist focused both on the extent of continuing influence of earlier socialization by parents and on the effects of economic and other conditions prevailing at the time. For example, perceived paternal support had an influence on occupational attainment, at least for upper middle class young men (Gecas & Seff, 1990) and young women's work and family aspirations were influenced by their mothers' values and choices related to employment and childbearing (Stewart & Healy, 1989). Less advantaged young adults were more strongly affected by shrinking job markets than those with better educational and economic opportunities, and their successful transition to marriage and parenthood was impeded by unemployment. The effects of off-time transition to adulthood (e.g., teenage parenting) were analyzed for young women but not young men; the results showed poor developmental outcomes for both mothers and babies unless the mothers finished high school, restricted further childbearing, and attained a stable marriage (Gecas & Seff, 1990).

Leading-edge Baby Boomers entered young adult romantic relationships in an era when both social mores and academic theory assigned them to traditional sequences and sex roles in marriage and parenting. Marriage was prescribed for those in their early 20s and parenthood was expected to follow marriage. Husbands worked outside the home; wives reared the children, and this pattern of maintaining "separate spheres" (Ferree, 1990) was expected to yield stable marriage and adaptive family development (Aldous, Osmond, & Hicks, 1979; Duvall, 1971). Compared to previous cohorts, however, young adults in the 1980s tended to delay marriage, create nonmarried cohabitating unions, pursue multiple marital-like relationships before marrying, and share breadwinning and household tasks across genders. Researchers began to recognize that legal marriage was not necessarily the sole indicator of successful, enduring romantic relationships and thus began to study topics such as sexuality and courtship in the context of multiple kinds of relationships (Surra, 1990).

During this time, research on young adult peer relationships focused almost exclusively on college students, with an exception being the *Four Stages of Life* study. This research included a group of middle class and lower-middle class newlyweds who were leading-edge Baby Boomers, the majority of whom were employed full-time (Lowenthal, Thurnher, & Chiriboga, 1975). Some analyses of peer relations among college students were conducted to assess the meaning of group pranks, such as contests to see how many dead bugs a person could swallow or how many people could stuff into a telephone booth (Lang & Lang, 1961), and of behaviors deemed counter-cultural at the time, such as nude streaking through public places on college campuses (Anderson, 1977). Studies of friendship per se focused on characteristics of the friendship networks of college students and newlyweds (e.g., descriptions of their size and homogeneity), typical interactions that took place among friends (e.g., frequency of contact, amount of self-disclosure, types of shared activities), and actual versus ideal qualities of friendship. It became apparent that young women and men experienced friendship differently, with women attending more to emotional aspects of friend interactions and men more focused on instrumental activities. Trust, mutual liking and respect, self-disclosure, and support were identified as important elements of friendship for both genders (Blieszner & Adams, 1992; Lowenthal et al., 1975).

CLOSE RELATIONSHIPS IN MIDLIFE

Our overview of the social and historical influences during formative teen and early adult years was designed to illustrate sources of the personal and relational characteristics exhibited by members of the baby-boom cohorts. That introduction sets the stage for an analysis of the ways Baby Boomers enact significant family and social relationships in their middle-aged years. In the following sections, we give attention to both intra- and intergenerational transactions, starting with romantic, friend, and sibling relationships and proceeding to discussion of parent–child and grandparent–grandchild ties. In the case of the latter two categories, note that most Baby Boomers are enacting parent and child roles simultaneously, and often are enacting grandparent and grandchild roles concurrently with the other two. Thus, they are experiencing unprecedented complexity in their constellations of family roles and relationships.

Romantic Relationship Types and Patterns

Diversity in Intimacy. In keeping with trends that would be expected based on their adolescent and young adult experiences, members of the baby-boom cohorts have experienced more diverse patterns of intimacy than ever before. For example in America, the number of persons cohabiting with someone of the opposite sex prior to marriage has quadrupled since the 1960s

(Edwards & Booth, 1994). Although 71% of Baby Boomers are married, their rate of divorce is higher (14.1% of those aged 35 to 54 and 15.7% of those aged 55 to 64 compared to 7.4% of those aged 65 and older) and a bigger proportion has never married (13.1% among 35- to 54-year-olds, 5.9% among 55- to 64-year-olds, and 3.6% among persons 65 or more years of age; U.S. Census Bureau, 2003a). Because not all individuals participating in gay, lesbian, bisexual, and transgendered relationships do so openly, it is difficult to calculate their incidence rates among the Baby Boomers. However, accounts of sexual identity and relational characteristics among such persons in midlife show similar developmental and life stage related concerns about personal identity, aging, and relational matters as found among those participating in heterosexual marriage (Kimmel & Sang, 1995; Mitchell, 2000; Weinberg, Williams, & Pryor, 2001). A study of a small sample of never-married midlife adults, presumably not involved in gay, lesbian, bisexual, or transgendered relationships, suggests that they might be more vulnerable than other Baby Boomers to fears about loneliness in old age and lack of sufficient planning for their retirement years. This is especially true for those reporting negative experiences and perceptions related to being single (Adelman & Bankoff, 1990). Analysis of a larger data set, however, revealed that ever-single midlife persons fared better than their married counterparts in autonomy and personal growth (Marks & Lambert, 1998).

Interaction Patterns and Outcomes.   A prospective longitudinal study of trailing-edge Baby Boomers in Sweden confirmed the early developmental influences theme presented in the introduction of this chapter. That is, persons who had reported warm and trusting relationships with their parents during their adolescent years were likely to report satisfaction with their partner relationships in midlife. Relationships of adolescent boys with their fathers are particularly influential in this regard (Möller & Stattin, 2001). A longitudinal follow-up investigation of middle-aged women who had all experienced a poor relationship with one or more of their parents in childhood or adolescence likewise yielded evidence of the effects of earlier experiences on midlife relationships. On the one hand, women who displayed insecure (avoidant or ambivalent) attachment styles had significantly greater negative functioning in romantic relationships than those with a secure attachment style, and were significantly more likely to have cohabited with a partner having a history of criminal offenses or substance abuse. On the other hand, women with secure attachment despite their childhood difficulties stated that they were more successful in their adult relationships (McCarthy, 1999).

Midlife Baby Boomers typically are balancing a variety of roles in the workplace, community, and family. This means that partners in intimate relationships need to coordinate roles and responsibilities with one another in order to enable both to function well in their relationship and all other domains (Sterns

& Huyck, 2001). Evidence of such coordination comes from a study of African American midlife baby-boom couples, for whom maintaining a strong commitment to the relationship as a friendship, to the larger family network, and to their faith promoted marital stability and harmony. Sharing these commitments prompted the partners to divide responsibilities as well as make time for each other, which in turn enabled them to deal effectively with the complexities of family life, occupation, community activities, and ongoing racism. These couples described increasing confidence, maturity, and relational stability as defining hallmarks of their current relationships (Carolan & Allen, 1999). Sexuality, too, plays an important role in sustaining satisfaction in intimate relationships. In a 3-wave national panel study involving midlife married couples of the baby-boom cohorts, Edwards and Booth (1994) found that decreased satisfaction with the sexual relationship and loss of interest in sexual activity were associated with reduced personal well-being and marital satisfaction over the course of the study. They reported gradual and modest declines in sexual activity and marital satisfaction as couples aged, but noted that the slope of decline was less steep for the younger portion of the middle-aged cohort as compared to the older couples. Indeed, marital satisfaction seems to be fairly stable through the midlife years (Antonucci, Akiyama, & Merline, 2001) and, in fact, analyses of data from five waves of the same national panel study showed that previous depictions of a sharp decline in marital satisfaction during midlife followed by a rise in the later years were artifacts of cross-sectional methods and failure to account for period and cohort effects (VanLaningham, Johnson, & Amato, 2001). In contrast, analyses of 7 cohorts over 17 years reflected a general pattern of decline in marital satisfaction with length of marriage, with sharp declines in the 1980s but only modest ones in the 1990s and more recent cohorts displaying lower marital satisfaction than older ones (VanLaningham et al., 2001).

In a longitudinal analysis of marital status continuity and change over a 5-year period, Marks and Lambert (1998) reported that marriage generally had beneficial effects on the psychological well being of midlife adults in the baby-boom cohorts, but the results varied according to whether marriage was experienced continuously or not. Those who remained married reported better well-being than those who transitioned out of marriage because of separation, divorce, or widowhood. Those whose marriages ended experienced decreasing psychological well-being over the study period. In addition, individuals who remarried had lower well-being than those who married for the first time.

Friendship Styles and Issues

Midlife Baby Boomers are good friends with up to seven people on average, most likely persons who are of the same sex and similar in age, race/ethnicity, class, education, employment status, and other social indicators (Blieszner &

Adams, 1992; Lowenthal et al., 1975). Some Baby Boomers are also friends with persons of the opposite sex, often met at work, despite numerous social and structural barriers to forming and sustaining such bonds. These friendships have some interesting features, including the fact that men tend to rate them higher than their same-sex friendships on overall quality, nurturance, emotional support, and enjoyment but women rate their same-sex friendships higher on these characteristics. Furthermore, men are more likely than women to see a sexual dimension to such friendships (Monsour, 2002).

Features deemed appealing in close friends and discriminating between friends and those who are not friends in a sample of White middle-class leading-edge Baby Boomers included being perceived as friendly, pleasant, polite, and easy to talk to and having similar values and background. The important background similarities were education, income, marital status, parental status, and shared interests in leisure, sports, and social activities (Johnson, 1989). As in other stages of life and cohorts, midlife Baby Boomers tend to be friends with those whom they like and trust, and who provide companionship and support. They are busy with family, work, and community activities, which could interfere with friendship but also might provide opportunities both to make new friends and to sustain existing ones (Adams & Blieszner, 1996; Rawlins, 1994).

An important dimension of friendship is self-disclosure of personal information for purposes of providing insight into one's feelings and emotions, being better understood, controlling relationship outcomes, and attaining social validation. In a study of self-disclosure with friends versus family among adults, leading-edge Baby Boomers were less likely than younger or older persons to distinguish between friends and family in the first three forms of self-disclosure but did confide in friends more than family for purposes of social validation (Parker & Parrott, 1995). Friendship has many benefits, not the least of which is social, emotional, and instrumental support. An investigation of Black professional women that included midlife Baby Boomers confirmed the importance of reciprocal friend-based caring for the women's well-being. Support was expressed in terms of social companionship, help with various tasks, emotional support, commitment, and encouragement (Denton, 1990).

Connections with Siblings

Sibling ties represent the longest enduring relationships experienced by most individuals, and Baby Boomers have more siblings than do individuals in earlier cohorts. Based on interviews with Baby Boomers who participated in the 1987–1988 National Survey of Families and Households, one half of early midlife respondents (aged 30 to 39) lived within 25 miles of a brother or sister and one third saw a sibling on a weekly basis (Bumpass & Aquilino, 1995). Similar proximity and contact patterns were noted for siblings at each age stage throughout mid- and later life.

Providing companionship and emotional support constitutes an important developmental task of sibling relationships over the life span (Goetting, 1986). Relationships with sisters tend to be emotionally closer than those with brothers, with the sister–sister tie viewed as the closest adult sibling bond (Bedford, 1996). Involvement with siblings in midlife provides beneficial social experiences and enhances personal well-being (Bedford, 1998; Cicirelli, 1996). Individuals who report positive feelings toward their siblings have more positive self-perceptions and are less lonely than individuals who have negative feelings about their sibling relationships (Paul, 1997).

A common concern that often brings siblings together in midlife is the care needs of their aging parents. Most of the existing literature suggests that in families with multiple siblings, one of them, usually a sister, takes on the primary caregiver role. However, other siblings may be directly or peripherally involved in the care network as well. Several factors influence the type and amount of help individual siblings are likely to provide including gender, proximity, marital status, and employment status (Cicirelli, 1995). For example, Matthews (1995) found that lone midlife sisters typically take charge of care provision while their brothers' contributions were less acknowledged by either brothers or sisters. In brother-only sibling groups, brothers met their parents' needs by performing "masculine" services, and their wives provided more nurturing types of assistance (Matthews & Heidorn, 1998).

Everyday demands (e.g., time, money, employment, and other relationships) often are sources of conflict as siblings attend to the care needs of their aging parents. Unresolved sibling rivalry, which may resurface in times of stress, also affects the support given to both the parent and the sibling–caregiver. Perceptions of parental unfairness in the past can interfere with adult children's current feelings of affection toward mothers and fathers (Bedford, 1992), which might influence their propensity to provide assistance to parents needing help (Gentry, 2001; Merrill, 1996).

As Parents and Children

Midlife Parents. The parent–child relationship continually reshapes itself over the life course, and often improves with age (Umberson, 1992). This is fortuitous, given that the lifestyles of midlife baby-boom parents revolve around their children. Fifty percent of householders aged 34 to 54 have children under age 18 living at home, ranging from a high of 67% among 35- to 39-year-olds to a low of 21% among 50- to 54-year-olds (Russell, 2001). Single parents dominate the 35- to 45-year-old group, with females more likely than their male counterparts to be raising children alone. Hispanic Baby Boomers are much more likely to have children under age 18 at home than White or

Black householders. They also tend to have larger families than White or Black Baby Boomers, thereby extending their child rearing years.

Although most of the children of midlife Baby Boomers are well beyond infancy (2%) and preschool (14%), the proportion of householders with children of any age at home remains above 50% even in the 45- to 54-year-old age group (Russell, 2001). In addition, as the proportion of young adults who live at home continues to rise, Baby Boomers in their late 40s and early 50s have extended their parental duties. Approximately 14% of men and 8% of women 18 to 34 years old are living with their parents (World Almanac and Book of Facts, 2003), a phenomenon referred to in the popular press as the "cluttered nest." Postponement of marriage, divorce, low wages, and unemployment have contributed to young adults remaining in or returning to their family home. Most midlife parents with adult children living in the home report being satisfied with the living arrangement and having a positive relationship with their children (Aquilino & Supple, 1991; U.S. Census Bureau, 2003b).

Investigators of social support between midlife parents and their adult children found that during the middle decades, parents continue to provide more help to their children than children report giving to their parents (Logan & Spitze, 1996; Rossi & Rossi, 1990). Help is most often given to single adult children or adult children who are single parents. The marital status of midlife parents also influences social support patterns between them and their adult children (Marks, 1995). Parents in first marriages are more likely than remarried or single parents to report giving, receiving, or giving and receiving support. In addition, providing social support to children, whether reciprocated or not, is associated with better psychological well-being.

Midlife Children.   Most Baby Boomers enter midlife in the role of adult children as well as in the role of parent. Although they have regular contact with their parents, a variety of factors influence interaction patterns including proximity, individual and family circumstances and history, and norms of filial obligation (Matthews, 2002; Mercier, Shelley, & Wall, 1997). Coresidence of midlife children and parents is typically assumed to be meeting the needs of aging parents; however, families involved in long-term coresident households tend to derive mutual financial, instrumental, and emotional benefits. When midlife children return to the home of their parents, it is usually because of a change in their marital, employment, or health status (Albrecht, Coward, & Shapiro, 1997; Aquilino, 1996). These are often less than equitable situations, with adult children benefiting greatly from the support of their parents. Men are far more likely than women to live with their parents as young adults, and the tendency continues through middle age. Approximately 6% of baby-boom men aged 35 to 54 live with their parents—double the figure for their female counterparts (Russell, 2001).

Adult children frequently report a mutual exchange of instrumental, financial, and emotional support with their parents and most often assess their interactions as positive (Lee & Aytac, 1998; Logan & Spitze, 1996; Silverstein & Bengtson, 1997). Positive relationships with parents contribute to a strong sense of self and emotional well-being in midlife (Welsh & Stewart, 1995). Conversely, unpleasant relationships with parents can lead to negative feelings (Cotton-Huston & Johnson, 1998) and stress (Huyck, 1991).

Similar to cohorts before them, midlife Baby Boomers are likely to witness progressive declines in the health and functioning of their aging parents that require them to take on added responsibilities of caring for one or more parents. This shift in their relationships is often gradual, starting with irregular provision of informal instrumental support (e.g., helping with transportation, running errands). According to a national survey conducted by AARP (2001), nearly 78% of Baby Boomers age 45 to 55 provide intermittent caregiving services to their parents or other older adults, but do not consider themselves to be caregivers. Of the 22% who identify themselves as caregivers for their parents, 17% provide personal assistance, while about 5% provide mainly financial support. Although both women and men provide a wide range of help, daughters rather than sons tend to be involved in more time-consuming tasks such as talking to doctors, arranging for home care, and helping with personal care.

Caregiving can have both negative and positive effects on the health and well-being of the Baby Boomers. Indicators of poor mental health, including depression, anger, and anxiety, are frequently found among midlife children who are providing care to their parents (Gallagher-Thompson & Powers, 1997; Raveis, Karus, & Pretter, 1999). The strains experienced by caregivers are not strictly internal but carry over to other roles and relationships. Midlife caregivers typically report: conflict among roles and relationships (Gerstel & Gallagher, 1993; Noonan, Tennstedt, & Rebelsky, 1997); the loss of normative roles within relationships (e.g., previous parent–child interactions; Pohl, Boyd, & Given, 1997; Walker, Martin, & Jones, 1992); and feeling that they have no time for themselves or others (Farkas & Himes, 1997). Among the most beneficial aspects of caregiving are the development of competence and effective coping skills that promote self-efficacy and the maintenance of positive attitudes (Gold et al., 1995; Noonan et al., 1997; Walker et al., 1992). Some midlife children discover that fulfilling the caregiving role also contributes positively to their own personal growth and development (Stephens & Franks, 1995) and strengthens emotional bonds with their parents (AARP, 2001).

Being a Grandparent and a Grandchild

Midlife Grandparents. Individuals generally become grandparents around the age of 45; thus, many members of the leading-edge Baby Boom are currently involved in these intergenerational relationships. Due to declines in family size and increases in longevity, baby-boom grandparents are likely to have fewer grandchildren than their grandparents or parents had, spend a longer duration in this prescribed family role, and share their role as grandparents with multiple others (Szinovacz, 1998).

The majority of midlife grandparents are married, employed, engaged in their communities, and actively parenting one or more of their own children. Personal responsibilities, as well as geographic proximity and the relationship with the parent generation, influence the role grandparents play in the daily lives of their grandchildren (Cherlin & Furstenberg, 1986; Kivett, 1991; Kivnick, 1983). Like their parents, the Baby Boomers' cadre of grandchildren frequently includes step-grandchildren. The norms, roles, and responsibilities of step-grandparents remain ambiguous, however, as the relationship between step-grandparents and step-grandchildren is only beginning to be recognized within the study of American families (Coleman, Ganong, & Cable, 1997).

Approximately 2.4 million grandparents have primary responsibility for their grandchildren, of whom 840,000 have been caring for their grandchildren for five or more years (U.S. Bureau of the Census, 2003b). The majority of grandparents rearing grandchildren are between the ages of 30 and 59 (60%), married (73%) and female (62%). More than one half of them are in the labor force and about one fifth have incomes below the poverty threshold. However, there is marked variation in income by household type, with grandmother-only households (the most common family structure) averaging $19,750 per year and households with two grandparents plus at least one parent averaging $61,632 (Bryson & Casper, 1999). Although Baby Boomers representing all race and ethnic groups are rearing grandchildren, grandparents belonging to minority groups are two to three times as likely as their White counterparts to assume the parenting role (Fuller-Thomson, Minkler, & Driver, 1997). Surrogate parenting by grandparents is a well established pattern in African-American families where grandparents and other family members assume parenting responsibilities for those children whose parents are temporarily or permanently unable to do so (Burton, 1996).

Few Baby Boomers, regardless of race, ethnicity, or social class, plan, anticipate, or are prepared for a second parenthood (Brown & Mars, 2000; Cox, Brooks, & Valcarcel, 2000). As they assume responsibility for rearing their grandchildren, Baby Boomers often confront several personal and social challenges in making adjustments in their daily lives to accommodate their acquired parental roles (Roberto & Qualls, 2003). Many baby-boom grandparents responsible for the care and well-being of their grandchildren perceive themselves as having to manage their situation alone and report feeling judged, criticized, and abandoned by their family, friends, and their communities.

Midlife Grandchildren. Little is known about relationships midlife Baby Boomers have with their grandparents. A national telephone survey of adult grandchildren conducted in 1990 revealed that young-adult grandchildren (ages 18 to 29) lived closer and had more frequent contact with their grand-parents than midlife grandchildren (ages 30 to 49; Hodgson, 1992). Using data from the University of Southern California Longitudinal Study of Gen-erations, Mills (1999) provided some initial insights into the solidarity be-tween midlife boomer grandchildren and their grandparents. When first interviewed in 1971, the young adult Baby Boomers (aged 17 to 30) reported an average of 30 contacts per year with their grandmothers and 40 contacts with their grandfathers. By 1994, the number of contacts had declined to about 24 contacts per year with grandmothers and 20 with grandfathers. As the Baby Boomers aged, they perceived less consensus with their grandfa-thers; aging, however, had little impact on consensus with grandmothers. In addition, grandchildren generally reported more affectional solidarity with grandmothers than with grandfathers, a trend that continued over time and that is consistent with research on younger cohorts (Hagestad, 1985; Roberto & Stoes, 1992).

A LOOK TO THE FUTURE: BABY BOOMERS' RELATIONSHIPS IN LATER LIFE

The Baby Boomers came of age in a context of extensive and powerful social and political change. The psychosocial transition from adolescence to young adulthood lengthened and youth strove to attain psychological maturity prior to moving toward marriage and economic independence from parents (Shulman & Ben-Artzi, 2003). Typically, although prior socialization by par-ents still had an impact on social competence with friends in adolescence, the direct influence of parents receded as that of peers increased (Steinberg & Morris, 2001). Nevertheless, most adolescents were not estranged from their parents and there was little evidence of a significant generation gap in values and norms (Gecas & Seff, 1990). As they moved into young adulthood, the in-fluence of early experiences with parents persisted, at least in terms of the val-ues they had acquired (Kasser, Koestner, & Lekes, 2002). The Baby Boomers tended to delay marriage until later in their 20s and to experiment with multi-ple cohabitation relationships before marrying (Surra, 1990). They turned to friends for social support and to professionals for help with problems, instead of relying exclusively on their spouses when they had problems (Stewart & Healy, 1989).

Now in midlife, the Baby Boomers are participating in complex and dy-namic social networks consisting of intimate partners, siblings, friends, par-ents, grandparents, children, and grandchildren. They are likely to have en-gaged in a series of romantic relationships, beginning with cohabitation prior to marriage and continuing through one or more marriages or nonmarital liai-sons. They had, on average, fewer than 2 children, whereas their parents gave birth to an average of 3.6. This means that they have more siblings than offspring. Most have living parents and many trailing-edge Baby Boomers still have living grandparents. The leading-edge Baby Boomers are now welcoming grandchildren to their family constellation. Concurrent with their family experiences, most Baby Boomers are sustaining multiple nonkin friendships in their midlife years. Some of them are engaged in compressing the generational span, as in the case of a midlife Baby Boomer whose son is two months older than her grandson or whose second wife is close in age to his daughter.

When they are old, the Baby Boomers will have more opportunities than any previous groups to participate in long-term, multi-generational family relationships. Just as in childhood and adolescence when their bulging numbers led to structural and functional changes in families and schools, and their attitudes and values fostered the emergence of new social movements, so too in old age they will chart new territory in family structures and relationships. As more generations coexist and people live more years than before in fairly good health, Baby Boomers will have new kinds of family ties to explore, such as with children who are three or more generations—60 or more years—younger, or with grandchildren who are themselves adults. The great-grandparent role will become more common, with perhaps attendant status and privilege within the family circle. Given the high rates of divorce and remarriage, blended families will increase in complexity, and more Baby Boomers will have step-children and step-grandchildren in their family circle. But these kinds of relationships blur the lines between obligation based on traditional family ties and voluntary associations, and society has not yet developed clear norms for such relationships (Ganong, Coleman, McDaniel, & Killian, 1998). It remains to be seen whether the Baby Boomers would be willing to rear step-grandchildren and whether their step-children and step-grandchildren would agree to provide them assistance in old age. The trend, likely to continue, of family members dispersing to seek employment and amenities in distant locales interferes with the possibility of having meaningful relationships with nuclear and extended kin. Although advances in transportation and communication technology will enable contact with relatives, Baby Boomers will be challenged to sustain more than acquaintance-level ties with those in younger generations with whom they spend little time.

Based on evidence from their early years of intimacy, it is expected that elderly Baby Boomers will continue to experiment with variety in their sexual expressions and some may remain open to extramarital relations (Edwards & Booth, 1994). If the economic and social trends of recent decades that have not been particularly supportive of marriage continue along with the decline in prohibition against divorce, it is possible that the divorce rate among aging Baby Boomers will be higher than for old couples in the past (VanLaningham et al., 2001).

Aged Baby Boomers are likely to rely on their siblings for assistance and social support more than those of previous cohorts did, particularly since they will have fewer children on whom to depend. Siblings who have never married or never had children, having been self-reliant throughout adulthood, may be especially adept at providing comfort to their widowed sisters and brothers and helping reduce their anxieties about growing older. These long standing and often very close bonds, nourished by shared history and ongoing involvement, will be particularly salient sources of emotional support as well as instrumental aid (Adelman & Bankoff, 1990).

Baby Boomers are also very likely to rely on their friends for instrumental aid and emotional sustenance when they are old, particularly because their shared experiences mean they will be able to understand one another's needs and values better than members of other generations could. Having been influenced by socially significant historical events that challenged the status quo, namely the Civil Rights and women's movements and the War on Poverty, old Baby Boomers are likely to pursue friendships based on equity, with less concern about homogeneity of social characteristics than in the past. They will use technology to retain many friendships, including those with people who live far away, and be less likely to follow traditional norms and rules in these relationships. They will probably be more emotionally expressive and more interested in dealing directly with friendship difficulties than today's elders (Adams & Blieszner, 1998). Because they have already engaged in cross-sex friendships, when they are old, the Baby Boomers will be more accepting of such relationships than those in previous cohorts (Monsour, 2002).

Although many of the relationship forms we imagine in the future exist today, their prevalence will grow with the large number of Baby Boomers moving into and through the later years of life. Therefore, diverse family and friend liaisons will become normative rather than exceptional. The range and length of relationships in which the Baby Boomers will be able to participate over the course of their lives will yield interesting developmental consequences at both the personal and relational levels. Both kin and nonkin ties have potential to provide aging Baby Boomers with ongoing opportunities to avoid past mistakes and repair damaged relationships, as well as chances to gain new social skills and emotional strengths. Thus, late life close relationships, the product of continuously evolving intra- and intergenerational ties, offer support for attaining vital involvement and positive well-being in old age.

REFERENCES

AARP. (2001). *In the middle: A report on multicultural boomers coping with family and aging issues.* Washington, DC: Author.

Adams, R. G., & Blieszner, R. (1996). Midlife friendship patterns. In N. Vanzetti & S. Duck (Eds.), *A lifetime of relationships* (pp. 336–363). Pacific Grove, CA: Brooks/Cole.

Adams, R. G., & Blieszner, R. (1998). Baby Boomer friendships. *Generations, 22,* 70–75.

Adelman, M. B., & Bankoff, E. A. (1990). Life-span concerns: Implications for mid-life adult sin-gles. In H. Giles, N. Coupland, & J. M. Wiemann (Eds.), *Communication, health, and the elderly* (Fullbright Papers, Vol. 8, pp. 64–91). Manchester, England: Manchester University Press.

Albrecht, S. L., Coward, R. T., & Shapiro, A. (1997). Effects of potential changes in co-residence on matched older parent–adult child dyads. *Journal of Aging Studies, 11,* 81–96.

Aldous, J., Osmond, M. W., & Hicks, M. W. (1979). Men's work and men's families. In W. R. Burr, R. Hill, F. I. Nye, & I. L. Reiss (Eds.), *Contemporary theories about the family* (Vol. 1, pp. 227–256). New York: Free Press.

Anderson, W. A. (1977). The social organization and social control of fad. *Urban Life, 6,* 221–240.

Antonucci, T. C., Akiyama, H., & Merline, A. (2001). Dynamics of social relationships in midlife. In M. E. Lachman (Ed.), *Handbook of midlife development* (pp. 571–598). New York: Wiley.

Aquilino, W. S. (1996). The returning adult child and parental experience at midlife. In C. D. Ryff & M. M. Seltzer (Eds.), *Parental experience in midlife* (pp. 423–458). Chicago: University of Chicago Press.

Aquilino, W. S., & Supple, K. R. (1991). Parent–child relations and parents' satisfaction with liv-ing arrangements when adult children live at home. *Journal of Marriage and the Family, 53,* 13–28.

Bedford, V. H. (1992). Memories of parental favoritism and the quality of parent–child ties in adulthood. *Journal of Gerontology: Social Sciences, 47,* S149–S155.

Bedford, V. H. (1996). Sibling relationships in middle and old age. In R. Blieszner & V. H. Bedford (Eds.), *Aging and the family: Theory and research* (pp. 201–222). Westport, CT: Praeger.

Bedford, V. H. (1998). Sibling relationship troubles and well-being in middle and old age. *Family Relations, 47,* 369–376.

Blieszner, R., & Adams, R. G. (1992). *Adult friendship.* Newbury Park, CA: Sage.

Brown, D. R., & Mars, J. (2000). Profile of contemporary grandparenting in African-American families. In C. Cox (Ed.), *To grandmother's house we go and stay: Perspectives on custodial grand-parents* (pp. 203–217). New York: Springer.

Bryson, K., & Casper, L. M. (1999). Coresident grandparents and grandchildren. (Publication No. P23-198). Retrieved March 23, 2004 from Current Population Reports at http://www.census.gov/prod/99pubs/p23-198.pdf.

Bumpass, L. L., & Aquilino, W. S. (1995). *A social map of midlife: Family and work over the middle life course.* Madison, WI: Center for Demography and Ecology.

Burton, L. (1996). Age norms, the timing of family role transitions, and intergenerational caregiving among aging African American women. *The Gerontologist, 36,* 199–208.

Cannon, K. L., & Long, R. (1971). Premarital sexual behavior in the sixties. *Journal of Marriage and the Family, 33,* 36–49.

Carolan, M. T., & Allen, K. R. (1999). Commitments and constraints to intimacy for African American couples at midlife. *Journal of Family Issues, 20,* 3–24.

Carruth, G. (1993). *What happened when* (Rev. ed.). New York: Harper Collins Publishers.

Cherlin, A., & Furstenberg, F. (1986). *The new American grandparent.* New York: Basic Books.

Chilman, C. S. (1980). Social and psychological research concerning adolescent childbearing: 1970–1980. *Journal of Marriage and the Family, 42,* 793–805.

Cicirelli, V. (Ed.). (1995). *Sibling relationships across the lifespan.* New York: Plenum Press.

Cicirelli, V. (1996). Sibling relationships in middle and old age. In G. Brody (Ed.), *Sibling relation-ships: Their causes and their consequences* (pp. 47–73). Norwood, NJ: Ablex.

Clayton, R. R., & Bokemeier, J. L. (1980). Premarital sex in the seventies. *Journal of Marriage and the Family, 42,* 759–775.

Clingempeel, W., Coylar, J., Brand, E., & Hetherington, E. (1992). Children's relationships with maternal grandparents: A longitudinal study of family structure and pubertal status effects. *Child Development, 63,* 1404–1422.

Coleman, M., Ganong, L., & Cable, S. M. (1997). Beliefs about women's intergenerational family obligations to provide support before and after divorce and remarriage. *Journal of Marriage and the Family, 59,* 165–176.

Cotton-Huston, A. L., & Johnson, D. V. (1998). Daughters and mothers: Age differences in relationship descriptions and communicative desires. *Journal of Adult Development, 5,* 117–123.

Cox, C., Brooks, L. R., & Valcarcel, C. (2000). Culture and caregiving: A study of Latino grandparents. In C. Cox (Ed.), *To grandmother's house we go and stay: Perspectives on custodial grandparents* (pp. 218–232). New York: Springer.

Denton, T. C. (1990). Bonding and supportive relationships among Black professional women. *Journal of Organizational Behavior, 11,* 447–457.

Dunn, J. (1993). *Young children's close relationships: Beyond attachment.* Newbury Park, CA: Sage.

Duvall, E. M. (1971). *Family development* (4th ed.). Philadelphia: Lippincott.

Edwards, J. N., & Booth, A. (1994). Sexuality, marriage, and well-being: The middle years. In A. S. Rossi (Ed.), *Sexuality across the life course* (pp. 233–259). Chicago: University of Chicago Press.

Erikson, E. H. (1950). *Childhood and society* (2nd ed.). New York: W. W. Norton.

Farkas, J. I., & Himes, C. L. (1997). The influence of caregiving and employment on the voluntary activities of midlife and older women. *Journal of Gerontology: Social Sciences, 52,* S180–S189.

Ferree, M. M. (1990). Beyond separate spheres: Feminism and family research. *Journal of Marriage and the Family, 52,* 866–884.

Fuller-Thomson, E., Minkler, M., & Driver, D. (1997). A profile of grandparents raising grandchildren in the United States. *The Gerontologist, 37,* 406–411.

Gallagher-Thompson, D., & Powers, D. V. (1997). Primary stressors and depressive symptoms in caregivers of dementia patients. *Aging & Mental Health, 1,* 248–255.

Ganong, L., Coleman, M., McDaniel, A. K., & Killian, T. (1998). Attitudes regarding obligations to assist an older parent or stepparent following later-life remarriage. *Journal of Marriage and the Family, 60,* 595–610.

Gecas, V., & Seff, M. A. (1990). Families and adolescents: A review of the 1980s. *Journal of Marriage and the Family, 52,* 941–958.

Gentry, D. B. (2001). Resolving middle-age sibling conflict regarding parent care. *Conflict Resolution Quarterly, 19,* 31–48.

Gerstel, N., & Gallagher, S. K. (1993). Kinkeeping and distress: Gender, recipients of care, and work–family conflict. *Journal of Marriage and the Family, 55,* 598–607.

Goetting, A. (1986). The developmental task of siblingship over the life cycle. *Journal of Marriage and the Family, 48,* 703–714.

Gold, D. P., Cohen, C., Shulman, K., Zucchero, C., Andres, D., & Etezadi, J. (1995). Caregiving and dementia: Predicting negative and positive outcomes for caregivers. *International Journal of Aging and Human Development, 41,* 183–201.

Hagestad, G. O. (1985). Continuity and correctness. In V. L. Bengtson & J. F. Robertson (Eds.), *Grandparenthood* (pp. 31–48). Beverly Hills, CA: Sage.

Hodgson, L. G. (1992). Adult grandchildren and their grandparents: The enduring bond. *International Journal of Aging and Human Development, 34,* 209–225.

Hodgson, L. G. (1998). Grandparents and older grandchildren. In M. Szinovac (Ed.), *Handbook on grandparenthood* (pp. 170–183). Westport, CT: Greenwood.

Huyck, M. H. (1991). Parents and children: Post-parental imperatives. In B. H. Hess & E. W. Markson (Eds.), *Growing old in America* (4th ed., pp. 415–426). New Brunswick, NJ: Transaction.

Jessor, R., & Jessor, S. L. (1977). *Problem behavior and psychological development.* New York: Academic.

Johnson, C. (1998). Effects of adult children's divorce on grandparenthood. In M. Szinovac (Ed.), *Handbook on grandparenthood* (pp. 184–199). Westport, CT: Greenwood.

Johnson, M. A. (1989). Variables associated with friendship in an adult population. *The Journal of Social Psychology, 129*, 379–390.

Kasser, T., Koestner, R., & Lekes, N. (2002). Early family experiences and adult values: A 26-year, prospective longitudinal study. *Personality and Social Psychology Bulletin, 28*, 826–835.

Kennedy, G. E. (1989). College students' relationships with the grandparents. *Psychological Reports, 64*, 477–478.

Kimmel, D., & Sang, B. (1995). Lesbians and gay men at midlife. In A. R. D'Augelli & C. J. Patterson (Eds.), *Lesbian, gay, and bisexual identities over the lifespan* (pp. 190–214). New York: Oxford University Press.

Kivett, V. (1991). The grandparent–grandchild connection. *Marriage and Family Review, 16*, 267–290.

Kivnick, H. (1983). Dimensions of grandparenthood meaning: Deductive conceptualization and empirical derivation. *Journal of Personality and Social Psychology, 44*, 1056–1068.

Lang, K., & Lang, G. (1961). *Collective dynamics.* New York: Thomas Y. Crowell.

Lawton, L., Silverstein, M., & Bengtson, V. (1994). Solidarity between generations in families. In V. Bengtson & R. Harootyan (Eds.), *Intergenerational linkages: Hidden connections in American society* (pp. 19–42). New York: Springer Publishing Company.

Lee, Y., & Aytac, I. (1998). Intergenerational financial support among Whites, African Americans, and Latinos. *Journal of Marriage & the Family, 60*, 426–441.

Logan, J. R., & Spitze, G. D. (1996). *Family ties: Enduring relations between parents and their grown children.* Philadelphia: Temple University Press.

Lowenthal, M. F., Thurnher, M., & Chiriboga, D. (1975). *Four stages of life.* San Francisco: Jossey-Bass.

Main, M., Kaplan, N., & Cassidy, J. (1985). Security in infancy, childhood, and adulthood: A move to the level of representation. *Monographs of the Society for Research in Child Development, 5*(Serial No. 209), 66–104.

Marks, N. F. (1995). Midlife marital status differences in social support relationships with adult children and psychological well-being. *Journal of Family Issues, 16*, 5–28.

Marks, N. F., & Lambert, J. D. (1998). Marital status continuity and change among young and midlife adults. *Journal of Family Issues, 19*, 652–686.

Matthews, S. H. (1995). Gender and the division of filial responsibility between lone sisters and their brothers. *Journal of Gerontology: Social Sciences, 50*, S312–S320.

Matthews, S. H. (2002). *Sisters and brothers/Daughters and sons: Meeting the needs of old parents.* Bloomington, IN: Unlimited Publishing.

Matthews, S. H., & Heidorn, J. (1998). Meeting filial responsibilities in brothers-only sibling groups. *Journal of Gerontology: Social Sciences, 53*, S278–S286.

McCarthy, G. (1999). Attachment style and adult love relationships and friendships: A study of a group of women at risk of experiencing relationship difficulties. *British Journal of Medical Psychology, 72*, 305–321.

Mercier, J. M., Shelley, M. C., & Wall, B. (1997). Quality of adult child-aging parent relationships: A structural equations approach using merged cross-generational data. *Consumer Sciences Research Journal, 26*, 160–192.

Merrill, D. M. (1996). Conflict and cooperation among adult siblings during the transition to the role of filial caregiver. *Journal of Social and Personal Relationships, 13*, 399–413.

Miller, B. C., & Moore, K. A. (1990). Adolescent sexual behavior, pregnancy, and parenting: Research through the 1980s. *Journal of Marriage and the Family, 52*, 1025–1044.

Mills, T. L. (1999). When grandchildren grow up: Role transition and family solidarity among Baby Boomer grandchildren and their grandparents. *Journal of Aging Studies, 13*, 219–239.

Mitchell, V. (2000). The bloom is on the rose: The impact of midlife on the lesbian couple. *Journal of Gay and Lesbian Social Services, 11,* 33–48.

Möller, K., & Stattin, H. (2001). Are close relationships in adolescence linked with partner relationships in midlife? A longitudinal, prospective study. *International Journal of Behavioral Development, 25,* 66–77.

Monsour, M. (2002). *Women and men as friends: Relationships across the life span in the 21st century.* Mahwah, NJ: Lawrence Erlbaum Associates.

Moss, J. J., Apolonio, F., & Jensen, M. (1971). The premarital dyad during the sixties. *Journal of Marriage and the Family, 33,* 50–69.

Noonan, A. E., Tennstedt, S. L., & Rebelsky, F. G. (1997). Making the best of it: Themes of meaning among informal caregivers to the elderly. *Journal of Aging Studies, 10,* 313–327.

Parker, R. G., & Parrott, R. (1995). Patterns of self-disclosure across social support networks: Elderly, middle-aged, and young adults. *International Journal of Aging and Human Development, 41,* 281–297.

Paul, E. L. (1997). A longitudinal analysis of midlife interpersonal relationships and well-being In M. E. Lachman & J. B. James (Eds.), *Multiple paths of midlife development* (pp. 171–206). Chicago: University of Chicago Press.

Peterson, A. C. (1988). Adolescent development. *Annual Review of Psychology, 39,* 583–607.

Pohl, J. M., Boyd, C., & Given, B. A. (1997). Mother–daughter relationships during the first year of caregiving: A qualitative study. *Journal of Women & Aging, 9,* 133–149.

Raveis, V. H., Karus, D., & Pretter, S. (1999). Correlates of anxiety among adult daughter caregivers to a parent with cancer. *Journal of Psychosocial Oncology, 17,* 1–26.

Rawlins, W. K. (1994). Being there and growing apart: Sustaining friendships during adulthood. In D. J. Canary & L. Stafford (Eds.), *Communication and relational maintenance* (pp. 275–294). San Diego, CA: Academic Press.

Roberto, K. A., & Qualls, S. (2003). Intervention strategies for grandparents raising grandchildren: Lessons learned from the late caregiving literature. In B. Hayslip & J. Hicks Patrick (Eds.), *Working with custodial grandparents* (pp. 13–26). New York: Springer.

Roberto, K. A., & Stoes, J. (1992). Grandchildren and grandparents—Roles, influences, and relationships. *International Journal of Aging and Human Development, 34,* 227–239.

Rogler, L. H. (2002). Historical generations and psychology: The case of the Great Depression and World War II. *American Psychologist, 57,* 1013–1023.

Rossi, A. S., & Rossi, P. H. (1990). *Of human bonding: Parent–child relations across the life-course.* Hawthorne, NY: Aldine de Gruyter.

Russell, C. (2001). *The Baby Boom: Americans aged 35 to 54* (3rd ed.). Ithaca, NY: New Strategist Publications.

Settersten, R. A., Jr. (1999). *Lives in time and place: The problems and promises of developmental science.* Amityville, NY: Baywood.

Shulman, S., & Ben-Artzi, E. (2003). Age-related differences in the transition from adolescence to adulthood and links with family relationships. *Journal of Adult Development, 10,* 217–226.

Silverstein, M., & Bengtson, V. L. (1997). Intergenerational solidarity and the structure of adult parent–child relationships in American families. *American Journal of Sociology, 103,* 429–460.

Silverstein, M., & Long, J. D. (1998). Trajectories of grandparents' perceived solidarity with adult grandchildren: A growth curve analysis over 23 years. *Journal of Marriage and the Family, 60,* 912–923.

Steinberg, L., & Morris, A. S. (2001). Adolescent development. *Annual Review of Psychology, 52,* 83–110.

Stephens, M. A. P., & Franks, M. M. (1995). Spillover between daughters' roles as caregiver and wife: Interference or enhancement? *Journal of Gerontology: Psychological Sciences, 50,* P9–P17.

Sterns, H. L., & Huyck, M. H. (2001). The role of work in midlife. In M. E. Lachman (Ed.), *Handbook of midlife development* (pp. 447–486). New York: Wiley.

Stewart, A. J., & Healy, J. M., Jr. (1989). Linking individual development and social change. *American Psychologist, 44*, 30–42.

Surra, C. A. (1990). Research and theory on mate selection and premarital relationships in the 1980s. *Journal of Marriage and the Family, 52*, 844–865.

Szinovacz, M. E. (1998). Grandparents today: A demographic profile. *The Gerontologist, 38*, 37–52.

Thompson, L., & Walker, A. (1987). Mothers as mediators of intimacy between grandmothers and their young adult granddaughters. *Family Relations, 36*, 72–77.

Tokuno, K. A. (1986). The early adult transition and friendships: Mechanisms of support. *Adolescence, 21*, 593–606.

Umberson, D. (1992). Relationships between adult children and their parents: Psychological consequences for both generations. *Journal of Marriage and the Family, 54*, 664–674.

U.S. Census Bureau. (2003a). *Statistical abstract of the United States: 2003* (Section 1. Population, No. 63. Marital status of the population by sex and age: 2002). Retrieved March 20, 2004 from http://www.census.gov/prod/www/statistical-abstract-03.html.

U.S. Census Bureau. (2003b, October). *Grandparents living with grandchildren: 2000* (Publication No. C2KBR-31). Retrieved November 15, 2003 from Census 2000 Briefs and Special Reports at http://www.ccnsus.gov/prod/2003pubs/c2kbr-31.pdf.

VanLaningham, J., Johnson, D. R., & Amato, P. (2001). Marital happiness, marital duration, and the U-shaped curve: Evidence from a five-wave panel study. *Social Forces, 78*, 1313–1341.

Walker, A. J., Martin, S. K., & Jones, L. L. (1992). The benefits and costs of caregiving and care receiving for daughters and mothers. *Journal of Gerontology: Social Sciences, 47*, S130–S139.

Walters, J., & Stinnett, N. (1971). Parent–child relationships: A decade review of research. *Journal of Marriage and the Family, 33*, 70–111.

Walters, J., & Walters, L. H. (1980). Parent–child relationships: A review, 1970–1979. *Journal of Marriage and the Family, 42*, 807–822.

Weinberg, M. S., Williams, C. J., & Pryor, D. W. (2001). Bisexuals at midlife: Commitment, salience, and identity. *Journal of Contemporary Ethnography, 30*, 180–208.

Welsh, W. M., & Stewart, A. J. (1995). Relationships between women and their parents: Implications for midlife well-being. *Psychology and Aging, 10*, 181–190.

White, K., & Riedmann, A. (1992). When the Brady Bunch grows up: Step/half and full-sibling relationships in adulthood. *Journal of Marriage and the Family, 54*, 197–208.

World Almanac and Book of Facts. (2003). *Young adults living at home in the U.S., 1960–2002.* Retrieved March 23, 2004 from Infoplease at http://www.infoplease.com/ipa/A0193723.html.

CHAPTER TWELVE

Employment and the Baby Boomers: What Can We Expect in the Future?

Sara J. Czaja
University of Miami

The aging of the baby-boom cohort coupled with changes in retirement policies, programs, and behavior and increased concerns about dwindling resources to support retirement incomes — all contribute to a renewed interest in the topic of aging and work. In the year 2002 there were about 61 million people aged 55+ in the U.S. and their numbers are expected to grow to 103 million representing 30% of the population (U.S. General Accounting Office, 2003). This change in the population demographics will have a significant impact on the composition of the labor force. By 2010 the number of workers aged 55+ will be about 26 million, a 46% increase since 2000, and by 2025 this number will increase to approximately 33 million. There will also be an increase in the number of workers over the age of 65 (Fullerton & Toossi, 2001; U.S. General Accounting Office, 2003). Although labor force participation rates are projected to be slightly greater for older women than older men in contrast to previous decades the labor force participation rates for older males is also increasing.

At the same time that the work force is aging there is also a slowed growth in the number of younger workers and slowing in the growth of the labor supply. Over the next few years the proportion of workers aged 25 to 44 years is expected to decrease; while those aged 45 to 54 will grow at a slower rate than in the past. This could create labor shortages, especially in skilled and managerial occupations. Thus employers are beginning to turn their attention to older workers as a potential resource to fill this gap. In this regard Baby Boomers represent an important economic resource for the country as this generation is better educated and highly skilled than previous generations.

Clearly, the topic of aging and work is a pertinent issue for policy makers, employers, researchers and society as a whole given the vast number of people who will be reaching the status of older worker. The goals of this chapter are: (a) to discuss future trends in work behavior and work environments that will affect the aging Baby Boomers; (b) summarize what is currently known about aging and work and; (c) highlight some important research questions that need to be addressed to help insure that the contributions and productivity of the baby-boom generation are maximized. An emphasis is given to the implications of information technologies for aging Baby Boomers as most current jobs do and future jobs will involve the use of some form of technology.

TRENDS IN WORK AND RETIREMENT BEHAVIOR

Prior to 1985, the U.S. experienced a steady downward trend in retirement age. Most older Americans exited the workforce well before their full eligibility for Social Security (Costa, 1998). Recently the trend of permanently leaving the workforce early has reversed (Purcell, 2002; Quinn, 2002). Traditional models of working life portray three distinct life stages, through which people progress sequentially: (1) childhood—an education period where one prepares for work; (2) adulthood—the time of one's working career; and (3) retirement—the time of leisure and departure from paid employment. Clearly, current data suggest that this model of working life no longer fits the experience of most workers. People make many more transitions throughout their working life and move in and out of the workforce in a variety of ways at a variety of age points (Wegman & McGee, 2004). For example, some people retire from the main career jobs and embark on a second career. In fact, instead of full-time leisure, workers and retirees in their 50s, 60s, and 70s are increasingly seeking more work options: reduced hours or days per week, more time off over the year, special project or contract work, greater flexibility, part-time work, and even the opportunity to start second (or third) careers, (including unpaid community service) (Moen, 2003). In fact, recently the terms *phased retirement* and *bridge employment* have emerged to describe current work practices. Phased retirement generally refers to staying with a particular job on a part-time or part-year schedule while phasing out employment over a number of years to retirement. Bridge employment generally refers to moving to another company or career before retirement; a practice that is common among today's workers. Currently about half of all workers aged 55 to 65 years have some sort of bridge job before seeking full retirement (Purcell, 2002). The trends toward phased retirement and bridge employment are likely to increase with the aging of the Baby Boomers as most people in this cohort desire to remain active and productive.

In fact, currently, many older workers, according to a variety of studies, say they would prefer to continue to be engaged in some kind of productive activity following their retirement, and a significant number of full-time retirees say they would like to be employed. For example, a recent survey of workers 45 and older found that 69% reported wanting to work into their retirement years (AARP, 2002). Work plays an important role in shaping physical and emotional health and also in defining personal and social roles. When people leave work their income and status generally decline as does their access to social participation (Wegman & McGee, 2004).

Many people also desire or need to continue working for financial reasons. The declines in the real value of pension benefits and in retiree health care coverage create a need for many older people to return to work after retirement from their primary occupation. Findings from the recent AARP survey indicate that money and health care coverage were cited as the major reasons for the desire to continue to work. These issues are likely to become even more relevant to Baby Boomers given current projections regarding health care and pension plans.

In the past few decades there have also been changes in laws and policies that have influenced retirement decisions. For example, because of the projected increase in the age dependency ratio and the average length of retirement, there have been several changes in retirement policies to create incentives to work longer. In 1983, the Social Security Act was amended to increase the minimum age of full benefits for retirement from 65 to 67. The practice of reducing Social Security benefits when a person has earnings and reached the normal retirement age has also been eliminated and the delayed retirement benefit for those who claim benefits after normal retirement age is steadily being increased. In addition, the Age Discrimination in Employment Act was amended in 1986 to eliminate a mandatory age for most occupational groups. Finally, the Americans with Disabilities Act (ADA), which became law in 1990, also has important implications for the employment of older people. The passage of the ADA shifted the focus of disability policy in the United States from eligibility for public income transfers to ending discrimination and removing barriers (employers are to make "reasonable accommodations") that prevent people with disabilities from obtaining or remaining in paid work (Burkhauser & Daly, 2002). Given that disabilities tend to increase with age the ADA does provide some protection for older workers.

Overall, the preceding discussion clearly suggests a need to develop strategies to prepare for and accommodate an aging workforce as the Baby Boomers reach retirement age. The development of these strategies requires understanding: (a) the characteristics of current and future cohorts of older workers; (b) the potential implications of aging for work and work environments; (c) the technological and social characteristics of jobs; (d) the conditions that contribute to the movement of people into and out of employment;

and (e) the development of methodologies that are ecologically valid and capture the complexities of work and work environments. It is also important to recognize that because of the diversity of older adult populations and the dynamic nature of work, issues related to aging and work are complex and present tremendous challenges and opportunities for researchers and policy makers. The next section will summarize demographic characteristics of the baby-boom generation and discuss the potential implications of aging for work and work environments.

IMPLICATIONS OF AN AGING POPULATION FOR WORK AND WORK ENVIRONMENTS

Who Are the New Elderly?

In general the baby-boom generation is healthier, more diverse, and better educated than previous generations. Overall, the baby-boom generation is the most highly educated in U.S. history. About 27% of people in this age group have four or more years of college. Higher levels of education are generally linked to higher income and increased employment opportunities. This is especially true in today's workplace where the demand for highly educated workers has increased and the demand for workers who perform physically demanding jobs has decreased. However, as will be discussed, most workers will need to have some degree of technical expertise and this will create an enormous need for worker training and retraining programs.

On some indices, Baby Boomers are also healthier than previous generations. Life expectancy is increasing and the number of people reporting very good health and improvements in physical functioning, such as ability to walk a mile or climb stairs, has increased in recent years. Disability rates among older people are also declining. The proportion of people 65 and older with a chronic disability declined from 24% in 1982 to 21% in 1994. Health status has an important influence on the decision to remain working at older ages. Thus data indicating that the health of older adults is improving suggests that compared to previous generations, the baby-boom generations should have increased capacity to work. However, it is also important to note that there has been a dramatic increase in the number of adults who are overweight or obese. The likelihood of developing a disability also increases with age. Currently, the majority of older people have at least one chronic condition with the most common being arthritis, diabetes, high blood pressure, sensory and orthopedic impairments. Cognitive and memory impairments also increase with age (Administration on Aging, 2002). Disability rates among older adults have important implications for workplace and job design. Employers need to adapt workplaces or provide adaptive equipment or technology (such as low vision aids) to workers who have functional limitations. Generally, labor force participation rates are lower and retirement rates are higher for people with chronic conditions.

Consistent with demographic changes in the U.S. population as a whole, the older population is becoming more ethnically diverse. Currently about 84% of people aged 65+ are non-Hispanic White; this proportion will drop to about 74% in 2030 and 64% by 2050. The greatest growth will be seen among Hispanic persons, followed by non-Hispanic Blacks. Work policies, programs and services will require greater flexibility to accommodate this diverse population. For example, individuals from ethnic minority groups are also less likely to own or use technologies such as computers. This implies that technology access training programs need to be targeted for minority populations.

Age-Related Changes in Abilities

Although the baby-boom generation is healthier than prior generations and there have been enormous medical innovations over the past decade, there still remain changes in abilities associated with normal aging that have implications for work. For example, currently, about 14 million people in the U.S. suffer from some type of visual impairment, and the incidence of visual impairment increases with age. Although the majority of older adults do not experience severe visual impairments, they may experience declines in eyesight sufficient to make it difficult to perceive and comprehend visual information. This has vast implications for today's computer-oriented workplace, given that interaction with computer systems is primarily based on visually presented information. Visual decrements may make it more difficult for older people to perceive small icons on toolbars, read e-mail, or locate information on complex screens or Web sites (Fisk, Rogers, Charness, Czaja, & Sharit, 2004). Age-related changes in vision also have implications for the design of written instructions and manuals and lighting requirements.

Declines in audition also occur with aging and have relevance to work settings. For example, older adults may find it difficult to understand synthetic speech, as this type of speech is typically characterized by some degree of distortion. High frequency alerting sounds such as beeps may also be difficult for older adults to detect. Changes in audition may also make it more difficult for older people to communicate in noisy work environments.

Aging is also associated with changes in motor skills, including slower response times, declines in ability to maintain continuous movements, disruptions in coordination, loss of flexibility, and greater variability in movement. The incidence of chronic conditions such as arthritis also increases with age. Changes in motor skills may make it difficult for older people to perform tasks, such as assembly work that requires small manipulation, or to use current input devices, such as a mouse or keyboard.

Older adults also tend to have reduced strength and endurance. Generally, by age 40, average muscle strength is about 95% of maximum in the late 20s; by age 50 it decreases to about 85%; and by age 65 only 75% of the maximum is available, with further declines thereafter (Whitbourne, 2002). These are population mean differences and there is a great deal of variability in muscle groups, in types of muscular performance, and between individuals. However, in general older adults are less willing and able to perform physically demanding jobs.

Age-related changes in cognition also have relevance to work activities, especially in tasks that involve the use of technology. Declines in working memory may make it difficult for older people to learn new concepts or skills or recall complex operational procedures. Declines in attentional capacity may also make it difficult for older adults to perform concurrent activities or switch attention between competing displays of information. They may also have problems attending to or selecting task targets on complex displays. Highly paced work may also be unsuitable for older workers.

However, these are primarily speculations. Although there is a great deal of information about aging as a process, there are limited data on the practical implications of aging for work activities. The majority of studies regarding the impact of age-related changes in abilities are based on laboratory tasks. As noted by Salthouse (1986), caution must be exercised when generalizing from laboratory findings to predict performance on real world tasks. Laboratory tasks do not capture the contextual elements that are present in work environments and may not allow older people to evoke compensatory strategies that they use in real world settings. Furthermore, many jobs do not require performance at full capacity. It is also important to recognize that aging is associated with substantial variability and older adults as a group are very heterogeneous. For many indices of performance there are greater differences within the older population than between older and younger age groups. Thus although we can discuss age-related trends in abilities, predictions about an individual's ability to learn a new skill or perform a particular job should be based on his/her functional capacity relative to the demands of that job or that skill rather than chronological age. This is especially true for the baby-boom generation who are healthier, more active and more highly educated than previous generations. Furthermore, medical innovations are continuing to evolve.

Aging and Work Performance

Common beliefs about older workers include that they are physically unable to do their job, have a high rate of absenteeism, have a high rate of accidents, are less productive, less motivated, and less receptive to innovations than younger people, and are unable to learn (Peterson & Coberly, 1989). These are rather commonly held beliefs, but there is little actual data to support these assumptions; in fact, most available research studies indicate that these stereotypes are inaccurate.

With respect to age and productivity, the available data are limited especially for technology-based jobs. Several extensive reviews of the aging and work performance literature have been conducted (e.g., Rhodes, 1983; McEvoy & Cascio, 1989; Avolio, Waldman, & McDaniel, 1990) and the general conclusion of these reviews is that there is little evidence to suggest that work performance declines with age. It appears that the relationship between age and work performance is dependent on the type of performance measure, the nature of the job, and other factors such as experience.

With respect to other measures of job behavior the findings, while limited, are more conclusive. Regarding accidents, older workers tend to have lower accident rates than younger workers; however, older workers tend to remain off the job longer if they are injured. Absenteeism and turnover rates also appear to be lower for older adults (Martocchio, 1989).

Overall, the relationship between age and work performance is complex and far from understood. Many of the existing studies involve small samples and restricted age ranges, or they are cross-sectional—which may confound age effects with factors such as experience, education or exposure to technology. Studies that rely on supervisory rating of performance may be biased if the rater has negative attitudes about older workers. The results also vary according to type of task and type of performance. Finally, the number of recent studies conducted in actual employment settings has been limited. Avolio (1992) points out that much of the research pertaining to aging and work performance has not included a detailed analysis of contextual factors, such as opportunities for retraining, which have an impact on work ability. He suggests that a "levels of analysis" framework would be useful when studying aging and work behavior, as it can be used to clarify links between individual changes and the context within which such changes take place within work settings. For example, grouping jobs according to job demands (e.g., complexity, pacing) may help explain variance in age performance relationships.

Occupational Trends

Older workers hold a wide variety of occupations; however, there is some variance according to age. For example, about the same percentage of workers in the age ranges of 40 to 54, 55 to 64, and 65+ are employed in white-collar occupations. However, as compared to younger workers, fewer workers age 65+ are in physically demanding blue-collar occupations. Specifically workers ages 55 to 64 tend to be in executive/management occupations and professional occupations whereas workers ages 65 to 74 are more likely to be employed in farming, fishing, and forestry, and then in sales, transportation and service jobs. In the future the percentage of older workers will increase in all occupational categories, with the greatest increase occurring in white-collar occupations such as managers, health care professionals, administrative support and sales (United States General Accounting Office, 2001).

General projections regarding the labor force can also be used to gain some understanding of employment opportunities for older people. In the next few years a gain of about 6.9 million jobs is projected for professional and related occupations such as computer and technical specialists, health care practitioners, and education-related occupations. The second largest growth rate will be seen in the service occupations, such as customer service representatives and health care support workers. Other occupations that will experience growth include: management and financial occupations, sales and related occupations, office and administrative support operations, and installation, maintenance and repair occupations especially within the telecommunications industry. If the labor force distribution of older workers remains the same, older people tend to be in industries that are likely to experience growth. However, this does not necessarily mean that employment opportunities will expand for older workers, as a number of other factors such as the job and skill requirements of these occupations and receptivity to older workers by employers and organizations influence this equation. Almost two thirds of the projected job openings in the next ten years will require on-the-job training. Because of existing stereotypes regarding older workers, they are often bypassed for participation in job training programs (Hamil-Luker & Uhlenberg, 2002).

There are other trends in working life that have particular relevance for older workers: increasing job insecurity and instability, longer working hours, teamwork and nonstandard work arrangements. Generally people in the United States work more hours than people in other industrialized countries, however, what is striking is that the average work hours among both males and females aged 65+ has increased as has the number of workers aged 55+ who work more than 40 hours per week. In addition, time pressure and work load demands for most jobs have increased. The effects of long work hours and time constraints on the health of older workers are largely unknown. The emphasis on teamwork and collaborative work is also increasing. There is a paucity of literature on older workers in collaborative work arrangements. There are also little data available regarding optimal training strategies for team work for older adults. The reliance by industry on nontraditional (work situations different from the standard full-time, year round job) work arrangements such as contingent and part-time work is also increasing. Increases in nontraditional work may be beneficial for older workers as many older people prefer part-time work arrangements; however, these types of arrangements may also have negative consequences for older workers as they may not have access to needed training and technical support (Wegman & McGee, 2004).

TECHNOLOGY AND OLDER WORKERS

Why Is This an Important Issue?

Concurrent with the changes in the demographic structure of the workforce, there are dramatic changes occurring in work environments. Computer, information, and automation technologies are increasingly being used in work settings. In 2001, within the United States, more than half of the workforce used a computer or some other form of technology at work and this number is continuing to grow with the greater scope and sophistication of new technologies in the workplace. Technology-based occupations are also expected to grow significantly in the upcoming decades. As noted, computer occupations will account for 8 out of the 20 fastest growing jobs. Furthermore, the number of people who are telecommuting is rapidly increasing. In 1995, at least three million Americans were telecommuting for purposes of work, and this number is expected to increase by 20% per year (Nickerson & Landauer, 1997). Telecommuting may be particularly appropriate for older adults, as they are more likely than younger people to be mobility impaired or engaged in some form of caregiving. Telecommuting also allows for more flexible work schedules and autonomy, and is more amenable to part-time work. These job characteristics are general preferred by older people.

The Potential Impact of Workplace Technology on Older Workers

Given the widespread use of technology in most occupations, one important issue concerns how the influx of technology into work settings will affect employment opportunities for older workers. Technology influences the types of jobs that are available, creating new jobs and opportunities for employment, and eliminating other jobs and creating conditions of unemployment for some classes of workers. Technology also changes the way in which jobs are performed and alters job content and job demands. Thus, existing job skills and knowledge become obsolete as new knowledge and skills are required. The influx of technology into the workplace is also creating a need for workers who are more highly skilled. Even workers in nontechnical jobs are expected to have some experience with computer applications. Although the baby-boom generation has more experience with technology, such as computers, than current older workers these issues will be critical given continual developments in technology.

To date, the issue of technological innovations and older workers has only received limited attention. For example, there have only been a handful of studies that have examined the ability of older people to perform computer-based tasks that are common in work settings. We conducted a series of studies examining age performance differences on a variety of simulated computer-based tasks (e.g., data entry, inventory management, customer service; Czaja & Sharit, 1993; Czaja & Sharit, 1998; Czaja, Sharit, Ownby, Roth, & Nair, 2001). Overall, the results of these studies indicate that older adults (60 to 75 years) are willing and able to perform these types of tasks. However, generally the younger adults (20 to 39 years) performed at higher levels than the older people. The data also indicate considerable variability in performance among the older people, and with experience those in their middle years (40 to 59 years) performed at roughly the same levels as the young adults. In fact, task experience resulted in performance improvements for people of all ages. The results also indicate that prior computer experience and cognitive abilities such as working memory and psychomotor speed were important predictors of performance. Finally, interventions such as redesigning the screen, providing on-screen aids and reconfiguring the timing of the computer mouse improved the performance of all participants.

In general, technology-based tasks place a greater emphasis on cognitive skills than do traditional work methods. This increase in dependence on technology may have a negative impact on the employment of older adults because of age-related changes in cognitive abilities (e.g., declines in processing speed) coupled with limited opportunities to offset declines in skill with experience. For example, component abilities such as psychomotor speed, memory, attention, and spatial abilities have been shown to be important predictors of performance of data entry tasks, computer-based information search and retrieval tasks, and text-editing (Egan & Gomez, 1985; Czaja & Sharit, 1998; Czaja, Sharit, Ownby, Roth, & Nair, 2001). Use of the Internet also requires higher level cognitive skills involving memory, reasoning, attention, learning, and problem solving (Marchionini, 1995).

Morrell and Echt (1996) posit that age-related declines in cognitive abilities are highly influential in age-related differences in the acquisition of computer skills. These concerns are likely to hold true for future generations of older adults, as technology by its nature is dynamic. For example, there have been dramatic changes in the design of cell phones, portable computers, input devices, and personnel organizers over the past several years.

Continuous changes in technology also imply that people will need to learn new systems and new activities at multiple points during their working lives. Workers not only have to learn to use technical systems, but they must also learn new ways of performing jobs. Issues of skill obsolescence and worker retraining are highly significant for older workers. Because of age-related role expectations on the part of employers and workers themselves, they are less likely than younger workers to participate in education and training (Hamil-Luker & Uhlenberg, 2002). A challenge for work organizations and policymakers is to develop strategies to insure that older adults are provided with equal access to the technology and training needed to acquire the skills to interact with these technologies.

Existing problems with usability have also made it difficult for older people to interact successfully with technology. Unfortunately, to date, designers of most systems have not considered older adults as active users of technology and thus many interfaces are designed without accommodating the needs of this population (Czaja & Lee, 2002). Usability problems relate to screen design, input device design, complex commands and operating procedures, and inadequate training and instructional support. Although the usability of systems has improved substantially, current interfaces still exclude many people, such as those who are older or people with disabilities, from effective interaction with technology (National Research Council, 1997). Hopefully, with the aging of the population, designers will need to rethink the issue of user group and recognize that older adults will be interacting with technology on an increasing basis.

On the positive side, because in many cases technology reduces the physical demands of work, employment opportunities for older people may increase with the influx of workplace technologies. As discussed, computer technology also makes work at home a more likely option and allows for more flexible work schedules.

Adaptive technologies may also make continued work more viable for older people especially those with some type of chronic condition or disability. The use of technology as an intervention tool for people with disabilities is expanding rapidly. There are a number of technologies such as low vision aids, speech recognition tools, and reminder systems that can improve the ability of older people with impairments to function in work environments (Czaja & Moen, 2003). However, the availability of these technologies does not guarantee their success. The degree to which these technologies improve the work life of older persons depends on the usability of these technologies, the availability of these technologies within organizations, the manner in which these technologies are implemented (e.g., training), and the willingness of older people and those with functional impairments to use these devices.

Use of Technology by Older Adults

Although there are a number of settings such as the workplace, the home, and health care and service settings where older people are likely to encounter technology such as computers, use of technology among people over the age of 55 is still low compared to other age groups. As shown in Fig. 12.1, about 26% of households of older people in the United States have a computer compared to about 55% of households of persons aged 35 to 54 years. The percentage of people who use a computer at work is also lower for older workers. Use

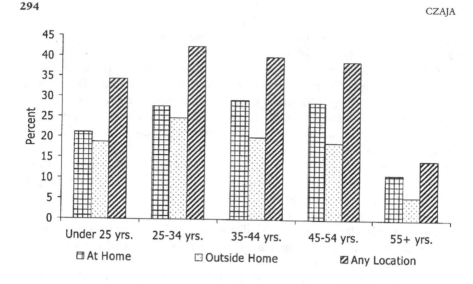

Source: Administration on Aging (2002)

FIG. 12.1.   Percent of U.S. persons using the Internet.

of the Internet among older people is also lower than that of younger age groups (UCLA Internet Report, 2003). Only 30% of people age 50+ were Internet users in 2000, and although the number of Internet users in this age group is increasing at the same rate as the overall population, Internet users age 50+ are still less than half of users age 16 to 40 years (U.S. Department of Commerce, 2002). Factors that limit the use of computers and other forms of technology by older people are: lack of access to the technology, lack of knowledge, and cost.

Older Adults and the Acquisition of Computer Skills

Given that the majority of older workers will need to interact with some form of computer technology, a critical issue is whether they will be able to acquire the skills necessary to interact successfully with these systems. Generally, the literature on aging and skill acquisition indicates that older people have more difficulty acquiring new skills than younger people and that they often achieve lower levels of performance (Park, 1992). This is especially true for tasks that represent unfamiliar domains.

A number of studies (e.g., Elias, Elias, Robbins, & Gage, 1987; Zandri & Charness, 1989; Czaja, Hammond, Blascovich, & Swede, 1989; Charness, Schumann, & Boritz, 1992; Morrell, Park, Mayhorn, & Echt, 1995; Mead, Spaulding, Sit, Meyer, & Walker, 1997) have examined the ability of older adults to learn to use new technologies such as computers. These studies span a variety of computer applications and also vary with respect to training strategies such as conceptual versus procedural training (Morrell, Park, Mayhorn, & Echt, 1995). The influence of other variables on learning, such as attitude towards computers and computer anxiety, has also been examined. Overall, the results of these studies indicate that older adults are, in fact, able to learn to use new technologies. However, they are typically slower to acquire new skills than younger adults and generally require more help and hands-on practice. Also, when compared to younger adults on performance measures, older adults often achieve lower levels of performance. However, age group comparisons must be interpreted with caution. The important issue is whether people, irrespective of age, are able to meet the performance demands of a task. In addition, the literature also indicates that training interventions can be successful in terms of improving performance for people of all ages. Essentially the critical issue is matching the training approach with the needs and characteristics of the trainee population.

Clearly, greater attention needs to be given to the design of training and instructional materials for older learners. The potential use of technology as a training aid also needs to be examined. For example, older people may benefit from multimedia systems or interactive online training programs as these programs allow for self-paced learning. However, careful attention needs to be given to the design of these types of packages. Finally, employers need to insure that older adults are provided with access to retraining programs and incentives to invest in learning new skills and abilities. Consideration also needs to be given to the scheduling and location of training programs and potential for partnerships between industries and communities. Issues related to interface workplace design are also critical to the successful adoption of technology by older people.

WHAT DO WE NEED TO DO AND KNOW TO ACCOMMODATE TO AN AGING WORKFORCE?

Areas of Needed Research

The topic of aging and work is increasingly important given current demographic trends, but the empirical data regarding the impact of aging on work performance are limited, especially for present day jobs and those likely to exist in the public sector in the future. There is a critical need for further research in this area.

Overall, we need more information on the relationship between age-related changes in functioning and the specific skill requirements of jobs. Although there are age-related declines in some functions, these changes are gradual and most jobs do not demand constant performance at the level of maximum capacity. The majority of the population of older adults remains healthy and functionally able until very late in life. One important area of needed research is developing a knowledge base that links age-related changes in skills and abilities to specific skill requirements of jobs. For example, currently, the relationships among aging, cognition, and work productivity are unclear. A more complete understanding of these relationships would help direct the development of intervention strategies for older workers. These interventions might include job redesign, workplace and equipment redesign, or the development of innovative training strategies.

We also need sound, research-based information about the impact of technology on the workforce of aging Baby Boomers and how technology might be used to promote employment opportunities for older people. In addition we need knowledge about how technology can be used to facilitate career and employment transitions. It is also important to understand how to design technology so that it is useful and usable for older adult populations especially those with some type of impairment. All too often designers restrict their vision of user groups to young, able-bodied populations. Research also needs to be directed towards examining the cost effectiveness of technological interventions.

Organizations and policymakers also need to turn their attention to issues related to successful retirement and recruitment of older workers. Issues of worker retraining and skill obsolescence are also critical. The work preferences of older people as well as the benefits of alternative work arrangements and financial incentives also need to be understood. In addition, the potential benefits and pitfalls of telecommuting for older workers should be investigated. There is also a need to identify strategies for ensuring that workers are provided with adequate training, technical support, and performance feedback for these types of tasks. In addition, we need information on how other factors such as family caregiving impact work performance. Currently an estimated 14.4 million workers are balancing work and caregiving responsibilities (National Alliance for Caregiving and American Association for Retired Persons 2004). This number is likely to increase as the Baby Boomers reach their 60s and 70s.

Finally, new methodologies need to be developed to examine age and work that capture the complexities of work and work environments. Careful consideration needs to be given to choice of outcomes measures including biologic markers that evaluate the impact of work.

In general, research attention directed toward those aspects of work that could become more difficult, less productive or less satisfying with age could make a worthwhile contribution to improving the work life of the Baby Boomers as they age. Such research would also help to assure the availability of appropriate employment opportunities for older people and broaden the pool of potential employees for public agencies competing for increasingly scarce labor.

REFERENCES

AARP. (2002). *Staying Ahead of the Curve: The AARP Work and Career Study.* Washington, DC: Author.

Administration on Aging. (2002). *A profile of older Americans: 2002.* Washington, DC: U.S. Department of Health and Human Services.

Avolio, B. J. (1992). A levels of analysis perspective of aging and work research. In K. W. Schaie & M. P. Lawton (Eds.), *Annual review of gerontology and geriatrics* (pp. 239–260). New York: Springer.

Avolio, B. J., Waldman, D. A., & McDaniel, M. A. (1990). Age and work performance in nonmanagerial jobs: The effects of experience and occupational type. *Academy of Management Journal, 33,* 407–422.

Burkhauser, R. V., & Daly, M. C. (2002). U.S. Disability Policy in a Changing Environment. *Journal of Economic Perspectives, 16*(1), 213–224.

Charness, N., Schumann, C. E., & Boritz, G. A. (1992). Training older adults in word processing: Effects of age, training technique and computer anxiety. *International Journal of Aging and Technology, 5,* 79–106.

Costa, D. L. (1998). *The Evolution of Retirement.* Chicago: University of Chicago Press.

Czaja, S. J., Hammond, K., Blascovich, J., & Swede, H. (1989). Age-related differences in learning to use a text-editing system. *Behavior and Information Technology, 8,* 309–319.

Czaja, S. J., & Lee, C. C. (2002). Designing computer system for older adults. In J. Jacko & A. Sears (Eds.), *Handbook of Human-Computer Interaction.* New York: Lawrence Erlbaum Associates.

Czaja, S. J., & Moen, P. (2004). Technology and employment. In R. Pew & S. Van Hamel (Eds.), *Technology and Adaptive Aging* (pp. 150–178). Washington, DC: National Research Council.

Czaja, S. J., & Sharit, J. (1993). Age differences in the performance of computer based work as a function of pacing and task complexity, *Psychology and Aging, 8,* 59–67.

Czaja, S. J., & Sharit, J. (1998). Ability-performance relationships as a function of age and task experience for a data entry task. *Journal of Experimental Psychology: Applied, 4,* 332–351.

Czaja, S. J., Sharit, J., Ownby, R., Roth, D., & Nair, S. (2001). Examining Age Differences in Performance of a Complex Information Search and Retrieval Task. *Psychology and Aging, 16,* 564–579.

Egan, D. E., & Gomez, L. M. (1985). Assaying, isolating, and accommodating individual differences in learning a complex skill. *Individual Differences in Cognition, 2,* 174–217.

Elias, P. K., Elias, M. F., Robbins, M. A., & Gage, P. (1987). Acquisition of word-processing skills by younger, middle-aged, and older adults. *Psychology and Aging, 2,* 340–348.

Fisk, A. D., Rogers, W. A., Charness, N., Czaja, S. J., & Sharit, J. (2004). *Designing for Older Adults. Principles and Creative Human Factors Approaches.* Boca Raton, FL: CRC Press.

Fullerton, H. N., & Toossi, M. (1991, November). Labor force projections to 2010: Steady growth and changing composition. *Monthly Labor Review,* 21–38.

Hamil-Luker, J., & Uhlenberg, P. (2002). Later Life Education in the 1990s: Increasing involvement and Continuing Disparity. *Journal of Gerontology, 57B,* S324–S331.

Marchionini, G. (1995). *Information seeking in electronic environments.* Cambridge: Cambridge University Press.

Martocchio, J. J. (1989). Age related differences in employee absenteeism: A meta-analysis, *Psychology and Aging, 4,* 409–414.

McEvoy, G. M., & Cascio, W. F. (1989). Cumulative evidence of relationship between employee age and job performance. *Journal of Applied Psychology, 74,* 11–17.

Mead, S. E., Spaulding, V. A., Sit, R. A., Meyer, B., & Walker, N. (1997). Effects of age and training on World Wide Web navigation strategies. *Proceedings of the Human Factors and Ergonomics Society 41st Annual Meeting, 152–156.*

Moen, P. (2003). "Midcourse: Navigating Retirement and a New Life Stage." In J. Mortimer & M. J. Shanahan (Eds.), *Handbook of the Life Course.* New York: Plenum.

Morrell, R. W., & Echt, K. V. (1996). Designing written instructions for older adults: Learning to use computers. In A. D. Fisk & W. A. Rogers (Eds.), *Handbook of Human Factors and the Older Adult* (pp. 335–361). San Diego: Academic Press.

Morrell, R. W., Park, D. C., Mayhorn, C. B., & Echt, K. V. (1995). *Older adults and electronic communication networks: Learning to use ELDERCOMM.* Paper presented at the 103 Annual Convention of the American Psychological Association. New York.

National Alliance for Caregiving and American Association for Retired Persons. (2004). *Caregiving in the U.S.* Washington, DC: Author.

National Research Council. (1997). *More than screen deep: Toward every-citizen interfaces to the nation's information infrastructure.* Washington, DC: National Academy Press.

Nickerson, R. S., & Landauer, T. K. (1997). Human-computer interaction: Background and issues. In M. G. Helander, T. K. Landauer, & P. V. Prabhu (Eds.), *Handbook of human-computer interaction* (2nd ed., pp. 3–32). Amsterdam: Elsevier.

Park, D. C. (1992). Applied cognitive aging research. In F. I. M. Craik & T. A. Salthouse (Eds.), *The handbook of aging and cognition* (pp. 449–494). Hillsdale, NJ: Lawrence Erlbaum Associates.

Peterson, D., & Coberly, S. (1989). The older worker: Myths and realities. In R. Morris & S. A. Bass (Eds.), *Retirement reconsidered: Economic and social roles for older people* (pp. 116–128). New York: Springer.

Purcell, P. J. (2002, October 18). *Older Workers: Employment and Retirement Trends.* Congressional Research Service Report for Congress. Washington, DC: Congressional Research Service.

Quinn, J. F. (2002). Retirement Trends and Patterns among Older American Workers. In S. H. Altman & D. Shactman (Eds.), *Policies for an Aging Society* (pp. 293–315). Baltimore: Johns Hopkins University Press.

Rhodes, S. R. (1983). Age-related differences in work attitudes and behavior: A review and conceptual analysis. *Psychological Bulletin, 93,* 328–367.

Salthouse, T. A. (1986, February). *On the leap from lab to life in perceptual cognitive aging.* Background Paper for the National Research Council Invitational Conference on Work, Aging, and Vision, Washington, DC.

UCLA Internet Report: *Surveying the Digital Future.* (2003, January 23). Retrieved September 10, 2004, from http://ccp.ucla.edu/pdf/UCLA-Internet-Report-Year-Three.pdf

United States General Accounting Office. (2001). *Older Workers: Demographic trends pose challenges for employers and workers.* Report to the ranking minority member, subcommittee or employer–employee relations, committee on education and the workforce, House of Representatives. Washington, DC.

United States General Accounting Office. (2003). *Older Workers: Policies of Other Nations to Increase Labor Force Participation.* Report to the ranking Minority Member, Special Committee on Aging. Washington, DC.

U.S. Department of Commerce. (2002). *A Nation online: How Americans are expanding their use of the Internet.* Washington, DC: Government Printing Office.

Wegman, D. H., & McGee, J. P. (2004). *Health and Safety Needs of Older Workers* (Eds.). Washington, DC: National Academies Press.

Whitbourne, S. K. (2002). *The aging individual: Physical and psychological perspectives* (2nd ed.). New York: Springer Press.

Zandri, E., & Charness, N. (1989). Training older and younger adults to use software. *Educational Gerontology, 15,* 615–631.

CHAPTER THIRTEEN

Summary and Future Directions

Susan Krauss Whitbourne
University of Massachusetts Amherst

Sherry L. Willis
Pennsylvania State University

The contributors to this volume have done a magnificent job of providing contemporary and comprehensive perspectives on the Baby Boomers as they proceed through midlife. They have reviewed extensive demographic data, analyzed social trends, reflected on psychological processes accompanying the transition through midlife, and given us many ideas about future directions for research, theory, and an understanding of social trends. Although there have been several recent volumes on middle age, this is one of the few volumes to focus exclusively on the Baby Boomers. The publication of this volume comes at a critical time as the Boomers prepare to enter old age. Our hope is to provide important insights into critical issues about aging with respect to this cohort. In this chapter, we summarize the major points of the book and attempt to reflect on the directions that research on this cohort might be taking especially with regard to middle age and the later adulthood years.

Section 1 of this volume presents the theoretical, social, and methodological overviews to the study of the Baby Boomers in middle age. In the first chapter, David J. Eggebeen and Samuel Sturgeon provide us with a comprehensive overview of the demographic phenomenon that took place from 1946–1962 in which the number of births wildly exceeded predictions. Why did it occur? What is its impact? From this chapter, we not only gain insight into these central questions but also learn about the many manifestations of the Baby Boom in the areas of marital status, living arrangements, education, income, and labor force status. The trends analyzed in this opening chapter set the stage for subsequent authors to explore the ways in which the demographic and social characteristics of this generation permeate all areas of life. Moreover, they make the key point that the Baby Boomers are not a uniform group—they vary in important ways by race and social class. Looking toward the future, Eggebeen and Sturgeon predict that many of the Baby Boomers now in middle age will weather successfully the potential turmoil of old age because they have built up a lifetime of economic and social resources. The danger will come, however, from those whose lack of access to these resources will strain both their own and society's ability to support them through the next few decades.

We turn next to the theoretical considerations. Abigail J. Stewart and Cynthia M. Torges in chapter 2 provide historical perspectives, including features of the shared experiences of the Baby Boomers that affect their lives in both direct and indirect ways. For example, a decision on the part of the American Gas Association to standardize the size of kitchen cabinets and appliances meant that the members of this generation would remember the same kitchen, if not the same political events. Of course, television, the Cold War, and the suburban lifestyle would also play a role in shaping the experiences of this generation. If you are a Baby Boomer yourself, some of these historical examples will probably bring a smile of recognition to your face such as the "duck and cover" that we practiced in our classrooms. However, as was pointed out by Eggebeen and Sturgeon, there are important variations within the baby-boom generation. With regard to the Vietnam War, for instance, some Baby Boomers experienced this historical event as soldiers and some as protesters. Similarly, the Civil Rights movement had a different impact on the lives of Blacks compared to Whites. Moreover, the early and late Baby Boomers would have had different experiences of these events based on their differing ages at the time.

Midlife as a period of development, similarly, is not a uniform time, and there are important differences between the 30s, the 40s, and the 50s. These differences notwithstanding, there are some generalities in the historical experiences of the Baby Boomers, such as having been children in a time of relative peace and prosperity and entering adolescence during the turbulent years of the Civil Rights movements and Vietnam War. There also was a kind of generational identity among the Baby Boomers, who were perhaps the first generation to think of themselves as sharing a common sense of self. This sense of identity as part of a generation carries into midlife. Stewart and Torges identify several important features of the baby-boom midlife identity including the ways that gender, social class, and race affect the particular identities that evolve through this period. At the conclusion of their insightful analysis of the interactions of cohort and historical era they suggest future studies that should be carried out to test both the unique and the common features of developmental processes characterizing this cohort during this historical period.

The importance of understanding cohort is the focus of chapter 3 on conceptual and methodological issues by Duane F. Alwin, Ryan J. McCammon, and Scott M. Hofer. Cohort effects are typically thought of as involving the impact of historical events on the lives of individuals, but as Alwin and his co-authors point out, these effects can cause individuals to change in ways that in turn affect the lives of others in a reciprocal process. Society is a reflection of the cohorts who compose it just as, conversely, cohorts are affected by the larger society. For example, cohorts reaching adolescence in the 1920s invented the phenomenon of dating; by the 1950s and 1960s, this was a normative pattern that in turn constrained the choices made by young women in those adolescent cohorts. Alwin and colleagues also provide the important distinction between the concept of *cohort* and the concept of *period*; if a social or historical event affects the young, it is a cohort effect, but if it affects all age groups, it is a period effect. They then illustrate in detail the problems in disentangling the effects of aging, period, and cohort on behavior, review cross-sectional, longitudinal, and cohort sequential designs, and present a contemporary summary of analytical models employing structural equations and latent growth. By employing these newer analytical models, particularly those focusing on within-individual changes, researchers can gain greater clarity into the interactions of aging, cohort, and period affecting the Baby Boomers as they develop through the midlife years.

In section 2, we turn to physical and mental health. Middle age is characterized by the gradual accumulation of physical changes, the onset of chronic disease, and also the stress of work and family. In the second section of the book, we examine these processes with regard to the baby-boom cohorts. Menopause is one of the few normative biological marker events in middle age. The Baby Boomers are a particularly interesting cohort to study in relation to menopause given that they have utilized hormones related to reproduction throughout their adult years and are the first cohort to enter old age with scientific findings regarding the pros and cons of hormone utilization in old age. In chapter 4 on the menopause, Nancy E. Avis and Sybil Crawford point out that in the past, this normative physiological transition was viewed as a deficiency disease but with the baby-boom generation, this approach is changing. Ethnic and racial variations, previously not examined in research on menopause, are now becoming the focus of several large-scale investigations. The onset of menopause is defined as twelve months following a woman's last menstrual period; however, current studies are attempting to distinguish the stages of menopause, using both chronological and endocrinological criteria. Researchers are also attempting to determine if there are secular trends in the age of menopause or whether there are racial and ethnic variations; so far, there does not appear to be evidence that the Baby Boomers are experiencing later menopause than was true for previous generations. Baby Boomers tend to have more positive attitudes toward the menopause than was true for previous generations, but there are significant variations within the U.S. among racial and ethnic groups. Moreover, there are also racial and ethnic differences in the experiencing of menopausal symptoms. Interestingly, despite the existence of more positive attitudes in Baby Boomers compared to previous generations, they have more symptoms and are more likely to report feeling depressed. A major focus of this chapter is the controversy surrounding Hormone Replacement Therapy (HT) and whether the benefits outweigh the risks. The authors provide an extensive review of HT and alternative therapies, concluding that as a treatment for menopausal symptoms HT is recommended, but there are more serious long-term negative consequences that warrant against its use. As these new large-scale studies of menopause in current middle-aged women continue, we will gain important new data on baby-boom women with varying demographic characteristics who adapt to this normative life transition.

Moving next to the mental health of the Baby Boomers, Jennifer R. Piazza and Susan Turk Charles in chapter 5 review the prevalence statistics for this cohort of major psychological disorders and then propose a set of psychosocial determinants that may be affecting current trends. They note that midlife adults currently score lower than older adults on a variety of measures of well-being, and have a lower sense of personal control. Studies of psychological disorders mirror these trends, and current middle-aged adults have higher rates of depression and substance abuse. These trends are not universal, however, and studies of non-Caucasian samples such as Mexican Americans, Puerto Ricans, and Koreans reveal differing trends by cohort in the prevalence of mental disorders. Large-scale prevalence studies, however, show a consistent pattern for post World War II cohorts. Looking at specific disorders, Piazza and Turk Charles report higher rates of depression, bipolar disorder, anxiety disorders, and substance use. Schizophrenia is not changing in prevalence, but there is evidence that the onset of schizophrenia has decreased from 1945 and on. Although not of major concern at present, Alzheimer's disease will become a mental health issue as the Baby Boomers enter later adulthood. However, the authors cite prevalence statistics that are far more conservative than those usually seen in the media, with the prediction of perhaps 25% of adults 85 and older being afflicted by this disorder rather than the 50% often seen in the popular press. In evaluating all prevalence data, it is important to keep in mind that estimates are affected by cohort and period effects, attrition, and faulty reporting of symptoms. We still lack the cohort sequential studies that would help to separate out some of these confounding influences on mental health statistics. Looking at psychosocial processes that could play a role in causing these cohort trends, Piazza and Turk Charles examine three factors: intragroup competition due to the large size of the cohort, increases in consumerism and hence the need to acquire wealth and the trappings of status, and feelings of alienation and personal threat associated with the protests of the 1960s and early 1970s. On the positive side, the Baby Boomers are more likely than preceding cohorts to take advantage of mental health services and they will be more knowledgeable about the risks associated with health and mental health problems. Such awareness may pave the way for future generations to benefit from psychological treatment and, just as importantly, prevention.

Psychosocial issues are the focus of section 3. We begin in the area of personality. Kelly M. Jones, Susan Krauss Whitbourne, and Karyn M. Skultety examine models of identity and development in chapter 6. After reviewing Erikson's theory of psychosocial development and studies that have focused specifically on identity, they summarize Identity Process Theory (IPT), an approach that examines the complex, reciprocal relationship between the individual and experiences in adulthood. IPT proposes that individual development in adulthood can best be understood by examining the relative use of identity assimilation (interpreting new experiences in terms of existing identity), identity accommodation (making changes in identity in response to new experiences), and identity balance (maintaining consistency in identity but making changes when necessary). Empirical tests of IPT in middle-aged Baby Boomers have shown that this population is more likely to use identity accommodation than are those in the older generation. Jones and colleagues interpret this and related findings to suggest that the Baby Boomers are more distraught over the lack of control they have over the aging process and are hence more likely to feel that there is little or nothing they can do to prevent loss. Furthermore, the thought of aging presents the Baby Boomers with a challenge to their self-concepts as youthful and vigorous. These challenges show significant gender differences due to the negative social stereotypes associated with aging for women. Aging self-stereotypes present another challenge for the Baby Boomers with their greater sensitivity to the changes associated with getting older. They are more likely than their elders to incorporate into their identities the view that they are unable to be as successful or competent as they were when they were younger. The focus of the baby-boom generation on youth and attractiveness should also make them more likely to incorporate into their sense of self any changes in outward appearance that begin to cause them to be labeled old. Similarly, concern in today's society about the prevalence of Alzheimer's disease which, as noted by Piazza and Turk Charles is misunderstood, may also lead the Baby Boomers to become overly sensitive even to minor memory failures. The concept of stereotype threat also seems relevant to the Baby Boomers, who when they begin to think of themselves as old may suffer needless deleterious changes in cognitive functioning. Such changes should be particularly likely to occur for those middle-aged adults who use identity accommodation. Unfortunately, because these negative stereotypes abound, and because the Baby Boomers seem particularly sensitive to age-related changes in physical and cognitive functioning, the risks are high that they will conclude that they cannot prevent or compensate for the age-related changes that are amenable to measures that maximize their health and functioning. However, it is also important to understand that, as other authors have pointed out, there are individual variations in the way that Baby Boomers approach the aging process. IPT provides a framework for organizing the way in which these variations are studied and understood.

The daily lives of Baby Boomers are thought by many popular writers to be filled with stress due to the multiple demands they face in the areas of family, work, community, and maintaining their physical health and fitness. David M. Almeida, Joyce Serido, and Daniel McDonald examine the sources of stress faced by current midlife adults in the area of daily life, stressors known as "hassles" in chapter 7. From the National Study of Daily Experiences (NSDE), a large-scale diary study of adults, Almeida and his colleagues examined the nature and impact of daily stressors. The most significant factor that predicted individual differences in daily stressors was year of birth. Early Baby Boomers had higher levels of education and fewer children living in the home. There were few differences between the early and late Baby Boomers in the number of stressors, but the older members of the generation were more likely to have stressors involving another person, such as a sick family member. The late Boomers were more likely to report interpersonal tensions. The younger Baby Boomers were also more likely to report suffering from stressors that disrupted their finances. In turn, they also had higher levels of psychological distress on a daily basis than the older Baby Boomers. Fleshing out these group differences, Almeida and colleagues provide narratives from the diaries of their respondents. The findings from the NSDE as analyzed in this chapter provide us with an in-depth understanding of how the types of social trends discussed by historians and demographers touch the lives of individuals as they adapt to the challenges involved in adapting to the multiple demands of daily experiences in middle adulthood.

Closely tied in with the concept of stress is sense of control. Marilyn McKeen Skaff in chapter 8 presents an analysis of how the Baby Boomers experience the extent to which they can control the events that take place in daily life, using a four-component model of control that incorporates subjective experience, multiple meanings of control, the dialectical nature of control, and the antecedents of the sense of control. Examining many of the historical events treated by other authors, Skaff provides an analysis of their particular impact on sense of control. Many of the events of the postwar period up through the 1960s could have had the effect of increasing the sense of control among the Baby Boomers. Increasing opportunities for education and economic security as well as a sense of political empowerment could have given the Baby Boomers greater feelings of personal control. The growth of the women's movement, and particularly the availability of the oral contraceptive, should theoretically have allowed women to feel more in control of their lives; however, empirical findings suggest that the opposite is the case—

women instead became more aware of the constraints that affected their lives. Changes in the family could also have an impact on sense of control, such as increases in the divorce rate, thus offsetting any positive changes left from an advantaged childhood. Skaff also points out that it is important to keep in mind diversity within the baby-boom population. Although even now many Baby Boomers express feelings of optimism as they face retirement, younger Baby Boomers feel that they have less control than do the older members of the baby-boom cohort. Furthermore, variations in sex, ethnicity, location, and social class add to the diversity of the population and, in turn, sense of control. Turning next to the theoretical model of primary versus secondary control, Skaff proposes that rather than assuming that primary control (i.e. having the ability to change one's environment) is superior to secondary control (changing oneself when the environment cannot be changed), there may be cultural variations that lead some subgroups to regard secondary control as a more adaptive and hence desirable strategy. As Baby Boomers age, there may also be changes in their sense of control with some factors leading to an increase (greater power and responsibility) and others to a decrease (feeling more overwhelmed by responsibilities). However, in examining control among the Baby Boomers, Skaff points out the necessity of keeping in mind that age, cohort, and period effects continue to be confounded in most of the available research. In addition, sense of control varies by domain, with Baby Boomers likely to experience greater control in some areas of life than others. Moreover, because social context also plays an important role in determining feelings of control, variations within the Baby Boomers by age, gender, occupation, education, race, and ethnicity must also be taken into account.

Cognitive functioning is clearly an important component of the aging process, and with regard to the baby-boom generation, the ability to maintain such skills as memory, the ability to learn, problem solving, and intelligence are critical both to well-being and to adaptive functioning. In their 40s and 50s, are the Baby Boomers technically at risk for significant cognitive declines? Sherry L. Willis and K. Warner Schaie review the evidence in chapter 9, drawing heavily from the Seattle Longitudinal Study (SLS). This large-scale investigation has followed a sequential design since its inception in 1955, allowing for inferences to be made about the relative contributions of age, cohort, and period effects, as well as to analyzing the nature of intraindividual variations in changes in intelligence. Using a measure of intelligence that provides separate estimates for *fluid* (unlearned, largely nonverbal) versus *crystallized* (learned, largely verbal) abilities, the SLS has examined thirteen 7-year cohorts with birth years 1889 to 1973. In addition to interest in the nature of change in the midlife years is the question of whether there have been "massive IQ gains" among post World War II cohorts, a phenomenon referred to as the *Flynn effect*. Based on data from the baby-boom cohorts of 1945 and 1952, data from the SLS support the existence of the Flynn effect for the fluid abilities of inductive reasoning and word fluency, but there are opposite findings for the crystal-lized abilities of number, which shows a negative cohort effect from the 1924 cohort and up. In terms of mean scores across midlife cohorts, evidence from the SLS has typically shown stability. However these aggregated scores disguise the fact that there are wide individual differences in patterns of change. Drawing from Bronfenbrenner's model of the environmental influences on development, Schaie and Willis examine the relative contributions to cognitive development of the Baby Boomers of family, education, and occupation, as well as the education and occupational experiences of their parents. Both individual differences, then, as well as sociohistorical influences on intelligence in midlife must be considered, and the Baby Boomers provide an excellent opportunity for the application of an understanding of these processes.

Context is a subtle theme of sections 1 to 3, but in section 4, we explicitly examine its role in the lives of the Baby Boomers. Continuing an examination of the parents of the Baby Boomers, but from the perspective of family relationships, Karen Fingerman and Megan Dolbin-MacNab in chapter 10 examine intergenerational ties and how they reflect the influences of cohort, social change, and inherent changes in the aging process. They begin by focusing on the life patterns of the parents and how these influenced relationships with their baby-boom children. For example, their parents were highly invested in their care, as indicated by the enormous success of Dr. Benjamin Spock's guide to child care. The parents themselves, in turn, had been raised by parents (particularly mothers) who had also sought advice on proper child care. By the time the parents were raising their baby-boom children, however, rigid child care standards had relaxed considerably, mainly under the influence of Dr. Spock's advice. Parents also wished to indulge their children, as evidenced by the success of toy companies who targeted these parents seeking to make their children happy. The Baby Boomers experienced a new sense of freedom in adolescence, continuing a trend begun in the early twentieth century. With the introduction of the term teenager, the Baby Boomers were now branded as a generation that would have even greater freedom from their parents who, in turn, encouraged and allowed them to avoid responsibility throughout their adolescent years. Currently, the Baby Boomers still receive more material, instrumental, and emotional support than they provide in return. As was pointed out by each of the other contributors to this volume, there are important differences within the baby-boom cohort; when examining parent–child relationships, these variations are made even more complex by the many possible permutations in social class, race, ethnicity, sexual orientation, marital status, employment status, and, of course gender. These variations aside, certain historical and social trends have had an impact on the lives of Baby Boomers and their children, although in differing ways. For example, increases in life expectancy meant that members of the parent generation, unlike their own parents, could envision relationships with their children enduring for many years. Similarly, the Baby Boomers grew up with a sense of time being expansive and their own lives reflecting a certain invulnerability; this, despite the fact that the Cold War was being fought with high intensity. Their sense of expansiveness of available time to spend with their parents may have given them the emotional freedom to rebel during their youth against the older generation's values, beliefs, and commitments. Today, the Baby Boomers themselves face conflicts with their own teenage children, but these tend not to revolve around core values. Of course, as parents grow older, caregiving issues become more prominent, but according to Fingerman and Dolbin-MacNab in chapter 10, these may not be significantly different for the baby-boom generation. Other social trends that have had an impact on parent–child ties are changes in mobility and economic patterns; as a result, there has been a weakening of family ties across generations from the 1900s through the present. Nevertheless, the Baby Boomers seem to value highly their family bonds, and remain emotionally tied to their parents. Changes in gender roles and sexuality have also had an impact on parent–child relationships for the Baby Boomers. Surprisingly, changes in gender roles have not had a strong impact on mother–daughter ties, nor have changes in attitudes toward sexuality. Fingerman and Dolbin-MacNab conclude their observations by noting that despite the many threats to parent–child relationships for the Baby Boomers, the bonds are strong, persistent, and reciprocal.

Moving beyond parent–child to other family relationships, Rosemary Blieszner and Karen Roberto in chapter 11 take us to the broader family context of the Baby Boomers. Referring to the familiar theme of the need to distinguish between leading-edge and trailing-Baby Boomers, the authors provide an insightful summary of the research on the Baby Boomers while they were in adolescence, which includes investigations of parent–child, grandparent–grandchild, siblings, romantic partners, and teen pregnancies. Little research exists on the development of relationships during the transition to adulthood of the Baby Boomers, but what is available suggests that young men and women experience friendship in ways that are more similar than different. Using this research as a backdrop, Blieszner and Roberto go on to examine the nature of close relationships in midlife. The baby-boom generation includes greater diversity in intimate relationships than has been true in the past, but relational patterns, as well as issues pertaining to sexuality, aging, identity, appear to be similar to the more traditional heterosexual marriage. It appears that early parent–child relationships characterized by warmth and trust play out in midlife to affect the nature of close relationships, so that adults who were securely attached to their parents also report having more satisfactory intimate relationships as adults. The intimate relationship in midlife appears, for the most part, to be stable in terms of satisfaction, but there are also effects of cohort and period such that more recent cohorts seem to have lower levels of satisfaction than their predecessors. However, for those couples who are able to maintain the relationships over the long term, there are benefits in terms of enhanced psychological well-being. Friendships in middle adulthood are also clearly of importance to midlife Baby Boomers. The average number of friendships is seven, and as at other stages in life, people in midlife share similar social characteristics and interests. Friendships, including opposite sex friendships at work, are an important source in midlife of companionship and support despite the fact that the Baby Boomers have many demands on their time. Sibling bonds also play important roles in the lives of midlife Baby Boomers, particularly those between sisters. One third of the late Baby Boomers see a sibling at least once a week. Sharing the care of an aging parent may present a source of tension in these relationships but also, surprisingly, sibling rivalries may still exist long after they have not shared the same household. Parenting, of course, is a major focus of the Baby Boomers, and although most midlife parents expect to be empty nesters, many increasingly are facing the return of children to the household, a phenomenon referred to as the "cluttered nest." Even if they are not living with them in the home, the Baby Boomers are continuing to provide help to their children, more in fact than they receive in return. At the same time, with the typical age of entry into grandparenthood at 45-years-old, many of the Baby Boomers are becoming grandparents. With the changing composition of families, grandchildren often include step-grandchildren, and increasingly, midlife grandparents are being asked to perform parenting functions. Approximately 1 million baby-boom grandparents, particularly those who are members of minority groups, have become surrogate parents. Looking at the other side of the grandparenting relationship, Baby Boomers tend to remain close to their own grandmothers, with the number of yearly contacts averaging 2 per month. Many of the baby-boom grandchildren state that they still feel emotionally connected to their grandmothers. Clearly, as Blieszner and Roberto point out, the Baby Boomers have complex and multifaceted closer relationships in midlife, a trend that will continue to give them the potential for rich and rewarding networks as they develop through the years of later adulthood.

With the aging of the Baby Boomers will come not only changes in family relationships, but also changes in the workplace. As the leading-edge of the Baby Boomers reaches the traditional retirement age of 65, there will also be large-scale economic and social changes that accompany the withdrawal of this large group from the labor force. Sara Czaja analyzes in depth the numerous ramifications of these changes in work and retirement patterns in chapter 12. Her discussion of these patterns makes clear the need for employers and policymakers to prepare for these shifts. The Baby Boomers are more likely than other cohorts to have received a college education and to be in good health, so they should be able to keep working longer and at higher capacity. On the other hand, the fact that rates of obesity have increased dramatically combined with the fact that disability rates rise with age means that there may also be higher rates of impairment within this aging workforce. Reviewing the data on aging and job skills, Czaja weighs the negative changes (such as loss of strength and visual acuity) against the mitigating factors (decrements shown in the laboratory may not show up as decrements on the job). In fact, older workers have lower rates of accidents and absenteeism. She makes the important point that ratings of job performance may be biased by negative attitudes toward older workers. The aging Baby Boomers will, however, be faced with challenges if current workplace trends continue into the future, such as long work hours and the need for retraining. At present, older workers have less experience with and exposure to technology, and this may be another challenge because jobs are likely to involve the reliance on advanced computer skills. Again, the Baby Boomers are a unique cohort in the study of work and aging, in that they have utilized computers in the workplace throughout their lives and enter old age computer literate. Of particular interest is how the Baby Boomers will continue to update their technical knowledge when out of the workplace—the major source of technical training and updating. However, in some ways, these demands may present less of a problem for older workers whose physical abilities and willingness to exert themselves may be lower than when they were younger. It is very likely that the Baby Boomers will need to receive training in order to remain able to carry out their jobs in an increasingly technological workplace. In addition to identifying the practical challenges that will face the Baby Boomers as their abilities change, Czaja raises empirical issues that will ultimately need to be addressed by researchers and planners. First, there is a tremendous gap in our knowledge about age-related changes in abilities and how these changes will impact job performance. In particular, we lack data about the impact of new technologies on the aging Baby Boomers in the workplace. Second, helping the Baby Boomers make the adjustment to the changing workplace through job training and recruitment will be needed to maximize their productivity and job satisfaction. Third, retirement planners need to take into account the differences between the Baby Boomers and previous generations of retirees in their interests, preferences, and financial status.

The contributors to this volume have each provided innovative and compelling ways to gain perspective on the aging of the baby-boom generation. The Baby Boomers' parents were the Greatest Generation in terms of their ability to cope with the calamities of severe economic depression and a long and brutal world war. Having faced both unparalleled challenges and advantages in their development through adulthood, the Baby Boomers are the "largest generation," and the most diverse. Given their place in history they have acquired many of the forms of cognitive and social reserves that current research suggests are associated with successful aging—high levels of education, high occupational status, technological competence, and stimulating environments. They have been the recipients of many of the health care advances (e.g., antibiotics) that have significantly reduced the effects of acute disease and moderated the effects of chronic disease. At the same time they are entering old age with fewer social supports because of the reduced birth rate, and they are experiencing economic uncertainty and increasing globalization. Just as they have paved new social paths in areas ranging from clothing styles to political activism to family structures, the Baby Boomers will surely in the future continue to chart new modes and ways of development. Of interest is the extent to which their advantaged early development will provide a buffer or support as they enter the challenging aging years. We will look to them (indeed, to us!) to define new ways of aging.

Author Index

Note: Page numbers in *italic* refer to reference pages. Those followed by "n" refer to footnotes.

A

AARP, 190, *202*, 223, 224, *230*, 272, *276*, 285, *297*
Abeles, R. P., 186, 187, 188, 200, *202*
Abma, J. C., *109*
Abraham, R., 90, *107*
Abraham, S., 84, *99*
Achenbaum, W. A., 219, *232*
Ackerman, R. J., 168, *182*
Adams, C., 90, *109*
Adams, R. G., 266, 269, 276, *276*, *277*
Adams, W., 127, *141*
Adams-Campbell, L. L., 93, 94, *101*
Adelman, M. B., 267, 276, *277*
Adler, N. E., 38, 39, *41*
Adler, S., 84, 86, *108*
Administration on Aging, 286, *297*
Agerbo, E., 133, *141*
Agronick, G., 28, *40*

Akiyama, H., 268, *277*
Albert, M. S., 214, 221, *230*
Albertazzi, P., 97, *99*
Albrecht, S. L., 271, *277*
Aldercreutz, H., 87, *99*
Alderman, E., 92, *109*
Aldous, J., 265, *277*
Aldwin, C. M., 122, 130, *142*
Allardyce, J., 127, *139*
Allen, K. R., 268, *277*
Almeida, D. M., 166, 169, 172, *182*, *183*
Alt, P. M., 6, *20*
Alwin, D. F., 46, 47, 50, 51, 52, 60, 65, 66, *67*, 68,
    71, 167, *182*, 208, 209, 219, 222, 225,
    230, *232*, 237, *256*
Amato, P., 47, 68, 268, 275, *281*
American Psychiatric Association, 113, *138*
Anderson, E., 65, *70*
Anderson, G. L., 91, *107*
Anderson, H., 93, *104*

Anderson, L., 95, 96, 97, 98, 106
Anderson, W. A., 266, 277
Andreasen, N. C., 111, 114, 115, 120, 130, 142, 144
Andres, D., 272, 278
Andrew, M., 131, 143
Angerer, P., 92, 99
Angst, J., 114, 138
Ansbacher, R., 95, 104
Anstey, K., 220, 221, 230
Anthony, J. C., 221, 232
Anthony, M. S., 93, 97, 100, 101
Antonucci, T. C., 219, 231, 268, 277
Apolonio, F., 264, 280
Applegate, W., 95, 102
Aquilino, W. S., 269, 271, 277
Aragaki, A. K., 94, 103
Arias, S., 82, 108
Arking, R., 206, 230
Ascensao, J., 93, 94, 101
Assaf, A., 92, 94, 105
Assmann, S. F., 81, 88, 100
Astin, J. A., 154, 164
Atkinson, M. P., 240, 241, 251, 256
Attwell, P., 224, 230
Avis, N. E., 76, 77, 81, 82, 84, 85, 86, 87, 88, 89,
     91, 99, 100, 104, 108
Avolio, B. J., 289, 297
Aykan, H., 66, 68
Aytac, I., 272, 279
Azen, S. P., 92, 93, 103

B

Bachman, J. G., 61, 70
Bachman, L., 207, 230
Baird, D. D., 80, 83, 101
Baker, D. P., 228, 230
Baldessarini, R. J., 145
Baldwin, C., 189, 202
Baltes, M. M., 186, 189, 202
Baltes, P. B., 55, 68, 186, 189, 202, 207, 219, 230
Bamrah, J. S., 127, 138
Banasik, B. L., 33, 41
Bandura, A., 161, 163, 187, 202
Bankoff, E. A., 267, 276, 277
Barbieri, R., 81, 101
Bardis, P. D., 250, 256

Barer, B., 243, 258
Barko, J. J., 221, 231
Barnes, L. L., 229, 234
Baron, J., 81, 99
Barrett-Connor, E., 92, 94, 102, 104, 107
Barroso, A., 82, 108
Barsky, A. J., 136, 138
Barton, D. L., 97, 106
Baruch, G., 38, 39
Bauman, K. E., 82, 99
Baumeister, R. F., 135, 138, 156, 163
Baumgardner, A. H., 156, 163
Beal, M. W., 96, 99
Bean, F. D., 5, 6, 20
Bebbington, P., 131, 145
Beck, A. T., 132, 139
Bedford, V. H., 270, 277
Beitins, I. Z., 81, 107
Bell, R. Q., 65, 66, 70
Bell, S., 76, 99
Bellah, R. N., 32, 39
Ben-Artzi, E., 274, 280
Benefice, E., 82, 108
Bengtson, V. L., 52, 68, 241, 245, 255, 256, 258,
     264, 272, 279, 280
Bengtsson, C., 82, 99, 107
Bennett, D. A., 229, 234
Beresford, S. A., 91, 107
Berg, G., 97, 103
Berg, S., 137, 141
Berglund, P., 114, 115, 120, 142
Berkman, L., 221, 230
Berkowitz, H., 29, 41
Berlin, J. A., 77, 103
Bermann, E., 246, 257
Bernis, C., 82, 108
Bertrand, R. M., 192, 193, 203
Biblarz, T. J., 52, 68
Bienias, J. L., 229, 234
Bifano, N. L., 81, 82, 105
Bird, H. R., 114, 139
Birditt, K. S., 241, 251, 252, 255, 257
Bittner, V., 92, 109
Black, H., 92, 105
Blair, C., 228, 230
Blanchard-Fields, F., 137, 139
Bland, D., 97, 100

Bland, R. C., *139*
Blascovich, J., 294, *297*
Blatter, C. W., 168, *182*
Blazer, D., 221, *230*
Blazer, D. G., 130, 136, 137, *139, 141*
Blieszner, R., 266, 268–269, 276, *276, 277*
Blocker, T. J., 33, 35, *42*
Bluck, S., 30, *42*, 188, 192, *204, 206, 207, 233*
Bobo, L., 47, *71*
Boersma, H., 82, *108*
Boggs, P., 98, *108*
Bokemeier, J. L., 264, *277*
Boldsen, J., 82, *99*
Bolger, N., 169, *182*
Bonaccorsi, G., 97, *99*
Bondarenko, I. V., 87, *95, 106, 107*
Bonetta, C., *95, 99*
Bonham-Leyba, M., 78, *102*
Booth, A., 47, *68*, 267, 268, 275, *278*
Boritz, G. A., 294, *297*
Bottner, M., 94, *109*
Boulet, M. J., 83, *99*
Bouvier, L. F., 3n, 4, 5, 8, 12, 15, *21*
Bowen, D., 78, 94, *105, 106*
Bowers, J., 28, *41*
Bowlby, J., 240, *256*
Boyce, T., 38, *39*
Boyd, C., 272, *280*
Boyd, J. H., 114, 130, *141, 144*
Boydell, J., 127, *139*
Boyle, M. H., *143*
Bradsher, J., 90, 91, *100*
Brambilla, D. J., 80, 81, 89, *100, 105*
Brand, E., 263, *277*
Brandt, D., 65, *71*
Brass, L., 92, *109*
Braun, M., 47, *71*
Bravo, M., 114, *139*
Breer, L., 86, *106*
Breines, W., 31, *39*
Brenner, R., 136, *139*
Breslau, E. S., *95, 100*
Brett, K., 83, *100*
Brody, E. M., 246, 249, *256*
Brokaw, T., 23, 33, *39*, 237, *256*
Bromberger, J., 81, 82, 83, 86, 87, 88, 89, 90, *99, 100, 102, 104*

Bronfenbrenner, U., 206, 217, *230*
Brookmeyer, R., 128, *141*, 160, *163*, 206, *230*
Brooks, L. R., 273, *278*
Brooks-Gunn, J., 38, *39*, 245, *257*
Brosnihan, K. B., 92, *103*
Brown, B., 97, *102*
Brown, D. R., 273, *277*
Brown, G., 132, *139*
Brown, G. W., 166, 170, *182, 183*
Brown, J. D., 157, *164*
Brown, J. S., *95, 102*, 132, *139*
Brown, R., 26, 27, *39*
Brown, W. J., 77, *100*
Brubaker, L., *95, 107*
Bruce, M. L., 111, *115*, 120, 129, 130, *142, 145*
Brumberg, J. J., 245, *256*
Brunner, R. L., 94, *103, 106*
Bryk, A. S., 66, *68*
Bryson, K., 273, *277*
Bryson, L., 77, *100*
Brzyski, R. G., 94, *103*
Buckley, H., 92, *101*
Bucur, A., 52, *68*
Buist, D. S., 96, *106*
Bumpass, L. L., 253, *256*, 269, *277*
Bungay, G. T., 80, *100*
Burger, H. G., 77, 81, 87, 90, *100, 101, 102, 103*
Burke, G. L., 97, *100*
Burke, J. D., 115, 120, 122, 129, 130, *139, 144*
Burke, K. C., 115, 120, 122, 129, *139*
Burkhauser, R. V., 285, *297*
Burnam, A., 122, *141*
Burnam, M. A., 114, 138, *141*
Burns, S., 205, *231*
Burton, L., 273, *277*
Busch, J. C., 194, *203*
Bush, T. L., 81, 92, *100, 104*
Butz, W. P., 6, *21*
Byles, J. E., 77, *100*
Bynner, J., 59, *68*

C

Cable, S. M., 273, *278*
Cain, V., 86, 87, *99*
Camburn, D., 60, *68*
Campbell, D., *143*

Campbell, J. D., 156, *163*
Campbell, L. D., 243, *256*
Campbell, R. T., 240, 241, 251, *256*
Canino, G. J., 114, *139*
Cannon, K. L., 264, *277*
Caputo, R. K., 36, *39*
Card, D., 167, *182*
Cardno, A., 131, *143*
Carolan, M. T., 268, *277*
Carroll, M. D., 82, *102*
Carruth, G., 262, *277*
Carstensen, L. L., 113, 137, *139, 140,* 187, 188, 191, 200, *202, 203,* 244, 250, *256*
Cascio, W. F., 289, *297*
Cashin-Hemphill, L., 92, *103*
Casper, L. M., 273, *277*
Cassidy, J., 261, *279*
Castle, D., 127, *139*
Castro, C. A., 78, *102*
Cauley, J. A., 92, 93, 94, *100, 104, 107*
Cavanaugh, J. T. O., 127, *139*
CBO (Congressional Budget Office), 24, *39*
CDC, 82, *101*
Center for Higher Education Support Services, 248, *256*
Chafe, W. H., 26, *39*
Charles, S. T., 113, 137, *139,* 244, 250, *256*
Charness, N., 287, 294, *297, 298*
Chen, C., 93, 94, *101*
Chen, K., 47, *68*
Chen, L. S., 221, *232*
Chen, P. C., 249, 250, *257*
Chen, Z., 93, *100*
Cherlin, A. J., 253, *256,* 273, *277*
Cherry, N., 92, *101*
Chesla, C., 186, *204*
Chesney, M. A., 38, *39*
Cheung, A. M., 95, *99*
Chilman, C. S., 264, *277*
Chiriboga, D. A., 168, *182,* 266, 269, *279*
Chlebowski, R. T., 93, 94, *101*
Christensen, H., 220, 221, *230*
Christensen, K. A., 195, *202*
Cichy, K. E., 249, 250, *257*
Cicirelli, V., 264, 270, *277*
Cicirelli, V. G., 246, *256*
Ciompi, L., 136, *139*

Clarke, R., 226, *230*
Clarke, S., 92, *101*
Clark-Plaskie, M., 189, 190, 192, *202*
Clarkson, T. B., 92, 93, *101, 103*
Clayton, P. J., 122, *143*
Clayton, R. R., 264, *277*
Climo, A. H., 29, *39*
Clingempeel, W., 263, *277*
Clipp, E. C., 136, 138, *139*
Cloninger, C. R., 122, *143*
Cloninger, R., *144*
Clydesdale, T. T., 190, *202,* 242, *256*
Cobb, F., 92, *109*
Coberly, S., 288, *298*
Cochran, V., 92, *106*
Cohen, C., 272, *278*
Cohen, C. I., 136, *139*
Cohen, L., 25, *39*
Cohen, P. C., 247–248, *258*
Cohen, R. L., 47, 60, *67*
Cohen, S., 38, *39*
Cohler, B. J., 254, *256*
Coker, L., 94, *106*
Colditz, G., 92, *108*
Cole, E. R., 33, 35, *39*
Coleman, M., 273, 275, *278*
Collins, A., 84, *106*
Collins, K. C., 157, 159, 160, *164*
Collins, W. A., 245, *258*
Conboy, L., 98, *101*
Connell, J. P., 193, 200, *204*
Connelly, M. T., 98, *101*
Connidis, I. A., 241, 243, 246, 252, 255, *256*
Connolly, L. A., 153, *164,* 206, *233*
Converse, P. E., 58, *68*
Conway, M., 32, 33, *40*
Cooke, D. J., 86, *102*
Coontz, S., 25, 31, *40,* 239, 242, 251, 252, *256*
Cooper, G., 80, 83, *100, 101*
Corbett, J., 122, 128, *144*
Cordal, A., 81, 88, 89, *100*
Cornman, J. M., 132, *139*
Corwin, S., 96, *107*
Coryell, W., *139*
Costa, D. L., 284, *297*
Costa, P. T., *232*
Costa, P. T., Jr., 172, *182,* 207, *230, 231*

Costanza, M., 82, 106
Cotton-Huston, A. L., 272, 278
Cowan, G., 84, 101
Coward, R. T., 271, 277
Cox, C., 273, 278
Coy, K. C., 245, 258
Coylar, J., 263, 277
Craik, F. I. M., 207, 231
Cramer, D. W., 80, 81, 101
Cranney, A., 93, 109
Crawford, S., 80, 81, 82, 83, 84, 86, 87, 91, 99, 101, 102, 108
Crimmins, E., 249, 257
Crimmins, E. M., 132, 140
Cronbach, L. J., 65, 68
Crosnoe, R., 138, 139
Cross-National Collaborative Group, 115, 140
Crouse, J., 92, 105
Crouter, A., 206, 217, 230
Crystal, S., 205, 231
Cummings, S. R., 93, 100
Curhan, G. C., 103
Curtin, S. C., 109
Cushman, M., 92, 105
Cyr, M. G., 101
Czaja, S. J., 287, 292, 293, 294, 297

D

Dailey, M., 94, 106
Daley, J., 83, 109
Daly, M. C., 285, 297
Darden, F. R., 83, 101
Darrow, C. M., 34, 41
Davis, K. E., 47, 68
Davis, W. W., 95, 100
Dawson, D., 82, 101
de Aloysio, D., 97, 99
Dean, J., 137, 142
Deeb-Sossa, N., 133, 141
de Frias, C., 207, 208, 224, 231
Deleon, H., 137, 143
DeLongis, A., 166, 182
de Meeus, T., 82, 108
Demler, O., 114, 115, 120, 142
Dennehy, C., 96, 104

Dennerstein, L., 77, 87, 90, 91, 101, 102, 103, 107
Denton, T. C., 269, 278
Der, G., 145
Derby, C., 90, 91, 102
Detrano, R., 92, 105
De Vita, C. J., 4, 5, 8, 12, 15, 21
Dibble, E., 145
Dickens, W. T., 208, 231
Dickstein, M., 33, 34, 35, 40
Diehl, M., 154, 163
Diener, E., 113, 140, 172, 183
Di Maggio, C., 127, 140
Dixon, R. A., 207, 208, 214, 231
Dobson, A. J., 77, 100
Doherty, W. J., 189, 202
Domar, A., 98, 101
Dominguez, J., 96, 109
Doner, L., 95, 100
Dooley, D., 132, 140
Dorland, M., 82, 108
Driver, D., 273, 278
Dubal, D., 94, 109
Dubas, J., 82, 108
Dudek, F. J., 215, 231
Dudley, E. C., 87, 90, 91, 101, 103, 107
Duncan, E. M., 129, 143
Duncan, G. J., 57, 62, 68
Duncan, L., 28, 40
Duncan, L. E., 252, 257
Dunn, J., 264, 278
DuPlessis, R. B., 36, 40
Durbin, C. E., 131, 142
Duvall, E. M., 265, 278

E

Eagles, J. M., 127, 140
Earles, J. L. K., 59, 71, 207, 233
Easterbrook, G., 133, 134, 140
Easterlin, R. A., 4, 5–6, 21, 24, 40, 48, 68, 132, 133, 140, 167, 182, 222, 231
Eaves, L. J., 131, 141, 169, 182
Ebrahim, S., 82, 105
Echols, A., 36, 40
Echt, K. V., 292, 294, 295, 298
Edelberg, R., 87, 108

Edwards, J. N., 267, 268, 275, *278*
Egan, D. E., 292, *297*
Eggebeen, D. J., 12, *21*, 238, 240, 242, 254, *257, 259*
Eidelson, J. I., 132, *139*
Eimicke, J., 136, *139*
Eisner, E. J., 95, *100*
Elder, G. H., 30, *40*, 134, 136, 138, *139, 140*, 168, *182*, 248, *258*
Elder, G. H. J., 189, *202*
Elder, G. H., Jr., 220, 227, *231, 232*, 238, *257*
Elias, M. E., 294, *297*
Elias, P. K., 294, *297*
Elkind, D., 244, *257*
Elliot, L. B., 29, *43*
Elstein, M., 92, *101*
Endicott, J., 111, 113, 114, 115, 120, 130, *139, 140, 142, 144*
Epstein, D., 65, *70*
Erikson, E., 28, 29, *40*
Erikson, E. H., 49, *68*, 149, *163*, 192, *202*, 261, *278*
Ernst, E., 97, *104*
Escobar, J. I., 114, 138, *141*
Eshleman, S., 113, 114, 115, 120, 128, 130, *142*
Espeland, M., 94, *106*
ESPRIT Team, 92, *101*
Essex, M. J., 249, *258*
Etaugh, C., 168, *182*
Etezadi, J., 272, *278*
Ettinger, B., 95, 96, 97, 98, *102*
Evans, D. A., 90, 91, *102, 105, 108, 234*
Everson-Rose, S. A., 90, *105*

F

Fahy, T. A., 131, *145*
Farber, D., 32, 33, 34, *40*
Farkas, G., 58n, *68*
Farkas, J. I., 272, *278*
Farmer, M. E., 221, *231*
Farrell, M. P., 38, *40*, 206, *232*
Fasick, F., 240, *257*
Faxon, D. P., 92, *103*
Featherman, D. L., 219, 222, *231*
Feldman, P., 38, *41*
Femia, E. E., 246, *257*

Ferrari, N., 98, *101*
Ferree, M. M., 265, *278*
Ferri, E., 59, *68*
Fields, J. M., 135, *142*, 251, *258*
Fienberg, S. E., 55, 57, 58, 58n, *70*
Fingerman, K. L., 240, 241, 245, 246, 249, 250, 251, 252, 253, 255, *257*
Firebaugh, G., 47, 52, 64, *68*
Fischer, S. A., 114, 128, 129, 130, *143*
Fisher, J. E., 137, *140*
Fisher, L., 186, *204*
Fishman, R., 115, 120, *144*
Fisk, A. D., 287, *297*
Flacks, R., 60, *70*
Flaherty, B. P., 61, *69*
Flegal, K. M., 82, *102*
Florio, L. P., 111, 115, *145*
Flynn, J. R., 206, 208, 209, 210, *231*
Fogel, C., 96, *102*
Folkman, S., 38, *39*, 166, *182*
Folnegovic, Z., *140*
Folnegovic-Smalc, V., *140*
Folsom, R., 122, *140*
Foner, A., 219, *232*
Fong, J., 92, *107*
Forini, E., 97, *99*
Foster, D. W., 80, *109*
Fouad, M., 78, *105*
Fozard, J., 128, *141*
Fraer, C., 81, *101*
Frank, E., 166, *183*
Frankenberg, R., 27, *40*
Franks, M. M., 195, 198, *204*, 272, *280*
Franz, C., 33, 35, *40*
Freedman, D., 60, *68*
Freedman, R. R., 97, *102*
Freedman, V. A., 66, *68*, 245, *258*
Freeman, E., 77, 95, 97, 98, *103, 106*
Freeman, H. L., 127, *138*
French, W. J., 92, *103*
Frere, G., 83, *102*
Frey, K., 84, *102*
Friedan, B., 25, *40*
Frieske, D., 59, *71*
Fugh-Berman, A., 96, 97, *104*
Fukuyama, F., 134, 135, *140*
Fuller-Thompson, E., 273, *278*

Fullerton, H. N., 252, *257*, 283, *297*
Fung, H. H., 137, *139*, 187, 188, 200, *202*
Furberg, C. D., 92, 94, *103*, *104*
Furby, L., *65*, *68*
Furedi, F., 135, *140*
Furstenberg, F., 273, *277*
Futterman, A., 132, 136, *145*

G

Gaarder, T. D., 92, *103*
Gage, P., 294, *297*
Gaines, C., 59, *71*
Gallagher, S. K., 272, *278*
Gallagher-Thompson, D., 132, 136, *145*, 272, *278*
Gamson, D. A., 228, *230*
Ganong, L., 273, 275, *278*
Ganz, P., 86, 87, 88, 90, *99*, *100*, *104*
Garcia-Espana, B., 77, *103*
Gardiner, *202*
Garrida-Latorre, F., 83, *102*
Garrison, D., 26, *40*
Gaskell, G. D., 34, *40*
Gass, M., 94, *101*, *106*
Gater, R., *144*
Gatz, M., 120, 137, *139*, *140*, *141*, 195, 197, *202*
Gavaler, J. S., 78, *102*
Gecas, V., 263, 265, 274, *278*
Geenens, D., *145*
Gentry, D. B., 270, *278*
George, V., 78, *105*
Gershon, E. S., 120, *140*, *145*
Gerson, K., 39, *40*
Gerstal, N., 272, *278*
Gerstel, *247*
Gerstenberg, E. P., 96, *103*
Gfroerer, J., 122, *140*
Ghosh, T., 83, *105*
Gilewski, M. J., 132, 136, *145*
Gilligan, M. A., *101*
Gilmour, K., 92, *101*
Gilvarry, K., 131, *145*
Gitlin, T., 32, 33, *40*
Giuffra, L. A., 129, *140*
Given, B. A., 272, *280*
Givens, D. H., 92, *103*
Gladney, E., 86, *106*

Glazer, G., 86, *108*
Gleason, P., 31, *40*
Glenn, N. D., *55*, *56*, 58n, 66, *69*, 208, 209, *231*
Goering, P., *143*
Goethe, J. W., *145*
Goetting, A., 270, *278*
Gold, D. P., 272, *278*
Gold, E., 81, 82, 83, 86, 87, 91, *102*, *108*
Goldberg, D. P., 127, *138*
Goldberg, J., 83, *109*
Goldenberg, R. L., 80, *102*
Goldstein, H., 66, *69*
Gomez, L. M., 292, *297*
Gonzalez, B., 82, *108*
Goodman, N. R., 95, *100*
Goodwin, D. C., *145*
Gorbach, S., 87, *99*
Gordon, D., 92, *109*
Gottesman, I. I., 131, *140*
Gould, S. J., 191, *202*
Goulden, J., 24, *40*
Gove, W. R., 208, 209, *234*
Graber, J. A., 245, *257*
Grady, D., 92, 94, 95, 96, 97, 98, *102*, *104*, *109*
Granek, I. A., 94, *103*
Grant, B. F., 122, *140*
Graves, A. B., 127, *143*
Gray, S., 128, *141*, 206, *230*
Green, A., 77, 87, *102*
Green, J., 90, *107*
Greenberg, D. F., *65*, *69*
Greenberger, E., 240, *257*
Greendale, G. A., 81, 82, 83, 91, *102*, *108*
Greene, J. G., 86, *102*
Greenough, W. T., 221, *231*
Griffin, L. J., 219, *232*
Grimes, D. A., 92, 93, *103*
Grisso, J., 77, 95, 97, 98, *103*, *106*
Grob, A., 193, 196, 200, *203*
Grodin, B., 87, *99*
Grodin, J. M., 80, *102*
Grodstein, F., 92, 93, 94, *103*
Gruenberg, E., 120, *144*
Grünendahl, M., 61, *69*
Guarnaccia, C. A., 136, *144*
Guegan, J., 82, *108*
Gullette, M. M., 29, 36, *40*

Gureje, O., *144*
Guroff, J. J., 120, *140*, *145*
Guthrie, J. R., 87, 90, 91, *101*, *103*, *107*
Guyatt, G., *93*, *109*
Guze, S. B., 122, *143*
Guzinski, 83

H

Haas, S., *96*, *103*
Haber, C., 245, *257*
HABIS Steering and Data Monitoring Committees, *93*, *104*
Hagan, J., *69*
Hagen, N., 98, *101*
Hagestad, G. O., 274, *278*
Hagnell, O., 114, 130, 132, *140*
Hall, R., 92, *106*
Hamagami, F., 65, *70*
Hamalainen, O., 87, *99*
Hamil-Luker, J., 290, 292, *297*
Hammar, M., 97, *103*, *104*, *109*
Hammond, K., 294, *297*
Hammoud, M., 95, *104*
Hamovit, J. H., 120, *140*, *145*
Hanford, G. H., 209, *231*
Hannaford, P., 92, *101*
Hardy, M. A., 6, *21*
Hardy, R., 82, *103*
Hareven, T. K., 245, *257*
Harford, T. C., 122, *140*
Harlow, B. L., 81, 83, *101*, *103*
Harlow, S., 87, 88, 89, 91, 95, *100*, *107*
Harlow, S. C., 81, 82, 83, *102*
Harlow, S. D., 87, *106*
Harman, S. E., 78, *102*
Harris, C. W., 65, *69*
Harris, F., 92, *107*
Harris, R., 93, 94, *101*
Harris, T. O., 166, 170, *182*
Harris, V., 91, *107*
Hartmann, S. M., 26, *40*, 247–248, *258*
Hasin, D., 129, *140*, *141*
Haskell, W., 94, *104*
Haukka, J. K., *145*
Hausdorff, J., 158, *164*
Hauser, R. M., 219, 222, *231*

Hautaniemi, S., 83, *107*
Hautzinger, M., 129, *143*
Hay, E. L., 241, 246, 249, 250, 255, *257*
Hayghe, H. V., 252, *257*
Haynie, D. A., 137, *141*
Hays, J., 94, *103*, *106*
Heagerty, A., 92, *101*
Heale, M. J., 167, *182*
Healy, J. M., 27, 28, 30, 34, *42*
Healy, J. M., Jr., 244, *258*, 262, 265, 274, *281*
Heart and Estrogen/Progestin Replacement Study Research Group, 94, 95, *102*, *104*
Heath, A. C., 131, *141*, 169, *182*
Heckbert, S., 92, *105*
Heckhausen, J., 136, *146*, 191, 192, 200, *203*, *204*
Hedera, P., 131, *141*
Heidorn, J., 270, *279*
Heimberg, R. G., 120, 128, *141*
Heise, D. R., 65, *69*
Helson, R., 29, 35, 36, *40*, *42*, 220, *231*
Helzer, J. E., 120, 122, *141*, *144*
Hencke, R., 158, *164*
Henderson, A. S., 128, *141*, 221, *230*
Henderson, V. W., 90, 94, *103*, *106*
Henderson, W., 83, *109*
Hendrix, S. L., 94, *101*, *107*
Hennekens, C., 92, *108*
Henry, D., *93*, *109*
Henshaw, S., *109*
Herberg, W., 135, *141*
Hernandez-Avila, M., 83, *102*
Herrington, D., 91, 92, 95, *103*, *104*, *107*
Hersh, A. L., *96*, *103*
Hertzog, C., 214, *231*
Herzog, A. R., 66, *71*, 136, *141*
Hesselbrock, V., 122, 128, *144*
Hetherington, E., 263, *277*
Hicks, M. W., 265, *277*
Higa, H., 82, *104*
Higgins, J., 83, *100*
Higginson, L., 92, *109*
Hillis, S., 83, *104*, *105*
Hilton, M. E., *140*, *141*
Himes, C. L., 272, *278*
Hine, T., 240, *257*
Hiripi, E., 120, 128, *141*

Hirschfield, R. M., 111, 114, 115, 120, 122, 128, 130, *142, 144*
Ho, J. E., 92, *103*
Hodgson, L. G., 264, 274, *278*
Hodis, H. N., 92, 93, *103, 104*
Hofer, S. M., 61, 66, *67, 69,* 237, *256*
Hoff, E., 194, 198, *203*
Hoffman, C., 246, 249, *256*
Hoge, D. R., 135, *141*
Hoge, J. L., *141*
Hohner, H., 194, 198, *203*
Holford, T. R., *145*
Holmberg, L., *93, 104*
Holmes-Rovner, M., 86, *104, 106*
Holzer, C. I., 111, 115, *145*
Homans, G. F., 241, *257*
Hooker, K., 160, *163,* 195, *203*
Hopper, J. L., 77, 87, *101, 102*
Horwitz, R., 92, *109*
Hough, R. L., 114, 138, *141*
Howard, B. V., 91, 92, *107, 109*
Howe, G. R., *93, 104*
Hox, J., 66, *69*
Hsia, J., 92, *105, 107, 109*
Hubbell, F. A., *93, 94, 101*
Hughes, M., 113, 114, 115, 120, 128, 130, *142*
Hulbert, A., 239, 252, *258*
Hulbert, K. D., 36, *40*
Hulka, B. S., 87, *107*
Hulley, S., 92, 94, *104, 107*
Hultsch, D. F., 214, *231*
Hunninghake, D., 94, *104*
Hunter, K., 29, *41*
Hunter, M. S., 84, 87, *104*
Huntley, A. L., 97, *104*
Huntley, M. S., *104*
Hurwicz, M., 137, *140*
Huyck, M. H., 268, 272, *278, 280*
Hwang, J., *93, 103, 104*
Hy, L. X., 160, *163*
Hybels, C. F., 136, 137, *141*
Hynes, E., 83, *109*

I

Ingegneri, D. G., 249, *257*
Inglehart, R., 47, *69*

Inui, T. S., 98, *101*
Isaacowitz, D. M., 137, *139,* 244, 250, *256*
Ivarsson, T., 97, *104*
Iwasaki, H., 83, *108*

J

Jackson, D. J., 65, *68*
Jackson, E. F., 135, *144*
Jackson, R. D., 91, 93, 94, *100, 107*
Jacobsen, J. J., 168, *182*
Jacomb, P. A., 221, *230*
Jagawa-Singer, M., 86, 87, *99*
James, J. B., 29, *41,* 168, *182*
Jaques, E., 29, *41*
Jefferys, M., 80, 86, *105*
Jennings, J. M., 207, *231*
Jennings, K., 33, 35, *41*
Jennings, M. K., 28, 38, *41*
Jensen, M., 264, *280*
Jessor, R., 265, *278*
Jessor, S. L., 265, *278*
Jeste, D. V., 122, 136, *143, 144*
Jeune, B., 82, *99*
Jin, R., 114, 115, 120, *142*
Jobst, K. A., 226, *230*
Johannes, C. B., 81, *104*
Johansson, B., 246, *257*
Johansson, G., 137, *141*
Johnson, C., 243, *258,* 264, *279*
Johnson, C. L., 82, *102,* 251, *258*
Johnson, D. R., 268, 275, *281*
Johnson, D. V., 272, *278*
Johnson, K., 91, 92, 94, *105, 106, 107*
Johnson, M. A., 269, *279*
Johnson, M. J., 219, *232*
Johnson, M. P., 247–248, *258*
Johnson, S., 92, *108*
Johnston, L. D., 61, *70*
Jones, B. III, 94, *107*
Jones, K., 221, *230*
Jones, L. L., 272, *281*
Jones, L. Y., 6, *21*
Jones, P., 131, *145*
Jöreskog, K. G., 65, *69*
Jorm, A. F., 128, *141*
Jorn, A. F., 221, *230*

Joyce, P. R., *141*
Justice, J., 90, *107*

K

Kaaks, R., 82, *108*
Kaelber, C. T., 114, 120, 127, *144*
Kagawa-Singer, M., 84, 86, *108*
Kahn, R. L., 38, *39*, 219, *231*
Kalish, R., 29, *41*
Kalton, G., 57, 62, *68*
Kam, I., 96, *104*
Kancler, C., 95, *107*
Kang, H., 95, *104*
Kaplan, C. P., 96, *103*
Kaplan, G. A., 137, *144*
Kaplan, G. D., 187, *204*
Kaplan, N., 261, *279*
Karel, M. J., 120, *140*, 195, 197, *202*
Karim, R., 93, *104*
Karno, M., 114, 138, *141*
Karus, D., 272, *280*
Kasimatis, M., 166, *182*
Kasl-Godley, J. E., 120, *140*
Kasser, T., 274, *279*
Katz, R., 131, *143*
Katz, S., *145*
Katzman, R., 221, *231*
Kaufert, P. A., 76, 82, 87, *99, 104*
Kaus, C. R., 160, *163*
Kawakami, N., 82, *106*
Kawas, C., 128, *141*, 160, *163*
Kawas, S., 206, *230*
Kay, C., 92, *101*
Kazadjian, 83
Keenan, N., 95, 96, 97, 98, *106*
Kehn, M., 136, *139*
Keister, L. A., 133, *141*
Keith, S. J., 122, *141*
Kelche, R. P., 81, *107*
Kelleher, J., 92, *101*
Keller, D. M., 160, *163*
Keller, M. B., 111, 113, 114, 115, 130, *139, 142*
Kellogg, S., 5, *21*
Kelly, A., 96, *109*
Kelsey, J. L., 87, 91, *102, 108*
Kelsey, S., 77, *105*

Kemmann, E., 87, *108*
Kemp, B. J., 132, *141*
Kendell, R. E., 127, *141*
Kendler, K. S., 113, 114, 115, 120, 128, 130, 131, *141, 142, 169, 182*
Kennedy, G. E., 263, *279*
Kerlikowski, K., 96, *103*
Kernan, W., 92, *109*
Kertzer, D. I., 49, *69*
Keshavarz, H., 83, *104*
Kessing, L. V., 133, *141*
Kessler, R. C., 65, *69*, 111, 113, 114, 115, 120, 128, 130, 131, *139, 141, 142, 146, 166, 169, 182, 183, 198, 203*
Keyes, C. L. M., 113, *142*
Khan, M. A., 92, *101*
Khandekar, J., *101*
Khuri, S., 83, *109*
Kidd, K. K., *145*
Kieke, B., 83, *104, 105*
Killian, T., 275, *278*
Killiany, R., 214, *230*
Kim, S., 92, *106*
Kimmel, D., 267, *279*
King, V., 248, *258*
Kingson, E. R., 132, *139*
Kitchener, H., 92, *101*
Kittner, S. J., 221, *231*
Kivett, V. R., 194, *203*, 240, 241, 251, *256*, 263, *273, 279*
Kivnick, H., 273, *279*
Kjerulff, 83
Kleban, M. H., 137, *142*, 246, 249, *256*
Klein, D. N., 131, *142*
Klein, E. B., 34, *41*
Klein, K., 91, 92, *103*
Klein, R., 95, *102*
Klerman, G. L., 111, 113, 114, 115, 120, 122, 128, 130, 135, *142, 144*
Kluckhohn, C., 38, *41*
Knaeuper, B., 111, *146*
Knoll, J., 86, *106*
Knopp, R., 94, *104*
Koenig, K. E., 60, *70*
Koestner, R., 274, *279*
Kohn, M. L., 198, *203*, 219, *231*
Kolarz, C. M., 113, *143*, 172, *182*

Kono, S., 82, *104*
Koonin, L., 83, *105, 109*
Kooperberg, C., 91, *107*
Kop, P. P., 132, *142*
Koretz, D., 114, 115, *142*
Korten, A. E., 128, *141*, 221, *230*
Kotchen, J. M., 91, 94, *103, 107*
Kothny, W., 92, *99*
Kotlikoff, L. J., 205, *231*
Kovak, Y. S., 114, *142*
Kowalchuk, G. J., 92, *103*
Kozin, M., 26, *42*
Kraines, R. J., 84, 86, *106*
Kramer, A. F., 220, *231*
Kramer, M., 130, *144*
Krause, C. R., 195, *203*
Krause, J. S., 132, *141*
Kravitz, H. M., 81, 88, 89, 90, *100, 104, 105*
Kreider, R. M., 135, *142*
Krieder, R. M., 251, *258*
Kristof, M., 94, *102*
Kroll, J., 86, *104*
Kronenberg, F., 86, 96, 97, *104, 109*
Kruse, K. S., 6, *21*
Krysan, M., 47, *71*
Kubler, J. W., 96, *105*
Kuh, D., 82, *103*
Kulcar, Z., *140*
Kulik, J., 26, 27, *39*
Kuller, L. H., 77, 82, 83, 87, *100, 105*
Kumakura, N., *145*
Kumka, D., 219, *232*
Kunda, Z., 156, *163*
Kunik, M. E., 137, *143*
Kuypers, J. A., 245, *256*
Kwawukume, E., 83, *105*

L

Lachman, M. E., 29, *41*, 113, *142*, 168, *182*, 186, 187, 189, 190, 192, 193, *195*, 197, 200, *202, 203*, 207, *231*
LaCroix, A. Z., 91, 93, 94, 95, 96, 97, 98, *100, 103, 106, 107*
Laird, N. M., *143*
Lambert, J. D., 267, 268, *279*
Lambri, M., 127, *139*

Landauer, T. K., 291, *298*
Landsverk, J. A., 138, *141*
Lane, D., 94, *101, 106*
Lang, G., 266, *279*
Lang, K., 266, *279*
Langenberg, 83
Langer, R. D., *101*
Lanke, J., 114, 130, 132, *140*
LaPietra, M. T., 80, 81, 90, 91, *108*
Larsen, R. J., 166, *182*
Larson, J. R., 221, *231*
Lascano-Ponce, E., 83, *102*
Lasch, C., 32, *41*
Lasch, K., 115, 129, 130, *142*
Lassern, N., 92, *105*
Laub, J. H., 225, *232*
Laursen, B., 245, *258*
Lautenschlager, G., 59, *71*
Lavallee, L. F., 156, *163*
La Vecchia, C., 81, *99*
Lavori, P. W., 111, 113, 114, 115, 130, *142*
Lawhorn, S., 92, *106*
Lawlor, D., 82, *105*
Lawson, A., 247–248, *258*
Lawton, L., 264, *279*
Lawton, M. P., 137, *142*
Lawton, P., 136, *142*
Lazarus, R. S., 132, *142*, 166, 169, *182*
Leaf, P. J., 111, 115, *145*
Leaf, P. L., *145*
Leary M. R., 135, *138*
LeBoff, M., 93, *100*
Leckman, J. F., *145*
Lee, C., 77, *100*
Lee, C. C., 293, *297*
Lee, K. C., 114, *142*
Lee, Y., 272, *279*
Lee, Y. H., 249, *258*
Lefkowitz, E. S., 249, 250, *257*
Legault, C., 94, 97, *100, 107*
Leggett, K., 97, *100*
Lehert, P., 83, *99*
Leighton, A. H., 115, *143*
Lekes, N., 274, *279*
Lemieux, T., 167, *182*
Lepine, L., 83, *105*
Lesthaeghe, R., 47, *69*

Leveille, S., 95, 97, 98, 106
Levenson, M. R., 122, 130, 142
Levi, F., 81, 99
Levinson, D. J., 34, 41
Levinson, M. H., 34, 41
Levy, B. R., 158, 161, 163, 164
Levy, F., 5, 21, 133, 143
Lewinsohn, P. M., 114, 128, 129, 130, 131, 142, 143
Lewis, C. E., 78, 93, 100, 105
Lewis, S., 131, 145
Lewis, S. K., 198, 203
Lezak, M. D., 214, 232
Li, D., 95, 102
Lieberburg, I., 94, 109
Lieberman, M. A., 201, 203
Lifford, K., 103
Light, P. C., 24–25, 41, 134, 135, 143, 223, 232
Lin, E., 143
Lin, F., 94, 102
Lin, G., 249, 258
Lindgren, R., 97, 103
Lindquist, E. F., 65, 69
Lindquist, O., 82, 99
Link, B., 129, 141
Linville, P. W., 156, 164
Little, R. J., 87, 106
Little, T. D., 193, 196, 200, 203
Liu, C.-H., 93, 103, 104
Liu, C.-R., 93, 103, 104
Llewellyn-Jones, D., 84, 99
Lloyd-Jones, H., 92, 101
Lo, A., 91, 108
Lobo, R. A., 92, 93, 103, 104
Locher, J. L., 191, 200, 204
Lock, M., 82, 87, 99
Lockenhoff, C. E., 191, 203
Logan, J. R., 271, 272, 279
Long, J. D., 264, 280
Long, R., 264, 277
Longcope, C., 81, 108
Lonnqvist, J. K., 145
Loomis, B., 84, 106
Lopez, S. R., 138, 143
Lopez-Carillo, L., 83, 102
Loprinzi, C. L., 96, 97, 105, 106
Lord, F. M., 65, 69
Lowenthal, M. F., 168, 182, 266, 269, 279

Lowery, M., 94, 104
Lu, Y., 47, 70
Luborsky, J. L., 87, 90, 105, 106
Lucas, R. E., 113, 140
Lucerno, M. A., 97, 105
Luescher, K., 241, 246, 255, 258
Lunt, M., 90, 107
Lyketsos, C. G., 221, 232

M

Macdonald, C., 167, 182
Macer, J. L., 96, 97, 98, 102
Mack, W. J., 92, 93, 103, 104
Mackinnon, A. J., 221, 230
MacMahon, B., 105
MacNeil, R. D., 137, 138, 143
Macunovich, D. J., 4, 6, 21, 133, 140, 167, 182
Madans, J. H., 83, 100
Madden, T., 84, 86, 90, 105, 108
Magai, C., 136, 139
Magursky, V., 80, 105
Mahrer, P. R., 92, 93, 103
Maides, S. A., 187, 204
Main, M., 261, 279
Maitland, S. B., 207, 208, 231
Malcolm, D. E., 127, 141
Mallars, M. C., 166, 182
Malley, J. E., 25, 42
Mannheim, K., 27, 41, 49, 50, 69
Manson, J. E., 92, 93, 94, 103, 105, 106, 108
Marchbanks, P., 83, 105
Marchionini, G., 292, 297
Marcia, J. E., 150, 164
Mariella, A., 80, 106
Marks, N. F., 267, 268, 271, 279
Markus, H. R., 136, 141
Mars, J., 273, 277
Marsh, J. V. R., 83, 100
Martin, L. G., 66, 68
Martin, M., 61, 69, 207, 214, 232
Martin, P., 61, 69
Martin, R. L., 122, 143
Martin, S. K., 272, 281
Martinez, M., 127, 140
Martinez, R., 114, 139
Martocchio, J. J., 289, 297

Mason, K. O., 47, 58n, 70
Mason, W. M., 55, 57, 58, 58n, 70
Matthews, K. A., 77, 82, 83, 84, 87, 91, 100, 105, 108
Matthews, S. H., 270, 271, 279
Maurin, E., 77, 103
May, E. T., 26, 31, 41
Mayhorn, C. B., 294, 295, 298
Mayr, U., 113, 139
McAdam, D., 33, 35, 41, 56, 70
McAdams, D. P., 29, 41
McAdams, L. A., 136, 144
McArdle, J. J., 65, 66, 70
McCallister, B., 92, 106
McCammon, R. J., 46, 50, 52, 66, 67, 68, 222, 230, 237, 256
McCarthy, G., 267, 279
McClelland, D. C., 33, 35, 40
McCloskey, W. W., 97, 105
McConnaughey, R., 82, 109
McCrae, R. R., 172, 182, 207, 230, 231, 232
McCrea, F., 105
McCreadie, R. G., 127, 139
McDaniel, A. K., 275, 278
McDaniel, M. A., 289, 297
McDermott, C., 33, 42
McEvoy, G. M., 289, 297
McEvoy, L. T., 122, 141
McGarry, K., 248, 258
McGee, J. P., 284, 285, 290, 298
McGlashan, T., 145
McGonagle, K. A., 113, 114, 115, 120, 128, 130, 139, 142, 247
McGowan, J., 93, 100
McGuffin, P., 131, 143
McIntosh, J. L., 133, 143
McKee, B., 34, 41
McKeown, R., 96, 107
McKinlay, J. B., 81, 82, 89, 105
McKinlay, S. M., 76, 77, 80, 81, 82, 84, 85, 86, 87, 89, 90, 91, 99, 100, 104, 105, 108
McMahon, D., 83, 96, 104
McMullin, J. A., 241, 246, 252, 255, 256
McNamee, R., 92, 101
McPherson, C. K., 80, 100
McTiernan, A., 101
Mead, S. E., 294, 298
Medinger, F., 198, 201, 203, 204

Mehra, A. O., 92, 103
Meilahn, E. N., 77, 82, 83, 87, 100, 105
Meissner, H. I., 95, 100
Melin, A., 97, 109
Menaghan, E. G., 201, 203
Menard, J. F., 127, 140
Mendes de Leon, Carlos, 229, 234
Mercier, J. M., 271, 279
Meredith, 65
Merikangas, K. R., 114, 115, 120, 142
Merline, A., 268, 277
Merrill, D. M., 270, 279
Mesko, M., 80, 105
Metlife Mature Market Institute, 205, 232
Meyer, B., 294, 298
Meyer, P. M., 84, 86, 88, 90, 100, 104, 105, 108
Miller, A., 84, 109
Miller, B. C., 264, 279
Mills, T. L., 274, 279
Miner-Rubino, K., 29, 35, 36, 37, 38, 41, 42
Minkler, M., 273, 278
Mintz, S., 5, 21
Mirowsky, J., 194, 198, 203, 204
Mishra, G., 77, 100
Mitchell, A., 90, 107
Mitchell, E. S., 77, 80, 90, 105, 106, 109
Mitchell, V., 267, 280
Miyazaki, Y., 66, 70
Moane, G., 220, 231
Modell, J., 48, 70
Moen, P., 189, 203, 206, 232, 243, 254, 258, 284, 293, 297, 298
Moldin, S. O., 128, 144
Moles, E. L., 249, 258
Molinari, V., 137, 143
Möller, K., 261, 267, 280
Monroe, S. M., 131, 143
Monson, R. R., 143
Monsour, M., 269, 276, 280
Montero, P., 82, 108
Montgomery, A., 84, 109
Moore, K. A., 264, 279
Morabia, A., 82, 106
Morgan, S. P., 51, 52, 70
Morgan, T. M., 93, 101
Morgan, T. N., 97, 100
Morgan, W. R., 219, 232

Morganstein, D., 91, *102, 108*
Morrell, R. W., 292, 294, 295, *298*
Morris, A. S., 265, 274, *280*
Morrow, B., 83, *105*
Morse, C., 77, 87, *102*
Mortensen, P. B., 127, 133, *141, 143*
Mortimer, J. A., 127, *143*
Mortimer, J. T., 219, *232*
Mosca, L., 92, *103*
Mosher, W., 82, *109*
Moss, J. J., 264, *280*
Moss, M. S., 249, *258*
Moss, S. Z., 249, *258*
Mouton, C., 84, 86, *108*
Moye, 83
Mroczek, D. K., 113, 137, *143,* 172, *182*
Mulatu, M. S., 224, *233*
Mullan, J. T., 186, 194, 195, 201, *203, 204*
Mullaney, J., *144*
Muller, T. E., 134, *143*
Munk-Jorgensen, P., 127, *143*
Murphy, J. M., 115, *143*
Murphy, P. A., 96, *109*
Murray, D. M., 82, *99*
Murray, H. A., 38, *41*
Murray, R. M., 127, *139*
Myers, J. K., 130, *144, 145*

N

Nagata, C., 82, *106*
Nair, S., 292, *297*
Nam, C. B., 225, 226, *232*
Narrow, W. E., 114, 120, 127, *144*
National Alliance for Caregiving and American Association for Retired Persons, 296, *298*
National Center for Complementary and Alternative Medicine (NCAAM), 96, *106*
National Center for Health Statistics, 4, *21*
National Committee for Quality Assurance, 97, *106*
National Research Council, 293, *298*
Naughton, M. J., 97, *100*
Neale, M. C., 131, *141,* 169, *182*
Nedstrand, E., 97, *109*

Neer, R., 91, *102, 108*
Neff, R. K., 115, *143*
Neighbors, H. W., 198, *203*
Neisser, U., 26, 33, *41*
Nelson, C. B., 113, 114, 115, 120, 128, 130, *142*
Nesselroade, J. R., 113, *139*
Neugarten, B. L., 29, *41,* 84, 86, *106*
Neuman, R. J., 122, 128, *144*
Neuner, J., 93, *100*
Neupert, S. D., 166, *182*
Newcomb, P., 94, *103*
Newcomb, T. M., 47, 60, 67, *70*
Newman, S. C., *139*
Newton, K., 95, 96, 97, 98, *106*
Nicholls, A., 90, *107*
Nickerson, R. S., 291, *298*
Nilsson, L. G., 207, *230*
Nisker, W., 185, 189, *203*
Noonan, A. E., 272, *280*
North American Menopause Society, 94, *106*
Nurmi, J., 195, *203*
Nurnberger, J. I., 120, *140*
Nussbaum, J., 252, *257*

O

Oates, G., 224, *233*
O'Brien, R. M., 58n, *70*
Ockene, J. K., 91, 94, *103, 107*
O'Connell, D., *109*
O'Connell, E., 98, *101*
O'Connell, H., 91, *107*
Oddens, B. J., 83, *99*
Oejesjoe, L., 114, 130, 132, *140*
Offord, D. R., *143*
Ofstedal, M. B., 66, *71*
Ogden, C. L., 82, *102*
O'Keefe, J. J., 92, *106*
O'Leary Cobb, J., 96, *104*
Olivier, D. C., 115, *143*
Olofsson, A. S., 84, *106*
O'Malley, P. M., 61, *70*
O'Neill, W., 25, 32, *41*
Orn, H., *139*
Ortega y Gasset, J., 49, *70*
Orvaschel, H., 120, *144*
Ory, M., 84, 86, *108*

Os, J. V., 132, *143*
Osmond, M. W., 265, *277*
Osteoporosis Research Advisory Group, 93, *109*
Ostrove, J., 29, 30, 33, 35, 36, 38, *39, 40, 41, 42, 43*
Ouyang, P., 92, *109*
Ownby, R., 292, *297*

P

Padmanabhan, V., 81, *107*
Padonu, G., 86, *104, 106*
Pampel, F. C., 48n, *70*
Pandey, D., 90, *105*
Pansini, F., 97, *99*
Park, D. C., 59, *71*, 294, 295, *298*
Parker, R. G., 269, *280*
Parrott, E., 80, *108*
Parrott, R., 269, *280*
Parsons, T., 241, *258*
Passerini, L., 23, *41*
Pasupathi, M., 113, *139*
Patterson, R. E., 94, *103*
Patterson, T. L., 122, 136, *143, 144*
Paul, E. L., 270, *280*
Pauls, D. L., *145*
Peacock, E. J., 195, *203*
Pearlin, L. I., 187, 194, 195, 198, 201, *203, 204*
Pemberton, M., 122, *140*
Pennak, S., 218, *233*
Penne, M., 122, *140*
Pennebaker, J. W., 33, *41*
Perz, J., 84, *99*
Petersen, R. C., 214, *232*
Peterson, A. C., 263, 265, *280*
Peterson, D., 288, *298*
Peterson, H., 83, *109*
Peterson, J., 93, *109*, 132, 136, *145*
Petit, M., 127, *140*
Petrovitch, H., *101*
Pettinger, M., 93, *100*
Pham, K. T. C., 95, 97, 98, *106*
Pieper, C. F., 136, 137, *141*
Pillemar, K., 6, *21*
Pillemer, D. B., 26, *41*
Pillemer, K., 241, 242, 246, 251, 255, *258*
Plantinga, P., 82, 83, 87, *100*
Pohl, J. M., 272, *280*

Pokras, R., 83, *109*
Poole, W. K., 58n, *70*
Porter, V., 78, *105*
Posner, J. G., 80, 86, *105*
Powell, L., 88, 90, 100, 104, *105*
Powers, D. V., 272, *278*
Prause, J., 132, *140*
Prentice, R. L., 91, *107*
Pressman, A., 96, 97, 98, *102*
Pretter, S., 272, *280*
Proschan, M., 92, *109*
Prusoff, B. A., *145*
Pryor, D. W., 267, *281*
Pulliainen, H., 195, *203*
Purcell, P. I., 284, *298*

Q

Qualls, S., 273, *280*
Quella, S. K., 97, *106*
Quinn, J. F., 284, *298*

R

Rabbani, R., 92, *103*
Racine, Y. A., *143*
Rae, D. S., 114, 115, 120, 122, 127, 129, 130, *139, 141, 144,* 221, *231*
Rajagopal, D., 137, *142*
Ramirez, P. M., 136, *139*
Randolph, J. R. Jr., 87, *106*
Ranson, S., 86, *106*
Rapp, S., 94, *106, 107*
Rasor, N. O., 84, 86, *108*
Rau, S., 94, *109*
Raudenbush, S. W., 66, 68, *70*
Raveis, V. H., 272, *280*
Rawlins, W. K., *280*
Reame, N. E., 81, *107*
Rcbar, R., 80, *108*
Rebelsky, F. G., 272, *280*
Reboussin, D. M., 92, 95, *103, 107*
Redvall, L., 82, *99*
Reece, S., 95, *107*
Reeve, J., 90, *107*
Refsum, H., 226, *230*

Regier, D. A., 114, 115, 120, 122, 127, 128, 129, 130, 138, *139*, *141*, *144*, 221, *231*
Reich, J. W., 136, *144*
Reich, T., 111, 113, 114, 115, 120, 130, *142*, *144*
Reid, J., 29, *43*
Reker, G. T., 195, *203*
Renaud, F., 82, *108*
Resnick, N. M., *103*
Reynolds, C. A., 137, *139*
Rheaume, C., 96, *107*
Rhee, H., 114, *142*
Rhodes, S. R., 289, *298*
Rice, J. P., 111, 113, 114, 115, 120, 122, 128, 130, *142*, *144*
Richards, C., 92, 94, *102*, *107*
Richter, D., 96, *107*
Riedmann, A., 264, *281*
Riesman, D., 32, *41*
Riggs, A., 34, *42*, 135, *144*, 190, *203*
Riggs, B., 92, *104*
Rijsdijk, F., 131, *143*
Riley, M. W., 53, 55, 59, 61, *71*, 219, *232*
Rimer, B. K., 95, *100*
Risch, N., 129, *140*
Ritenbaugh, C., 93, 94, *101*
Roark, J. L., 247–248, *258*
Robbins, J., 93, *100*
Robbins, M. A., 294, *297*
Roberto, K. A., 263, 273, 274, *280*
Roberts, R. E., 137, *144*
Robins, L. N., 120, 128, *144*
Robinson, R. V., 135, *144*
Robinson, V., 93, *109*
Rochberg, N., 122, 128, *144*
Rockwell, R. C., 168, *182*
Rodabough, R. J., 93, 94, *101*
Rodbard, D., 80, *102*
Rodgers, B., 221, *230*
Rodgers, W. L., 66, *71*
Rodin, J., 187, *204*
Rodstrom, K., 82, *107*
Rogers, W. A., 287, *297*
Rogers, W. J., 92, *103*, *109*
Rogerson, P. A., 249, *258*
Rogler, L. H., 262, *280*
Rogosa, D., 65, *71*
Rohan, T. E., 93, *104*

Rohde, P., 114, 128, 129, 130, 131, *142*, *143*
Rollins, B. C., 168, *182*
Roof, W. C., 47, *71*
Rorsman, B., 114, 130, 132, *140*
Roscow, I., 50, *71*
Rosenberg, C. A., 93, 94, *101*
Rosenberg, H. J., 206, *232*
Rosenberg, S., 38, *40*
Rosenberg, S. D., 206, *232*
Rosner, B., 92, *108*
Ross, C. E., 189, 193, 194, 195, 198, *203*, *204*
Ross, G. T., 80, *102*
Rossi, A. S., 29, *42*, 52, *71*, 240, 241, 251, 253, 254, 255, *258*, 271, *280*
Rossi, P. H., 52, *71*, 240, 241, 251, 253, 254, 255, *258*, 271, *280*
Rossouw, J. E., 91, 92, 95, *100*, *105*, *107*
Rostosky, S. S., 76, 80, *107*
Roth, D., 292, *297*
Rothert, M., 86, *104*, *106*
Rotter, J. B., 187, *204*
Rovner, D. R., 86, *104*, *106*
Rowe, J. W., 221, *230*
Rubin, D., 26, *42*
Rubio-Stipec, M., 114, *139*
Rush, A. J., 114, 115, *142*
Russell, A., 131, *145*
Russell, C., 6, *21*, 133, 135, 137, 138, *144*, 270–271, *280*
Russell, L., 90, *107*
Russell, L. B., 6, *21*
Rutter, C., 95, 97, 98, *106*
Ryan, M., 77, 87, *102*
Ryder, N. B., 47, 52, 55, *71*
Ryff, C. D., 29, *42*, 113, *142*, 249, *258*

S

Saccone, N. L., 122, 128, *144*
Sales, E., 168, *183*
Salmela-Aro, K., 195, *203*
Salthouse, T. A., 129, *144*, 288, *298*
Sampselle, C., 91, 95, *107*
Sampson, R. J., 225, *232*
Samuels, S., 81, 82, 83, *102*
Sandler, D. P., 82, *109*
Sang, B, 267, *279*

Sanmarco, M. E., 92, *103*
Santana, F., 114, *141*
Santoro, N., 80, *108*
Sarrel, P., 92, *109*
Sartorius, N., *144*
Sastry, J., 189, 194, 198, *204*
Satterfield, S., 94, *104*
Savage, C. R., 221, *230*
Savin-Williams, R. C., 254, *258*
Sawaya, G., 94, *109*
Sayer, A. G., 65, 66, *71*
Schaeffer, C. M., 133, *140*
Schaie, K. W., 55, 64, *71*, 205, 206, 207, 208, 210, 211, 213, 214, 215, 218, 219, 224, 227, *231, 232, 233, 234*
Schatzberg, A. F., 114, 120, 127, *144*
Scheider, J. A., 229, *234*
Schiff, I., 97, 98, *108*
Schmitt, N., 86, *106*
Schmitt, P., 92, *99*
Schmutte, P. S., 249, *258*
Schocken, M., 81, 88, *100*
Schoeni, R. F., 245, 248, *258*
Schofiel, P. M., 92, *101*
Schofield, M., 77, *100*
Schooler, C., 187, 190, 191–192, 198, *203, 204*, 219, 224, *231, 233*
Schoonover, C. B., 246, 249, *256*
Schor, J., 133–134, *144*
Schrott, H., 94, *104*
Schulz, R., 136, *146*, 191, 200, *204*
Schuman, H., 28, *42*, 47, *71*
Schumann, C. E., 294, *297*
Schuster, D. T., 36, *40*
Schwartz, C. E., 154, *164*
Schwingl, P. J., 87, *107*
Sciolla, A., 136, *144*
Scott, J., 28, *42*, 47, *68, 71*
Seeley, J. R., 114, 128, 130, 131, *142, 143*
Seeman, T., 221, *230*
Seff, M. A., 263, 265, 274, *278*
Seidl, M., 96, *107*
Seif, M., 92, *101*
Seligman, M. E. P., 135, *144*
Seltzer, M. M., 29, *42*
Selzer, R. H., 92, 93, *103*
Settersten, R. A., 262, *280*

Settles, I. H., 32, *42*
Sevanian, A., 92, 93, *103, 104*
Shajahan, P. M., 127, *139*
Sham, P., 131, 132, *143, 145*
Shanas, E., 249, *258*
Shapiro, A., 271, *277*
Shapiro, D. H., 154, *164*
Sharit, J., 287, 292, *297*
Sharp, P. C., 92, 95, *103, 107*
Shea, B., 93, *109*
Shea, D., 205, *231*
Shelley, M. C., 271, *279*
Shema, S. J., 137, *144*
Shepherd, P., 59, *68*
Sherburn, M., 91, *107*
Sherkat, D. E., 33, 35, *42*
Sherman, A., 95, *107*
Sherman, S., 80, 91, *108*
Shields, J., 131, *140*
Shil, A. B., 92, *103*
Shimizu, H., 82, *106*
Shook, T. L., 92, *103*
Shortle, B., 96, *109*
Shoupe, D., 92, 93, *103*
Shroute, P. E., 114, *139*
Shulman, K., 272, *278*
Shulman, S., 274, *280*
Shumaker, S. A., 92, 94, 95, *103, 106, 107*
Sievert, L., 83, *107*
Signorello, L., 83, *103*
Silverstein, M., 241, 255, *258*, 264, 272, *279, 280*
Silverstone, B., 137, *144*
Simon, G. E., *144*
Simon, J., 92, *107*
Simons, A. D., 131, *143*
Sit, R. A., 294, *298*
Skaff, M. M., 186, 194, 195, 201, 202, *203, 204*
Skinner, E. A., 186, 187, 191, 193, 198, 200, 201, *204*
Skultety, K. M., 154, 155, 157, *164*
Skurnick, J., 81, 82, 83, 95, *102, 107*
Slack, M., 92, *101*
Sliwinski, M. J., 61, *69*
Sloan, J. A., 96, *105*
Small, B. J., 214, *231*
Smetana, J. G., 245, *258*
Smith, A. D., 59, *71*, 207, 226, *230, 233*

Smith, A.M. A., 77, 87, *102*
Smith, G., 82, *105*
Smith, H. L., 113, *140*
Sneed, J. R., 154, 155, 156, *164*
Snitow, A., 36, *40*
Snow-Turek, A. L., 137, *143*
Snyder, T. D., 168, *183*
Snyder, T. E., 92, 95, *102, 103*
Sobol, A. M., 115, *143*
Sokolik, L, 80, *105*
Solano, N. H., 136, *144*
Somerfield, M. R., 172, *182*
Sommer, B., 84, 86, 88, *100, 108*
Sotelo, M., 92, *108*
Soules, M. R., 80, *108*
Sowers, M., 80, 81, 87, 90, 91, *106, 107, 108*
Spaulding, V. A., 294, *298*
Speizer, E., 92, *108*
Spetz, A. C., 97, *104*
Spiro, A., 113, 122, 130, 137, *142, 143*
Spitze, G. D., 271, 272, *279*
St. Aubin, E., 29, *41*
Stafford, R. S., 96, *103*
Stage, S., 247–248, *258*
Stahl, S. M., 136, *145*
Stampfer, M., 92, 94, *103, 108*
Standing, T. S., 86, *108*
Stanton, A. K., 129, *143*
Stattin, H., 261, 267, *280*
Staudinger, U. M., 30, *42,* 188, 192, *204,* 206, 207, *233*
Steeh, C., 47, *71*
Steele, C. M., 161, *164*
Steer, R. A., 132, *139*
Stefanick, M. L., 91, 93, 94, 96, *100, 101, 103, 106, 107*
Steffes, M., 92, *109*
Stein, E., 92, *105*
Stein, M. B., 120, 128, *141*
Stein, S., *145*
Steinberg, L., 240, *257,* 265, 274, *280*
Stellato, R., 81, 86, 87, *99, 108*
Stephens, M. A. P., 195, 198, *202, 204,* 272, *280*
Sternfeld, B., 87, 91, *102, 108*
Sterns, H. L., 267, *280*
Stewart, A. J., 24, 25, 27, 28, 29, 30, 32, 33, 34, 35, 36, 37, 38, 39, *39,* 40, 41, 42, 43,

220, *233,* 244, 252, *257, 258,* 262, 265, 272, 274, *281*
Stewart, D. E., 95, 96, *99, 107*
Stinnett, N., *281*
Stoes, J., 263, 274, *280*
Stoker, L., 28, *41*
Stoll, A. L., *145*
Stolley, 83
Stone, A. A., 166, *183*
Stork, S., 92, *99*
Strauss, L., 83, *109*
Strawbridge, W. J., 137, *144*
Strickland, O., 92, *105*
Stuckey, T. D., 92, *103*
Sturt, E., *145*
Suchindran, C. M., 82, *99*
Suh, E. M., 113, *140*
Suissa, S., 92, *109*
Suitor, J. J., 6, *21,* 242, 248, 251, 253, *258*
Sunagawa, H., 82, *104*
Sunagawa, Y., 82, *104*
Sundel, M., 29, *41*
Supple, K. R., 271, *277*
Surra, C. A., 265, 274, *281*
Sutton, L., 226, *230*
Sutton-Tyrrell, K., 88, 90, *100, 104*
Suvisaari, J. M., *145*
Swartz, M. S., 130, *139*
Swartzman, L. C., 87, *108*
Swede, H., 294, *297*
Sweet, J. A., 253, *256*
Swinson, R. P., *145*
Syme, S. L., 38, *39*
Szinovacz, M. E., 273, *281*

T

Talarczyk, G., 86, *104, 106*
Tamada, T., 83, *108*
Tamborini, R., 135, *145*
Tanskanen, A. J., *145*
Tardif, J., 92, *109*
Tarter, R. E., 132, *145*
Taylor, K., 95, 97, 98, *107, 108*
Taylor, S. E., 157, *164*
Taylor, V. M., 93, 94, *101*
Teitelbaum, M. S., 51, *71*

Tennstedt, S. L., 272, *280*
te Velde, E., 82, *108*
Thal, L., 94, *107*
Theroux, R., 95, 97, 98, *107, 108*
Thibaut, F., 127, *140*
Thomas, D. L., 172, *183*
Thomas, F., 82, *108*
Thompson, B., 80, *105*
Thompson, E. H. Jr., 36, *42*
Thompson, L., 253, *259*, 264, *281*
Thompson, L. W., 132, 136, *145*
Thompson, P., 92, *109*
Thompson, W. D., *145*
Thomson, C. A., *101*
Thorne, S., 228, *230*
Thornton, A., 60, *68*, 225, *230*
Thurnher, M., 266, 269, *279*
Thurstone, L. L., 214, *233*
Thurstone, T. G., 214, *233*
Tice, D. M., 135, *138*
Timbers, D. M., 114, 138, *141*
Tisek, *65*
Tohen, M., *145*
Tokuno, K. A., 265, *281*
Toone, B., 131, *145*
Toossi, M., 283, *297*
Torges, C., 37, 38, *42*
Torres, M., 92, *103*
Tosteson, A. N., 96, 97, 98, *102*
Townsend, A. L., 195, 198, *202, 204*
Travis, C. B., 76, 80, *107*
Treloar, A. E., 80, *108*
Trevisan, M., 92, *105*
Troll, L. E., 245, 253, *258*
Trzcinski, E., 247, *259*
Tsourounis, C., 96, *104*
Tugwell, P., 93, *109*
Turner, B. S., 34, *42*, 135, *144*, 190, *203*
Turner, R. S., 131, *141*
Twenge, J. M., 30, 31, 36, 39, *42*, 114, 120, 134, 135, *145*

U

U. S. Bureau of the Census, 12, 13, *21*, 205, 222, 223, *233*, 248, 252, *259*, 267, 271, 273, *281*

U. S. Department of Commerce, 294, *298*
U. S. Department of Education, 227, *233*
U. S. Department of Health and Human Services, 114, 115, 120, 122, 127, *145*
U. S. Department of Justice, 135, *145*
U. S. Department of Labor, 246, *259*
U. S. General Accounting Office, 283, 290, *298*
UCLA Internet Report, 294, *298*
Ueland, P. M., 226, *230*
Uhlenberg, P., 290, 292, *297*
Umberson, D., 255, *259*, 270, *281*
Urban, N., 78, *105*
Ustun, B., *144*
Utian, W., 80, 97, 98, *108*

V

Valanis, B. G., 94, *103*
Valcarcel, C., 273, *278*
Vandewater, E. A., 29, 30, 37, *42*
Van Eerdewegh, P., 115, 120, *144*
VanLaningham, J., 268, 275, *281*
van Noord, P., 82, *108*
Van Os, J., 127, 131, *139, 145*
Varea, C., 82, *108*
Varghese, R., 198, 201, 203, *204*
Varner, E., 95, *102*
Vass, K., 82, 87, *99*
Vemer, H. M., 83, *99*
Ventura, S., 82, *109*
Verter, J., 92, *109*
Vessey, M. P., 80, *100*
Vial, V., 135, *145*
Vinocour, S. M., 226, *233*
Viscoli, C., 92, *109*
Visser, A., 83, *99*
Vitolins, M. Z., 97, *100*
Vittinghoff, E., 92, 94, 95, *102, 104*
Vogelbach, K. H., 92, *103*
Vonkorff, M., *144*
von Schacky, C., 92, *99*

W

Wactawski-Wende, J., 93, 94, *100, 101*
Wade, C., 96, *109*
Wadsworth, M. E. J., 60, *71*

Wakshlag, J., 135, *145*
Waldman, D. A., 289, *297*
Walker, A. J., 253, *259*, 264, 272, *281*
Walker, N., 294, *298*
Walkup, M., 95, *107*
Wall, B., 271, *279*
Wallace, R., 94, *107*
Wallace, R. B., 245, *258*
Wallston, B. S., 187, *204*
Wallston, K. A., 187, *204*
Walters, E. E., 114, 115, 120, *142*
Walters, J., 263, *281*
Walters, L. H., 263, *281*
Walton, L., 90, *107*
Wang, P. S., 114, 115, *142*
Wanner, B., 193, 196, 200, *203*
Ward, M. P., 6, *21*
Wardley-Smith, B., 90, *107*
Warren, L. G., 84, *101*
Warren, N., 96, *109*
Warwick, D. P., 60, *70*
Washburn, S. A., 97, *100*
Wassertheil-Smoller, S., 94, *107*
Waterman, A. S., 29, *43*
Waters, D., 92, *103*, *109*
Watson, J. A., 194, *203*
Watts, N. B., 93, *100*
Weaver, F., 83, *109*
Weaver, S. L., 113, *142*, 187, 189, 195, 200, *203*
Wegman, D. H., 284, 285, 290, *298*
Wei, J. Y., 158, *164*
Weinberg, C. R., 82, *109*
Weinberg, M. S., 267, *281*
Weiss, G., 91, *108*
Weissman, M. M., 111, 114, 115, 120, 128, 129, 130, 135, *142*, *144*, *145*
Welch, F., 24, *43*
Wells, G., 93, *109*
Welsh, W. M., 272, *281*
Westoff, C. F., 5, *21*
Wetherell, J. L., 136, *144*
Wethington, E., 166, 169, *182*, *183*, 189, *203*, 206, *232*, 243, *258*
Whalley, L. J., 127, *140*
Wheaton, B., 169, *183*
Whelan, E. A., 82, *109*
WHI Investigators, *101*

Whitbourne, S. K., 29, *43*, 136, *144*, *145*, 151, 152, 153, 154, 155, 157, 159, 160, 164, 201, *204*, 206, *233*, 288, *298*
White, E., 93, 94, *101*
White, H., 49, *71*
White, K., 264, *281*
Whyte, W. H., 32, *43*
Wickramaratne, P. J., 120, 129, 130, *142*, *145*
Wijma, K., 97, *109*
Wilbur, J., 84, *109*
Wilcox, L., 83, *105*, *109*
Wiley, D. E., 65, *71*
Wiley, J. A., 65, *71*
Wilkins, S., 131, *145*
Willett, J. B., 65, 66, *71*
Willett, W., 92, *108*
Williams, C. J., 267, *281*
Williams, W., 137, *143*
Willis, S. L., 29, *43*, 206, 208, 213, 214, 215, 218, 220, *231*, *232*, *233*, *234*
Wilson, J., 83, *105*
Wilson, J. A., 208, 209, *234*
Wilson, J. D., 80, *109*
Wilson, M., 94, *109*
Wilson, R. S., 90, *105*, 229, *234*
Wing, R. R., 77, 82, 83, 87, *100*, *105*
Winsborough, H. H., 58n, *70*
Winter, D. G., 29, 35, 36, *41*
Winter, J. M., 51, *71*
Winter, N. J. G., 32, *42*
Wise, P., 94, *109*
Withers, G. S., 221, *231*
Wittchen, H. U., 111, 113, 114, 115, 120, 128, 130, *142*, *146*
Wohl, R., 23, 33, *43*
Wolman, R., 90, *107*
Women's Estrogen-Progestin Lipid-Lowering Hormone Atherosclerosis Regression Trial Research Group, 92, *103*
Women's Health Initiative Investigators, 91, 92, 93, 94, *100*, *101*, *103*, *105*, *107*
Women's Health Initiative Memory Study Investigators, 94, *106*
Wong, M., *143*
Wong, N., 92, *105*
Wong, P. T. P., 195, *203*

Wood, V., 84, *106*
Woods, N. F., 77, 80, 90, 96, *102, 105, 106, 108, 109*
Woodward, S., 97, *102*
Worcester, J., 83, *105*
World Almanac and Book of Facts, 271, *281*
World Health Organization, 80, 81, 82, 86, *109*
Wright, D. B., 34, *40*
Wrosch, C., 136, *146*

X

Xia, Z., 83, *109*
Xu, H., 80, 81, *101*

Y

Yaffe, K., 94, *102, 109*
Yesavage, J. A., 128, *146*
Younes, N., 92, *109*
Young, J. L., 84, *101*
Young-DeMarco, L., 60, *68*

Yu, M. Y., 81, *107*

Z

Zandri, E., 294, *298*
Zanotti, L., 97, *99*
Zarit, S. H., 137, *141*, 240, 242, 245, 246, *257, 259*
Zautra, A. J., 136, *144*
Zawacki, C. M., 81, *107*
Zeiss, A. M., 137, *140*
Zhao, S., 113, 114, 115, 120, 128, 130, *142*
Zimowski, M., 65, *71*
Zimprich, D., 207, 214, *232*
Zonderman, A., 128, *141*
Zucchero, C., 272, *278*
Zucker, A. N., 29, 33, 35, *39, 43*
Zuckerman, A., 169, *182*
Zuschlag, M. K., 29, *43*
Zwahr, M., 59, *71*
Zytaruk, N., 93, *109*

Subject Index

Note: Page numbers in *italic* refer to figures; those in **boldface** refer to tables.

A

Accidents, occupational, 289
ADA, 285
Adolescence
  historical trajectory of, 239–240
  psychology of, 32–34
  relationships in, 263–265, 267
Adult Identity Interview, 154
Age Discrimination in Employment Act, 285
Age effects
  in data analysis, 62–66, **63**
  described, 53–55, *54*
  in identity processes, 154–155
  in mental health research, 128–130, 136–138
  in research design issues, 55–62, **56**
Agent of control, 186
Age structure, of Boomers, 6, *7*

Aging parents
  control beliefs and, 194
  intergenerational ties and, 245–247
  as midlife issue, 29, *36*
  relationship changes and, 272
  sibling relationships and, 270
Aging self-stereotypes, 158–159
AHEAD study, 248
Alcohol abuse, 122, **123–124**
Alienation, 134–135
Alzheimer's disease, 127–128, 160, 206
Ambivalence model, of intergenerational ties, 241
American Gas Association, 24
Americans with Disabilities Act (ADA), 285
Annual Demographic File, 8
Anxiety disorders, 120, **121**
Appearance, physical, 159–160
Attrition, in mental health research, 129

B

Baby Boom generation. *See also* Birth cohorts
  causes of, 4–6
  consequences of, 6, 24–25
  defined, 24, 52
  future for, 20
  future research on, 38–39
  generation units within, 26–28, 37
Bereavement, 136
Bipolar disorders, 115–120, **119**
Birth cohorts. *See also* Cohort effects
  within Baby Boom generation
    cohabiting status in, 10, **10**
    cultural contrasts of, 261–262
    defined, 4, 52, 167
    education levels of, 12–13, **13,**
        167–168, 172–173, **173**
    family income of, 15–17, **16, 18–19**
    living arrangements of, 10–12, **11**
    marital status in, 9–12, **9**
    occupational status of, 13–15, **14,** 168
  versus generations, 48–51
  size consequences of, 5–6, 48
Birth control, 189, 253
Birth rates, declining, 4, 51
Blended families, 275
Bone density, 90–91, 93
Breast cancer, 93
Bridge employment, 284

C

Cardiovascular disease, 92–93
Caregiving. *See* Aging parents
Child-focused society, 239
Childhood, psychology of, 30–32
Chronosystem, in cognitive functioning, **218,**
        219–220, 226–227
Civil Rights movement, 32, 50
Cluttered nests, 271
Cognitive functioning
  cohort effects in, 208–212, *211*
  hormone therapy and, 94
  identity processes and, 160–161
  influences on
    chronosystem, 226–228

    exosystem, 225–226
    mesosystem, 221–224
    overview, 218–220, **218**
  in menopause, 90
  midlife changes in, 213–217, *213, 215, 216, 217*
  occupational status and, 288
  prior midlife research in, 206–209
  significance of in Boomers, 205–206
Cohabitation, 10, **10,** 253, 266–267
Cohort effects
  in cognitive functioning
    Boomers versus previous cohorts,
        208–212, *211*
    environmental influences on,
        217–228, **218**
  in control beliefs, 186, 190–191, 197–198
  in daily stressors, 167–168, 174–178, **174, 176**
  in data analysis, 62–66, **63**
  described, 26, 27–28, 47–48, 53–55, *54*
  in identity processes, 155
  in intergenerational ties, 241–242
  in mental health research, 128–130 (*See
        also specific disorders*)
  in relationships, 261–262, 265–266
  in research design issues, 55–62, *54,* **56**
Cohort replacement, 47, 53, 62–64
Cohort research design
  age-period-cohort identification problem
        in, 56–58, **56**
  data analysis in, 62–66, **63**
  types of, 58–62
Cohorts, defined, 45–46. *See also* Birth cohorts
Cohort sequential research design, 61–62
Cold War, impact on Boomers, 25, 26, 244
Collectivist values, 34–35
Colorectal cancer, 94
Competition, impact on Boomers, 31–32,
        132–134
Compulsory schooling, 227
Computers. *See* Technology
Consumerism, 133–134
Control beliefs
  across life span, 195–197
  cohort effects on, 186, 190–191, 197–198
  historic and social influences on, 188–191
  life span theories of, 191–192, 199–201
  in midlife, 192–195

models of, 186–188
paradox of, 198–199
CPS, 8
Crime rates, 135
Cross-sectional research design, 58–59
Crystallized intelligence, 208–214, 221
Current Population Surveys (CPS), 8

D

Daily life stressors. See Stress
Dating, as cohort effect, 48. See also Romantic relationships
Dementia, 127–128, 160, 206
Demobilization, as cause of Baby Boom, 4–5, 25–26
Demographic characteristics
    of aging Boomers, 283, 286–287
    of Baby Boom, 4–7, 7
    of midlife Boomers
        data sources for, 8
        education, 12–13, 13
        income, 15–17, 16
        marriage and living arrangements, 8–11, 9, 10, 11
        occupational status, 13–15, 14, 15
Demographic predictions, pre-1946, 4
Demographic surveys, 8
Depression
    in menopause, 88–90, 89
    in old age, 137
    prevalence of, 114–115, 116–118
Developmental stages. See Life span development
Diathesis/stress model of mental health, 131–132
Disidentification, 161–162. See also Identity
Diversity among Boomers, 17, 138. See also Racial/ethnic differences
Divorce rates, 190, 251, 267, 275
Domain specific control beliefs, 186–187
Drug abuse, 122, 123–124
"Duck and cover, " 26, 244

E

Easterlin effect, 5–6, 48, 48n, 132
Economy

as cause of baby boom, 5–6, 25–26
impact on Boomers
    competition, 132–134
    control beliefs, 189
    early versus late Boomers, 168
    intergenerational ties, 247–248
    psychology, 31, 34
Education levels
    in Boomers versus previous cohorts, 286
    cognitive functioning and, 221–223
    in early versus late Boomers, 167–168, 172–173, 173
    federal funding and, 227–228
    gender differences in, 167–168, 173, 173, 226
    GI Bill role in, 225–226, 248
    intergenerational ties and, 248–249, 265
    legislation affecting, 227
    menopause and, 89
    racial/ethnic differences in, 12–13, 13, 222
    stress reactivity and, 177–178, 178, 179
Employment. See Occupational status
Erikson's theory of identity, 149–150
Exosystem, in cognitive functioning, 218, 219, 225–226

F

Family and household size
    as cause of Baby Boom, 4–5
    declining, 274–275
    in early versus late Boomers, 172–173, 173
    in middle age, 12
    parental investment and, 250
Family structures
    control beliefs and, 190
    intergenerational ties and, 250–252, 273, 275
Feminism. See Women's movement
Fertility, unwanted, 5
Financial risk, 175
Fluid ability, 208–214, 221
Flynn effect (IQ gains), 208–212
Four Stage of Life study, 266
Friendships

in adolescence, 264–265
in midlife, 268–269
in old age, 276
in young adulthood, 266

G

Gender differences
in control beliefs, 189, 193–194, 198
in education levels, 167–168, 173, **173**, 226
in friendships, 266
in identity processes, 155
in marriage and living arrangements, 10–12
in occupational status, 14–15, **15**
post WWII, 25–26
Gender roles, 252–253, 265
Generations
versus birth cohorts, 48–51
as kinship term, 50–51
Generation units, 26–28, 50. *See also* Birth cohorts
Generativity, 29, 36, 37
Genetics, mental health and, 131–132
Geographic separation, parent-child, 249–250, 275
GI Bill, 225–226, 248
Global control beliefs, 186–187
Grandparent relationships, 263–264, 272–274, 275
Growth curve models, 64–66

H

Health issues. *See* Mental health; Physical health
Hearing impairment, 287
Hormone therapy
alternatives to, 96–98
benefits and risks of, 91–96
Hot flashes, 86–88, **88,** 94–97
Household size. *See* Family and household size
Housing boom, 24
Hysterectomy, 81, 83

I

IAE, 156–157
Identity
generational, 28, 33–34
personal
midlife changes and, 157–162
as midlife issue, 29, 36
models of, 149–157
social, 38
Identity accommodation
described, 152–153
midlife changes and, 157–162
self-esteem and, 156
Identity and Experience Scale–General (IES–G), 154
Identity assimilation
age and, 154–155
described, 152
gender and, 155
midlife changes and, 157–162
self-esteem and, 156
Identity Assimilation Effect (IAE), 156–157
Identity balance
age and, 154–155
described, 153–154
gender and, 155
midlife changes and, 157–162
self-esteem and, 156
Identity Experience Scale–Specific Aging (IES–SA), 154
Identity Process Theory (IPT)
age effects in, 154–155
cohort effects in, 155
described, 151–154
gender differences in, 155
self-esteem in, 155–157
tests of, 154
Identity statuses, 150–151
IES–G, 154
IES–SA, 154
Income
control beliefs and, 190
racial/ethnic differences in, 15–16, **16, 19**
workers in family and, 16–17, **18**
Individual differences, in cognitive functioning, 214–217, *215, 216, 217*

Inductive reasoning, 210–212, *211*
Intergenerational conflicts, 244–245, 263
Intergenerational ties. *See also* Relationships
     of Boomers
   in adolescence, 263–264
   complexity of, 241–242
   historical influences on, 238–240
   in midlife, 270–274
   in old age, 275
   social changes and
      economic changes, 247–248
      educational opportunities, 248–249,
         265
      family structures, 250–252
      gender roles, 252–253
      geographic separation, 249–250
      life expectancy, 243–247
      occupational status, 249
      sexuality and sexual identity, 253–254
   theories of, 240–241
   in young adulthood, 265–266
Intermediate Boomers, defined, 4
Intracohort change, 53, 62–64
IPT. *See* Identity Process Theory (IPT)
IQ gains, 208–212

K

Kennedy assassination, 26, 28
Kinship, 50–51
Kitchen cabinet standardization, 24

L

Labor force participation. *See* Occupational
     status
Leading-edge Boomers, defined, 4
Legacies, midlife concern with, 29
Life expectancy, intergenerational ties and,
     243–247
Life span development. *See also* Midlife
   environmental systems in, **218,** 219–220
   psychological implications of
      adolescence, 32–34
      childhood, 30–32
      middle age, 35–37
      young adulthood, 34–35

Living arrangements, 10–12, **10, 11.** *See also*
     Marriage
Locus of control (LOC), 187, 197

M

Marcia's identity statuses, 150–151
Marriage
   cohort differences in, 265–266
   control beliefs and, 193–194
   declining, 10–12, **9**
   gender differences in, 10–12
   psychological effects of, 268
   racial/ethnic differences in, 9–10, **9**
   satisfaction in, 268
   trend changes in, as cause of baby boom,
      5–6
McArthur Study of Midlife, 195–196
Medicare, 205
Memory ability, 215–216, *215*
Menopause
   age of, 81–83
   attitudes towards, 84–86, **85**
   changing views of, 76–79
   defined, 79–81
   impact on chronic conditions, 90–91
   importance of, 75–76
   racial/ethnic differences in, 77–78, 83, 86,
      87
   surgical, 81, 83
   symptoms of, 86–90, **88, 89**
   treatments for, 91–98
Mental health
   age-related trajectory of, 136–138
   diathesis/stress model of, 131–132
   historical context of research in, 112–113
   methodological issues in, 128–130
   psychological disorders
      anxiety disorders, 120, **121**
      dementia, 127–128
      mood disorders, 114–120, **116–119**
      schizophrenia, 122–127, **125–126**
      substance use disorder, 122, **123–124**
      trends in, 113–114
   psychosocial correlates of
      alienation and personal threat,
         134–135

competition, 132–133
consumerism, 133–134
racial/ethnic differences and, 114, 138
well-being, 113
Mesosystem, in cognitive functioning
    described, **218,** 219
    educational influences in, 221–223
    occupational influences in, 223–224
Midlife
    cognitive function changes in, 213–217,
            213, 215, 216, 217
    control beliefs in, 192–197
    early versus late, 30, 37
    generational units in, 37
    lack of research on, 192, 206–207
    psychology of, 29–30, 35–37
    relationships in
            friendship, 268–269
            grandparent-grandchild, 272–274
            parent-child, 270–272
            romantic, 266–268
            sibling, 269–270
Mobility, intergenerational ties and, 249–250,
        275
Mortality, midlife concern with, 29, 36
Mother-daughter relations, 252–253. *See also*
        Intergenerational ties
Motor skills, changes in, 287
Multiple cohort research design, 61
Muscle strength, reduced, 288

N

National Defense Education Act, 227–228
National Study of Daily Experiences (NSDE),
        169–172, **171,** 180–181
Number ability, *211,* 212, 216, *217*

O

Obsessive-compulsive disorder, 120
Occasion-based models, 66
Occupational status. *See also* Income
    of aging work force
            future research in, 295–296
            health changes and, 287–288
            technology and, 291–295

trends in, 284–286, 289–290
    work performance and, 288–289
as cognitive function influence, 223–224
control beliefs and, 194
demographic changes and, 283–284
of early versus late Boomers, 168
gender differences in, 14–15, **15**
increase in, 13
intergenerational ties and, 249, 265
racial/ethnic differences in, 14, **14**
Old age
    depression in, 137
    relationships in, 275–276
Overcrowding, 12, 24–25, 222–223

P

Panic disorder, 120
Parent-child relations. *See* Intergenerational
        ties
Parenting
    child-focused, 238–239
    control beliefs and, 194
    family size and, 250
    as midlife relationship, 270–271
    surrogate, by grandparents, 273
Peace, impact on Boomers, 31
Perimenopause, defined, 80–81. *See also*
        Menopause
Period effects
    in data analysis, 62–66, **63**
    described, 55
    in intergenerational ties, 238
    in mental health research, 128–130
    in relationships, 261–262
    in research design issues, 55–62, **56**
Personal fable, 244
Personal threat, 134–135
Phased retirement, 284
Physical health
    in Boomers versus previous cohorts,
            286–287
    control beliefs and, 195
    identity processes and, 159–160
    mental health and, 136
    occupational status and, 287–288
    social class impact on, 38

Political environment, in young adulthood, 34
Primary control, 191

R

Racial/ethnic differences
  among Boomers, 17, 138
  in Boomers versus previous cohorts, 287
  control beliefs and, 198
  in education levels, 12–13, **13**, 222
  as generation unit, 27
  in income, 15–16, **16, 19**
  in marriage, 9–10, **9**
  in menopause, 77–78, 83, 86, 87
  in mental health, 114, 138
  in occupational status, 14, **14**
  in parenting, 270–271, 273
Recall bias, in mental health research, 129
Regret, 37–38
Relationships of Boomers. See also Intergenerational ties
  in adolescence, 263–265, 267
  cohort and period effects on, 261–262
  in midlife
    friendship, 268–269
    grandparent-grandchild, 272–274
    parent-child, 270–272
    romantic, 266–268
    sibling, 269–270
  in old age, 275–276
  in young adulthood, 265–266
Religious participation, 33, 135
Repeated measures research designs, 62–65
Research design. See Cohort research design
Retirement
  as cognitive functional influence, 223–224
  trends in, 284–286
Roles
  changes in, 168
  control beliefs and, 193–195, 198, 199
  romantic relationships and, 267–268
Romantic relationships
  in adolescence, 264
  in midlife, 266–268
  in young adulthood, 265

S

SAT scores, declining, 208–209
Schizophrenia, 122–127, **125–126**
Schools, impact on, 12. See also Education levels
Seattle Longitudinal Study (SLS)
  cohort effect findings, 210–212, *211*
  longitudinal effect findings, 213–217, *215, 216, 217*
Secondary control, 191
Self-complexity, in identity processes, 155–157
Self-efficacy, 187, 197
Self-esteem, in identity processes, 155–157
Sense of control theory, 187. See also Control beliefs
Sexuality, sexual identity
  in adolescence, 264
  effect on intergenerational ties, 253–254
  in midlife, 267, 268
Sibling relationships
  in adolescence, 264
  in midlife, 269–270
  in old age, 275–276
Single cohort research design, 59–61
Sleep difficulties, in menopause, 90
SLS
  cohort effect findings, 210–212, *211*
  longitudinal effect findings, 213–217, *215, 216, 217*
Smoking, menopause and, 81, 87
Social change
  as cause of baby boom, 5–6
  cohort effect and, 52–55, *54*
Social comparison, 133
Social crowding, 12, 24–25, 222–223
Social experiences. See Cohort effects
Social Security, 205, 285
Social support, menopause and, 89
Socioeconomic differences
  among Boomers, 17–20, **18**
  control beliefs and, 198
  menopause and, 87
  physical health and, 38
Solidarity theory, 240–241
Spatial orientation, *211*, 212

Status, midlife concern with, 29, 36
Stereotypes, of aging, 158–159
Stereotype threats, 161–162
Stress
    control beliefs and, 201
    in early versus late Boomers
        characteristics and meaning of,
            174–175, **174**
        cohort effects and, 167–168
        exposure and reactivity to, 168–169,
            176–178
        NSDE study anecdotes, 180–181
        NSDE study description, 169–172,
            171
        sociodemographic differences and,
            172–173, **173, 176, 178,**
            179
    identity processes and, 156
    menopause and, 87, 89
    mental health and, 131–132
    minor versus major, 166
Stress process model, 201
Student activism, 32–35, 189
Study of Women's Health Across the Nation
    (SWAN), 78–79
Substance use disorders, 122, **123–124**
Suburbanization, post WWII, 25–26, 247–248
Surrogate parenting, 273
SWAN, 78–79
Synthetic cohorts, 58–59

T

Technology
    as cognitive function influence, 223
    impact on aging work force, 291–293
    skill acquisition by older adults, 294–295
    use of by older adults, 293–294, *294*

Telecommuting, 291
Television, 223
Time-based models, 66
Trailing-edge Boomers, defined, 4
Trust, breakdown in, 134–135

U

Unemployment rates, 168
Urinary incontinence, 95

V

Verbal ability, *211, 212*
Vietnam War
    cohort differences and, 50
    education levels and, 167
    versus WWII, 33, 134
Visual impairment, 287

W

Well-being, 113
Within-person change, 64–66
Women's movement
    control beliefs and, 189, 199
    as formative event, 32
    view of menopause and, 76–77
Word fluency, *211,* 212, 216, *216*
Work., Occupational status

Y

Young adulthood
    psychology of, 34–35
    relationships in, 265–266
Youth-oriented values, 159–160, 162–163